Communications in Computer and Information Science 997

Commenced Publication in 2007
Founding and Former Series Editors:
Phoebe Chen, Alfredo Cuzzocrea, Xiaoyong Du, Orhun Kara, Ting Liu,
Krishna M. Sivalingam, Dominik Ślęzak, Takashi Washio, and Xiaokang Yang

More information about this series at http://www.springer.com/series/7899

Dominique Bechmann ·
Manuela Chessa · Ana Paula Cláudio ·
Francisco Imai · Andreas Kerren ·
Paul Richard · Alexandru Telea ·
Alain Tremeau (Eds.)

Computer Vision, Imaging and Computer Graphics Theory and Applications

13th International Joint Conference, VISIGRAPP 2018
Funchal–Madeira, Portugal, January 27–29, 2018
Revised Selected Papers

 Springer

Editors
Dominique Bechmann
University of Strasbourg
Strasbourg, France

Ana Paula Cláudio
University of Lisbon
Lisbon, Portugal

Andreas Kerren (iD)
Linnaeus University
Växjö, Kronobergs Län, Sweden

Alexandru Telea
University of Groningen
Groningen, The Netherlands

Manuela Chessa
University of Genoa
Genoa, Italy

Francisco Imai
Research Innovation Center
Apple Inc.
San Jose, CA, USA

Paul Richard
LISA - ISTIA
University of Angers
Angers, France

Alain Tremeau
Jean Monnet University
Saint-Etienne, France

ISSN 1865-0929   ISSN 1865-0937   (electronic)
Communications in Computer and Information Science
ISBN 978-3-030-26755-1   ISBN 978-3-030-26756-8   (eBook)
https://doi.org/10.1007/978-3-030-26756-8

Preface

The present book includes extended and revised versions of a set of selected papers from the 13th International Joint Conference on Computer Vision, Imaging and Computer Graphics Theory and Applications (VISIGRAPP 2018) held in Madeira, Portugal, during January 27–29, 2018.

The purpose of the 13th International Joint Conference on Computer Vision, Imaging and Computer Graphics Theory and Applications (VISIGRAPP 2018) was to bring together researchers and practitioners interested in both theoretical advances and applications of computer vision, computer graphics, and information visualization. VISIGRAPP is composed of four co-located conferences, each specialized in at least one of the aforementioned main knowledge areas.

VISIGRAPP 2018 received 317 paper submissions from 52 countries, of which 6% are included in this book. The papers were selected by the event program co-chairs based on a number of criteria that include the reviews and suggested comments provided by the Program Committee members, the session chairs' assessments, and also the program chairs' global view of all papers included in the technical program. The authors of selected papers were then invited to submit a revised and extended version of their papers having at least 30% new material.

The papers selected to be included in this book contribute to the understanding of relevant trends of current research on image and video formation, preprocessing, analysis, and understanding; motion, tracking, and stereo vision; visual data analysis and visualization; visual representation and interaction; interactive environments and user interfaces; haptic and multimodal interaction; human and computer interaction; and user experience. The richness and the variety of theoretical advances and research results highlighted by these selected papers reflect the vitality and the prevalence of the research areas covered by the VISIGRAPP conference.

We would like to thank all the authors for their contributions to this book and also to the reviewers who helped ensure the quality of this publication.

January 2018

Dominique Bechmann
Ana Paula Cláudio
Paul Richard
Manuela Chessa
Alexandru Telea
Andreas Kerren
Francisco Imai
Alain Tremeau

Organization

Conference Chair

Jose Braz   Escola Superior de Tecnologia de Setúbal, Portugal

Program Co-chairs

GRAPP

Dominique Bechmann   CNRS-Université de Strasbourg, France
Ana Paula Cláudio   Universidade de Lisboa, Portugal

HUCAPP

Paul Richard   University of Angers, France
Manuela Chessa   University of Genoa, Italy

IVAPP

Alexandru Telea   University of Groningen, The Netherlands
Andreas Kerren   Linnaeus University, Sweden

VISAPP

Francisco Imai   Apple Inc., USA
Alain Tremeau   Université Jean Monnet in Saint Etienne, France

GRAPP Program Committee

Francisco Abad	Universidad Politécnica de Valencia, Spain
Marco Agus	King Abdullah University of Science and Technology, Saudi Arabia
Lilian Aveneau	University of Poitiers, France
Gérard Bailly	University Grenoble-Alpes/CNRS, France
Thomas Bashford-Rogers	The University of the West of England, UK
Bedrich Benes	Purdue University, USA
Gonzalo Besuievsky	Universitat de Girona, Spain
Carla Binucci	Università degli Studi di Perugia, Italy
Venceslas Biri	University of Paris Est, France
Fernando Birra	UNL, Portugal
Kristopher Blom	Virtual Human Technologies, Czech Republic
Carles Bosch	Eurecat, Spain
Stephen Brooks	Dalhousie University, Canada
Maria Beatriz Carmo	Universidade de Lisboa, Portugal

L. G. Casado	University of Almeria, Spain
Eva Cerezo	University of Zaragoza, Spain
Parag Chaudhuri	Indian Institute of Technology Bombay, India
Antoni Chica	Universitat Politecnica de Catalunya, Spain
Hwan-gue Cho	Pusan National University, Korea, Republic of
Miguel Chover	Universitat Jaume I, Spain
Teodor Cioaca	University Politehnica Bucharest, Romania
António Coelho	Universidade do Porto, Portugal
Sabine Coquillart	Inria, France
António Costa	ISEP, Portugal
Vasco Costa	INESC-ID, Portugal
Rémi Cozot	IRISA, France
Luiz Henrique de Figueiredo	IMPA, Brazil
Bailin Deng	Cardiff University, UK
Fabian Di Fiore	Hasselt University, Belgium
Paulo Dias	Universidade de Aveiro, Portugal
Thierry Duval	IMT Atlantique, France
Marius Erdt	Fraunhofer IDM@NTU, Singapore
Petros Faloutsos	York University, Canada
Pierre-Alain Fayolle	University of Aizu, Japan
Francisco R. Feito	University of Jaén, Spain
Dirk Feldmann	na, Germany
Jie Feng	Peking University, China
Pablo Figueroa	Universidad de los Andes, Colombia
Ioannis Fudos	University of Ioannina, Greece
Davide Gadia	Università degli Studi di Milano, Italy
Arturo Garcia	University of Salford, UK
Alejandro García-Alonso	University of the Basque Country, Spain
Miguel Gea	University of Granada, Spain
Djamchid Ghazanfarpour	University of Limoges, France
Stephane Gobron	HES-SO/Arc, Switzerland
Alexandrino Gonçalves	Polytechnic Institute of Leiria, Portugal
Laurent Grisoni	University of Lille Science and Technologies, France
Marcelo de Paiva Guimaraes	Federal University of São Paulo, Brazil
James Hahn	George Washington University, USA
Vlastimil Havran	Czech Technical University in Prague, Czech Republic
Nancy Hitschfeld	University of Chile, Chile
Ludovic Hoyet	Inria Rennes, Centre Bretagne Atlantique, France
Andres Iglesias	University of Cantabria, Spain
Insung Ihm	Sogang University, Korea, Republic of
Alex James	Nazarbayev University, Kazakhstan
Jean-Pierre Jessel	IRIT, Paul Sabatier University, France
Juan Jiménez Delgado	Universidad de Jaen, Spain
Xiaogang Jin	Zhejiang University, China

Robert Joan-Arinyo	Universitat Politecnica de Catalunya, Spain
Chris Joslin	Carleton University, Canada
Cláudio Jung	Universidade Federal do Rio Grande do Sul, Brazil
Mubbasir Kapadia	Rutgers University, USA
Josef Kohout	University of West Bohemia, Czech Republic
Maciej Kot	Tokyo Institute of Technology, Japan
Alexander Kulik	Bauhaus-Universität Weimar, Germany
Richard Kulpa	Université Rennes 2, France
Miguel Leitão	ISEP, Portugal
Alejandro León	University of Granada, Spain
Ligang Liu	University of Science and Technology of China, China
Marco Livesu	Italian National Research Council, Italy
Hélio Lopes	PUC-Rio, Brazil
Pedro Lopes	ISCTE-IUL, Portugal
Joaquim Madeira	University of Aveiro, Portugal
Luís Magalhães	University of Minho, Portugal
Stephen Mann	University of Waterloo, Canada
Michael Manzke	Trinity College Dublin, Ireland
Ricardo Marroquim	Rio de Janeiro Federal University, Brazil
Belen Masia	Universidad de Zaragoza, Spain
Nelson Max	University of California, USA
Daniel Meneveaux	University of Poitiers, France
Stéphane Mérillou	University of Limoges, France
Eder Miguel	Universidad Rey Juan Carlos, Spain
José Molina Massó	Universidad de Castilla-la Mancha, Spain
Ramon Molla	Universitat Politècnica de València, Spain
David Mould	Carleton University, Canada
Adolfo Muñoz	Universidad de Zaragoza, Spain
Lidia M. Ortega	University of Jaén, Spain
Georgios Papaioannou	Athens University of Economics and Business, Greece
Giuseppe Patané	Italian National Research Council, Italy
Daniel Patel	University of Bergen, Norway
Félix Paulano-Godino	University of Jaén, Spain
Aruquia Peixoto	CEFET/RJ, Brazil
João Pereira	Instituto Superior de Engenharia do Porto, Portugal
João Pereira	INESC-ID at IST, Portugal
Sinésio Pesco	PUC-Rio Institute, Brazil
Ruggero Pintus	Center for Advanced Studies, Research and Development in Sardinia, Italy
Paulo Pombinho	Universidade de Lisboa, Portugal
Tomislav Pribanic	University of Zagreb, Croatia
Anna Puig	University of Barcelona, Spain
Luís Reis	University of Porto, Portugal
Inmaculada Remolar	Universitat Jaume I, Spain
Mickael Ribardière	University of Poitiers, XLIM, France
Nuno Rodrigues	Polytechnic Institute of Leiria, Portugal

Inmaculada Rodríguez	University of Barcelona, Spain
Przemyslaw Rokita	Warsaw University of Technology, Poland
Teresa Romão	Universidade de Nova Lisboa, Portugal
Isaac Rudomin	BSC, Spain
Wang Rui	Zhejiang University, China
Holly Rushmeier	Yale University, USA
Basile Sauvage	University of Strasbourg, France
Vladimir Savchenko	Hose University, Japan
Rafael J. Segura	Universidad de Jaen, Spain
Ari Shapiro	University of Southern California, USA
Frutuoso Silva	University of Beira Interior, Portugal
A. Augusto Sousa	FEUP/INESC Porto, Portugal
Ching-Liang Su	Da Yeh University, India
Matthias Teschner	University of Freiburg, Germany
Daniel Thalmann	Ecole Polytechnique Federale de Lausanne, Switzerland
Juan Carlos Torres	Universidad de Granada, Spain
Alain Tremeau	Université Jean Monnet in Saint Etienne, France
Hassan Ugail	Centre for Visual Computing, UK
Torsten Ullrich	Fraunhofer Austria Research, Austria
Anna Ursyn	University of Northern Colorado, USA
Cesare Valenti	Università degli Studi di Palermo, Italy
Luiz Velho	Instituto de Matematica Pura e Aplicada, Brazil
Andreas Weber	University of Bonn, Germany
Thomas Wischgoll	Wright State University, USA
Burkhard Wuensche	University of Auckland, New Zealand
Lihua You	Bournemouth University, UK
Jian Zhang	Bournemouth University, UK
Yayun Zhou	Siemens AG, Germany

GRAPP Additional Reviewers

Shujie Deng	Bournemouth University, UK
Saket Patkar	Google Inc., USA
Ana Serrano	Universidad de Zaragoza, Spain
Zhao Wang	Bournemouth University, UK

HUCAPP Program Committee

Andrea Abate	University of Salerno, Italy
Federica Bazzano	Politecnico di Torino, Italy
Yacine Bellik	LIMSI-CNRS, Orsay, France
Frank Biocca	New Jersey Institute of Technology, USA
Leon Bodenhagen	University of Southern Denmark, Denmark
Gunnar Bolmsjö	University West, Sweden
Daniel Cermak-sassenrath	University of Copenhagen, Denmark

Jessie Chen	U.S. Army Research Laboratory, USA
Yang-Wai Chow	University of Wollongong, Australia
José Coelho	University of Lisbon, Portugal
Cesar Collazos	Universidad del Cauca, Colombia
André Constantino da Silva	Instituto Federal de São Paulo, Brazil
Alma Culén	University of Oslo, Norway
Kerstin Dautenhahn	University of Hertfordshire, UK
Damon Daylamani-Zad	University of Greenwich, UK
Lucio Tommaso De Paolis	University of Salento, Italy
Larbi Esmahi	Athabasca University, Canada
Tom Garner	University of Portsmouth, UK
Luis Gomes	UNL/UNINOVA, Portugal
Andrina Granic	University of Split, Croatia
Toni Granollers	University of Lleida, Spain
Gareth Jones	Dublin City University, Ireland
Koji Kashihara	Tokushima University, Japan
Chee Weng Khong	Multimedia University, Malaysia
Uttam Kokil	Kennesaw State University, USA
Heidi Krömker	Technische Universität Ilmenau, Germany
Fabrizio Lamberti	Politecnico di Torino, Italy
Tsai-Yen Li	National Chengchi University, Taiwan
Flamina Luccio	Università Ca' Foscari Venezia, Italy
Sergio Luján-Mora	University of Alicante, Spain
Nadia Magnenat-Thalmann	NTU, Singapore and MIRALab, University of Geneva, Switzerland
Célia Martinie	University of Toulouse 3, France
Maristella Matera	Politecnico di Milano, Italy
Troy McDaniel	Arizona State University, USA
Vincenzo Moscato	Università degli Studi di Napoli Federico II, Italy
Keith Nesbitt	University of Newcastle, Australia
Nuno Otero	Linnaeus University, Sweden
Evangelos Papadopoulos	NTUA, Greece
Ioannis Paraskevopoulos	University of Greenwich, UK
Gianluca Paravati	Polytechnic University of Turin, Italy
James Phillips	Auckland University of Technology, New Zealand
Armelle Prigent	University of La Rochelle, France
Nitendra Rajput	IBM Research, New Delhi, India
Arcadio Reyes Lecuona	University of Málaga, Spain
Antonio Rinaldi	University of Naples Federico II, Italy
Otniel Rodriguez	Universidad Autonóma del Estado de México, Mexico
Juha Röning	University of Oulu, Finland
Paul Rosenthal	Germany
José Rouillard	Université des Sciences et Technologies de Lille, France
Sandra Sanchez-Gordon	Escuela Politecnica Nacional, Ecuador

Antonio-José Sánchez-Salmerón	Universitat Politecnica de Valencia, Spain
Andrea Sanna	Politecnico di Torino, Italy
Corina Sas	Lancaster University, UK
Trenton Schulz	Norwegian Computing Center, Norway
Berglind Smaradottir	University of Agder, Norway
Fabio Solari	University of Genoa, Italy
Daniel Thalmann	Ecole Polytechnique Federale de Lausanne, Switzerland
Godfried Toussaint	New York University Abu Dhabi, UAE
Eulalie Verhulst	University of Angers, France
Windson Viana	Federal University of Ceará, Brazil
Kostas Vlachos	University of Ioannina, Greece

HUCAPP Additional Reviewers

| Patricia Acosta-Vargas | Universidad de Las Américas, Ecuador |
| Cristiano Russo | Université Paris-est, France |

IVAPP Program Committee

Jürgen Bernard	TU Darmstadt, Germany
Rita Borgo	King's College London, UK
David Borland	University of North Carolina at Chapel Hill, USA
Massimo Brescia	Istituto Nazionale di AstroFisica, Italy
Ross Brown	Queensland University of Technology, Brisbane, Australia
Maria Beatriz Carmo	BioISI, Universidade de Lisboa, Portugal
Daniel Cernea	University of Kaiserslautern, Germany
Guoning Chen	University of Houston, USA
Yongwan Chun	University of Texas at Dallas, USA
Joao Comba	UFRGS, Brazil
Christoph Dalitz	Niederrhein University of Applied Sciences, Germany
Robertas Damasevicius	Kaunas University of Technology, Lithuania
Mihaela Dinsoreanu	Technical University of Cluj-Napoca, Romania
Georgios Dounias	University of the Aegean, Greece
Achim Ebert	University of Kaiserslautern, Germany
Ronak Etemadpour	City College, CUNY, USA
Chi-Wing Fu	The Chinese University of Hong Kong, SAR China
Randy Goebel	University of Alberta, Canada
Martin Graham	University of Edinburgh, UK
Daniel Griffith	University of Texas at Dallas, USA
Torsten Hopp	Karlsruhe Institute of Technology, Germany
Alfred Inselberg	Tel Aviv University, Israel
Tobias Isenberg	Inria, France
Won-ki Jeong	UNIST, Korea, Republic of

IVAPP Additional Reviewers

Florian Evequoz	University of Fribourg, Switzerland
Kostiantyn Kucher	ISOVIS Group, Linnaeus University, Sweden
Rafael Martins	Linnaeus University, Sweden
Jorge Ono	NYU, USA

VISAPP Program Committee

Davide Moroni	Institute of Information Science and Technologies CNR, Italy
Amr Abdel-Dayem	Laurentian University, Canada
Ilya Afanasyev	Innopolis University, Russian Federation
Palwasha Afsar	Algorithmi Research Center, Uminho, Portugal
Vicente Alarcon-Aquino	Universidad de las Americas Puebla, Mexico
Mokhled Al-Tarawneh	Mu'tah University, Jordan
Hugo Alvarez	Vicomtech-Ik4, Spain
Djamila Aouada	University of Luxembourg, Luxembourg
Angelos Barmpoutis	University of Florida, USA
Giuseppe Baruffa	University of Perugia, Italy
Ardhendu Behera	Edge Hill University, UK
Saeid Belkasim	Georgia State University, USA
Fabio Bellavia	Università degli Studi di Firenze, Italy
Olga Bellon	Universidade Federal do Paraná, Brazil
Achraf Ben-Hamadou	Digital Research Center of Sfax, Tunisia
Neil Bergmann	University of Queensland, Australia
Adrian Bors	University of York, UK
Arnaud Boucher	Université Paris Descartes, France
Marius Brezovan	University of Craiova, Romania
Valentin Brimkov	State University of New York, USA
Arcangelo Bruna	STMicroelectronics, Italy
Vittoria Bruni	University of Rome La Sapienza, Italy
Alice Caplier	GIPSA-lab, France
Franco Cardillo	Consiglio Nazionale delle Ricerche, Italy
Satish Chand	Netaji Subhas Institute of Technology and Jawaharlal Nehru University Delhi, India
Jocelyn Chanussot	Grenoble Institute of Technology Institut Polytechnique de Grenoble, France
Samuel Cheng	University of Oklahoma, USA
Manuela Chessa	University of Genoa, Italy
Chia Chong	Sunway University, Malaysia
Michal Choras	University of Technology and Life Sciences Bydgoszcz and ITTI Poznan, Poland
Laurent Cohen	Université Paris Dauphine, France
Sara Colantonio	ISTI-CNR, Italy
Carlo Colombo	Università degli Studi di Firenze, Italy

Richard Connor	University of Strathclyde, UK
Donatello Conte	Université de Tours, France
António Cunha	Universidade de Trás-os-Montes e Alto Douro, Portugal
Boguslaw Cyganek	AGH University of Science and Technology, Poland
Larry Davis	University of Maryland, USA
Kenneth Dawson-Howe	Trinity College Dublin, Ireland
Anselmo Cardoso de Paiva	Universidade Federal do Maranhao, Brazil
Emmanuel Dellandréa	Ecole Centrale de Lyon, France
Thomas Deserno	Technische Universität Braunschweig, Germany
Michel Devy	LAAS-CNRS, France
Sotirios Diamantas	University of Nevada, Reno, USA
Yago Diez	Yamagata University, Japan
Jana Dittmann	Otto-von-Guericke-Universität Magdeburg, Germany
Mahmoud El-Sakka	The University of Western Ontario, Canada
Ulrich Engelke	CSIRO, Australia
Grigori Evreinov	University of Tampere, Finland
Giovanni Farinella	Università di Catania, Italy
Aaron Fenster	Robarts Research Institute, Canada
Stefano Ferilli	University of Bari, Italy
Jorge Fernández-Berni	Institute of Microelectronics of Seville, CSIC - Universidad de Sevilla, Spain
Gernot Fink	TU Dortmund, Germany
David Fofi	Le2i, France
Tyler Folsom	QUEST Integrated Inc., USA
Gian Foresti	Unversity of Udine, Italy
Mohamed Fouad	Military Technical College, Egypt
Juan Francisco Garamendi	Universitat Pompeu Fabra, Spain
Antonios Gasteratos	Democritus University of Thrace, Greece
Claudio Gennaro	CNR, Italy
Przemyslaw Glomb	IITiS PAN, Poland
Seiichi Gohshi	Kogakuin University, Japan
Herman Gomes	Universidade Federal de Campina Grande, Brazil
Juan A. Gómez-Pulido	University of Extremadura, Spain
Amr Goneid	The American University in Cairo, Egypt
Manuel González-Hidalgo	Balearic Islands University, Spain
Nikos Grammalidis	Centre of Research and Technology Hellas, Greece
Michael Greenspan	Queen's University, Canada
Levente Hajder	MTA SZTAKI, Hungary
Ju Han	Lawrence Berkeley National Lab, USA
Daniel Harari	Weizmann Institute of Science, Israel
Walid Hariri	University of Cergy Pontoise, France
Wladyslaw Homenda	Warsaw University of Technology, Poland
Hui-Yu Huang	National Formosa University, Taiwan
Céline Hudelot	Ecole Centrale de Paris, France
Chih-Cheng Hung	Kennesaw State University, USA

Laura Igual	Universitat de Barcelona, Spain
Francisco Imai	Apple Inc., USA
Jiri Jan	University of Technology Brno, Czech Republic
Tatiana Jaworska	Polish Academy of Sciences, Poland
Xiuping Jia	University of New South Wales, Australia
Xiaoyi Jiang	University of Münster, Germany
Zhong Jin	Nanjing University of Science and Technology, China
Leo Joskowicz	The Hebrew University of Jerusalem, Israel
Paris Kaimakis	University of Central Lancashire, Cyprus
Ratheesh Kalarot	The University of Auckland, USA
Martin Kampel	Vienna University of Technology, Austria
Mohan Kankanhalli	National University of Singapore, Singapore
Asma Kerbiche	University of Tunis El Manar, Tunisia
Etienne Kerre	Ghent University, Belgium
Anastasios Kesidis	National Center for Scientific Research, Greece
Nahum Kiryati	Tel Aviv University, Israel
Mario Köppen	Kyushu Institute of Technology, Japan
Andreas Koschan	University of Tennessee, USA
Constantine Kotropoulos	Aristotle University of Thessaloniki, Greece
Arjan Kuijper	Fraunhofer Institute for Computer Graphics Research and TU Darmstadt, Germany
Paul Kwan	University of New England, Australia
Gauthier Lafruit	Université Libre de Bruxelles, Belgium
Mónica Larese	National University of Rosario, Argentina
Denis Laurendeau	Laval University, Canada
Sébastien Lefèvre	Université Bretagne Sud, France
Daw-Tung Lin	National Taipei University, Taiwan
Huei-Yung Lin	National Chung Cheng University, Taiwan
Giosue Lo Bosco	University of Palermo, Italy
Liliana Lo Presti	University of Palermo, Italy
Angeles López	Universitat Jaume I, Spain
Bruno Macchiavello	Universidade de Brasilia, Brazil
Ilias Maglogiannis	University of Piraeus, Greece
Baptiste Magnier	LGI2P de l'Ecole des Mines d'Ales, France
András Majdik	MTA SZTAKI, Hungary
Francesco Marcelloni	University of Pisa, Italy
Mauricio Marengoni	Universidade Presbiteriana Mackenzie, Brazil
Emmanuel Marilly	NOKIA - Bell Labs France, France
Jean Martinet	University of Lille 1, France
José Martínez Sotoca	Universitat Jaume I, Spain
Mitsuharu Matsumoto	The University of Electro-Communications, Japan
Javier Melenchón	Universitat Oberta de Catalunya, Spain
Jaime Melendez	Universitat Rovira i Virgili, Spain
Radko Mesiar	Slovak University of Technology, Slovak Republic
Leonid Mestetskiy	Lomonosov Moscow State University, Russian Federation

Cyrille Migniot   Université de Bourgogne - le2i, France
Dan Mikami   NTT, Japan
Nabin Mishra   Stoecker & Associates, USA
Pradit Mittrapiyanuruk   Srinakharinwirot University, Thailand
Birgit Moeller   Martin Luther University Halle-Wittenberg, Germany
Thomas Moeslund   Aalborg University, Denmark
Bartolomeo Montrucchio   Politecnico di Torino, Italy
Kostantinos Moustakas   University of Patras, Greece
Dmitry Murashov   Federal Research Center Computer Science
                                     and Control of Russian Academy of Sciences,
                                     Russian Federation
Lazaros Nalpantidis   Aalborg University, Denmark
Marcos Nieto   Vicomtech-ik4, Spain
Mikael Nilsson   Lund University, Sweden
Nicoletta Noceti   Università di Genova, Italy
Takahiro Okabe   Kyushu Institute of Technology, Japan
Yoshihiro Okada   Kyushu University, Japan
Akshay Pai   University of Copenhagen, Denmark
Gonzalo Pajares   Universidad Complutense de Madrid, Spain
Félix Paulano-Godino   University of Jaén, Spain
Francisco Perales   UIB, Spain
Felipe Pinage   Federal University of Parana, Brazil
Stephen Pollard   HP Labs, UK
Giovanni Puglisi   University of Cagliari, Italy
Bogdan Raducanu   Computer Vision Center, Spain
Giuliana Ramella   Istituto per le Applicazioni del Calcolo M. Picone, Italy
Ana Reis   Instituto de Ciências Biomédicas Abel Salazar,
                                     Portugal
Huamin Ren   Inmeta Consulting AS, Norway
Phill Rhee   Inha University, Korea, Republic of
Neil Robertson   Queen's University, Belfast, UK
Joao Rodrigues   University of the Algarve, Portugal
Bart Romeny   Eindhoven University of Technology, The Netherlands
Paolo Rota   IIT, Italy
Ramón Ruiz   Universidad Politécnica de Cartagena, Spain
Silvio Sabatini   University of Genoa, Italy
Farhang Sahba   Sheridan Institute of Technology and Advanced
                                     Learning, Canada
Ovidio Salvetti   National Research Council of Italy, Italy
Andreja Samcovic   University of Belgrade, Serbia
K. C. Santosh   The University of South Dakota, USA
Ilhem Sboui   La Manouba University, Tunisia
Gerald Schaefer   Loughborough University, UK
Siniša Šegvic   University of Zagreb, Croatia
Shishir Shah   University of Houston, USA
Gaurav Sharma   University of Rochester, USA

Désiré Sidibé   Université de Bourgogne, France
Luciano Silva   Universidade Federal do Parana, Brazil
Ömer Soysal   Southeastern Louisiana University, USA
Tania Stathaki   Imperial College London, UK
Mu-Chun Su   National Central University, Taiwan
Tamás Szirányi   MTA SZTAKI, Hungary
Ryszard Tadeusiewicz   AGH University of Science and Technology, Poland
Norio Tagawa   Tokyo Metropolitan University, Japan
Tolga Tasdizen   University of Utah, USA
Yubing Tong   University of Pennsylvania, USA
Alain Tremeau   Université Jean Monnet in Saint Etienne, France
Vinh Truong Hoang   Ho Chi Minh City Open University, Vietnam
Yulia Trusova   Federal Research Center Computer Science
                                  and Control of the Russian Academy of Sciences,
                                  Russian Federation
Du-Ming Tsai   Yuan-Ze University, Taiwan
Aristeidis Tsitiridis   University Rey Juan Carlos, Spain
Cesare Valenti   Università degli Studi di Palermo, Italy
Vassilios Vonikakis   Advanced Digital Sciences Center, Singapore
Frank Wallhoff   Jade University of Applied Science, Germany
Tao Wang   BAE Systems, USA
Wen-June Wang   National Central University, Taiwan
Layne Watson   Virginia Polytechnic Institute and State University,
                                  USA
Quan Wen   University of Electronic Science and Technology
                                  of China, China
Laurent Wendling   LIPADE, France
Christian Wöhler   TU Dortmund University, Germany
Stefan Wörz   University of Heidelberg, Germany
Yan Wu   Georgia Southern University, USA
Pingkun Yan   Rensselaer Polytechnic Institute, USA
Guoan Yang   Xian Jiaotong University, China
Vera Yashina   Dorodnicyn Computing Center of the Russian
                                  Academy of Sciences, Russian Federation
Lara Younes   Inria, France
Hongfeng Yu   University of Nebraska - Lincoln, USA
Yizhou Yu   University of Illinois, USA
Pietro Zanuttigh   University of Padua, Italy
Huiyu Zhou   Queen's University Belfast, UK
Yun Zhu   UCSD, USA
Zhigang Zhu   City College of New York, USA
Peter Zolliker   Empa, Swiss Federal Laboratories for Materials
                                  Science and Technology, Switzerland
Ju Zou   University of Western Sydney, Australia
Tatjana Zrimec   University of Primorska, Slovenia

VISAPP Additional Reviewers

João Almeida	Federal University of Maranhaão, Brazil
Júlio Batista	IMAGO Research Group, Brazil
Tiago Bonini	Federal University of Maranhão, Brazil
Geraldo Braz Júnior	Universidade Federal do Maranhão, Brazil
Xavier Cortés	Université Francois Rabelais, France
Juan Galan	Universidad de las Americas Puebla, Mexico
Bingchen Gong	The University of Hong Kong, SAR China
Dong Han	University of Oklahoma, USA
Otilia Kocsis	University of Patras, Greece
Victor Kyriazakos	University of Patras, Greece
Aris Lalos	Visualization and Virtual Reality Group, Greece
Guanbin Li	HKU, Hong Kong, SAR China
Mohamed Masoud	Georgia State University, USA
Alessandro Ortis	University of Catania, Italy
Simara Rocha	Federal University of Maranhão, Brazil
Fernando Rueda	Technische Universität Dortmund, Germany
Oleg Seredin	Tula State University, Russian Federation
Sebastian Sudholt	Technische Universität Dortmund, Germany
Flávio Zavan	Universidade Federal do Paraná, Brazil
Yanjun Zhao	Troy University, USA

Invited Speakers

Carol O'Sullivan	Trinity College Dublin, Ireland
Alexander Bronstein	Israel Institute of Technology, Tel Aviv University and Intel Corporation, Israel
Falk Schreiber	University of Konstanz, Germany and Monash University Melbourne, Australia
Catherine Pelachaud	CNRS/University of Pierre and Marie Curie, France

Contents

Computer Vision Theory and Applications

Computer Graphics Theory and Applications

Sensor-Fusion-Based Trajectory Reconstruction for Quadrotor Drones

Jielei Zhang$^{(\boxtimes)}$, Jie Feng, and Bingfeng Zhou

Institute of Computer Science and Technology, Peking University, Beijing, China
{zjl1992,feng_jie,cczbf}@pku.edu.cn

Abstract. In this paper, we propose a novel sensor-fusion-based method to eliminate errors of MEMS IMUs, and reconstruct trajectory of quadrotor drones. MEMS IMUs are widely equipped in quadrotor drones and other mobile devices. Unfortunately, they carry a lot of inherent errors, which cause poor results in trajectory reconstruction. To solve this problem, an error model for accelormeter signals in MEMS IMUs is established. In this model, the error is composed of a bias component and a noise component. First, a low-pass filter with downsampling is applied to reduce the noise component. Then, the bias component is detected and eliminated dynamically with the assistance of other sensors. Finally, the trajectory of the drone is reconstructed through integration of the calibrated accelormeter data. We apply our trajectory reconstruction method on Parrot AR.Drone 2.0 which employs a low-cost MEMS IMU. The experimental results prove its effectiveness. This method can theoretically be applied to any other mobile devices which are equipped with MEMS IMUs.

Keywords: MEMS IMUs · Sensor fusion · Inertial navigation · Trajectory reconstruction

1 Introduction

As one kind of mobile devices, the quadrotor drone has the characteristics of wide application, small size, flexible movement, and so on. A large amount of methods have been proposed for the application of comsumer-level drones these years. Trajectory reconstruction is one of the most important basis for drone applications.

The trajectory reconstruction has a wide application in computer graphics. The self-location information can provide important camera parameters, which could be applied in 3-D reconstruction [1] or image-based rendering. It also can be applied in self-localization and map building [2]. Additionally, the drone cinematography could utilize reconstructed trajectory as virtual rail [3].

Methods based on IMU (inertial measurement unit) is one of options for trajectory reconstruction. The position can be calculated through the second-order integration of accelerometer signals in IMU Data [4].

© Springer Nature Switzerland AG 2019
D. Bechmann et al. (Eds.): VISIGRAPP 2018, CCIS 997, pp. 3–24, 2019.
https://doi.org/10.1007/978-3-030-26756-8_1

However, due to the character of MEMS, significant errors occur in measured IMU data, especially low-cost MEMS IMU. Those errors usually take the form of *noise* and *bias* [5].

A number of methods have been proposed to reduce errors in MEMS signals [6–8]. For instance, Kalman Filter is a common estimation approach. Usually, through Kalman Filter, IMU data is combined with computer vision, GPS or other sensors, which can also reconstruct trajectory directly or indirectly. However, the reconstruction results through Kalman Filter depends on the error-staute estimation, which is estimated in advance. Such methods may fail, if the error statue is estimated incorrectly.

Take those limitations into consideration, we focus on the trajectory reconstruction based on IMU. An effective method is proposed to reduce errors in MEMS sensors in this paper.

We establish an error model, which consists of the types of MEMS errors, i.e., the noise and the bias. Different from traditional methods that eliminate bias just once at the static beginning, we process the two components separately and dynamically without highly depending on the priori error-state estimation. For the noise component, errors are treated as high-frequency signals, which can be reduced by a low-pass filter with downsampling. For the bias componet, errors occur in a form of *data drifting*. Thus, we adopt a sensor-fusion method to detect and eliminate the bias. We first detect the event timestamps with the help of multiple auxiliary sensors. The accelerometer data is then segmented into sections according to those timestamps, and the bias is corrected in each section. After that, the calibrated data is obtained.

The pipeline of our method is as follows: First, IMU sensor data is collected and preprocessed, including coordinate transformation between body frame and inertial frame. Then, errors, both noise and bias, are eliminated according to the established error model. Finally, the trajectory is reconstructed through the second-order integration of calibrated accelerometer data. The effectiveness of our method is proved by experimental results.

The main contributions of this paper include:

1. A novel method aiming to estimate errors in MEMS is proposed in this paper. Errors in different types are eliminated seperately and dynamically. This method relies less on priori error estimation.
2. The sensor-fusion-based bias elimination algorithm in our paper is highly adaptive. The type of combined sensors is not limited to what we applied in this paper. In fact, it can be extended to any other sensors.
3. Our method works effectively even on low-cost MEMS IMU which produces more instable errors, while most previous work relies on MEMS IMU with higher precision.
4. In theory, our method can be applied not only to quadrotor drones but also to other mobile devices, as long as they are equipped with MEMS IMU.

2   Related Work

2.1   Trajectory Reconstruction Method Based on Sensors

Plenty of sensors, equipped on mobile devices, can be used in trajectory reconstruction. There are lots of trajectory reconstruction methods based on sensors, such as follows:

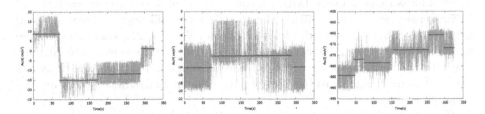

Fig. 1. Raw accelerometer signals of 3 axes (X, Y and Z) collected from a static device. The significant noise and data drifting in the signal will lead to wrong results in trajectory reconstruction [30]. (Color figure online)

GPS-Based Localization. The principle of localization method based on GPS is that, a GPS receiver monitors several satellites and solves equations to determine where the receiver is in real time. Due to the low accuracy and limitations of GPS, many methods are raised to improve accuracy, such as D-GPS [9], aided navigation [10] and so on. However, GPS is not available around large obstacles such as tall buildings and tunnels [11], and thus this kind of method will be invalid in many cases.

Visual Odometry. Visual odometry is a method to determine the position and orientation of a robot by analyzing the associated camera images [12]. It is a localization method based on computer vision. Lots of methods adopt camera in trajectory reconstruction. The method in [13] locates two surveillance cameras and simultaneously reconstructs object's 3D trajectories. Silvatti et al. utilizes submerged video cameras in an underwater 3D motion capture system to reconstruct 3D trajectory [14]. Nevertheless, computer vision methods are not effective in textureless environment usually, such as wide snowfield or dark night.

Wireless-Based Localization. Wireless-based localization is mainly applied in indoor situations. There are many wireless devices. The most widely-used wireless devices are Wi-Fi and Bluetooth [15,16]. A most common wireless localization technique is called "fingerprinting" for getting position information [17]. One can calculate its location according to the magnitude of received signals from several base stations. The inconvenience of these wireless approaches is that they require base stations set up in advance in the scene. Hence, the Wi-Fi/Bluetooth signal is not always available for most common situations.

Ultrasonic Sensor/LIDAR-Based Localization. The principles of localization through LIDAR [18] and ultrasonic sensors [19] are similar. They measure the distance to a certain target by calculating time between when emit a pulse and when receive echoes. Nonetheless, LIDAR is so expensive that most mobile devices are not equipped with it, while the measuring range of ultrasonic sensors is too limited to cover most area [20].

Inertial Navigation. Inertial navigation is to get one's location through IMU (inertial measurement unit). IMU is a combination of 3-axis accelerometers and 3-axis gyroscopes. It can measure the specific force and angular velocity of an object. According to the work of Titterton and Weston [21], trajectory can be reconstructed through the second-order integration of the accelerometer signals. The attitude information could be obtained through gyroscopes, which assists the accelerometer signals to be transformed from the body frame to the inertial frame [22].

Some work studies how to utilize the IMU signals to reconstruct trajectory [4]. For example, writing trajectory based on IMU is reconstructed through a pen tip direction estimation method in the work of Toyozumi et al. [23]. An error compensation method and a multi-axis dynamic switch developed by Wang et al. to minimize the cumulative errors caused by sensors [24].

Because of the merits of MEMS IMU, such as low-cost, light weight and small size, most mobile devices are equipped with MEMS IMU. But the main disadvantage of the MEMS IMU is its low accuracy on account of errors [25].

Taking into account the advantages and disadvantages, MEMS IMU signals are employed as a main source of data for reconstructing trajectory in our work. IMUs depend less on the environment. IMU-based trajectory reconstruction methods are quite practicle for MEMS IMU is commonly equipped in mobile devices. However, it is impossible to reconstruct trajectory by IMU alone due to the errors carried in MEMS IMU. Therefore, we propose a sensor-fusion-based method to eliminate errors in MEMS IMU signals.

2.2   Methods to Calibrate IMU Signals

Recent advances in MEMS (Micro-Electro-Mechanical Systems) technique bring possibility of producing small and light inertial navigation systems. On the other hand, the main problem of MEMS devices is its low accuracy. The error, as illustrated in Fig. 1, is indicated by bias and noise in their measurements as elaborated in the work of Woodman [5]. During trajectory reconstruction, the accelerometer signals are integrated twice, which makes the error grow even rapidly.

Many researchers study on reducing errors caused by IMU devices. A zero velocity compensation (ZVC) mechanism to reduce the accumulative errors of IMUs proposed by Yang et al. [6]. Pedley applies linear least squares optimization to compute the recalibration parameters from the available measurements to reduce errors [7].

Some other methods adopt Kalman Filter to combine IMU with computer vision to improve accuracy. For instance, a VISINAV algorithm is presented to enable planetary landing, which utilizes an extended Kalman filter (EKF)

to reduce errors [26]. Additionally, a state space model is applied to estimate
the navigation states in an extended Kalman filter [8]. However, the error-state
vector, which is estimated in advance, has a direct impact on the result, that is,
large deviation of error-state estimation leads to poor results.

Most of the works mentioned before do not aim at low-cost MEMS devices
which carry much more errors, while low-cost MEMS devices are commonly used
because of convenience.

Consequently, we focus on the trajectory reconstruction from low-cost MEMS
IMU in this paper. A type of quadrotor drone is taken as an example of mobile
devices. During the course, different error models are designed for different types
of errors, so that diverse errors can be eliminated in targeted ways.

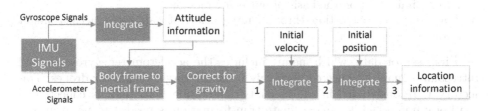

Fig. 2. The principle of trajectory reconstruction based on IMU. In the figure, 1.
Accelerometer data in inertial frame; 2. Velocity calculated from accelerometer data;
3. Location information calculated from velocity.

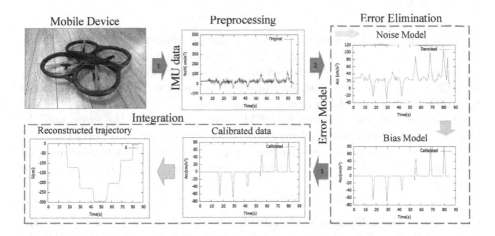

Fig. 3. The pipeline of our method: (1) Data collection and preprocessing; (2) Error
elimination according to error model; (3) Integration and trajectory reconstruction.

3   IMU-Based Trajectory Reconstruction

Trajectory can be reconstructed from IMU signals shown in Fig. 2 in ideal status. The measured accelerometer data is transferred from the body frame to

the inertial frame according to the attitude estimation calculated by gyroscope signals. The accelerometer data is then corrected for gravity. Next, velocity is obtained from the integration of the accelerometer data. Finally, trajectory is reconstructed from the integration of the velocity, that is, the second-order integration of the accelerometer data [5].

However, inevitable errors exist in MEMS IMU signals. That's why the trajectory reconstruction cannot be directly calculated in such ideal way.

Thus, we propose a trajectory reconstruction method for quadrotor drones in this paper, which utilizes the measurement of IMU and other sensors. The pipeline of our method is illustrated in Fig. 3. It consists of three phases:

1. Sensor data collection and preprocess;
2. Error elimination on the basis of our error model;
3. Trajectory reconstruction through integration of calibrated accelerometer data.

First, sensor data, which mainly includes the accelerometer, gyroscope and ultrasonic signals, is collected discretely from the target quadrotor drones. Trajectory is reconstructed in the inertial frame while IMU data is collected in the body frame [27], so a coordinate transformation is needed to perform in a preprocessing phase.

We denotes the raw measured accelerometer data at time point t in the body frame as $a^0(t) = (a^0_x(t), a^0_y(t), a^0_z(t))^T$, and its correspondence in the inertial frame as $\tilde{a}(t) = (\tilde{a}_x(t), \tilde{a}_y(t), \tilde{a}_z(t))^T$. Thus, the coordinate transformation can be formulated as

$$a^0(t) = R(\phi, \theta, \varphi) \cdot \tilde{a}(t), \tag{1}$$

where $R(\phi, \theta, \varphi)$ is the rotation matrix from the inertial frame to the body frame [28]; ϕ, θ and φ stand for the three Euler angles between the two frames.

Because the raw IMU signals contain a lot of errors due to the low accuracy of MEMS, the most important step in our pipeline is to eliminate those errors before the data is used for trajectory calculation.

As mentioned above, errors in MEMS are comprised of the noise and the bias. Different from traditional methods which process the two parts together, we divide the error model into a noise component $\epsilon_n(t)$ and a bias component $\epsilon_b(t)$, and process them separately in the second step. So we design the error model as,

$$\tilde{a}(t) = \alpha \cdot a(t) + \epsilon_n(t) + \epsilon_b(t) - H \cdot g, \tag{2}$$

where $a(t)$ is the calibrated accelerometer data, α is a scale factor between the measured inertial data and the actual data, $H = (0, 0, 1)^T$, and g stands for the gravitational acceleration.

The two parts are processed separately in the next phase with accordance to our error model. We first reduce the noise, then eliminate the bias. Thus, a set of calibrated accelerometer data $a(t)$ is obtained.

Finally, the calibrated accelerometer data is integrated over time to obtain the 3D trajectory. Hence, the 3D position at time t_i, noted as $S_i = (S_{ix}, S_{iy}, S_{iz})^T$, which is calculated as follows:

$$S_i = V_i * \Delta t_i + S_{i-1} = \sum_{k=0}^{i} v_k * \Delta t_k = \sum_{k=0}^{i} (\sum_{j=0}^{k} a(t_j) \Delta t_j) \Delta t_k, \qquad (3)$$

where $a(t_i)$ represents the ith signal of the calibrated accelerometer data, and Δt_i is the time interval between t_i and t_{i-1}. V_i stands for the velocity calculated from $a(t)$. Thence, $\{S_i | i = 1, 2, ..., n\}$ composes the reconstructed trajectory.

4   Reducing Noise

According to the previous analysis, the errors can be classified into two types, noise and bias. As shown in Fig. 1, the measured accelerometer signals seriously oscillate at a large amplitude around certain values (marked by red lines). This serious vibration results in noise. On the other hand, even when the device remains still while its signals are being collected, the red line keeps drifting from its true value, and presents a step shaped line instead of a straight line. This kind of data drifting is called bias.

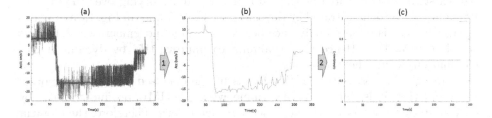

Fig. 4. Eliminating noise and bias errors in the accelerometer data. (a) Raw measured accelerometer signals collected from a static devices; (b) After reducing noise; (c) After eliminating bias [30].

Here, in this section, we focus on how to reduce noise, and the other type of the errors will be discussed in the following section.

The noise in the MEMS IMU data could be regarded as a high frequency signal superimposed on the real signal, while the real signal is in low frequency. Therefore, valid data could be obtained by filtering out the noise through a low-pass filter.

Since the measured data is in the discrete form, the low-pass filter can be designed through FIR (finte impulse response filter) [29].

Hence, given the measured raw accelerometer signals $\{\tilde{a}(t_i) | i = 1, 2, ..., n\}$, the denoised accelerometer data $\{\hat{a}'(t_i)\}$ is filtered out by

$$\hat{a}'(t_i) = \sum_{k=0}^{n} h(t_k) \tilde{a}(t_i - t_k), \qquad (4)$$

where $h(.)$ is the impulse response function of the low-pass filter. The filter is presented in a convolution form in the time domain. Here we adopt Rectangular as the low-pass window function. The parameters in Rectangular will be adjusted to a proper value.

In order to achieve a better denoised result, a down sampling is applied to the filtered data, which could reduce the amount of the following calculation as well. Thus, the final denoised accelerometer data set $\{\hat{a}(t)\}$ is a subset of $\{\hat{a}'(t)\}$, which is down sampled at a certain period δ. In our current implementation, we adopt $\delta = 100$ ms.

In fact, the high-frequency noise also exists in the signals of other sensors, such as gyroscopes and ultrasonic sensors, and thus the data of these sensors should also be denoised in the similar way. After denoising, the smoother result will be used in the following bias elimination method.

5 Eliminating Bias

Figure 4(b) shows that, a relatively smooth curve of the accelerometer data is obtained after filtering the noise. But the value is not correct yet for bias errors still exist. It is represented as the data drifting. It is varying over time in low frequency [5], as demonstrated by the change of the red lines in Fig. 1. In previous works, the bias is removed only once before the whole movement, which ignores the dynamical bias. Hence we are aiming to improve this by dynamical bias elimination during the movement.

Through the observation of the details in the denoised accelerometer data, we found that it is difficult to determine when the IMU produces a bias by only analyzing the absolute value of accelerometer data. Therefore, the moment when a bias happens should be found out, in order to eliminate bias correctly and dynamically during the movement of the device.

Although bias may occur on all MEMS sensors aperiodically, it is less probably to occur on multiple sensors at the same time. Hence, a sensor-fusion-based method is proposed to detect the moment when bias occurs.

The denoised accelerometer data can be segmented into a series of sections along the timeline, according to these moments. In each section, we consider the device maintaining the same motion status, which means the accelerometer value should be a constant.

Here, we define each section on the timeline as an *event*, and the beginning moment of each *event* is called an *event timestamp*.

We then take different strategies to eliminate bias errors according to different *event* tags. This method, through segmentation on the timeline, will effectively compensate for the accumulation of bias errors over time.

5.1 Event Detection

For the sake of event timestamps detection, we first inspect the derivative of the accelerometer data over time, which indicates the vibration of the accelerometer data. If the absolute derivative value is greater than a certain positive threshold

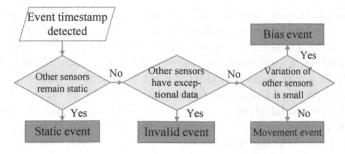

Fig. 5. Determining the type of an event according to the status of multiple sensors [30].

τ, it indicates the status of the IMU is being changed, i.e., an event is happening. Hence, this particular moment is recorded as an event timestamp, the beginning of a new event.

However, the initially detected events are not necessarily the bias events that aimed to process. Maybe the event timestamp is when a real movement happens. Sometimes, exception events will also occur. Because the possibility of bias occurring simultaneously in multiple sensors is extremely low, we refer to the status of multiple different sensors as an assistant, e.g. gyroscopes and ultrasonic sensors. Therefore, different types of the events are discriminated through this way.

By analyzing the data status from other sensors, initial events can be classified into the following four types, as illustrated in Fig. 5:

Bias Event. Bias event is when the device produces bias errors. The accelerometer data in this event needs to be corrected. If the variation of other sensors is small at the event timestamp while the event still happen, the bias is considered to happen. For instance, the accelerometer data has an intense change while other sensors data remains stable, which indicates bias occurs to the accelerometer sensor. Therefore, the event is marked as a bias event.

Movement Event. This type of event indicates that the device is in a movement, that is, the device is moving in a certain direction. In this case, the change of the accelerometer data is caused by a real movement, and other sensors data should correspondingly show reasonable variations. For instance, the accelerometer data has an intense change while other sensors data also has a coordinated change in the correspond direction, which indicates the device is taking an action. Therefore, the event is marked as a movement event.

Static Event. In this case, the mobile device is actually in a static status, i.e., its accelerometer data and speed should be zero. That can be deduced by Euler angles (attitude angles: picth, roll, yaw) ϕ, θ and φ of the device. If the values of the picth, roll and the change of yaw are all very near to zero, and the status lasts a period time with the data of other sensors also has little variation, the event is regarded as a static event. Additionally, the static event should last for a little while.

Invalid Event. In some special cases, we may encounter invalid data occasionally. For instance, when the value exceeds the measuring range, or the data is in a violent shaking, those cases cannot present the real status. Therefore, if other sensors exhibit an irregular status, e.g. the gyroscope data vibrates frequently and severely in a very short period, the event is marked as an invalid event.

Here, bias event and movement event are regarded as regular types, while static event and invalid event are considered as handful types, which happens occasionally. Besides, we may design that some static events happen on purpose in order to eliminate cumulative errors.

5.2   Processing Algorithm

The accelerometer data can be segmented into events after the detection of event timestamps. Then, the accelorometer data is calibrated in each event, according to the type of the event. Consequently, bias errors will all be eliminated. The bias elimination algorithm is listed as Algorithm 1.

Here, we denote the calibrated accelerometer value in the previous section as *PreAcc*, and the bias value of current section as *BiasValue*, both initialized as zero.

If the event corresponds to a bias event, the motion status of the device is not actually changing although a data drifting is occurring. Hence, we correct the accelerometer data in this event to the calibrated data in the previous section (Fig. 6(b)). Meanwhile, the bias value, i.e., the difference between the measured data and the calibrated data, is updated and recorded as *BiasValue*. It will be applied in the processing of the subsequent events.

If the event corresponds to a movement event, the variation of the accelerometer data is caused by a real movement. Then, the calibrated accelerometer value can be calculated as the median of the data in this event subtracting current recorded *BiasValue* (Fig. 5(c)). After that, *PreAcc* is updated as the same value for the calculation of the following events.

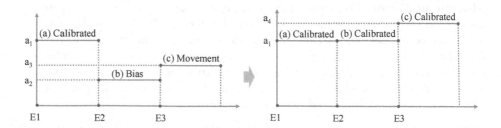

Fig. 6. An example of event processing [30]. Accelerometer data is calibrated by sections according to different event types.

Algorithm 1. Bias Elimination Algorithm.

Input:

1. Denoised accelerometer data $\{\hat{a}(t)|t = 1, 2, ..., n\}$;
2. Detected events $\{E_i|i = 1, 2, ..., m\}$;

Output:

1. Calibrated accelerometer data $\{a(t_i)|i = 1, 2, .., n\}$;

Definition:

1. t_i: the event timestamp of E_i.
2. $median(.)$: a function returns the median value of a data set.
3. $BiasValue$: the bias value of the accelerometer data, initialized as zero;
4. $PreAcc$: the calibrated accelerometer data of the prevoius event, initialized as zero;

Algorithm:

1: **for** i from 1 to m **do**
2:     **if** $E_i == static$ **then**
3:         **while** $t \in [t_i, t_{i+1})$ **do**
4:             $a(t) = 0.0$
5:         **end while**
6:         $PreAcc = 0.0$
7:         $BiasValue = median(\hat{a}(t), t \in [t_i, t_{i+1}))$
8:     **else if** $E_i == invalid$ **then**
9:         All parameters remain unchanged.
10:     **else if** $E_i == bias$ **then**
11:         **while** $t \in [t_i, t_{i+1})$ **do**
12:             $a(t) = PreAcc$
13:         **end while**
14:         $curAcc = median(\hat{a}(t), t \in [t_i, t_{i+1}))$
15:         $BiasValue = curAcc - PreAcc$
16:     **else if** $E_i == movement$ **then**
17:         $curAcc = median(\hat{a}(t), t \in [t_i, t_{i+1}))$
18:         **while** $t \in [t_i, t_{i+1})$ **do**
19:             $a(t) = curAcc - BiasValue$
20:         **end while**
21:         $PreAcc = curAcc - BiasValue$
22:     **end if**
23: **end for**

In the case of a static event, the device stays still and motionless. Hence, the accelerometer data in this event should be reset to zero. $PreAcc$ is also cleared to zero, and the median of the accelerometer data in this event is recorded as the $BiasValue$.

Finally, for an invalid event, it can be view as the same as the previous event because of the very short time. Thus, the process of this event follows the previous event, and all parameters remain unchanged.

Therefore, the output of the algorithm is the final calibrated accelerometer data, which could be directly applied in trajectory reconstruction.

Table 1. Onboard sensors of AR. Drone 2.0 [30].

Sensors	Specifications
3-axis accelerometers	Bosch BMA 150, Measuring range: ± 2g
2-axis gyroscopes	Invensense IDG500, Measuring rate: up to 500 deg/s
1-axis gyroscope	Epson XV3700, On vertical axis
Ultrasonic sensor	Measuring rate: 25 Hz
Vertical camera	64° diagonal lens, Frame rate: 60 fps
Front camera	93° wide-angle diagonal lens, Frame rate: 15 fps

6   Experiments

We have proposed trajectory reconstruction method for quadrotor drones so far. The data from the accelerometer and other sensors on the device is utilized in the reconstruction in a manner of sensor-fusion. In order to validate the effectiveness of our method, we apply it to several quadrotor drones with the same type, which are equipped with low-cost MEMS IMU and other sensors.

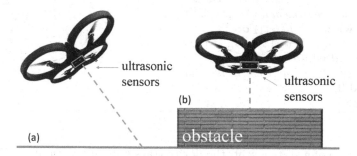

Fig. 7. The ultrasonic measurement may deviate from the actual height during movement or flying over obstacles [30]. (The red rectangels stand for the ultrasonic sensor on the drone, and the red dotted lines indicate the ultrasonic measurements). (Color figure online)

6.1 Implementations

In our experiments, we adopt the Parrot AR. Drone 2.0 as the target quadrotor drones. AR. Drone 2.0 is a lightweight quadrotor. A Linux based real-time operating system and multiple onboard sensors are equipped on it. The sensors and their specifications are listed in Table 1.

Accelerometers provide the major data for the calculation of the trajectory among all these sensors, while the others are used as auxiliary sensors in the bias elimination method.

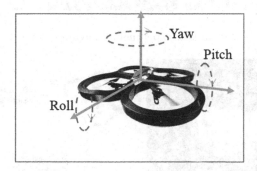

Fig. 8. Euler angles on quadrotor drones.

The gyroscope data is applied for attitude estimation, i.e., calculate the euler angel: pitch, roll and yaw (shown in Fig. 8). It can also be used for event timestamp detection on the X or Y axis, because the drone would tilt if there is a movement on the X - Y plane, and that will result in a variation of the gyroscope measurement.

There is an ultrasonic sensor on the bottom of the AR. Drone. It measures the distance from the drone to the ground. The absolute derivative of the ultrasonic data is utilized in event detection on the Z-axis. However, it is not directly used as the trajectory on the Z-axis, because when the drone tilts during its movements, the angle of the ultrasonic sensor would also change. Therefore, its measurement can not reflect the actual height of the drone (Fig. 7(a)). Besides, when the drone flies over a series of obstacles, large variations may also occur in its measurement (Fig. 7(b)).

In addition, we perform our experiments indoor for the ultrasonic sensor has a limited range. Indoor experiments can also simplify the flight condition, like the absence of wind. On the other hand, indoor localization is more difficult for there is no GPS signals indoors.

6.2 Experimental Environment

We apply our experiments indoors, where there is no GPS signals for reference. Moreover, indoor environments may avoid the influence of winds and other

Fig. 9. Our experimental environment.

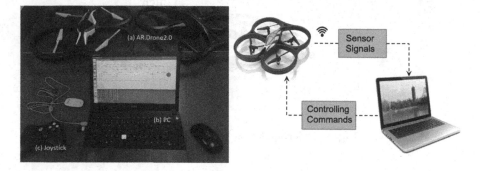

Fig. 10. Drone Control Technique.

affects. The experimental environment is shown in Fig. 9 left, where the floor is relatively flat. Note that surfaces of obstacles in the environment are relatively flat as well, so that the ultrasonic sensor can work effectively as an assist of accelerometer data in Z-axis.

Flight Route Control

As shown in Fig. 10, the Parrot AR.Drone 2.0 communicates with PC through Wi-Fi. We control the automatic flight route of the drone through its SDK[1]. A joystick is also used to avoid emergencies, e.g., that the drone hits the wall or breaks the window. The controlling commands of the joystick are sent to the drone by means of PC.

Trjactory Groud-Truth Measurement

The ground-truth of our experiment is measured in a manual way. Several rulers are fixed in the environment, as shown in Fig. 11. At the same time, a laser range finder is applied to sample the distance between the drone and the ground or between the drone and the staring position (shown in Fig. 9(b)). Since the flight route is determined by programming, we could approximate the movement of the

---

[1] http://developer.parrot.com/products.html.

drone, which makes our measurement easier. Besides, because the drone itself may be influenced by the environment, such as the temperature and its battery power, the drone cannot be controlled accurately. That's why the drone routes do not perfectly match the designed route.

Fig. 11. Measure the distance by a laser ranger.

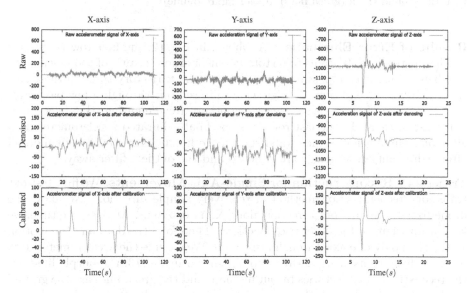

Fig. 12. The result of error elimination for the accelerometer data on three axes [30]. The first row is the raw accelerometer data collected from a quadrotor drone. The second row shows the signal after denoising by a low-pass filter and down sampling. The last row is the final calibrated output of accelerometer data after bias elimination.

6.3 Experimental Results

A large amount of experiments are performed in order to verify the effectiveness of the proposed algorithm. Here are some experimental results demonstrated in this section.

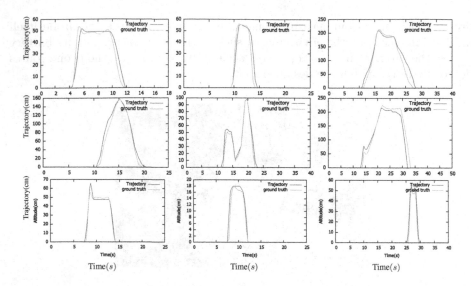

Fig. 13. Trajectory reconstruction results on a single-axis (purple lines), comparing with the ground truth (green lines). (Color figure online)

Results of Error Elimination. As shown in Fig. 12, the first row is the raw accelerometer data. It seems to be totally out of order because of too much noise and bias. Thus, it is impossible to reconstruct the trajectory through these raw signals. In the second row, the signals are filtered out through a low-pass filter with down sampling, which becomes smoother after denoising. But bias errors still exist in there. In the last row, it is the final calibrated accelerometer data after bias elimination. Hence, valid signals are finally extracted by our method after redundant error signals are removed and the outliers filter away.

Trajectory Reconstruction for Single-Axis Movements. We first test our trajectory reconstruction method in relatively simple direction. We allow the drone to move in only one direction along X, Y, or Z axis. At the same time, we keep it invariant in the other two directions. Therefore, the data and the motion status is on only one axis through inspection. We assume the accelerometer data on the other two axes are always zero. As shown in Fig. 13, the purple lines are the reconstructed trajectories by our method, and the green lines are the ground truth trajectory. Through the comparison, we can see that our result is close to the actual movement. The errors of reconstruction are controlled within 10 cm in each axis.

Algorithm Calibration. In order to obtain better results, the event detection thresholds τ for the accelerometer or other sensors' data, together with the window size of low-pass filter, need to be adjusted to a proper value. In fact, this parameters adjustment of algorithm can be adaptively accomplished in our method. We first pick a small part of the data at the beginning of the flight, and obtain the optimal thresholds interactively. Then, the rest of the trajectory can be automatically reconstructed with these thresholds.

An example is given in Fig. 14, only the red part of the result is the one after the algorithm calibration is accomplished interactively. The purple line is the result when the parameters are fixed before. The final result is similar with what we designed in advance, which shows the adaptability of our method.

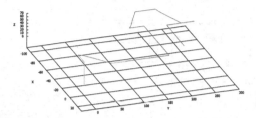

Fig. 14. Algorithm calibration [30]. Optimal parameters are interactively searched for using the first part of data (red line), and then the whole trajectory (purple line) can be automatically reconstructed. (Color figure online)

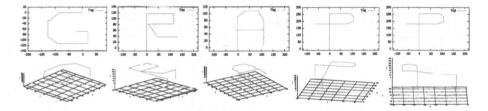

Fig. 15. Trajectories reconstructed from Ar.drone. We design target trajectories as the letters of "GRAPP". And the results match the targets well. The first row is the trajectory in X-Y plane. The second row is each corresponding one in three-dimensional space [30].

Trajectory Reconstruction for Multiple-Axis Movements. After the success of single-axis tests, we carry out more complicated experiments of reconstructing trajectory on multiple axes. Drones fly along given routes with various shapes. The drone is controlled by PC through Wi-Fi. The route is designed in advance by a program so that it can fly at a relatively constant speed, and fly straightly in the given directions.

Several groups of reconstruction results are given in Figs. 15, 16, 17 and 18. Target trajectories are designed as meaningful letters. We can see that, the reconstructed routes are close to what we designed. After denoising and bias elimination, the valid accelerometer data can be extracted from the raw signal. The 3D trajectories of the drone can be correctly reconstructed. The reconstructed trajectories (purple lines) coincide with the ground truth routes (green lines).

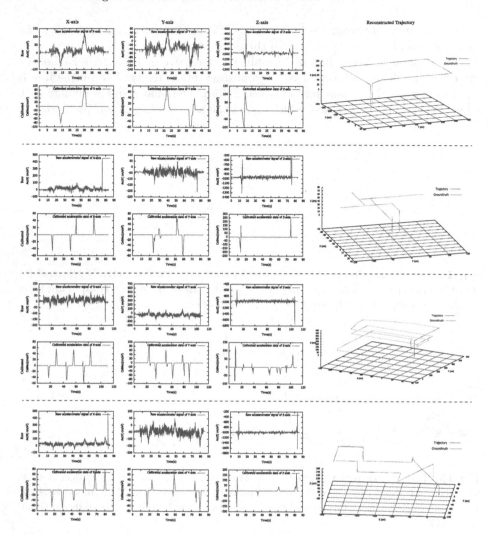

Fig. 16. Multi-axis trajectory reconstruction results. In each group, the left three columns show the raw and calibrated accelerometer data on X, Y and Z axis. The last column illustrates the final 3D reconstructed trajectories of the drone (purple line), comparing with the ground truth (green line). (Color figure online)

However, due to the instability of the controlling algorithm inside the drone, the actual flying route of the drone may have a little slight offsets. The offsets are too small to be detected due to the low accuracy of onboard sensors, hence they would be ignored by our algorithm. It is the reason that reconstructed trajectory is a little smoother and straighter than the actual trajectory.

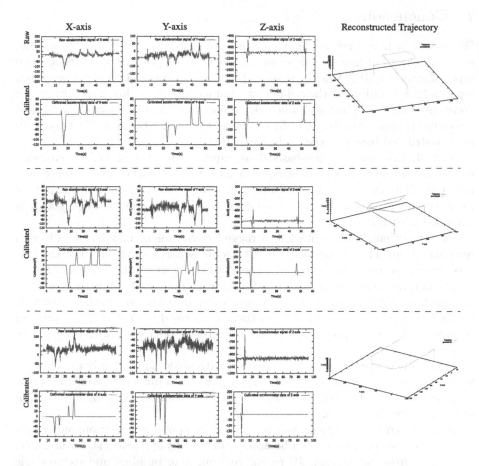

Fig. 17. Reconstructed trajectory "PKU", which is the abbreviation of our school. In each group, the left three columns show the raw and calibrated accelerometer data on X, Y and Z axis. The last column illustrates the final 3D reconstructed trajectories of the drone (purple line), comparing with the ground truth (green line). (Color figure online)

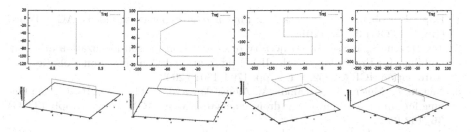

Fig. 18. Reconstructed trajectory "ICST", which is the abbreviation of our institute.

7 Conclusions

We present a novel method for trajectory reconstruction of quadrotor drones, which suffers from unavoidable errors of low-cost MEMS IMUs. There are two types of errors in MEMS IMUs: noise and bias. In our method, they are processed separately, according to their different characteristics. A low-pass filter with downsampling is applied to reduce the noise, and then a sensor-fusion-based algorithm is applied to dynamically eliminate the bias. Therefore, the trajectory is reconstructed based on the calibrated data.

In fact, this sensor-fusion-based bias elimination method can be extended to employ various kinds of sensors, such as cameras, gradienters, magnetometers, etc. That makes the method more practical. Theoretically, the trajectory reconstruction method can also be applied to any mobile device as long as it is equipped with IMUs.

In our current implementation, a rugged environment may cause failure in reconstruction. That is because the ultrasonic senor, as one of auxiliary sensors, would become invalid in such cases. In our future work, we will try to enroll more auxiliary sensors to handle more complicated conditions, so that our method may be applied to more scenarios. Besides, our method performs better in reconstructing straight lines than in curves due to the low accuracy of sensors. To solve this problem, we can approximate the curves with a set of line segments.

On another aspect, the flight routes of the drone do not perfectly match what we design, for the environment and battery power will influence the flying status of drone. Thus, we will put emphasis on the route controlling module as well, in order to make the drone fly more steadily.

Since the trajectory can provide important viewpoint information, our trajectory reconstruction method can be applied in various applications, for instance, automatic drone navigation, 3D reconstruction, map building and stereoscopic video synthesizing.

Acknowledgements. This work is partially supported by National Key Research and Development Program of China (2016QY02D0304) and NSFC grants (61602012).

References

1. Kopf, J., Cohen, M.F., Szeliski, R.: First-person hyper-lapse videos. ACM Trans. Graph. (TOG) **33**, 78 (2014)
2. Ten Hagen, S., Krose, B.: Trajectory reconstruction for self-localization and map building. In: Proceedings of the IEEE International Conference on Robotics and Automation, ICRA 2002, vol. 2, pp. 1796–1801 (2002)
3. Nägeli, T., Meier, L., Domahidi, A., Alonso-Mora, J., Hilliges, O.: Real-time planning for automated multi-view drone cinematography. ACM Trans. Graph. (TOG) **36**, 132 (2017)
4. Suvorova, S., Vaithianathan, T., Caelli, T.: Action trajectory reconstruction from inertial sensor measurements. In: 2012 11th International Conference on Information Science, Signal Processing and their Applications (ISSPA), pp. 989–994 (2012)

5. Woodman, O.J.: An introduction to inertial navigation. Technical report, University of Cambridge, Computer Laboratory (2007)
6. Yang, J., et al.: Analysis and compensation of errors in the input device based on inertial sensors. In: Proceedings of the International Conference on Information Technology: Coding and Computing, ITCC 2004, vol. 2, pp. 790–796 (2004)
7. Pedley, M.: High precision calibration of a three-axis accelerometer. Freescale Semicond. Appl. Note **1** (2013)
8. Fredrikstad, T.E.N.: Vision aided inertial navigation. Master's thesis, NTNU (2016)
9. Kee, C., Parkinson, B.W., Axelrad, P.: Wide area differential GPS. Navigation **38**, 123–145 (1991)
10. Farrell, J.: Aided navigation: GPS with high rate sensors (2008)
11. Kleusberg, A., Langley, R.B.: The limitations of GPS. GPS World **1** (1990)
12. Huang, A.S., et al.: Visual odometry and mapping for autonomous flight using an RGB-D camera. In: Christensen, Henrik I., Khatib, Oussama (eds.) Robotics Research. STAR, vol. 100, pp. 235–252. Springer, Cham (2017). https://doi.org/10.1007/978-3-319-29363-9_14
13. Pflugfelder, R., Bischof, H.: Localization and trajectory reconstruction in surveillance cameras with nonoverlapping views. IEEE Trans. Pattern Anal. Mach. Intell. **32**, 709–721 (2010)
14. Silvatti, A.P., Cerveri, P., Telles, T., Dias, F.A., Baroni, G., Barros, R.M.: Quantitative underwater 3D motion analysis using submerged video cameras: accuracy analysis and trajectory reconstruction. Comput. Methods Biomech. Biomed. Eng. **16**, 1240–1248 (2013)
15. Biswas, J., Veloso, M.: Wifi localization and navigation for autonomous indoor mobile robots. In: 2010 IEEE International Conference on Robotics and Automation (ICRA), pp. 4379–4384 (2010)
16. Faragher, R., Harle, R.: Location fingerprinting with bluetooth low energy beacons. IEEE J. Sel. Areas Commun. **33**, 2418–2428 (2015)
17. Chen, Y., Kobayashi, H.: Signal strength based indoor geolocation. In: IEEE International Conference on Communications, ICC 2002, vol. 1, pp. 436–439 (2002)
18. Amzajerdian, F., Pierrottet, D., Petway, L., Hines, G., Roback, V.: Lidar systems for precision navigation and safe landing on planetary bodies. In: Proceedings of the SPIE, vol. 8192, pp. 819202 (2011)
19. Hazas, M., Hopper, A.: Broadband ultrasonic location systems for improved indoor positioning. IEEE Trans. Mob. Comput. **5**, 536–547 (2006)
20. Rencken, W.D.: Concurrent localisation and map building for mobile robots using ultrasonic sensors. In: Proceedings of the 1993 IEEE/RSJ International Conference on IROS, vol. 3, pp. 2192–2197 (1993)
21. Titterton, D., Weston, J.L.: Strapdown Inertial Navigation Technology, vol. 17 (2004)
22. Suh, Y.S.: Attitude estimation using low cost accelerometer and gyroscope. In: Proceedings KORUS 2003 the 7th Korea-Russia International Symposium on Science and Technology, vol. 2, pp. 423–427 (2003)
23. Toyozumi, N., Takahashi, J., Lopez, G.: Trajectory reconstruction algorithm based on sensor fusion between IMU and strain gauge for stand-alone digital pen. In: 2016 IEEE International Conference on Robotics and Biomimetics (ROBIO), pp. 1906–1911 (2016)
24. Wang, J.S., Hsu, Y.L., Liu, J.N.: An inertial-measurement-unit-based pen with a trajectory reconstruction algorithm and its applications. IEEE Trans. Ind. Electron. **57**, 3508–3521 (2010)

25. Park, M., Gao, Y.: Error and performance analysis of mems-based inertial sensors with a low-cost GPS receiver. Sensors **8**, 2240–2261 (2008)
26. Mourikis, A.I., Trawny, N., Roumeliotis, S.I., Johnson, A.E., Ansar, A., Matthies, L.: Vision-aided inertial navigation for spacecraft entry, descent, and landing. IEEE Trans. Robot. **25**, 264–280 (2009)
27. Lee, T., Leoky, M., McClamroch, N.H.: Geometric tracking control of a quadrotor UAV on SE (3). In: 2010 49th IEEE Conference on Decision and Control (CDC), pp. 5420–5425 (2010)
28. Bristeau, P.J., Callou, F., Vissiere, D., Petit, N.: The navigation and control technology inside the AR. Drone micro UAV. In: IFAC Proceedings, vol. 44, pp. 1477–1484 (2011)
29. Antoniou, A.: Digital Signal Processing. McGraw-Hill, New York (2016)
30. Zhang, J., Feng, J., Zhou, B.: Sensor-fusion-based trajectory reconstruction for mobile devices. In: Proceedings of the 13th International Conference on Computer Graphics Theory and Applications, pp. 48–58 (2018)

3D Articulated Model Retrieval Using Depth Image Input

Jun-Yang Lin[1], May-Fang She[1], Ming-Han Tsai[1](✉), I-Chen Lin[1],
Yo-Chung Lau[2], and Hsu-Hang Liu[2]

[1] Department of Computer Science, National Chiao Tung University,
1001 University Rd., Hsinchu, Taiwan
g83u6219@hotmail.com, may930451.cs96@nctu.edu.tw, parkertsai@gmail.com,
ichenlin@cs.nctu.edu.tw
[2] Telecommunication Laboratories, Chunghwa Telecom Co., Ltd.,
99 Dianyan Rd., Yangmei District, Taoyuan, Taiwan
{lyc0326,hsuhang}@cht.com.tw

Abstract. In this paper, a novel framework to retrieve 3D articulated models from a database based on one or few depth images is presented. Existing state-of-the-arts retrieval approaches usually constrain the view points of query images or assume that the target models are rigid-body. When they are applied to retrieving articulated models, the retrieved results are substantially influenced by the model postures. In our work, we extracts the limbs and torso regions from projections and analyzes the features of local regions. The use of both global and local features can alleviate the disturbance of model postures in model retrieval. Experiments show that the proposed method can efficiently retrieve relevant models within a second, and provides higher retrieval accuracy than those of compared methods for not only rigid body 3D models but also models with articulated limbs.

Keywords: 3D object retrieval · Depth image analysis ·
Shape matching

1 Introduction

With the popularity of depth sensor and 3D modeling tools, more and more 3D models are designed and uploaded by creators and vendors. People can use their own smart phone to build a 3D model without prior knowledge. In order to effectively use the numerous models, various kinds of methods were proposed to improve the efficiency of 3D model retrieval from a large dataset. Searching by keywords is the most common way to retrieve desired models, but it can be

---

Electronic supplementary material The online version of this chapter (https://doi.org/10.1007/978-3-030-26756-8_2) contains supplementary material, which is available to authorized users.

D. Bechmann et al. (Eds.): VISIGRAPP 2018, CCIS 997, pp. 25–47, 2019.
https://doi.org/10.1007/978-3-030-26756-8_2

difficult for a user to figure out appropriate keywords describing the variety of model shapes. Therefore, most successful 3D model retrieval systems adopted content-based search and required users to input sketches or images as queries. Funkhouser et al. [17] presented a shape-based query engine, supporting queries based on keywords, 2D sketches, 3D sketches, and 3D models. The LightField descriptor proposed by Chen et al. [8] projects each 3D model onto silhouette images from vertices of an enveloping dodecahedron. It then evaluates the similarities between query images and silhouettes of database models.

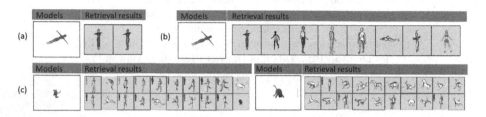

Fig. 1. (a) Retrieval results using one global shape depth image only. (b) Retrieval results of our proposed method. (c) Top 20 retrieval results of our method for articulated models and non-rigid quadruped animal models in one random view.

Nevertheless, most existing methods assume that the 3D models are rigid or the viewpoint of input images are constrained, e.g. the frontal or side views. In the case of querying by views, they compared two projected shapes based on shape features extracted from the whole projected silhouette or depth images. When a user takes a articulated model with limbs as the input, the retrieved results can be substantially influenced by the limb postures of models or view points. Therefore, we propose evaluating not only the global projected shapes but also local features. As shown in Fig. 1, if we only considered the global shapes, it led to the result Fig. 1(a). However, if we compared the local information extracted from torso and limb regions combining with previous global shape features, more relevant models can be retrieved as shown in Fig. 1(b).

Based on the aforementioned concept, we measured different combinations of global and local features and developed a prototype system. Given one or multiple depth images as query inputs, the proposed system can efficiently retrieve relevant models from a dataset extended from publicly used databases. Our experiments also demonstrate that it can retrieve more accurate results than results by comparative methods, for not only rigid body 3D models but also models with articulated limbs.

This paper is an extend version of Lin et al. [1]. We introduce more features for object retrieval and examine which combination of features is suitable in our application. We also compare the state-of-the-art methods to our method in different database. The results shows our method performs well not only in articulated model database, but also in rigid body model database.

2   Related Work

To intuitively assign input queries, several research works adopted view-based matching methods to retrieve models from sketch or image inputs. View-based retrieval systems usually assume that 3D shapes can be represented by several 2D projections from different views. Chen et al. [8] thought that if two 3D models are similar, their projected views from various angles are similar as well. They compared the Zernike moment [2] and the Fourier descriptor between two projected silhouettes. Daras and Axenopoulos [9] extended the view-based concept and measured multiple shape features and their combinations. However, the models in the database and from input queries need to be aligned in a standard viewpoint set. Wu et al. [18] used the view-based matching for object pose tracking. In our work, we allow users to record depth images of an input in an arbitrary viewpoint.

Existing view-based systems usually analyze the global shapes of projections. It implicitly assumes that the models in the same category have similar poses, but in reality there are plenty of models with joints and their limb postures are changeable. Skeleton-based measures are capable of dealing with the deformation and articulation of shape data. Bai and Latecki [3] computed skeleton similarity by comparing geodesic paths between skeleton endpoints, and did not consider the topological structure of the skeleton graphs or trees. Shen et al. [14] extended the previous work [3] to do shape clustering according to the similarity of each shape. They proposed the distance measurement between shapes and clusters according to the correspondence of skeleton endpoints and junction points.

To extract skeleton from 2D contours, Igarashi et al. [20] presented an extraction method in the famous Teddy system. The method first performs Delaunay triangulation to generate triangles covering the shape. Then, it approximates the medial axis and extracts the skeleton of the contour according to the connectivity between triangles. However, skeleton extraction is usually sensitive to the boundary noise. In order to prune the spurious skeleton branches, Shen et al. [19] evaluated the contribution of contour segment to the whole shape, and presented a novel method for skeleton refinement. In the case of 3D skeleton extraction, Hasler et al. (2010) inspected examples of different subjects at the same time, and then improved the robustness of shape skeleton estimation. Wang and Lee [21] applied iterative least squares optimization to shrink models and preserves their geometries and topologies.

Several works decompose a 3D model into parts or skeletons for similarity measures or other applications. Mohamed and Hamza [22] matched two 3D shapes by comparing their relative shortest paths between the skeleton endpoints. Kim et al. [23] partitioned a collection of models into clusters and generated consistent segmentations and correspondences for all the models with similar parts. Instead of analyzing geometric structures of shapes, Kim et al. [24] and Xie et al. [25] analyzed 3D shapes based on the interactions between 3D models and human postures. These methods can be extended for 3D shape retrieval and correspondence estimation. Kleiman et al. [26] presented a novel approach to quantify shape similarity based re-arrangements, additions, and removals of parts. López-Sastre et al. [27] employs a 3D spatial pyramid representation for 3D shape categorization and classification. Sipiran et al. [28] represents a 3D shape by its global descriptions and partition descriptions. However, these methods were designed for 3D shape matching, and they cannot be directly applicable to sparse depth image inputs, since the 3D parts or limbs can partially be occluded during projection.

3   Overview

Our goal is to efficiently retrieve 3D models with one or few input images, especially for 3D objects with articulated limbs. In order to acquire the information and details of the object surfaces, we selected depth images as our inputs rather than silhouette binary images in related methods. We used Xtion PRO [4] as our live depth image capture device, and it can be replaced by other low-cost depth cameras off the shelf, such as Kinect [5].

The flow chart of our proposed method is shown in Fig. 2. For more efficient online retrieval, we divided our system into two stages: offline analysis and online retrieval. In the offline analysis stage, for each model in the database, we generated a set of 2D projected depth images. Then, we extracted features with rotation-invariant and perspective-insensitive properties for these projected images. These feature coefficients were regarded as the global information. We then further segmented each projected depth images into the main torso (body) and limb regions. These parts (torso and limb regions) can provide local information, respectively. Finally, we can get global and local features to build our feature database.

In the online retrieval part, our system first loads the descriptors(global and local features) databases, and then a user can input one or multiple depth images loaded from files or captured from a real 3D object. The proposed system then evaluates the minimum matching distance between the input and each model in database according to global and local features. The retrieval results are sorted according to their distance scores. A complete online retrieval process can be finished within a second for the database containing about 18,000 images.

4   Offline Analysis

This section describes how we extract different shape descriptors to represent the complex 3D models and the properties of these features are introduced as well. Figure 3 shows the flowchart of our offline analysis.

4.1   Extraction of Projected Views and Regions

The pioneer view-based matching method by Chen et al. [8] extracted features from the whole projected silhouette images. By contrast, we make use of projected depth images to acquire more details from the model surfaces, and segment parts from the whole shape for local information analysis. Figure 4 shows an example of a 3D ox model and four of its projected depth images.

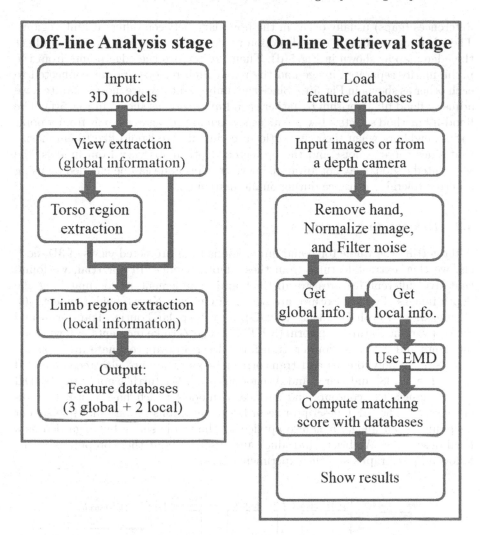

Fig. 2. The flow chart of the proposed system [1].

For a model with limbs, generally the limb regions are located as prominent regions in global projected images. Therefore, we first find the body part from the projected image. Our initial thought is to apply the mathematical morphology operations (erosion and dilation) to the whole projected image, and leave the torso region. Then, we can obtain the preliminary limb regions by subtracting the torso region form the global region. However, we found that the limbs may be still connected with the torso or other limbs by such a method because of overlapping, as in Fig. 5(c).

We have to further analyze the preliminary limb region for more accurate region separation. The depths within each limb region are similar, abrupt depth differences (gaps) usually occur in the boundary between different limb regions. Therefore, we use Canny edge detection to the preliminary limb images, and get the edge map as shown in Fig. 5(d). Then, we remove the edge points from the preliminarily separated image and the result limb regions are not connected to each other as shown in Fig. 5(e). Since the limbs and torso are most separated, we adjust a flood fill algorithm to gather each limb region as shown in Fig. 5(f). The flood-fill method selects a few points as seeds and propagates labels from a point to its neighbors when their properties are similar. We would like to emphasize that since there is noise and the projected depth maps vary from models, the segmented regions may not always be perfect. This issue can be mended by using an error-tolerable distance during online matching.

4.2   Extraction of Features

After getting the whole torso and limb regions from projected views of 3D models, we then extract features from these depth regions. In our trial, we found that five different features are distinct and complementary for matching the depth images. The five features are Zernike moments, Krawtchouk moments [6], Histogram of Depth Gradient (HODG), and 2D-polar Fourier Transform, and Scale-invariant feature transform (SIFT) [7]. The Zernike moments, Krawtchouk moments and 2D-polar Fourier Transform descriptor approximate image shape structure by polynomials and transformed bases. They are also recommended in Chen et al. [8] and Daras and Axenopoulos [9]. We further apply the HODG to distinguish the contours and surface of models which have distinct gradient vectors. The SIFT descriptor records the variations around multiple salient keypoints in an image. It is also applied to the whole shape but regarded as a local descriptor. We briefly introduce and discuss about their properties in the following paragraphs and the experiment section.

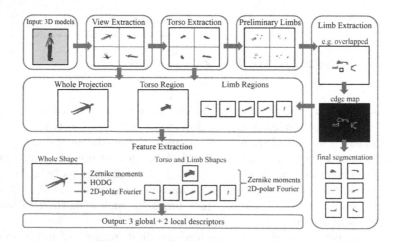

Fig. 3. Overview of offline analysis [1].

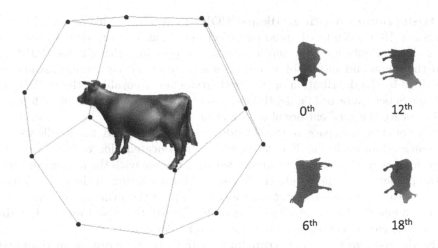

Fig. 4. An example of an ox model and its projected depth images at 0th, 6th, 12th, 18th vertices of a dodecahedron.

Zernike moments are a set of orthogonal moments. They have the properties of rotation invariance and efficient construction. Moreover, they can effectively resist image noise. Due to the above properties, Zernike moments are ideal features for shape representation in shape classification problems. Please refer to [2] and [8] for more details.

Krawtchouk moments are a set of Krawtchouk polynomials, which are discrete orthogonal polynomials associated with the binomial distribution. We utilize the rotation invariant Krawtchouk moments proposed by Yap et al. (2003). Please refer to [6] for more details.

2D-polar Fourier Transform is a variant of the Discrete Fourier Transform (DFT). This approach first transforms an input image into a 2D-polar image by mapping the (θ, r) onto the (x, y) coordinate. We can then apply popularly used Fast Fourier Transform (FFT) to the 2D-polar image. It is also applied in [9].

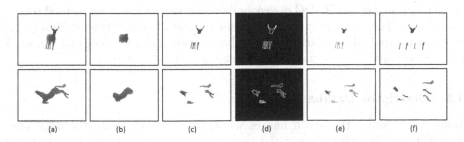

Fig. 5. Extracting the limb regions of two models. (a) Input depth images. (b) The torso region by mathematical operations. (c) The preliminary limb regions by subtraction. (d) The edge map of the preliminary limb regions. (e) The results of subtracting the edge points from the preliminarily separated image. (f) The final results of limb regions.

Histogram of depth gradients (HODG) is variant of histogram of image gradients (HOG) commonly used for object detection. It counts the occurrences of gradient orientation in a depth image. The principal thought for HODG is that the shape and surface of an object in a certain view can be approximately described by the distribution of the depth gradients. To evaluate the HODG, we first use Sobel operator in a depth image to get the depth gradient of each pixel, and evaluate the gradient orientation and magnitude.

The orientation space is then divided into 36 bins, and the gradients are accumulated for each bin. The descriptor is the concatenation of these bins. To keep this descriptor rotation-invariant, we align the bin with the maximum value as the primary one, and rotate the following bins according to the order. When we want to match two histograms, we can compare the primary bin first, and then compute the following bins sequentially. The HODG is suitable to describe the various changes of surface appearance and contours.

Scale-invariant feature transform (SIFT) is an algorithm in computer vision to detect and describe local features in 2D images [7]. SIFT method first generate a Gaussian pyramid, and then subtracts each layer with its adjacent layers to get the Difference of Gaussian (DoG). The keypoints are then be extracted with extremal values of the Difference of Gaussian. The SIFT descriptor is rotate-invariant and scale-invariant. In our work, we apply SIFT method to each whole projected image. It can catelog local salient variations, e.g. corners, depth gaps. For an articulate model, if there is a salient feature on its leg, it can still be matched when the leg pose is changed (as long as the local projections are similar).

In our early trial, we found that for an articulated model, because the local projections of each body part may not similar and the poses of each body part may different, SIFT features of two depth images captured from the same model but different poses are hard to be matched. At the meanwhile, both Zernike moments and Krawtchouk moments extract the shape of object, for efficiency, we choose Zernike moments as the main feature representing shape. Those feature performs well on whole depth images, but for part regions (torso and limb region), only Zernike moments and 2D-polar Fourier features are still capable of approximating the shapes of local regions. The areas of limbs are relatively small and it makes the HODG occasionally sensitive to noise or segmented region boundaries. Therefore, only Zennike moments and 2D-polar Fourier Transform features are applied to local regions. In short, three global features and two local features are applied to describe depth images in the database.

4.3   Descriptor Database

When we generate the depth images which are projected from the dodecahedron vertices, in order to keep the images scale and translation invariant, we translate the depth images to the center of an image and normalize their sizes. Moreover, the aforementioned descriptors are all rotation-invariant. We then use these features to build the compact feature databases.

Zernike moments are useful in discriminating the whole appearance of images in these three descriptors. However, as shown in Fig. 6, while only using Zernike moments, sometimes we may retrieve some unexpected results when the poses of articulated models, such as human beings or animals, are similar to that of a plane. In order to reduce the failure results, we apply the 2D-polar Fourier Transform. It can retain more detailed contour shapes. By constrast, HODG is suitable for analyzing the surface orientation and sharp contour changes as shown in Fig. 7. In summary, our global feature set is composed of Zernike moments, Histogram of Depth Gradient, and 2D-polar Fourier Transform; our local feature set consists of Zernike moments and 2D-polar Fourier Transform for torso and limb regions. The recommended combination of these features is analyzed in the experiment section.

5   Online Model Retrieval

This section introduces our interactive 3D model retrieval system. Figure 8 shows the flow chart about our online retrieval system.

5.1   Acquiring Input Depth Images

After the system initialization, a user can input one or multiple depth image files or live capture inputs from a depth camera. Figure 9 shows different ways to get the query inputs. Before capturing the live depth images, we need to take an initial frame as the background region. Pixels with large depth differences between the initial and current frames are regarded as the foreground. This step can be improved by advanced segmentation methods, e.g. [10], [11]. For the live

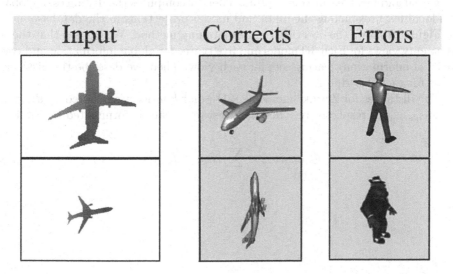

Fig. 6. The retrieval results of zernike moments. Left: the input image. The middle and the right are the correct and wrong searching results of Zernike moments.

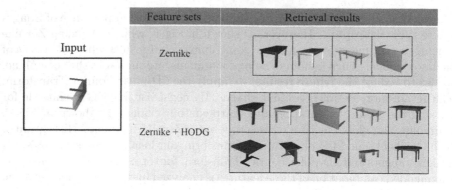

Fig. 7. Different retrieval results by using Zernike moments with and without HODG [1].

captured depth images, a user can hold an object in front of the camera in hand. According to the recorded color histogram, our system can detect and remove user's hand region and leave the grabbed object for model query. Since there is always noise disturbing a live captured image, we apply connected component labelling to gather pixels and omit the scattered groups without sufficient pixel numbers.

5.2   Matching Distances

After acquiring the refined depth images, similar to Sect. 4.1, our system automatically segments the torso and limb regions from the whole shape, and extracts the global and local feature descriptors. Then, it computes the distances of global and local features among the input and model projections in the database.

Figure 10 shows the overview of our matching method. We can see that there are twenty views for each 3D model and five (three for global information and two for local information) feature sets for each view. Then, we describe the distance terms for each descriptor.

The distances for Zernike moments, 2D-polar Fourier are denoted by d_{Zernike} and $d_{\text{PolarFourier}}$ respectively. These two distances can be formulated by Eq. 1.

$$d_{\text{set}_{in},\text{set}_{obj}} = \sum_{i=1}^{N} |f_{in_i} - f_{obj_i}|, \tag{1}$$

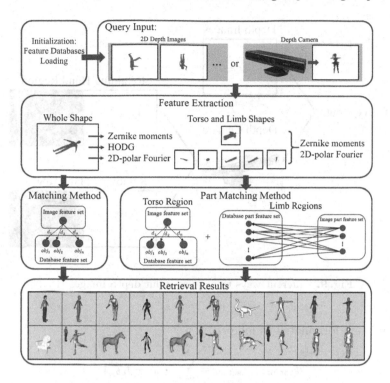

Fig. 8. Overview of online model retrieval [1].

where f_{in_i} is the ith feature coefficient of a query image, f_{obj_i} is the ith coefficient of one of the objects in our 3D model database, and N is 35 for Zernike moments and 78 for 2D-polar Fourier descriptors.

The distance for Histogram of Depth Gradient is denoted by d_{HODG}, and it is formulated as follows:

$$d_{\text{HODG:set}_{in},\text{set}_{obj}} = \frac{1}{\sum_{i=1}^{N}\left(f_{in_i} \cap f_{obj_i}\right) + \varepsilon}, \tag{2}$$

where f_{in_i} is the ith feature coefficient of a query image, f_{obj_i} is the ith coefficient of one of the objects in our 3D model database, and we set ε to 0.001, N to 36. The denominator of Eq. 2 is the sum of intersection operations for histogram bin values.

On the other hand, the local feature sets (ZernikePart and PolarFourierPart) comprise features for torso and limb regions. For example, if a whole projected depth image can be divided into one torso and three limb regions, there are four parts in this shape. Since a torso and limbs have different properties, these two kinds of regions are handled and matched separately. The distances for torso and limb regions are denoted by d_{Torso} and d_{Limb}, and the distance between two

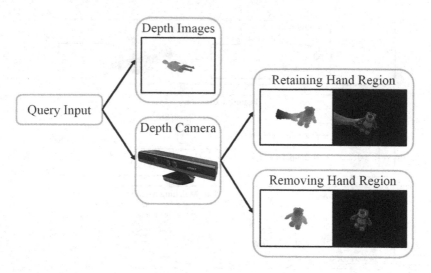

Fig. 9. Different ways to acquire input depth images [1].

feature sets are formulated as follows:

$$
\begin{aligned}
d_{\text{Torso}:\text{set}_{in},\text{set}_{obj}} &= \sum_{i=1}^{N} |f_{in_i} - f_{obj_i}|, \\
d_{\text{Limb}:\text{set}_{in},\text{set}_{obj}} &= \text{EMD}\left(f_{in}, f_{obj}\right), \\
d_{\text{Part}} &= \frac{d_{\text{Torso}} + n \times d_{\text{Limb}}}{n+1},
\end{aligned}
\tag{3}
$$

where f_{in_i} is the ith feature coefficient of query image, f_{obj_i} is the ith coefficient of one of the objects in our 3D model database, and N is 35 for ZernikePart and 78 for PolarFourierPart. The computing way between Zernike moments and ZernikePart for torso region is the same because there is only a torso region in each shape, and so do 2D-polar Fourier Transform and PolarFourierPart for the torso region. f_{in} is a sequence of limb features of query image, and f_{obj} is a sequence of limb features of an object in our 3D model database. The EMD function is the earth mover's distance proposed by Rubner et al. [29]. n is the number of limb regions in a projected image, and d_{Part} is weighted average of d_{Torso} and d_{Limb}.

The earth mover's distance (EMD) is a method to evaluate dissimilarity (distance) between two multi-dimensional distributions, and here we use ZernikePart and PolarFourierPart. Figure 11 shows an example. The EMD estimates the minimum moving distance between two feature sets, and the EMD is formulated as follow:

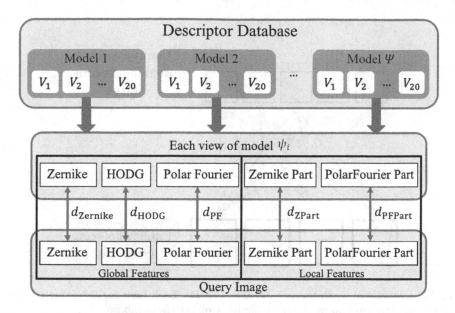

Fig. 10. Overview of the matching method. Ψ is the set of all 3D models in our database. ψ_i is one of the 3D models. The left three global feature works on whole depth region, and the right two local features works on parts (torso and limbs) regions.

$$\sum_{i=1}^{m}\sum_{j=1}^{n} a_{ij} = \min\left(\sum_{i=1}^{m} wP_i, \sum_{j=1}^{n} wQ_j\right),$$
$$\mathrm{EMD}\,(P,Q) = \frac{\sum_{i=1}^{m}\sum_{j=1}^{n} d_{ij}a_{ij}}{\sum_{i=1}^{m}\sum_{j=1}^{n} a_{ij}},$$

(4)

where P is the first feature set with m limb regions, Q is the second feature set with n limb regions, a_{ij} is the optimal work amount between P and Q, and d_{ij} is the ground distance between P and Q.

Finally, the distance between two views (input and a projected view of a database model) becomes:

$$d_{\mathrm{view:set_1,set_2}} = w_{\mathrm{Zernike}}d_{\mathrm{Zernike}} + w_{\mathrm{HODG}}d_{\mathrm{HODG}} + w_{\mathrm{PF}}d_{\mathrm{PF}}$$
$$+ w_{\mathrm{ZPart}}d_{\mathrm{ZPart}} + w_{\mathrm{PFPart}}d_{\mathrm{PFPart}},$$

(5)

where w_{Zernike}, w_{HODG}, w_{PF}, w_{ZPart}, and w_{PFPart} are the normalized weights for corresponding distances. These distances have the same weights by default. If a user turns off one of the distances, the corresponding weight term is set to zero.

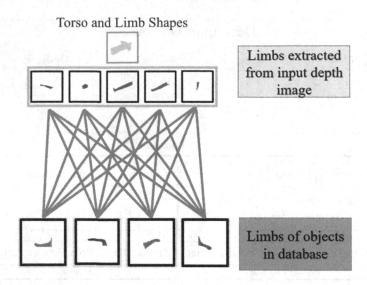

Fig. 11. Example of earth mover's distance (EMD). Each limb region extracted from input image tries to find most similar limbs of objects in database.

5.3   Model Query

Since our system does not constrain the viewing angle of the query input, we do not have information about the viewpoints or other spatial relationship among the input images. Therefore, the distance between an input depth image and a database model is set as the distances between the inputs and the most similar view of that model. The equation is as follows:

$$obj = \arg\min_{o} \sum_{i=1}^{N_{in}} \min_{j} \left(d_{\text{view}:in,j} \right),$$
(6)

where o represents the index of an object model in database; i is the index of an input image; j is the index of a view belonging to o; N_{in} is the number of input images.

Our system allows users inputting one or more query images. Figure 12 shows different results with one, two, and four query inputs, and we can find that the results are more accurate with more input views.

6   Experiment

6.1   Retrieval System

Our prototype system is developed in C/C++ language, with OpenCV, OpenGL, and OpenNI libraries. The experimental database derived from two famous 3D model datasets. The NTU dataset is published by Chen et al. [8], and

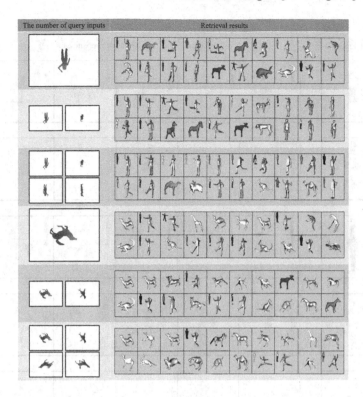

Fig. 12. Left: Examples of query by different numbers of input images. Right: The corresponding retrieval results [1].

SHREC15 [12] dataset contains a variety of non-rigid 3D models. Since one of our comparison methods, shape clustering proposed by Shen et al. [14], is only suitable for retrieving the silhouette images with extractable skeletons, we chose 573 models from NTU database which have complete and noiseless meshes. Since there are few postured models in NTU dataset, we therefore chose 42 human models and required users to edit their postures with Maya [13]. Each human model has 5 different postures. Several examples are shown in Fig. 13. Also, we take 97 non-rigid quadruped animal models from SHREC15 [12]. There are 880 models in total. In Table 1, we list the time spending in the offline and online stages. It shows that our method is efficient in online retrieval. Please refer to the supplementary video to see the demo for online retrieval. The retrieval system is shown in Fig. 14.

Fig. 13. Left: The original human models from NTU database [8]. Right: The corresponding models in random postures [1].

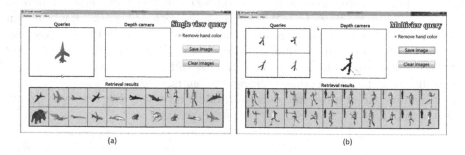

Fig. 14. Our retrieval system. Query depth image comes from (a)depth image files or (b)depth camera. System applies single or multiple depth images to retrieve target models.

6.2   Performance Evaluation

We compared three different methods. The method proposed by Shen et al. [14] is denoted by "SC". SC computes the similarity between two skeleton paths of silhouette images. It finds the correspondence of endpoints and junction points, and calculates path distances as the similarity measurement of shapes. SC can advantageously retrieve shapes with the presence of joint movement, stretching, and contour deformation, so we took this method as one of our comparisons for retrieving models with articulated limbs. The feature set proposed by Chen et al. [8] is denoted by "LFD". LFD feature set is combination of Zernike moments and Fourier Transform, and it is known for its capability for searching 3D models with sparse inputs. Our proposed method is denoted by "Our Method". However, since the two related methods do not consider the depth information, during our experiments we also turned off the HODG term to

Table 1. The spending time in the offline and online stages [1].

Process	Time (seconds)
Extract projected views	309.685
Extract local info. and features	1746.443
Load feature databases	4.366
Retrieve per image	0.539

Table 2. The precision-recall area and F-measure of articulated categories (human and uadruped animal).

Random 1 view	F-measure	Area
Our (without HODG)	0.504932889	0.580003589
Our (with HODG)	0.496679571	0.572922307
SC [14]	0.447445817	0.47332525
LFD [8]	0.418556555	0.417046229
Random 4 views	F-measure	Area
Our (without HODG)	0.521221525	0.633340893
Our (with HODG)	0.512510686	0.623152318
SC [14]	0.481085013	0.550202734
LFD [8]	0.440714983	0.466291704
All 20 views	F-measure	Area
Our (without HODG)	0.521740861	0.653806268
Our (with HODG)	0.522987381	0.658021439
SC [14]	0.497486855	0.592502025
LFD [8]	0.452905746	0.499051089

42   J.-Y. Lin et al.

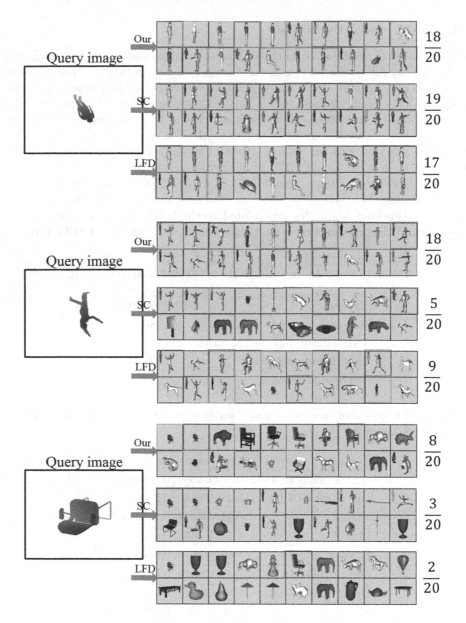

Fig. 15. The results of retrieving articulated models and rigid objects. Target model with red square means the retrieval result is correct [1]. (Color figure online)

demonstrate the capability without using depth information. Our method without HODG is denoted by "Our Method (without HODG)".

Before the precision-recall analysis, we demonstrate the results of articulated and rigid model retrieval. Since the articulated models may have diverse motions

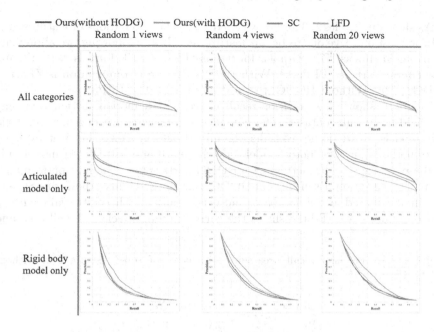

Fig. 16. The precision-recall curves of both rigid and articulated categories (32 categories). Top: Database contains all categories. Middle: Database contains articulated model only Bottom: Database contains rigid body model only. The number of query images from left to right is Left: random 1 view. Middle: random 4 views. Right: all 20 views.

Table 3. The precision-recall area and F-measure of top-4 feature sets with HODG [1].

Feature sets	F-measure	Area
Z+HODG+PF	0.337945	0.362754
ZPart+HODG+PF	**0.353717**	**0.380994**
Z+HODG+PFPart	0.339882	0.365623
ZPart+HODG+PFPart	0.351692	0.376325

of torso parts or limbs, we want to retrieve models which have diverse motions compared to the input. Figure 15 shows the retrieved results. Since our method includes not only global but also local information, the proposed method can get human or quadruped animal models in different postures.

In order to evaluate these methods, we use three popularly used measures: precision-recall diagram, the area under precision-recall curve, and F-measure. To calculate the Precision-Recall, we separated the dataset into 32 categories, and used the leave-one-out method to evaluate the retrieval accuracy. Table 2 shows the F-measure of articulated categories.

As shown in Tables 2, 3 and 4, we tried various combinations of features, and find the most effective one to be our feature sets. In the following, we abbreviate Zernike moments as "Z", 2D-polar fourier as "PF", ZernikePart as "ZPart", and PolarFourierPart as "PFPart". With HODG, the best combination is ZPart + HODG + PF. Without HODG, the best one is ZPart + PFPart.

Figure 16 shows the precision-recall curves of all models, articulated only and rigid-body only dataset. The comparison methods are designed for rigid body models, so we do not consider the mixed database only, but also evaluate those methods on rigid body model only database and articulated model only database. In Fig. 16, our method with HODG parts gets the highest performance at any view situation. Even without HODG, our method still outperforms SC and LFD in articulated model database, and gets evenly matched retrieval results in rigid body database. Table 5 shows the corresponding precision-recall area and

Table 4. The precision-recall area and F-measure of top-4 feature sets without HODG [1].

Feature sets	F-measure	Area
Z+PF	0.320841	0.312618
ZPart+PF	0.352201	0.354703
Z+PFPart	0.325695	0.321335
ZPart+PFPart	**0.354193**	**0.357654**

Table 5. The precision-recall area and F-measure of both rigid and articulated categories (32 categories) [1].

Random 1 view	F-measure	Area
Our (without HODG)	0.351801	0.352638
Our (with HODG)	0.352834	0.37696
SC [14]	0.317446	0.301876
LFD [8]	0.304962	0.286351
Random 4 views	F-measure	Area
Our (without HODG)	0.370055	0.40825
Our (with HODG)	0.372430	0.441786
SC [14]	0.343624	0.363110
LFD [8]	0.328067	0.34843
All 20 views	F-measure	Area
Our (without HODG)	0.375983	0.429935
Our (with HODG)	0.379451	0.467065
SC [14]	0.355618	0.395940
LFD [8]	0.335435	0.372276

F-measure. We show the precision-recall curves of random one view, random four views and all twenty views.

In Figs. 17 and 18, we give different numbers of inputs, and find that the performance improvement converges with 8 or more inputs.

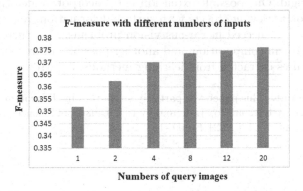

Fig. 17. The F-measure scores in different numbers of inputs [1].

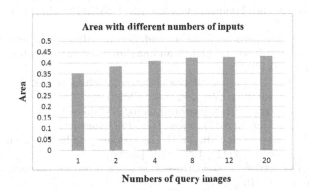

Fig. 18. The area scores in different numbers of inputs [1].

7   Conclusion

In this paper, we propose a novel method to retrieve rigid or articulate 3D models by using both global and local information. The global information is retrieved from the original projected views. Since the articulate 3D models may have various poses, we propose using the additional local information from segmented torso and limb regions. We estimate the Zernike moments, HODG and PF features for local salient variations on global shape and limb regions to get the posture-invariant features from few input. This method does not require a well-aligned model pose or viewpoints. Experiments show that our method get more accurate results than two known methods in both rigid and articulate model databases, and each query can be finished within a second by our current system without carefully code optimization. The performance can even be improved with parameter-space partition method, e.g. the K-D tree or data clustering.

Currently, our retrieval method is designed for articulated objects in which the limbs are rigid. One possible extension is to incorporate deformation methods, e.g. [15], for retrieving objects with surface deformation. Recently, the deep learning techniques succeed in various vision problems. Our current method is relatively low-cost in computation, and another possible future work is to incorporate the features extracted from learning methods, e.g. [16].

Acknowledgement. This paper was partially supported by Telecommunication Laboratories, Chunghwa Telecom Co., Ltd., and by the Ministry of Science and Technology, Taiwan, under grant no. 106-2221-E-009 -178 -MY2.

References

1. Lin, J.Y., She, M.F., Tsai, M.H., Lin, I.C., Lau, Y.C., Liu, H.H.: Retrieving 3D objects with articulated limbs by depth image input. In: Proceedings of the 13th International Joint Conference on Computer Vision, Imaging and Computer Graphics Theory and Applications - Volume 1: GRAPP, INSTICC, pp. 101–111. SciTePress (2018)
2. Canterakis, N.: 3D Zernike moments and Zernike affine invariants for 3D image analysis and recognition. In: 11th Scandinavian Conference on Image Analysis In 11th Sc, pp. 85–93 (1999)
3. Bai, X., Latecki, L.J.: Path similarity skeleton graph matching. IEEE Trans. Pattern Anal. Mach. Intell. **30**(7), 1282–1292 (2008)
4. ASUS Inc.: Xtion pro (2011). www.asus.com/3D-Sensor/
5. Microsoft Corp.: Kinect (2011). www.xbox.com/Kinect
6. Yap, P.T., Paramesran, R., Ong, S.H.: Image analysis by Krawtchouk moments. Trans. Image Process. **12**(11), 1367–1377 (2003)
7. Lowe, D.G.: Distinctive image features from scale-invariant keypoints. Int. J. Comput. Vis. **60**(2), 91–110 (2004)
8. Chen, D.Y., Tian, X.P., Shen, Y.T., Ouhyoung, M.: On visual similarity based 3D model retrieval. Eurographics **22**(3), 223–232 (2003)
9. Daras, P., Axenopoulos, A.: A 3D shape retrieval framework supporting multimodal queries. Int. J. Comput. Vis. **89**(2–3), 229–247 (2010)
10. Rother, C., Kolmogorov, V., Blake, A.: GrabCut: interactive foreground extraction using iterated graph cuts. ACM Trans. Graph. **23**(3), 309–314 (2004)
11. Lin, I.C., Lan, Y.C., Cheng, P.W.: SI-Cut: Structural inconsistency analysis for image foreground extraction. IEEE Trans. Vis. Comput. Graph. **21**(7), 860–872 (2015)
12. Lian, Z., Zhang, J.: SHREC15 non-rigid 3D shape retrieval (2015). www.icst.pku.edu.cn/zlian/shrec15-non-rigid/data.html
13. Autodesk Inc.: Maya (1998). www.autodesk.com/products/maya/
14. Shen, W., Wang, Y., Bai, X., Wang, H., Jan Latecki, L.: Shape clustering: common structure discovery. Pattern Recogn. **46**(2), 539–550 (2013)
15. Chen, C.H., Tsai, M.H., Lin, I.C., Lu, P.H.: Skeleton-driven surface deformation through lattices for real-time character animation. Vis. Comput. **29**(4), 241–251 (2013)

16. Su, H., Maji, S., Kalogerakis, E., Learned-Miller, E.G.: Multi-view convolutional neural networks for 3D shape recognition. In: Proceedings of the IEEE International Confererence on Computer Vision, pp. 945–953 (2015)
17. Funkhouser, T., et al.: A search engine for 3D models. ACM Trans. Graph. **22**(1), 83–105 (2003)
18. Wu, L.C., Lin, I., Tsai, M.H.: Augmented reality instruction for object assembly based on markerless tracking. In: Proceedings of the 20th ACM SIGGRAPH Symposium on Interactive 3D Graphics and Games, I3D 2016, pp. 95–102. ACM (2016)
19. Shen, W., Bai, X., Hu, R., Wang, H., Latecki, L.J.: Skeleton growing and pruning with bending potential ratio. Pattern Recogn. **44**(2), 196–209 (2011)
20. Igarashi, T., Matsuoka, S., Tanaka, H.: Teddy: a sketching interface for 3D freeform design. In: Proceedings of SIGGRAPH, pp. 409–416 (1999)
21. Wang, Y.S., Lee, T.Y.: Curve-skeleton extraction using iterative least squares optimization. IEEE Trans. Visual Comput. Graphics **14**(4), 926–936 (2008)
22. Mohamed, W., Hamza, A.B.: Reeb graph path dissimilarity for 3D object matching and retrieval. Visual Comput. **28**(3), 305–318 (2012)
23. Kim, V.G., Li, W., Mitra, N.J., Chaudhuri, S., DiVerdi, S., Funkhouser, T.: Learning part-based templates from large collections of 3D shapes. ACM Trans. Graph. **32**(4), 70:1–70:12 (2013)
24. Kim, V.G., Chaudhuri, S., Guibas, L., Funkhouser, T.: Shape2pose: Human-centric shape analysis. ACM Trans. Graph. **33**(4), 120:1–120:12 (2014)
25. Xie, Z., Xiong, Y., Xu, K.: AB3D: action-based 3D descriptor for shape analysis. Vis. Comput. **30**(6–8), 591–601 (2014)
26. Kleiman, Y., van Kaick, O., Sorkine-Hornung, O., Cohen-Or, D.: SHED: shape edit distance for fine-grained shape similarity. ACM Trans. Graph. **34**(6), 235:1–235:11 (2015)
27. López-Sastre, R.J., García-Fuertes, A., Redondo-Cabrera, C., Acevedo-Rodríguez, F.J., Maldonado-Bascón, S.: Evaluating 3D spatial pyramids for classifying 3D shapes. Comput. Graph. **37**(5), 473–483 (2013)
28. Sipiran, I., Bustos, B., Schreck, T.: Data-aware 3D partitioning for generic shape retrieval. Comput. graph. **37**(5), 460–472 (2013)
29. Rubner, Y., Tomasi, C., Guibas, L.J.: The earth mover's distance as a metric for image retrieval. Int. J. Comput. Vision **40**(2), 99–121 (2000)

Human Computer Interaction Theory and Applications

Haptic and Touchless User Input Methods for Simple 3D Interaction Tasks: Interaction Performance and User Experience for People with and Without Impairments

Mirjam Augstein[1(✉)], Thomas Neumayr[1], Thomas Burger[2], Josef Altmann[1], Werner Kurschl[1], and Stephan Vrecer[1]

[1] University of Applied Sciences Upper Austria, Hagenberg, Austria
{mirjam.augstein,thomas.neumayr,josef.altmann,werner.kurschl,
stephan.vrecer}@fh-hagenberg.at
[2] LIFEtool, Linz, Austria
thomas.burger@lifetool.at

Abstract. The sense of touch is of crucial importance for humans, especially those with impairments. Traditionally, most input devices (e.g., mice, joysticks or touchpads) accounted for this by involving at least a certain amount of a haptic experience during human-computer interaction processes. However, during the past years, also touchless input devices that enable user input without physical contact between human and device, became popular and available for mass markets. While these input devices such as Microsoft Kinect or the Leap motion controller bear high potential for certain settings (e.g., therapeutic ones) and usually support more than two degrees of freedom, they also involve new challenges like missing borders and thus physical restrictions of the interaction space. This chapter summarizes two investigations around the actual relevance of a haptic experience in user input for people with and without known impairments. Both studies focused on simple input tasks in a 3D interaction space and involve an analysis of interaction performance and User Experience, comparing three input devices with varying amount of haptics.

Keywords: Haptic interaction · Touchless interaction · Comparative study

1 Introduction

In the past decades, user input seemed to be coupled with at least a certain haptic experience. The most widely used input devices like mice, keyboards, touch screens, joysticks or game controllers have in common that they involve direct physical contact between the user and the device. Touch-based or haptic input

© Springer Nature Switzerland AG 2019
D. Bechmann et al. (Eds.): VISIGRAPP 2018, CCIS 997, pp. 51–80, 2019.
https://doi.org/10.1007/978-3-030-26756-8_3

techniques however often suffer from limited interaction options through physical/technological constraints. For instance, the interaction with a (hardware) button is restricted by its physical resistance and movement range. Also, most touchscreens only allow for two-dimensional input because the physical device is a flat surface which makes movement along the third axis mostly irrelevant (although this might be up to changes since the advent of 3D touch capabilities with the latest generations of smart phones). Yet, these physical restrictions also provide a certain amount of guidance and haptic input devices mostly offer inherent haptic feedback mechanisms.

During the past few years, touchless input methods and devices, e.g., Microsoft Kinect (further referred to as "Kinect") or the Leap motion controller (further referred to as "Leap") that theoretically allow for nearly unlimited input options (e.g., the human hand theoretically has 27 degrees of freedom [15]) became attractive, e.g., in game-based scenarios that involve physical engagement like sports applications or in therapeutic settings. Touchless input surely offers high potential for a number of selected application fields where other input approaches are difficult to apply (e.g., sports applications that involve whole body interaction or therapeutic applications with specifically tailored physical tasks). However, touchless input also bears potential shortcomings that should be considered, e.g., connected to haptic perception mentioned before or missing physical constraints that could provide orientation for the user during input. Although there are approaches to overcome these risks (through haptic feedback for touchless input scenarios, e.g., via focused ultrasound [8]), most readily-available touchless input devices do not yet support such mechanisms.

We consider a missing haptic experience as a potentially critical problem due to the following considerations. The sense of touch is formed at a very early stage of prenatal development, long before other senses such as sight or hearing. It is a sense that helps humans to perceive not only their surroundings but also themselves which makes it a connecting element responsible for interactions between humans and their environment [3]. For most people without impairments, other senses become more and more important throughout their further development. However, for many people with impairments the sense of touch remains most crucial because it is so fundamental and physically familiar and they particularly rely on it. We believe that for any kind of interaction technique and related devices, the appropriate amount of haptics involved in the process must be carefully considered. Due to the considerations mentioned above, we believe that the importance of haptics must be determined for both potential user groups, people with and without known impairment, separately.

This chapter describes two exemplary studies with the aforementioned two groups, aiming at investigating actual relevance of a haptic experience during user input. As this relevance might differ with varying complexity of input tasks, we focus on a small predefined set of simple input tasks in a 3D interaction space (see a description of the tasks in Sect. 4). The first study was conducted with 25 participants without known impairments (see Sect. 5.1), the second (qualitative) study involved five selected people with impairments (see Sect. 5.2). In both studies we compared three input techniques: (i) touchless input, (ii) "touchful" input (relying on application of physical pressure to a surface), and (iii) semi-touchless input (combining characteristics of the previous two). We use Leap as touchless input device and two device prototypes [3] that have been developed specifically to fit the requirements of this and similar studies. The touchful input device can be considered isometric, i.e., connecting human limb and the device through force [19] while the other two can be considered isotonic, i.e., connecting the interacting hand and the device through movement [19].

The studies are targeted to analyze (i) users' interaction performance and (ii) User Experience (UX) with each of the three input techniques. The main aim behind is to study the actual relevance of haptics during user input for the respective target group (and, secondarily, also the potentials of isometric and isotonic input devices) for the selected category of tasks. We believe that the combined findings comprising objective criteria and subjective ones are more conclusive than any of the two in isolation. A good interaction performance does not necessarily have to imply a good UX and vice versa (which is confirmed by the results of our study where we identified contradictions between performance and UX). In our study we introduce so-called interaction tests the users have to take. Based on the raw input data we compute metrics indicative of interaction performance (e.g., time or interaction regularity). To measure UX, the standardized User Experience Questionnaire is used. We expect the results to be interesting for researchers and practitioners conceptualizing and designing interactive environments or input devices.

This chapter is an extended version of [5] (where the results of the study with 25 participants without impairments have been discussed) and, in order to be able to compare the findings for the two user groups, also contains elements of [3][1] (where the results of the tests with selected people with impairments have been discussed).

2 Related Work

Related work on 3D input as well as studies comparing different input techniques for 3D input tasks similar to the tasks used in our two studies by analyzing interaction performance on the one hand, and UX on the other is discussed in this section.

Fröhlich et al. [11] suggest a classification for 3D interaction into (i) navigation and travel, (ii) selection, (iii) manipulation (e.g., of an object's position) and (iv) system control. Accordingly, the interaction tasks described in this chapter (see Sect. 4) can be regarded as manipulation tasks (specifically, positioning) and selection tasks. Furthermore, Fröhlich et al. divide devices and sensors into isotonic (measuring movement), isometric (measuring force) and elastic (allowing

---

[1] Reprinted from Harnessing the Power of Technology to Improve Lives, Volume 242, Mirjam Augstein, Thomas Neumayr & Thomas Burger, The Role of Haptics in User Input for People with Motor and Cognitive Impairments, 2017, with permission from IOS press. Available at http://ebooks.iospress.nl/publication/47269.

for movement and providing a counterforce) sensors. Zhai [19] categorizes elastic input sensors as devices with varying resistance "between the isometric (infinite resistance) and the isotonic (zero or constant resistance)". The devices we used for our studies can be considered isometric (see "touchful input" in Sect. 3.2) and isotonic (see touchless and semi-touchless input in Sects. 3.1 and 3.3). Bowman et al. [7] note that many input devices are actually a combination of different types of input sensors. They coined this combination "multisensory input". While we agree on the value of multisensory input for practical use we explicitly tried to avoid combinations in our studies to be better able to compare.

Zhai [19] compiled an exhaustive list of studies comparing isometric and isotonic input devices. Thereby, he comes to the conclusion that the literature on the relative advantages and disadvantages of isometric vs. isotonic devices has not been very conclusive and argues that the definite answer may depend on (among others) the concrete interaction tasks. This led us to a careful selection of the tasks for our studies and guaranteeing the uniformity of the tasks for all three input devices.

Bowman et al. [7] also argue that haptics is "one of the most important types of sensory feedback" and distinguish between "active haptic feedback" and "passive" or "pseudo-haptics". Our touchful input technique can be considered passive haptic input, our touchless input technique intentionally does not involve any haptic experience and our semi-touchless input technique is situated somewhere in between. The comparison of input techniques involving a differing amount of haptics was our main focus. Zhai [19] further distinguishes between position control, i.e., "control mechanisms by which the human operator controls object positions directly" and rate control, i.e., mapping "human input into the velocity of the object movement". In the two studies presented in this chapter, all three input techniques and all the interaction tasks are based on position control.

More recently, Tscharn et al. [18] have evaluated two isotonic input devices (Leap and the 3D mouse SpaceNavigator) for real world navigation tasks. Their study participants were asked to solve four different interaction tasks in Google Earth (general movement, targeted movement, specified coordinate movement and specified trajectory movement). They evaluated navigation efficiency (measured by the task time) and UX (based on the analysis of facial expressions and the AttrakDiff questionnaire). As in our own research, they also follow the idea of comparing touchless and touch-able input devices along interaction performance metrics and UX. Although their approach differs regarding domain and UX indicators, some of the interaction tasks and performance metrics are similar. Tscharn et al. found interaction with Leap to be less accurate for complex tasks, compared to SpaceNavigator while it had a good UX for simple tasks (which is in line with our findings).

Another study on interaction performance and UX related to touchless (using a ceiling-mounted gesture recognition device prototype) and touch-able (using SpaceNavigator) input has been conducted earlier by Stannus et al. [17]. They found that the interaction performance and UX indicators (e.g., naturalness, strain, speed, and accuracy) participants scored with the touchless device could not keep up with touch-able devices. Interestingly, similar to our findings, for touchless input, UX-related metrics (e.g., naturalness) were scored relatively better compared to the pure performance indicators. Although the study aims were similar, the study design described by Stannus et al. differs from ours drastically as we analyze objective interaction performance metrics automatically while Stannus et al. asked the participants to rate these metrics. We believe these "objective" results reported by users subjectively might be easily biased by users' UX-related impressions and are thus less reliable.

Dangeti et al. [10] discuss bare-hand in-air gesture-based interaction vs. object-in-hand tangible interaction for navigation of 3D objects. They present the technological differences between the approaches and announce a user study in which they plan to compare three different interaction methods (traditional mouse/keyboard interaction, bare hand in-air and object-in-hand interaction) along objective criteria like interaction speed and accuracy and UX-related aspects based on interviews. Thus, the planned methodology seems to be similar to ours, unfortunately, they did not publish any results, yet.

Coelho and Verbeek [9] conducted a study with a traditional mouse and Leap for pointing tasks similar to ours in a 3D virtual environment. They describe two different tasks their participants had to perform. The first task consisted of simple pointing (start point to target point) while the second task was more complex (start point to first target point to second target point). For the simpler task, Leap outperformed the mouse while for the more complex task, the outcome was contrary. The authors state that the z-axis can be controlled by the "roll of the mouse", which we assume to be the mouse wheel and can therefore be manipulated isolated from the x- and y-axes. Our assumption is that there is a major difference for 3D pointing tasks when using Leap, where all axes are controlled through the same mechanism (i.e., movement of fingers or the hand). In our studies, we tried to avoid such general differences (not related to haptics) among the input techniques. To measure usability (and UX), Coelho and Verbeek used the System Usability Scale (SUS) questionnaire where Leap scored better than the mouse which is partly in line with our results.

Hürst and Helder [12] investigated navigation and selection tasks in a 3D space using mobile devices for moving around virtual objects. However, while we varied the extent of haptics, they varied the type of visualization. Thus, the results are not directly related to our work but the study setup is similar. They measured objective values from log data and obtained information about UX.

Another similar approach was applied by Atkins et al. [1] who compared the three interaction techniques mouse wheel, mouse dragging, and a jog wheel to navigate through a stack of medical 3D images, however the navigation itself was two-dimensional. They also used interaction accuracy, time, and navigation paths as objective measures and qualitatively evaluated participants' preferences.

Although we found several studies with aims similar to ours, we did not find a comparison where input activities with different devices have been aligned in a way that the actual difference between settings is the amount of haptics involved. Most studies compared Leap to a (3D) mouse, however, although both isotonic, interaction with Leap inherently differs from interaction with a mouse e.g., regarding hand movement, interaction space and DoF. We aimed at comparing the input techniques using devices that allow for almost identical input activities (with the amount of haptics involved being the actual difference and hence, an independent variable). We expect the results to be better generalizable and more interesting for designers of interactive environments for both people with and without known impairments.

3   Input Techniques

The three input techniques that were subject to comparison in our two studies have several aspects in common. They all involve small movements of the dominant hand in a three-dimensional interaction space and are based on position control. The 3D interaction tasks used in the studies (see Sect. 4) only require the input devices to analyze the user's hand position within a predefined 3D space but allow for users to choose the most comfortable hand orientation and posture. The tasks require movement in the directions left/right, forward/backward and down/up, see Fig. 1 [5]. The interaction space should be the same for all settings (thus, the devices have been calibrated within pre-tests prior to the studies). The major differences between the devices can be seen in the amount of haptics involved. Further, our touchless and semi-touchless input techniques and devices can be described as isotonic while touchful input is isometric.

3.1   Touchless Interaction

Touchless interaction is interaction that "can take place without mechanical contact between the human and any part of the artificial system" [6]. In such settings, the absence of direct haptic guidance during the interaction is a major challenge that can also cause confusion or uncertainty regarding the space sensitive to the user's actions. This also leads to users being informed about the effects of their actions via the system's output (e.g., visually) only. This visual information is present for the other two techniques (i.e., touchful and semi-touchless interaction) as well, for touchless input it is, however, the only source of feedback. We implemented our touchless setting with Leap which relies on infrared technology for measurement. It has a size of $8 \times 3 \times 1$ cm and is usually placed on the table or other surface in front of the user. In our studies, it was used to track the position of the wrist. Here, the user holds his/her hand above the device (see Fig. 1(c)) and moves it according to the tasks. The provision of a hand rest was not possible as this would have (i) interfered with accurate tracking of the user's hand (this was found during the pre-tests) and (ii) reduced the "touchless" impression for the users (which was actually the main reason why we did not want any kind of touch to occur during the tests).

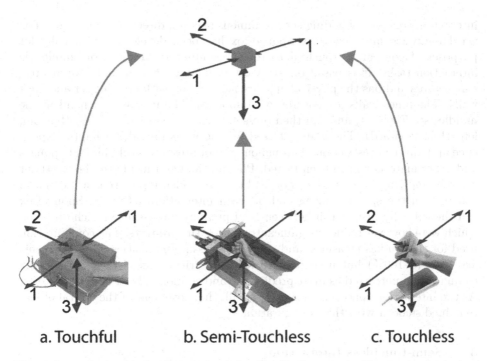

Fig. 1. Input devices and techniques and the three DoF as required by the manipulation tasks during our user studies [5].

3.2 Touchful Interaction

Touchful interaction can be seen as the opposite of touchless interaction, i.e., interaction which involves thorough mechanical contact between human and device during the whole interaction process. Thus, it generally includes the majority of the most widely used input methods and devices such as mice or joysticks. Touchful interaction allows for a direct haptic experience and can help the user to orientate and correctly assess the interaction options and limitations (e.g., the physical resistance of a button indicates that applying stronger pressure will make no difference). Yet, these generally helpful boundaries also limit the interaction range (e.g., a hardware button can only be pressed to its physical limit or it will break). The concrete manifestation of touchful input used in our work can be described as *three-dimensional pressure-based interaction*. This technique aims to combine the advantages of 3D interaction (as also enabled by touchless techniques) and pressure-based interaction while reducing the respective short-comings. It ties in with previous approaches to one-dimensional pressure-based interaction, see [2] and [13]. This technique allows application of different pressure intensities to a specified target area (in our studies, the walls of a box (see below)).

The device used for our studies was "SpongeBox" (introduced and described in further detail in [3]), which extends the one-dimensional pressure-based interaction concept by adding several dimensions and directions: left/right, forward/backward and down/up. SpongeBox has been developed specifically for purposes of comparing touchful to touchless input techniques for simple 3D interaction tasks. It is based on an Arduino microcontroller and several pressure sensors and has the physical appearance of a box with open upper and back walls. The inner walls are covered with sponges. The user puts a hand in the middle (see Fig. 1(a)) and can then press against four sides of the box (bottom, left, right, forward). The material used for the walls provides a haptic experience and physical restriction. Throughout the pre-tests several different sponges and other materials have been tested. Placing the hand inside the box without actively applying pressure does not lead to unintended input, thus a user's arm can rest on the sponge during and between interaction activities. SpongeBox can theoretically distinguish between 1024 pressure intensities in each direction which were however reduced significantly during the pre-tests. The configuration used for the studies measured and collected pressure intensities on the percentage level (0–100%) but used only 13 levels to trigger activities (this was the configuration perceived as most predictable and comfortable by the pre-testers). As the interaction space was relatively small, the movement of the digital object remained smooth with this configuration.

3.3   Semi-touchless Interaction

Semi-touchless interaction can be defined as a cross between the touchless and touchful interaction concepts. It joins the following characteristics: (i) physical constraints and (ii) touchless position/movement analysis. As for the touchless and touchful interaction settings in our studies, input is done via small movements of the interacting hand. The directions are equal to those used for the other two techniques and physical borders around the area sensitive to input are provided. The input device used in our study is "SquareSense" (introduced and described in further detail in [3]). Similar to SpongeBox, it has been developed specifically for purposes of comparing semi-touchless to touchless input techniques for simple 3D interaction tasks. It consists of a box with highly sensitive capacitive side, bottom and front walls the user can freely move the hand within. The device can recognize touchless movements but also pressure intensities if the walls are touched. Thus the device is isometric-isotonic generally, however, we did not use application of pressure for the study described here as the devices were configured in a way that the physical borders marked the interactive area (which was also aligned to the digital interaction space).

As with the touchful setting, the user's arm can rest on a sponge placed in the rear part of the box which reduces the physical strain often involved with touchless input. Similar to SpongeBox, SquareSense is based on an Arduino microcontroller but uses capacitive sensors and copper plates fixed to the walls of the box. Similar to SpongeBox, SquareSense was configured in an iterative process during the pre-tests and used an equal number of 13 distinct proximity levels for each direction.

4 Interaction Tests and Performance Metrics

Our user studies consider several objective metrics indicative of interaction performance. These metrics have been selected specifically to fit simple 3D interaction tasks. To be able to compute values for these metrics, our users of both studies perform identical so-called "interaction tests" with each input technique. We consider the metrics to be interesting individually and do not aim at computing an overall index of performance in the first study, but make use of such an overall index for the study with people with impairments as this facilitates the comparison within subjects on a more qualitative level (e.g., the existing impairments might be relevant for interpreting individual results with the three different input techniques there). We thus utilize a user modeling framework [4] which offers an infrastructure for defining, maintaining and analyzing an arbitrary number of individual metrics. Each test (see the following sections) requires the user to move a red cube (see Fig. 2 [5]) which acts as a cursor in a 3D space according to a particular task. All devices were used for absolute positioning of the cube in the digital space.

4.1 Reach and Regularity

The first test (and corresponding metric) is called *Reach*. Here, the user has to move the red interactive cube to the personal maximum comfortable position in the directions left, right, forward and down (in all cases starting from the same position in the center of the interaction space). The metric *Reach* has been selected because the mobility and strength of a user's dominant hand (which are decisive for the values achieved for *Reach*) are highly individual and could be significantly reduced for users with (temporary) motor impairments which again can strongly influence interaction performance. For people without motor imparments we expected *Reach* within our relatively small physical interaction space to be about equally high. The test is similar to the "straight navigation task" used by Tscharn et al. [18] in their study on 3D map navigation.

At the touchful (isometric) setting, a user has to apply the highest amount of pressure he/she can (comfortably) achieve in all four directions to move the cube in the respective direction. The maximum values achieved for the four directions are stored as *ReachLeft*, *ReachRight*, *ReachDown*, and *ReachForward*. At the (semi-)touchless (isotonic) settings, the test requires a user to move the cube by moving the hand. The values are stored in percent of the system's global maximum (the red cube cannot be moved out of the interaction space, if it has reached the maximum position, the resulting *Reach* value is 100% and the cube will stop there). The results could also be used to individually adapt the *ContinuousRegularity* and *Time* test (see Sects. 4.2 and 4.3) which was done for the study with people with impairments (see Sect. 5.2) where *Reach* was quite diverse. For the study with people without impairments (see Sect. 5.1) we did not use this individual adaptation of the *ContinuousRegularity* task in order for the values of the *ContinuousRegularity* and *Time* metrics (see Sect. 4.3) to be better comparable.

Within the same test used to compute *Reach*, the system analyzes deviations from the straight-most path between initial and maximum position and uses it to compute a *Regularity*[2] metric (again, for all interaction directions and measured in percent). A straight path would result in a *Regularity* of 100%. The path (including the respective target and actual positions) is analyzed at every time stamp between initial and end position. The deviation from the straight path is averaged over all time stamps and subtracted from an initial value of 100%. *Regularity* is computed for each direction (*RegularityLeft*, *RegularityRight*, *RegularityDown*, *RegularityForward*).

4.2   Continuous Regularity

The second test *ContinuousRegularity*[3] shares some characteristics with the "rotation navigation task" used by Tscharn et al. [18] and requires users to follow a green target cube (see Fig. 2 [5]) over a path that reaches all relevant areas of the 3D interaction space. The target path starts at the initial position in the center of the interaction space, then moves around.

The computation algorithmically matches the one of *Regularity*, which is, however, tested for each of the four directions individually only while *ContinuousRegularity* requires a user to perform a coordinated, continuous and interruption-free movement that covers all directions. To be able to identify preferred directions (e.g., left or right) or dimensions (e.g., left/right or down/up), we compute individual metrics (*ContinuousRegularityLeftForward*, *ContinuousRegularityLeftDown*, *ContinuousRegularityRightForward* and *ContinuousRegularityRightDown*) in addition to the general *ContinuousRegularity* metric which considers the whole path.

For the study with people with impairments (see Sect. 5.2), we used the values of the *Reach* metric to automatically configure the path that should be followed by the user. This was done mainly to aviod paths that confront the users with (due to their impairment) unsolvable tasks. Figure 3 shows an example path the users had to take in a 3D coordinate system. The path starts at the green dot in the middle of the left area. From there, the users follow the path as indicated by the numbered arrows (subpaths 1 to 7).

4.3   Time

Finally, the third test called *Time* requires users to reach target cubes that consecutively appear in each of the four directions after a certain delay as quickly

---

[2] This metric was named "Accuracy" in [3]. After this publication we found out that for many, the wording was misleading which is why we changed it before the publication of the second study in [5].

[3] This metric was named *Coordination* in [3]. As we later decided to rename *Accuracy* to *Regularity* (as explained in Sect. 4.1), we concluded to use the name *Continuous-Regularity* introduced in [5] to keep it consistent with *Regularity*, a stronglly related metric.

as possible. Again, the red interactive cube is positioned in the center of the interactive space initially and is moved back there after a target cube has been reached. The target cubes are big enough to be easily reached as it was not the aim to find out the optimum size of the target area but the interaction speed in case the target is of sufficient size. For the study with people with impairments, we again personalized this test based on the results for *Reach* so that the cube was in a reachable area for every participant. The metrics are called *TimeLeft*, *TimeRight*, *TimeForward*, and *TimeDown*.

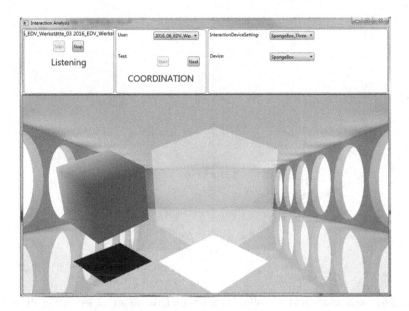

Fig. 2. Visualization users see during interaction [5].

5 User Studies

This section describes research questions, procedure and methodology, and participants of the two user studies on the role of haptics in user input. One study has been designed for people without known impairments (see Sect. 5.1), the other has been designed for and conducted with people with motor and cognitive impairments (see Sect. 5.2).

5.1 Study with People Without Impairments

Research Questions. This user study was tailored to evaluate two aspects related to the three input techniques and devices. First, it should identify strengths and weaknesses of the individual devices/techniques, based on the

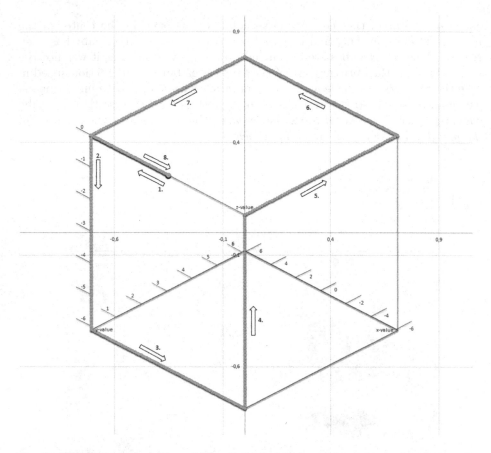

Fig. 3. The path users had to follow the interactive target object cube during the Continuous Regularity tests.

interaction performance indicators *Reach, Regularity, ContinuousRegularity* and *Time* (see Sects. 4.1, 4.2 and 4.3). In the second part, UX related to each of the input devices/techniques should be evaluated, using the categories *Efficiency, Perspicuity, Dependability, Stimulation* and *Novelty* defined by the standardized User Experience Questionnaire (UEQ)[4] and described later.

We designed our study so that the interaction tests were identical for all devices (see Sect. 4), the users' required interaction activities were comparable for all techniques and the users had enough time to get familiar with the input techniques prior to the actual tests. Thus we consider the main difference between the three input techniques to be the degree of haptics involved. An additional difference can be seen between touchful and the other two techniques as it relies on force application (isometric) whereas the other two rely on movements (isotonic). Based on our expectations and findings of related studies, we formulated seven hypotheses:

----

[4] http://www.ueq-online.org.

- H1: We expect users to be able to interact fastest with touchless input.
- H2: We expect *Reach* to be about equally high with all three input techniques.
- H3: We expect interaction *Regularity* to be better with input techniques that involve haptics.
- H4: We expect *ContinuousRegularity* to be better with input techniques that involve haptics.
- H5: We expect *UX* to be generally better with input techniques that involve haptics.
- H6: We expect *Stimulation* to be better with input techniques that involve haptics.
- H7: We expect *Dependability* to be better with input techniques that involve haptics.

Regarding H1, we found divergent results in related studies, e.g., Tscharn et al. [18] found users to be slower with Leap for navigation tasks, compared to a 3D mouse whereas in the study of Coelho and Verbeek [9] who compared Leap to a common mouse, users were faster with Leap at tasks comparable to ours. Although Zhai [19] concludes that "human response with an isometric device is faster than with a comparable isotonic one since no transport of limb or device is needed" we expected users to be faster with touchless input in our study. First, because they did not have to overcome physical resistance to hit the target and second, the distance users had to transport limb (i.e., their hand) over was equal for all three input techniques. Regarding H2, we expected *Reach* to be about equally high with all input techniques as the participants of this study did not have any known impairments (reducing interaction range) and analyzed it just to confirm this assumption. Further, we wanted to be able to compare the related results to those gained within the second study (see Sect. 7). Regarding H3 and H4, we expected *(Continuous)Regularity* to be better with input techniques that provide physical restrictions which constitute some form of guidance. Regarding H5, H6 and H7, we expected general UX, and *Dependability* and *Stimulation* in particular to be better with input techniques that involve a haptic experience because prior research suggests that even simple haptic stimulation can contribute to the communication of emotional information, see, e.g., Salminen et al. [16].

Procedure and Methodology. The study followed a within-subjects design and took place in a controlled lab setting. The participants were asked to do the three interaction tests with all devices. We used a counterbalanced order (latin square) in which the devices were presented to the users to prevent a bias due to practicing effects and control other position effects like fatigue. Before the tests, users got an introduction by the test supervisor, explaining device and input technique, and could become familiar with it. When they were ready, the tests started. The results were automatically recorded and analyzed. In total, 25 users did 27 interaction tasks each (9 tasks with three devices), resulting in a total number of 675 tasks that were analyzed. The interaction during the phase of getting familiar with the individual settings was not recorded.

After the tests with each device, users answered the standardized UEQ, see e.g., [14]. The UEQ aims at (i) enabling quick assessment, (ii) capturing comprehensive impression of UX, and (iii) encouraging simple and immediate feedback [14]. It is available in 15 languages and comprises the following UX aspects (so-called "scales"): attractiveness, perspicuity, efficiency, dependability, stimulation, and novelty. Each scale is represented by a number of "items" that have the form of a semantic differential, using a seven-point scale ranging from -3 to 3. For our study we excluded the scale *attractiveness* as we considered the related items less important for our objectives (after making sure that the UEQ allows for reduction of categories). Thus, our users answered 20 items related to the remaining five scales for each interaction setting:

- *Perspicuity*: Is it easy to get familiar with the product? Is it easy to learn how to use it? Example items are *not understandable/understandable* or *easy/difficult to learn*.
- *Efficiency*: Can users solve their tasks without unnecessary effort? Example items for this category are *fast/slow* or *impractical/practical*.
- *Dependability*: Does the user feel in control of the interaction? Example items are *unpredictable/predictable* or *meets expectations/does not meet expectations*.
- *Stimulation*: Is it motivating to use the product? Example items for this category are *not interesting/interesting* or *motivating/demotivating*.
- *Novelty*: Is the product innovative and creative? Does the product catch users' interests? Example items are *creative/dull* or *conservative/innovative*.

The procedure was repeated for all input techniques. Afterwards, we collected basic demographic data (e.g., gender and age) and some additional information we considered relevant (e.g., whether the participants had previous experiences with input techniques and devices similar to those that were used in the study). The tests took 15 to 30 min per person.

Participants. We recruited 25 participants who volunteered for the task. They were aged between 19 and 49 ($AV = 34.12$, $SD = 9.35$), 8 were male and 17 female. All participants were right-handed and used the right hand for interaction (thus, all interaction data was produced using the dominant hand). Most participants were staff or students of the university. The user group was exceptionally diverse regarding experiences with alternative input techniques, e.g., there was a professor for UX and interaction design but also an office assistant who did not have any previous experiences with input devices other than mouse, keyboard and touch screen. About 24% of the users had previous experience with Leap (however, only three users had used it more thoroughly before). Also 24% had used SpongeBox once before (they participated in an earlier user test). In order not to cause a bias based on previous experiences, we allowed all participants to get familiar with the respective device as long as they needed before the test.

5.2 Study with People with Motor Impairments

The study conducted with people with motor impairments has been described in [3]. It is summarized in this section (whereas the according results can be found in Sect. 7) in order to draw conclusions about the importance of haptics for people with and without impairments in comparison.

Research Questions. According to the previous study with people without known impairments, haptics plays an important role primarily on the side of interaction performance, while to UX it seems not to be the most important characteristic. However, for people with impairments interaction performance might be more important (i.e., how well they can work with some input device) than the UX (i.e., how much they like working with some input device) – at least compared to the balance people without known impairments might experience in this regard. Additionally, haptics is considered more important in earlier stages of development and for people with certain kinds of impairments [3]. Therefore, a qualitative user test with five carefully selected participants with motor and cognitive impairments was conducted in a facility, where people with impairments work, to investigate possible differences of the two target groups in regard to their reliance on haptics.

Procedure and Methodology. The participants were presented with a laptop computer running our prototype application and were asked to fulfill the different interaction tests using the three input devices described above. The typical study setting can be seen in Fig. 4.

Each participant followed the same set of tasks with each of the three input devices (again, the order of devices was changed via the Latin Square method to account for training effects). The study made use of a within-subjects design that aimed at comparing the three different interaction devices that provide a varying amount of haptics. Like in the other study, all tasks were centered around the controlling of a virtual red cube in a 3-dimensional space according to the different tasks described in Sect. 4.

Data for the analysis was gathered in three different forms: **(1)** Automated analysis of interaction data leading to the derivation of performance metrics. **(2)** The interaction performance was additionally evaluated (rated on a 5-point scale between 1-very good and 5-very poor) by the observers. **(3)** The participants were asked how they would describe each of the devices using one or more predefined or self-determined adjectives (multiple answers possible, e.g., funny and exhausting, complicated, or easy).

Participants. The selection process was done with the help of caretakers and the head of the facility to account for the participants' current health, mood or other conditions. The five participants (whose names were changed) were aged between 25 and 48 years ($AV = 33.80$, $SD = 7.83$), 4 male and 1 female, and are described in the following:

Fig. 4. A participant interacting with the touchful SpongeBox prototype during the instructions for our user tests [3].

1. Anton (29 years old, male)
   - Impairments: spastic tetraplegia, occasional epileptic seizures
   - Interactions: usually interacts with the computer using a trackball
   - Common Activities: maintains the facility's Facebook group
2. Boris (48, m)
   - Impairments: meningomyelocele and hydrocephalus, short-sighted, strabismus
   - Interactions: works with a common laptop
   - Common Activities: manages photos, writes the weekly menu plan, responsible for cash desk billing process
3. Chris (25, m)
   - Impairments: spastic tetraplegia
   - Interactions: interacts with the computer using a special keyboard, trackball and two hardware switches
   - Common Activities: edits slides in Photoshop
4. Debbie (32, f)
   - Impairments: spastic tetraplegia
   - Interactions: uses special software MULTiTEXT[5] with voice output
   - Common Activities: creates symbol boards, photo-based rosters, alternative communication concepts for apartments and other workshops at the facility

---

[5] http://hindelang-software.de, last access 22nd April 2018.

5. Evan (35, m)
   - Impairments: spastic tetraplegia
   - Interactions: uses special keyboard with bigger keys and trackball
   - Common Activities: digitalizes slides and supports CMS-based websites.

6   Results of the Study with People Without Impairments

This section summarizes the results of our first study, conducted with people without known impairments, following the study design described in Sect. 5.1. The results have been previously published in [5].

6.1   Interaction Performance

Here we describe the results related to users' interaction performance and analyzed the metrics introduced earlier in Sect. 4. The detailed results are listed in Tables 1 and 2 (both originally published in [5]).

We conducted a statistical analysis running Friedman's tests for the comparison of *Reach*, *Regularity*, *ContinuousRegularity* and *Time* between the three input techniques. We used the Friedman's test because our data partly violated the normal distribution assumption of ANOVA (which we would have generally preferred due to its higher stability). In order to examine the statistical results further, we additionally ran a repeated-measures ANOVA which confirmed all occurrences of statistical significance that were found by the Friedman's tests.

The Friedman's tests revealed statistically significant[6] differences between the three input techniques regarding *Reach* ($\chi^2(2) = 13.317$, $p = .001^*$), *Regularity* ($\chi^2(2) = 44.163$, $p = .000^{**}$), and *ContinuousRegularity* ($\chi^2(2) = 13.520$, $p = .001^*$) while the differences for *Time* were not significant ($\chi^2(2) = 5.040$, $p = .08$). We further conducted a post-hoc analysis with Wilcoxon signed-rank tests with a Bonferroni correction applied, resulting in a significance level set at $p < .017$. More detailed results related to the individual performance metrics are reported in the following sections.

Reach. The results for the *Reach* metric are reported in Table 1 (distinguishing between the four interaction directions) and Table 2 (aggregating the results for the four directions). Statistically significant differences for *Reach* were found only between the semi-touchless and touchful ($Z = -2.947$, $p = .003^7$) techniques. Differences between touchful/touchless and semi-touchless/touchless were not significant ($Z = -2.130$, $p = .033$ and $Z = -2.060$, $p = .039$). The results generally suggest that participants could reach the maximum positions well in all directions and with all techniques.

---

[6] * denotes a significance level set at $p < .05$, ** a significance level set at $p < .001$.

[7] As a significance level of $p < .017$ has been identified, we do not use the standard APA notation ($p < .05$).

Table 1. The computed values for mean, median and standard deviation of all metrics averaged for 25 participants [5], are measured in percent. LF stands for left forward, LD for left down, RF for right forward and RD for right down respectively.

Metric	Touchful			Semi-Touchless			Touchless		
	M	Mdn	SD	M	Mdn	SD	M	Mdn	SD
ReachDown	100.00	100.00	0.00	100.00	100.00	0.00	98.33	100.00	4.08
ReachLeft	95.33	100.00	19.73	100.00	100.00	0.00	99.00	100.00	4.90
ReachRight	91.33	100.00	12.80	100.00	100.00	0.00	99.67	100.00	1.63
ReachForward	100.00	100.00	0.00	100.00	100.00	0.00	100.00	100.00	0.00
RegularityDown	86.87	100.00	21.70	84.26	100.00	34.28	28.78	28.24	21.97
RegularityLeft	91.85	100.00	22.00	100.00	100.00	0.00	60.48	66.97	26.61
RegularityRight	72.30	93.13	34.31	95.30	100.00	14.81	62.11	72.50	32.21
RegularityForward	77.49	100.00	30.20	95.15	100.00	19.87	24.25	19.89	22.74
Cont.RegularityLF	82.18	83.84	6.12	83.58	84.46	3.40	81.43	85.10	14.02
Cont.RegularityLD	87.67	88.30	3.57	86.41	87.95	4.67	82.50	91.40	23.05
Cont.RegularityRF	76.47	75.92	4.44	72.89	73.38	3.75	79.61	82.20	6.56
Cont.RegularityRD	83.05	82.84	4.61	75.68	80.26	13.02	82.08	91.13	24.36
TimeDown	1272	1002	901	1391	1156	856	1832	1251	1681
TimeLeft	795	653	353	940	801	458	1679	1100	2729
TimeRight	1114	1107	466	978	900	380	1797	950	3862
TimeForward	1356	1014	1032	1451	1151	783	2819	1401	3024

Table 2. Aggregated results for mean, median and standard deviation of Reach, Regularity, ContinuousRegularity and Time averaged for the 25 participants [5], measured in percent (or milliseconds, for time).

Aggregated metric	Touchful			Semi-touchless			Touchless		
	M	Mdn	SD	M	Mdn	SD	M	Mdn	SD
Reach	96.67	100.00	6.36	100.00	100.00	0.00	99.25	100.00	1.85
Regularity	82.13	86.76	14.94	93.68	100.00	11.04	43.91	47.30	16.90
ContinuousRegularity	82.34	82.41	3.84	79.64	80.45	4.10	81.41	86.68	16.49
Time	1134	1026	466	1190	1081	484	2032	1250	2442

Regularity. We again measured *Regularity* related to four directions (see Table 1) and aggregated the results for an overall *Regularity* result (see Table 2). We can generally summarize that the semi-touchless technique clearly outperformed the other two. It resulted in a mean value of 93.68% ($SD = 11.04$), while the touchful technique gained 82.13% ($SD = 14.94$) and touchless input resulted in a mean of 43.91% ($SD = 16.9$). 20 of 25 participants gained their individually best result with the semi-touchless input technique, two with the touchful technique, and the remaining three gained equally good results with the semi-touchless and touchful techniques. Consequently, none of the 25 participants gained their individually best result with the touchless setting. The differences between the input techniques were significant for touchful and semi-touchless ($Z = -3.072, p = .002$), touchful and touchless ($Z = -4.372, p = .000$) and semi-touchless and touchless ($Z = -4.372, p = .000$) input.

For three directions (left, right, forward), *Regularity* was best with semi-touchless input (with means between 95.15% and 100%, however with a high standard deviaion in two cases, see Table 1). The touchful technique was best for *RegularityDown* ($M = 85.87\%$, which is slightly better than the average result with the semi-touchless setting, $M = 84.26\%$, both however with high variation). The touchless technique was worst for all directions (with means between 24.25% and 62.11% for forward and right). This global trend is confirmed by the participants' individual results: no user gained any of their individually best results with touchless input.

Continuous Regularity. We measured continuous regularity for all four directions individually (see Table 1) and further aggregated the results to *Continuous-Regularity* (see Table 2). As all participants had to follow the same path (non-individualized version), we consider the results comparable. The mean results for touchful input for the different directions were between 76.47% (right forward) and 87.67% (left down). For semi-touchless input, the results were between 72.89% (right forward) and 86.41% (left down). For touchless input, the results ranged from 79.61% (right forward) to 82.50% (left down).

Interestingly, even if the differences were moderate in most cases, the coordinated movement was most difficult in the direction right/forward with all devices and least difficult in the direction left/down for all 25 participants. We assume that the reason for this is that for right-handed people a movement (or force application) of the right hand to the left (i.e., towards the body) is easier than to the right (away from the body). For the aggregated *Continuous-Regularity* metric, touchful input was best on average, resulting in a mean of 82.34% ($SD = 3.84$). The touchless technique was slightly worse ($M = 81.41\%$, $SD = 16.49$) and semi-touchless was last ($M = 79.64\%$, $SD = 4.1$). The statistical analysis showed that the differences between touchful and semi-touchless input were significant ($Z = -2.4082$, $p = .016$). The other comparisons revealed no significant differences ($Z = -1.574$, $p = .115$ for touchful/touchless and $Z = -2.301$, $p = .021$ for semi-touchless/touchless).

Time. In the related test, we measure the average time a user took to reach each of the target cubes. Again, we consider the results for *Time* to be comparable here because all participants had to move the cube over equal distances. In opposition to our expectation (but consistent with the findings of some of the related studies we found, see Tscharn et al. [18] and Stannus et al. [17]), users were not fastest with touchless input. The statistical analysis did actually not reveal any significant differences. We initially expected users to be faster with touchless input due to the absence of physical resistance. Based on the results we assume that this missing resistance led to an uncertainty regarding whether the goal had already been reached or not (although we visualized this in the user interface). Due to the high variation we searched for outliers and found a user who seemed to have troubles with touchless input in general. Removing this user from the data set reduced the variation considerably but does have influence on statistical significance.

6.2   User Experience

We primarily utilized the customized data analysis tool and methodology provided by UEQ for the analysis of our results. Additionally we ran a statistical analysis of the UEQ data, in order to be better able to judge the actual differences between the settings. For this analysis we used a repeated-measures ANOVA (as the UEQ part of our data met the ANOVA's assumptions).

UEQ Summary. The summarized results for the UEQ are reported in Fig. 5 and Table 3 [5]. The scale ranges from −3.0 (which is considered "horribly bad") to 3.0 (considered "extremely good"). However, the authors of the UEQ consider it "extremely unlikely" to observe values < −2.0 or > 2.0 in real applications. Values between −0.8 and 0.8 represent a neutral evaluation (visualized yellow in Fig. 5), values > 0.8 represent a positive (green) and values < −0.8 a negative one (red). Thus we can summarize that touchful input was evaluated positively for the categories *Perspicuity*, *Stimulation* and *Novelty* and neutrally for *Efficiency* and *Dependability*. For semi-touchless input, the results were neutral for *Dependability* and positive for all other categories (especially for *Stimulation* and *Novelty*). For touchless input, all categories were evaluated positively.

Table 3. UEQ results averaged for the 25 participants [5].

UEQ-category	Touchful	Semi-touchless	Touchless
Perspicuity	1.560	1.520	1.740
Efficiency	0.670	0.873	1.140
Dependability	0.670	0.790	1.430
Stimulation	1.390	1.570	1.140
Novelty	1.440	1.580	1.170

Statistical Analysis. The ANOVA revealed significant differences for *Dependability* ($p = .022^{*8}$) and *Novelty* ($p = .036^*$). The pairwise comparison showed significant differences only between the touchful and the touchless input technique ($p = .031^*$). The differences for *Novelty* were significant at the group level only, pairwise comparisons did not reveal significant differences. The statistical results seem to lower the significance of the UEQ results drastically at first

---

[8] Greenhouse-Geisser correction was applied because *Dependability* data violated ANOVA's sphericity prerequisite.

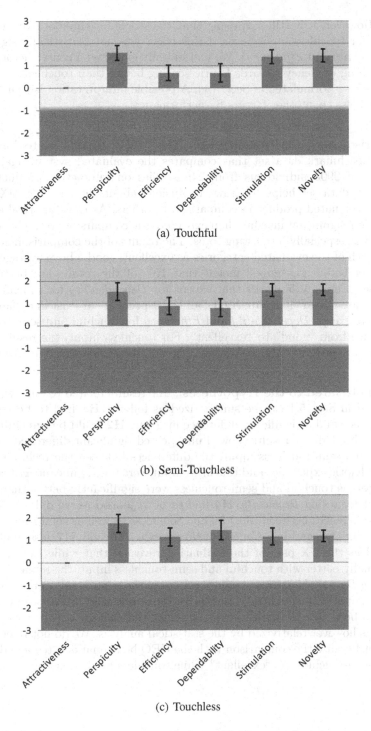

(a) Touchful

(b) Semi-Touchless

(c) Touchless

Fig. 5. The UEQ results for all input techniques [5]. The error bars represent the 95% confidence intervals of the scale means.

glance. However, it is still surprising that the scores for three of five categories are best for touchless input (even if this effect was not statistically significant for *Perspicuity* and *Efficiency*). We had initially expected a contradictory result with a strong tendency towards haptic scoring better than touchless input (see the hypotheses formulated in Sect. 5.1). A possible interpretation is that UX was influenced less than other factors by performance.

Comparison to UEQ Benchmarks. The UEQ data analysis tool also provides a benchmark data set that compares the evaluated system against the responses of 9905 individuals from 246 studies on interactive products. The benchmark data set helps to draw conclusions about the relative (UX) quality of the evaluated product in comparison to others. As the statistical analysis revealed less significant insights than expected, the comparsion to the benchmark data set was especially interesting to us. The results of the comparison generally classify each of the evaluated categories as excellent, good, above average, below average, or bad (e.g., "good" means that 10% of the results are better, 75% are worse). Figure 6 [5] shows that except for *Dependability* for touchful input (which is rated "bad" in comparison), all UX aspects are at least in a "fair" area. All aspects except *Dependability* and *Efficiency* for touchful and semi-touchless input range from "good" to "excellent". For touchless input, the results for all categories are at least "above average" ("good" for *Perspicuity* and *Novelty*).

Findings Related to the Hypotheses. The results related to our hypotheses introdcued in Sect. 5.1 can be summarized as follows. **H1** had to be **rejected** as we did not find a significant difference in *Time*. **H2** could be **partially confirmed**. Although the results showed unexpected significant differences between touchful and semi-touchless input, the differences between the techniques that involve a haptic experience and touchless input were not significant. **H3** could be **confirmed** as touchful and semi-touchless were significantly better than touchless input regarding *Regularity*. **H4** had to be **rejected** as we did not find significant differences between touchful and touchless as well as semi-touchless and touchless input regarding *ContinuousRegularity*. **H5** and **H7** also had to be **rejected** as the UX part of the evaluation revealed that while two categories were actually better with touchful and semi-touchless input, the remaining three (including *Dependability* that was in the focus of the hypothesis) were better with touchless input. **H6** could **only partially be confirmed**. *Stimulation* actually tended to be better for both input techniques that involve a haptic experience which was however relativized by the statistical analysis. We do not reject H6 at this point because the comparison with the UEQ benchmarks categorized touchful and semi-touchless as "excellent" while touchless input was only "good".

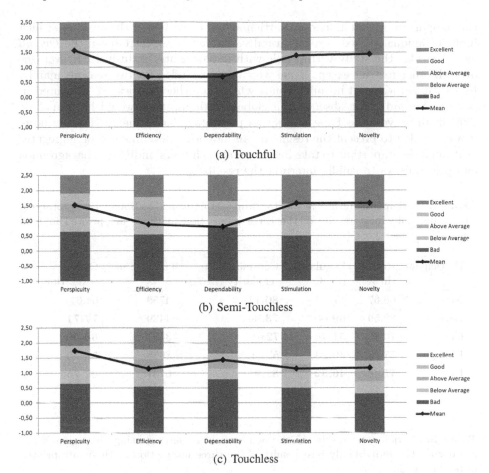

(a) Touchful

(b) Semi-Touchless

(c) Touchless

Fig. 6. Comparison with the benchmark data set [5].

7 Results of the Study with People with Impairments

To allow a better comparison in this book chapter, the following sections summarize the results of our study with people with impairments that were previously described in [3].

7.1 Interaction Performance

The results of the automatically determined performance metrics are depicted in Table 4 for the touchful input technique, Table 5 for the semi-touchless input technique, and Table 6 for the touchless input technique. All metrics except *Time* (measured in milliseconds) are measured in percent. In order to allow for an easy comparison, each user's individually best results among the three different input devices/techniques are formatted in bold. To further facilitate the comparison within individual participants (i.e., to answer the question, which input technique worked best on an individual level), we introduced the *Overall* evaluation for the study with people with impairments, exclusively. It averages over all other metrics except *Time* which was excluded for two reasons mainly. Firstly, it is measured in milliseconds while the other metrics are measured in percent. Secondly, the absence of a global maximum time would have made it difficult to convert the Time values to a percentage-based metric. Furthermore, it was decided to present the results on an individual level instead of aggregates as it might be important to take into account each users' individual backgrounds and prerequisites to validly interpret the results.

Table 4. Participants' results in the Touchful setting using the SpongeBox prototype. The individually best results of the three interaction methods are printed in bold type [3].

Participant	Reach (in %)	Regularity (in %)	Continuous regularity (in %)	Time (in ms)	Overall (excl. time)
Anton	66.67	**47.04**	**80.11**	4759	64.61
Boris	89.59	**69.60**	**73.94**	4429	**77.71**
Chris	70.83	**51.44**	72.61	13582	**64.96**
Debbie	77.08	**40.24**	52.04	8078	**56.45**
Evan	**75.00**	**46.32**	**81.95**	6731	**67.75**

Table 5. Participants' results in the Semi-touchless setting using the SquareSense prototype. The individually best results of the three interaction methods are printed in bold type [3].

Participant	Reach (in %)	Regularity (in %)	Continuous regularity (in %)	Time (in ms)	Overall (excl. time)
Anton	**100.00**	3.37	52.23	**3931**	51.87
Boris	**100.00**	54.19	67.88	11256	74.02
Chris	72.92	14.27	66.10	**3431**	51.09
Debbie	83.33	13.77	**69.46**	17142	55.52
Evan	64.58	37.23	68.07	16141	56.63

7.2   Observation and Subjective Impressions

The results of the observers' impressions regarding how well the interaction worked and the participants' subjective impressions are depicted in Table 7. Some additional information gathered during the observations concerning problems or characteristics are described in the following.

Table 6. Participants' results in the Touchless setting using the Leap. The individually best results of the three interaction methods are printed in bold type [3].

Participant	Reach (in %)	Regularity (in %)	Continuous regularity (in %)	Time (in ms)	Overall (excl. time)
Anton	**100.00**	25.86	79.59	6617	**68.48**
Boris	85.42	32.45	69.32	**3790**	62.39
Chris	**93.75**	20.62	**78.04**	7614	64.14
Debbie	**89.58**	0.00	57.30	**3789**	48.96
Evan	27.08	42.86	15.37	*n/a*	28.44

Anton. The *Regularity* interaction test, where the target cube has to be followed along a predefined path appeared to be difficult for Anton with both the touchful and semi-touchless input technique, but worked considerably better with the touchless input technique, according to the observer. Interestingly, the other interaction tests, where the aim is primarily to reach single targets, worked very well with the two prototypes.

Boris. As the observer noted, Boris had problems positioning his hand. This was connected to the restricted movement range of Boris' fingers, where it showed that the application of pressure (touchful) with the hand was especially difficult and exhausting, as he had to be apply pressure with only one finger due to the limited flexibility/mobility. Additionally, Boris had more problems moving in the direction forward because of this condition compared to the other directions.

Chris. Concerning the directional movement, for Chris, this was more difficult in the directions forward and down while it worked generally better left and right. For the test run with the touchless input technique, Chris had to take off his arm splint because of an interference with the infrared-based recognition technology of the Leap.

Debbie. For Debbie, the observer noted general challenges with the *Continuous Regularity* tasks (especially in the direction forward).

Evan. The physical characteristics (e.g., width and depth) of the two prototypes for touchful and semi-touchless input were suboptimal for Evan and at this early stage of development could only be marginally adjusted to better fit his hand size. Because of Evan's spastic tetraplegia, he could not pull his fingers into the palm of his hand, which led to one finger being outside the devices during operation. Yet, Evan achieved the best results according to the observer's rating with the touchful input technique as the haptic guidance of the material made it easier for him to orient the hand inside the device. The semi-touchless input technique posed an additional challenge for Evan (which was further accentuated with the Leap), because the permanent spreading of fingers led to some fingers being recognized by the touchless technology unintendedly. This oftentimes resulted in the device recording a movement where it shouldn't have. Finally, the test leader had to give support to Evan at the direction down with the Leap motion controller.

Table 7. Results of the observation and subjective impressions [3].

Participant	Device	Input worked ... (1 = very well, 5 = very poorly)	Assignment of adjectives	Additional comments
Anton	SpongeBox	4	Funny, easy	"happy to participate again"
	SquareSense	4	Exhausting, complicated	
	Leap	2	–	
Boris	SpongeBox	2	Exhausting, complicated	Previous experiences with Leap
	SquareSense	3	–	
	Leap	2	Funny, easy	
Chris	SpongeBox	4	Funny	"happy to participate again"
	SquareSense	3	Funny, exhausting	
	Leap	2	Funny, easy	
Debbie	SpongeBox	3	–	Previous experiences with Leap
	SquareSense	4	Exhausting, complicated	
	Leap	3	Funny, easy	
Evan	SpongeBox	2	Funny, easy	–
	SquareSense	4	–	
	Leap	5	Exhausting, complicated	

8   Discussion

In this section we will discuss the findings of both studies individually (some comparing conlusions will be drawn in Sect. 9).

Regarding the study with people without any know impairments (see Sects. 5.1 and 6), we found an unexpected discrepancy in the results between interaction performance and UX. Touchless interaction was largely outperformed by the other two techniques regarding users' interaction performance, especially related to *Regularity*. We consider *Regularity* one of the most important metrics because it is more relevant for everyday interaction settings than e.g., *Continuous Regularity* (which might be relevant for everyday interaction settings only with gesture-based input). *Reach* is most relevant for users whose movement range deviates from the average significantly as input devices and techniques are usually designed to be operable without problems by a "standard user". For our first study, the participants did not have such constraints, thus also the results did not vary much. *Time* is relevant for interaction efficiency also in everyday settings, however regarding *Time* we did not find significant differences between the three input techniques which leaves us with *Regularity* that revealed the most important insights related to interaction performance. While we did actually expect *Regularity* to be better for input techniques that provide physical restrictions and thus also some kind of guidance (see hypothesis H3), we expected UX to reveal correlated results. Yet, not only did we find touchless interaction to yield positive results for all UX categories, we could also draw the conclusion that *a bad interaction performance does not necessarily have to imply a bad UX and vice versa.* We consider this one of the most important findings of our first study. Another finding is that *for the target group without impairments, presence of a haptic experience does not necessarily be a prerequisite for a good UX* (this was also unexpected, see hypotheses H5 to H7).

Further, our second user study revealed that *for the target group of people with impairments, haptics is more important than for people without impairments regarding interaction performance.* All of our five participants gained their invididually best result for *Regularity* with the touchful input technique that relies on permanent phyiscal contact between user and device. Further, three of the five participants additionally gained their individually best result for *Continuous Regularity* with the touchful input technique and for four of five, the best individual overall interaction performance result was obtained with this setting.

However, for the target group of people with impairments, we also found some limiting factors related to the touchful interaction setting. First, *Time* (for all five participants) and *Reach* (for four of five participants) were better with the semi-touchless or touchless settings. We attribute this to the physical resistance of the material that had to be overcome when interacting with the touchful input device (however, the same resistance might have allowed for the good *Regularity* with this setting). This is in line with the subjective impressions we discussed with the participants (e.g., Boris described interaction with SpongeBox as "exhausting", an adjective he did not choose for any of the other two settings). In conclusion, we can note that *the selection of the material involved in touchful input settings is of tremendous importance for people with impairments.* While *it can facilitate interaction performance and also UX* (e.g., Anton and Evan found interaction with SpongeBox to be "easy"), *it can also cause severe exhaustion* if not individually suitable (see Boris).

9   Conclusions

In this chapter, we described two user studies on the importance of a haptic experience for interaction performance and UX and for people with and without known impairments. Due to the differences between the two target groups we used different study designs (see Sects. 5.1 and 5.2), thus we cannot compare the results on the statistical level. Further, we only had five participants for the second study, which was another reason why we focused on qualitative insights for the target group of people with impairments while the first study with people without impairments largely was of quantitative nature. Further, it would not have been possible for the second study to use the standardized UEQ due to the cognitive impairments of our participants. We discussed and adapted our study design in beforehand with the head of the facility where our participants work and asked him to judge the cognitive demand our questions would impose for them. Thus we ended up with a reduced, general questionnaire that asked the participants to assign one or more pre-defined attributes (such as "easy" or "complicated") to the three input techniques. This worked well for our participants and provides enough information to draw individual conclusions.

Nevertheless we want to draw some general conclusions that can help to put the findings (see Sects. 6 and 7) into context with each other as well and summarize them as follows (major conclusions in italic). *The presence of a haptic experience can influence interaction performance and UX* (while it is *more important for interaction performance than for UX for people without impairments,* it is *relevant for interaction performance as well as UX for people with impairments.* Especially for people with impairments, we found immense differences in the results (e.g., for *Regularity* for all five participants). Generally, *people with impairments were considerably more diverse regarding their interaction-related preferences and requirements, compared to people without impairments* (this leads to a need for personalizability of interaction solutions for this target group). Further, *for people with impairments, haptic interaction that requires application of force is more easily perceived as exhausting* (this was not observed for people without impairments in the setting with our touchful input technique). At least *for some people with impairments, the results suggest a correlation between interaction performance and UX which was not true for our participants without impairments* (e.g., Evan and Anton had a more positive subjective impression of the devices that worked well for them regarding interaction performance). This was, however, not the case for all of our five participants (e.g., Boris represented an exception). This again suggests that the preferences are highly individual for this target group. Another important finding for both groups is that *most participants with or without impairments gained their individually best overall interaction performance result with devices that involve haptics.*

We believe that these insights can help other researchers and practitioners to design and evaluate input devices and techniques. However, we also want to shortly discuss limitations related to the results presented in this chapter. The input devices and interaction tests used for both studies were restricted to a 3DoF interaction setting and the results should not be generalized to settings involving considerably more (as e.g., present in interaction with full body movement) or fewer (e.g., for conventional mouse/keyboard or touchscreen-based input) DoF. Similarly, we intendedly used rather simple interaction tasks throughout our study and consequently, the results should not be generalized for significantly more complex or less complex tasks. Our expectation is that the importance of haptics (and thus a haptic guidance and physical restrictions) increases with task complexity and number of DoF for both target groups, especially related to interaction performance (however, even more for the target group of people with impairments that generally relies more strongly on haptics than the group of people without impairments).

References

1. Atkins, M.S., Fernquist, J., Kirkpatrick, A.E., Forster, B.B.: Evaluating interaction techniques for stack mode viewing. J. Digit. Imaging **22**(4), 369–382 (2009)
2. Augstein, M., Kern, D., Neumayr, T., Kurschl, W., Altmann, J.: Measuring physical pressure in smart phone interaction for people with impairments. In: Mensch und Computer 2015, Workshopband. Oldenbourg Wissenschaftsverlag, Stuttgart (2015)
3. Augstein, M., Neumayr, T., Burger, T.: The role of haptics in user input for people with motor and cognitive impairments. In: Harnessing the Power of Technology to Improve Lives. Studies in Health Technology and Informatics, vol. 242, pp. 183–194 (2017). Reprinted with permission from IOS Press
4. Augstein, M., Neumayr, T., Kern, D., Kurschl, W., Altmann, J., Burger, T.: An analysis and modeling framework for personalized interaction. In: IUI 2017 Companion: Proceedings of the 22nd International Conference on Intelligent User Interfaces, Limassol, Cyprus (2017)
5. Augstein, M., Neumayr, T., Vrecer, S., Kurschl, W., Altmann, J.: The role of haptics in user input for simple 3D interaction tasks. An analysis of interaction performance and user experience. In: Proceedings of the 2nd International Conference on Human Computer Interaction Theory and Applications, Funchal, Madeira, Portugal (2018)
6. de la Barré, R., Chojecki, P., Leiner, U., Mühlbach, L., Ruschin, D.: Touchless interaction-novel chances and challenges. In: Jacko, J.A. (ed.) HCI 2009. LNCS, vol. 5611, pp. 161–169. Springer, Heidelberg (2009). https://doi.org/10.1007/978-3-642-02577-8_18
7. Bowman, D., et al.: 3D user interfaces: new directions and perspectives. IEEE Comput. Graph. Appl. **28**(6), 20–36 (2008)
8. Carter, T., Seah, S.A., Long, B., Drinkwater, B., Subramania, S.: Urtra haptics: multi-point mid-air haptic feedback for touch surfacces. In: Proceedings of the 26th Annual ACM UIST Symposium. ACM (2013)
9. Coelho, J.C., Verbeek, F.: Pointing task evaluation of leap motion controller in 3D virtual environment. In: Proceedings of the ChiSparks 2014 Conference, The Hague, Netherlands (2014)
10. Dangeti, S., Chen, Y.V., Zheng, C.: Comparing bare-hand-in-air gesture and object-in-hand tangible user interaction for navigation of 3D objects in modeling. In: Proceedings of the TEI 2016. ACM (2016)
11. Fröhlich, B., Hochstrate, J., Kulik, A., Huckauf, A.: On 3D input devices. IEEE Comput. Graph. Appl. **26**(2), 15–19 (2006)
12. Hürst, W., Helder, M.: Mobile 3D graphics and virtual reality interaction. In: Proceedings of the 8th International Conference on Advances in Computer Entertainment Technology, p. 28. ACM (2011)
13. Hwang, S., Bianchi, A., Ahn, M., Wohn, K.: MagPen: magnetically driven pen interaction on and around conventional smartphones. In: Proceedings of the 15th International Conference on Human-Computer Interaction with Mobile Devices and Services, Munich, Germany (2013)

14. Laugwitz, B., Held, T., Schrepp, M.: Construction and evaluation of a user experience questionnaire. In: Holzinger, A. (ed.) USAB 2008. LNCS, vol. 5298, pp. 63–76. Springer, Heidelberg (2008). https://doi.org/10.1007/978-3-540-89350-9_6
15. Rehg, J.M., Kanade, T.: Visual tracking of high DOF articulated structures: an application to human hand tracking. In: Eklundh, J.-O. (ed.) ECCV 1994. LNCS, vol. 801, pp. 35–46. Springer, Heidelberg (1994). https://doi.org/10.1007/BFb0028333
16. Salminen, K., et al.: Emotional and behavioral responses to haptic stimulation. In: Proceedings of CHI 2008. ACM (2008)
17. Stannus, S., Rolf, D., Lucieer, A., Chinthammit, W.: Gestural navigation in Google earth. In: Proceedings of the 23rd Australian Computer-Human Interaction Conference (2011)
18. Tscharn, R., et al.: User experience of 3D map navigation - bare-hand interaction or touchable device? In: Mensch und Computer 2016. GI (2016)
19. Zhai, S.: Human performance in six degree of freedom input control. Ph.D. thesis, University of Toronto (2008)

Recommendations from a Study of a Multimodal Positive Computing System for Public Speaking

Fiona Dermody$^{(\boxtimes)}$ and Alistair Sutherland$^{(\boxtimes)}$

Dublin City University, Dublin, Ireland
fiona.dermody3@mail.dcu.ie, alistair.sutherland@dcu.ie

Abstract. We review some existing multimodal systems for Public Speaking. We then present two versions of a multimodal system for Public Speaking based on Positive Computing. The system uses the Microsoft Kinect to detect voice, body pose, facial expressions and gestures. The system is a real-time system, which gives users feedback on their performance while they are rehearsing a speech. We discuss a study comparing two versions of the system. One version displays a live video-stream of the user. The other displays a computer-generated avatar, which represents the user's body movements and facial expressions. We discuss user reactions to both versions of the system and make recommendations for future multimodal systems for public speaking.

Keywords: Public speaking · Positive Computing ·
Real-time feedback · Multimodal interfaces · HCI

1 Introduction

A fear of public speaking can have a significant impact on a person's success in education or enterprise [1–3]. To date, there have been a number of multimodal systems for public speaking developed, which we discuss later. Our own multimodal system for public speaking has been developed based on the principles of Positive Computing. Within a framework of Positive Computing, self-awareness is described in the context of reflection and getting to know oneself. In regard to public speaking, this implies a speaker's awareness of how they appear to an audience. For instance, some speakers may not be aware of the importance of using gestures to engage an audience [4]. The systems presented in this paper make the user aware of their speaking through feedback. They utilise different approaches for relaying this feedback to users.

This material is based upon works supported by Dublin City University under the Daniel O'Hare Research Scholarship scheme. System prototypes were developed in collaboration with interns from École Polytechnique de l'Université Paris-Sud and l'École Supérieure d'Informatique, Électronique, Automatique (ESIEA) France.

© Springer Nature Switzerland AG 2019
D. Bechmann et al. (Eds.): VISIGRAPP 2018, CCIS 997, pp. 81–92, 2019.
https://doi.org/10.1007/978-3-030-26756-8_4

We present two versions of our multimodal Positive Computing System for Public Speaking. The system is a real-time system which gives users feedback on their performance while they are rehearsing a speech. One version of the system displays a live video-stream of the user. The other displays a computer-generated avatar which represents the user's body movements and facial expressions. In all other aspects, the two versions are identical. In both versions of the system, feedback is displayed using visual icons in proximity to the speaking modality it relates to (Figs. 1 and 4). We discuss a study comparing these two versions of this system. The objective of the study was to see which version of the system made the users more aware of their performance. We also discuss user reactions to both versions of the systems and make recommendations for future multimodal systems for public speaking.

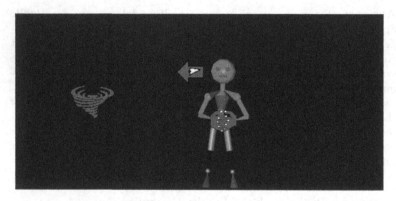

Fig. 1. System avatar with indicative visual feedback on gaze direction, agitation and hands touching. The avatar represents the user. The visual feedback icons are positioned in proximity to the area they relate to [5].

2   Related Work

There are other systems that have focused on awareness in the context of public speaking and communications skills development. AwareMe utilises a vibrating wristband and a coloured display (Fig. 4). As they are speaking, it provides speakers with haptic and visual feedback as they are speaking on speaking rate, voice pitch and filler words [6].

Cicero:Virtual Audience Framework utilises a virtual audience comprising avatars to convey non-verbal feedback to speakers [7–9]. As can be seen in Fig. 3, feedback is relayed to the speaker by engaged or disengaged body poses of the virtual audience and through a coloured bar at the top of the screen.

In other systems, the user is represented using an avatar or video stream. A Virtual Rehearsal educational application gives feedback to users in real-time on open and closed gestures using the Microsoft Kinect 2 skeletal view avatar [10], [11]. Presentation Trainer, for instance, enables users to view real-time feedback using a live video representation of the user [12].

Fig. 2. Video stream with visual feedback on gaze direction and hands-touching. The user is represented in the video. The visual feedback icons are positioned in proximity to the area they relate to [5].

Fig. 3. Cicero - virtual audience framework [8].

Fig. 4. AwareMe [6].

Fig. 5. Presentation trainer [12].

Presentation Trainer utilises the Microsoft Kinect 2 to track the user's body and voice. When delivering feedback, one nonverbal speaking modality is presented at a time with a gap of a minimum of six seconds between feedback displays. The feedback could be described as interruptive and directive because it directs the user to stop and adjust their speaking behaviour, if they are deemed to have exhibited an undesirable speaking behaviour. As can be seen in Fig. 5, the feedback is displayed as text eg. 'reset posture'. The feedback provided by these systems can make users aware of their speaking behaviour and this awareness can aid in the development of communication skills.

3   Positive Computing

Positive Computing is a paradigm for human-computer interaction. Its main aim being to boost the well-being of the user. It includes many themes, among them competence, self-awareness, stress-reduction and autonomy. [13–15]. Throughout this paper we will focus predominantly on self-awareness. We will explore some of the other themes in the section on Future Work. Becoming aware of speaking performance is the first step for the user when embarking on increasing their competence in public speaking. Important aspects of public speaking to consider include body posture, gestures and gaze direction [4,16]. In the past, the only options for a user to gain this awareness was to either practise in front of a mirror or in front of a human mentor. Each of these methods can cause both anxiety and stress for the user. The aim of our system is to give the user the opportunity to gain this awareness privately without being exposed to stress or anxiety. Awareness will be achieved through users looking at a representation of themselves as they speak. In the system, users have the choice to view themselves as an avatar or a live video stream. Their chosen representation will appear with real-time feedback superimposed on it. Central to our recent paper is the research question: which of these two representations makes the user more aware of their performance? [5].

4 Utilising Video

In social skills development it has been found beneficial for individuals to observe their own behaviour on video. Video is a useful medium for the user to see their own facial expressions, gestures, body pose and gaze direction in granular detail. However, users' reaction to observing themselves on video can often be negative. 'The cognitive dissonance that can be generated from the discrepancies between the way persons think they come across and the way they see themselves come across can be quite emotionally arousing and, occasionally, quite aversive' [17]. In addition, Dowrick and Biggs have reported that people may become conscious of their nonverbal communication while oberving themselves on video and are often not satisfied with what they see [17]. Furthermore while observing themselves on video, they may focus on and become distracted by the physicality of their appearance and their perceived physical attractiveness or lack thereof as opposed to their behaviour. If the person has a negative self-perception of themselves on video, then this can impact on their reaction to the video [18].

5 Utilising an Avatar

An avatar displays an abstract representation of the user and this form of abstract representation allows the user to observe their facial expressions, body pose and gestures in 3D. Considering the drawbacks to using video noted in Sect. 4, this type of abstract representation could be advantageous to the user due to the lessening of distractions caused by details of their physical appearance.

5.1 Avatars and Public Speaking

Studies exploring the fear of public speaking have confirmed that users do respond positively to virtual agents. This has been found to be the case 'even in the absence of two-way verbal interaction, and despite knowing rationally that they are not real' [19,20]. Virtual agents have been used effectively in multi-modal systems for public speaking, most notably, Cicero [9]. Virtual agents in the aforementioned systems were used to simulate an audience that responded to the user's speaking performance. In the system described here and in our previous paper, the avatar represents the user themselves [5].

6   System Description

The focus of our aforementioned paper is a multimodal Positive Computing system which delivers feedback in real-time on different modalities simultaneously. When referring to 'multimodal' we are describing the functionality of the system which detects multiple speaking modes in the speaker such as voice, eye contact and gestures. The interface allows users to choose whether they receive feedback on all speaking modes or a subset of them. It is of paramount importance that the user can speak freely using the system without being distracted, interrupted or confused by the visual feedback on the screen. A more in-depth description of the system can be found here: [21]. The system consists of a Microsoft Kinect 1 connected to a laptop. Users' interactions such as body movements, facial expressions and voice are detected by the Microsoft Kinect. The user stands in front of the system and speaks. A laptop screen in front of the user displays feedback.

6.1   System Feedback

Real-time visual feedback is displayed as follows, see Figure 6:

The system displays arrows around the user' or avatar's head to prompt the user to change their view direction. The pitch of the user's voice is indicated via a rolling graph above the user's head The frequency of the peaks in the graph indicate the speech rate. This enables the user to monitor how fast they are talking. The user can gauge whether they are speaking in a monotone voice or using a lot of vocal variety by observing the slope of the graph which indicates rising and falling tones. An icon is displayed over the avatar's hands to alert the user to when their hands are touching. An icon is displayed to indicate when the user has crossed their arms. An icon is displayed to indicate if the user is agitated or moving too quickly. The icon is positioned next to the avatar's body. An icon is displayed to indicate whether the user is smiling or surprised. The icon is located next to the avatar's face.

These particular speaking behaviours were selected because they were high-lighted as important by public speaking experts [4,16].

6.2   Avatar and Video Stream

A central tenet of positive computing is to provide users with more autonomy or choice when interacting with computer systems [14,15,22,23]. As such, our system can be configured according to users' preferences. For instance, a user can configure the system to use an avatar, see Fig. 1, or video stream, see Fig. 2.

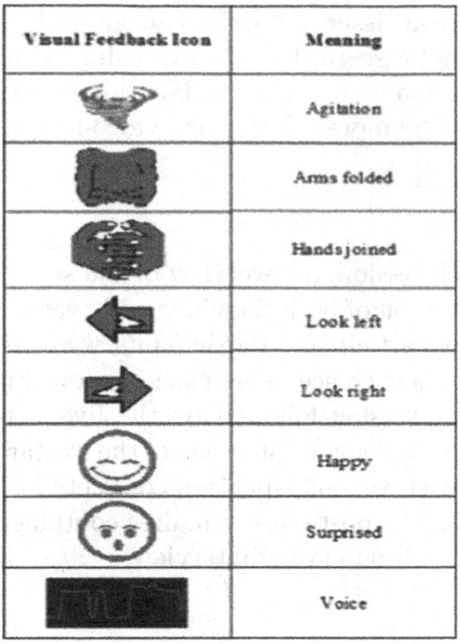

Visual Feedback Icon	Meaning
	Agitation
	Arms folded
	Hands joined
	Look left
	Look right
	Happy
	Surprised
	Voice

Fig. 6. Visual feedback icons that are displayed in proximity to the area they relate to in [5].

7   Study Design

The study consisted of 10 participants (4M, 6F). We drew participants from both the staff and student body at our university, Dublin City University. They came from various faculties across the Humanities, Science, Computing and Business. Each participant was recruited on a one-time basis with a duration of 25 min each. A preliminary questionnaire on demographic information was completed by each participant. At the end of each session each participant completed a post-questionnaire. Participants were all novice speakers who had done some public speaking but wished to improve their skills in this area. None of the participants had previously used a multimodal system for public speaking. The post-questionnaire consisted of eight items. It was based on the ACM ICMI Multimodal Learning Application Evaluation and Design Guide[1]. In order to evaluate user experience, three questions were put to users concerning (i) naturalness, (ii) motivation to use the application again and (iii) stress experienced using the application. Awareness was evaluated using four questions on distraction, body awareness, awareness of feedback and awareness of speaking behaviour. An open question was included for additional remarks and comments. The questionnaire prompted speakers to rate different aspects of the version which they had just used, on a scale from 1 to 10. Users were also given the opportunity to submit additional comments following each question if they so wished.

---

[1] http://sigmla.org/mla2015/ApplicationGuidelines.pdf accessed on January 2016.

A pretest uncovered an issue with the background colouring. Participants stated that they could not discern their dark clothing against a dark background in the video-stream version of the system. For this reason a white background was tested and found to be more effective for video-stream.

7.1 Study Format

At the beginning of each session, an overview of the study was presented to the participant. A demonstration of both the video and avatar versions of the system was then given to each participant. Participants were asked to speak for one minute on a subject of their choice using each version. Five of the participants initially used the avatar version followed by the live video. Then the other 5 participants used the video version followed by the avatar version. Immediately following their trial of each version, speakers completed a post-questionnaire to capture users' reactions. The post-questionnaires contained the same items each time. Finally, there was a brief closing interview.

8 Results

Our methodology regarding each question involved comparing and contrasting a boxplot of the responses for both the avatar and video versions. The most dramatic difference was observed for the question on distraction, Fig. 7. The video version was consistently rated more distracting than the avatar version according to users. This score correlates with that given to awarenesses of feedback and awareness of speaking performance. The trend was for users to allocate a greater score to the avatar system for awareness of speaking performance and awareness of feedback.

The experimental design was a standard hypothesis test, in which the independent variable was the version of system (avatar or live video) and the dependent variable was the level of distraction. Scores ranged from 1 for no distraction to 10 for very distracting.

It was pertinent to consider that the order in which the participants used the versions (avatar first or video) could potentially be a confounding variable. Consequently, the users were split into two equal-sized groups (avatar first and video first), in order to measure any effect that this variable might have. An Analysis of Variance was performed which revealed no statistically significant difference between the two groups.

The p-value for the difference between the distraction levels for the video version and the avatar version was 0.04, which indicates that there was a significant difference between the responses to the two versions.

Based on user comments and analysis, we concluded that the live video image was distracting users from their performance and from the system feedback. This assertion was further confirmed by the users' remarks in the closing interview. Of the ten users nine reported that the live video stream was very distracting. They said that they were more aware and conscious of their personal appearance

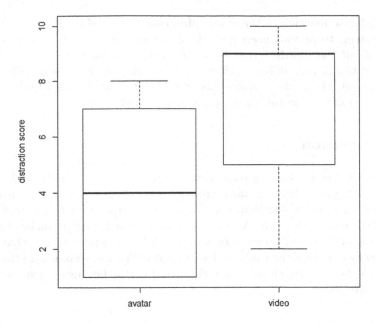

Fig. 7. Boxplots of the responses for the avatar version and the video version in answer to the question of distraction. The higher the score, the more distracting was the version. As can be seen, participants reported that the video version was more distracting [5].

than of their performance or of the system feedback. All participants reported that they would be motivated to use the system again, both avatar and video versions. Participants reported that they experienced elevated stress while using the video version of the system.

9   Discussion

The fact that all participants reported that they would use the system again highlights the need for multimodal systems for communication skills development. Overwhelmingly, the majority of participants preferred the avatar version of the system because they found it less distracting. However, there are some caveats to this finding as discussed below. Participants, on the whole did not like seeing themselves in video mode. They made comments such as 'I did not like seeing myself in this situation' and 'I felt awkward looking at myself'. However, three participants did report that they could discern their facial expressions more clearly in video mode. Furthermore, one participant reported that using the system in avatar mode 'made the act of talking feel too disembodied and therefore harder to relate to the information/feedback provided by the system'. This participant also stated 'that I was less focused on my speaker behaviour and more inclined to feel distracted by the avatar'. The fact that one user had such an adverse reaction to the avatar illustrates the need for interactive multi-modal systems to provide users with the autonomy or the option to choose the appearance of the interface that they are using. The participant who disliked the avatar had a very different experience of using the system in video mode reporting that 'the systems seems easy and fun to use, I would find this very helpful for preparing lectures and conference presentations'.

10 Conclusion

Based on our study, we can recommend that future multimodal systems for public speaking include an avatar representing the user. It was evident from this study that most users find it distracting or even unpleasant to see themselves represented in video stream. As an avatar is more abstract, it makes the user more aware of their body movements and facial expressions rather than being distracted by details of their personal appearance. We also recommend that users are given a choice between using live video and avatar because at least one user preferred live video.

11 Future Work

Work will focus on the following areas. Does the colour of the feedback affect the users evaluation? Would users prefer a more human-looking avatar? Some research shows that users find such avatars more sympathetic especially if the avatar resembles the user themselves [24,25]. We intend to conduct a longitudinal study to evaluate how the users' speaking performance changes if they use the system over a period of time. We want to investigate how users evaluate a statistical analysis of their performance e.g. recording how many times the system identified particular events such as hands touching, arms crossed, changing view direction etc.

We will evaluate other aspects of Positive Computing with respect to our system: Do users have autonomy i.e. can they select the feedback that they want when they want it? With regard to stress, is the system stressful to use? Does it become less stressful with practice? Does it reduce the stress of live public performance? Does the users' competence in public speaking increase with use of the system?

References

1. Dwyer, K.K., Davidson, M.M.: Is public speaking really more feared than death? Commun. Res. Rep. **29**, 99–107 (2012)
2. McCroskey, J.C., Booth-Butterfield, S., Payne, S.K.: The impact of communication apprehension on college student retention and success. Commun. Q. **37**, 100–107 (1989)

3. Harris, S.R., Kemmerling, R.L., North, M.M.: Brief virtual reality therapy for public speaking anxiety. Cyberpsychol. Behav.: Impact Internet Multimed. Virtual Reality Behav. Soc. **5**, 543–550 (2002)
4. Toastmasters International: Gestures: Your Body Speaks (2011)
5. Dermody, F., Sutherland, A.: evaluating user responses to avatar and video speaker representations a multimodal positive computing system for public speaking. In: Proceedings of the 13th International Joint Conference on Computer Vision, Imaging and Computer Graphics Theory and Applications (VISIGRAPP 2018), Volume HUCAPP, Madeira, pp. pp. 38–43. INSTICC (2018)
6. Bubel, M., Jiang, R., Lee, C.H., Shi, W., Tse, A.: AwareMe: addressing fear of public speech through awareness. In: Proceedings of the 2016 CHI Conference Extended Abstracts on Human Factors in Computing Systems, pp. 68–73. ACM (2016)
7. Batrinca, L., Stratou, G., Shapiro, A., Morency, L.-P., Scherer, S.: Cicero - towards a multimodal virtual audience platform for public speaking training. In: Aylett, R., Krenn, B., Pelachaud, C., Shimodaira, H. (eds.) IVA 2013. LNCS (LNAI), vol. 8108, pp. 116–128. Springer, Heidelberg (2013). https://doi.org/10.1007/978-3-642-40415-3_10
8. Chollet, M., Morency, L.P., Shapiro, A., Scherer, S., Angeles, L.: Exploring feedback strategies to improve public speaking: an interactive virtual audience framework. In: Proceedings of the 2015 ACM International Joint Conference on Pervasive and Ubiquitous Computing, UbiComp 2015, pp. 1143–1154 (2015)
9. Chollet, M., Stefanov, K., Prendinger, H., Scherer, S.: Public speaking training with a multimodal interactive virtual audience framework - demonstration. In: Proceedings of the 2015 ACM International Conference on Multimodal Interaction, ICMI 2015, pp. 367–368 (2015)
10. Barmaki, R., Hughes, C.E.: Providing real-time feedback for student teachers in a virtual rehearsal environment. In: Proceedings of the 2015 ACM International Conference on Multimodal Interaction, ICMI 2015, pp. 531–537 (2015)
11. Barmaki, R.: Improving social communication skills using kinesics feedback. In: Proceedings of the 2016 CHI Conference Extended Abstracts on Human Factors in Computing Systems, CHI EA 2016, pp. 86–91. ACM, New York (2016)
12. Schneider, J., Börner, D., Van Rosmalen, P., Specht, M.: Presentation trainer, your public speaking multimodal coach. In: Proceedings of the 2015 ACM on International Conference on Multimodal Interaction, pp. 539–546. ACM (2015)
13. Calvo, R.A., Peters, D.: Introduction to positive computing: technology that fosters wellbeing. In: Proceedings of the 33rd Annual ACM Conference Extended Abstracts on Human Factors in Computing Systems, CHI EA 2015, pp. 2499–2500. ACM, New York (2015)
14. Calvo, R.A., Peters, D.: Positive Computing: Technology for Wellbeing and Human Potential. MIT Press, Cambridge (2014)
15. Calvo, R.A., Peters, D.: Designing technology to foster psychological wellbeing. In: Proceedings of the 2016 CHI Conference Extended Abstracts on Human Factors in Computing Systems, CHI EA 2016, pp. 988–991. ACM, New York (2016)
16. Toastmasters International: Competent Communication A Practical Guide to Becoming a Better Speaker (2008)
17. Dowrick, P.W., Biggs, S.J.: Using Video: Psychological and Social Applications. Wiley, Hoboken (1983)
18. Dowrick, P.W.: A review of self modeling and related interventions. Appl. Prevent. Psychol. **8**, 23–39 (1999)

19. Garau, M.: Selective fidelity: investigating priorities for the creation of expressive avatars. In: Schroeder, R., Axelsson, A.S. (eds.) Avatars at Work and Play: Collaboration and Interaction in Shared Virtual Environments. Computer Supported Cooperative Work, pp. 17–38. Springer, Dordrecht (2006). https://doi.org/10.1007/1-4020-3898-4_2

20. Pertaub, D.P., Slater, M., Barker, C.: An experiment on public speaking anxiety in response to three different types of virtual audience. Presence: Teleoper. Virtual Environ. **11**, 68–78 (2002)

21. Dermody, F., Sutherland, A.: Multimodal system for public speaking with real time feedback: a positive computing perspective. In: Proceedings of the 18th ACM International Conference on Multimodal Interaction, pp. 408–409. ACM (2016)

22. Calvo, R.A., Peters, D.: Positive computing: technology for a wiser world. Interactions **19**, 28–31 (2012)

23. Calvo, R.A., Peters, D., Johnson, D., Rogers, Y.: Autonomy in technology design. In: Proceedings of the Extended Abstracts of the 32nd Annual ACM Conference on Human Factors in Computing Systems - CHI EA 2014, pp. 37–40 (2014)

24. Baylor, A.L.: Promoting motivation with virtual agents and avatars: role of visual presence and appearance. Philos. Trans. Roy. Soc. London B: Biol. Sci. **364**, 3559–3565 (2009)

25. Suh, K.S., Kim, H., Suh, E.K.: What if your avatar looks like you? Dual-congruity perspectives for avatar use. MIS Q. **35**, 711–729 (2011)

Utilisation of Linguistic and Paralinguistic Features for Academic Presentation Summarisation

Keith Curtis[1]([✉]), Nick Campbell[2], and Gareth J. F. Jones[1]

[1] ADAPT Centre, School of Computing, Dublin City University, Dublin, Ireland
Keith.Curtis@adaptcentre.ie, Gareth.Jones@dcu.ie
[2] ADAPT Centre, School of Computer Science and Statistics,
Trinity College Dublin, Dublin, Ireland
nick@tcd.ie

Abstract. We present a method for automatically summarising audio-visual recordings of academic presentations. For generation of presentation summaries, keywords are taken from automatically created transcripts of the spoken content. These are then augmented by incorporating classification output scores for speaker ratings, audience engagement, emphasised speech, and audience comprehension. Summaries are evaluated by performing eye-tracking of participants as they watch full presentations and automatically generated summaries of presentations. Additional questionnaire evaluation of eye-tracking participants is also reported. As part of these evaluations, we automatically generate heat maps and gaze plots from eye-tracking participants which provide further information of user interaction with the content. Automatically generated presentation summaries were found to hold the user's attention and focus for longer than full presentations. Half of the evaluated summaries were found to be significantly more engaging than full presentations, while the other half were found to be somewhat more engaging.

Keywords: Video summarisation · Classification · Evaluation · Eye-tracking

1 Introduction

Online archives of multimedia content are growing rapidly. Every minute in 2017, 4.1 million videos were viewed on *YouTube*, while 70,017 h of video were watched on *NETFLIX*. It is time consuming and a growing challenge for users to be able to browse content of interest in such large multimedia archives - either in response to user queries or in informal exploration of content. The goal of this work is to provide an effective and efficient way to summarise audio-visual recordings where the significant information is primarily in the audio stream, based on both linguistic and paralinguistic features.

© Springer Nature Switzerland AG 2019
D. Bechmann et al. (Eds.): VISIGRAPP 2018, CCIS 997, pp. 93–117, 2019.
https://doi.org/10.1007/978-3-030-26756-8_5

Current methods for accessing and browsing digital video archives include scene type classification [1], for finding relevant content, research has primarily focused on matching text queries against written metadata or transcribed audio [2]. These methods are limited by available low-level metadata descriptions and transcripts when browsing content such as lectures or presentations, where typically little information is available in the visual stream and most of the information exists in the audio track. Matching of the visual component of these queries is generally complemented by text search against a transcript of any available spoken audio and any meta-data provided [3].

However, significant amounts of multimedia content does not have these features; Presentations from academic conferences are potentially of great interest to researchers working in the area of the presentations. However, viewing full academic presentations can be time consuming, and, while keywords can give an indication of just how relevant each presentation is to the researcher, they do not know the value of a presentation until they actually watch it. There are other situations where they may wish to catch up on an academic presentation, and simply do not have the time to spare to watch it in its entirety. Suitably constructed automatically generated summaries of academic presentations could save users from needing to view full presentations in order to gauge their utility and access the information contained in them.

The work described in this paper contributes to addressing these limitations by classifying high-level paralinguistic features in such content, which can then be used to assist in the summarisation of lectures or presentations. We address the following research question "Can areas of special emphasis provided by the speaker, combined with detected areas of high audience engagement and high levels of audience comprehension, be used for effective summarisation of audio-visual recordings of presentations?" We evaluate this summarisation approach using eye-tracking and by questionnaire.

This paper revises and extends our earlier conference paper [4]. It is structured as follows: Sect. 2 introduces related work in video summarisation and describes the high level feature classification process. Section 3 introduces the multimodal corpus used for our experiments, while Sect. 4 describes the procedure for creating automatic summaries. This is followed by Sect. 5 which describes the evaluation tasks performed and their results. Finally, conclusions and considerations of possible extensions of this work are offered in Sect. 6 of this paper.

2   Previous Work

2.1   Related Work on Summarisation

This section looks at related work on summarisation and skimming of audio-visual recording of academic presentations.

The use of motion estimation techniques for analysing and annotating video recordings of technical talks was investigated in [5]. They used a robust motion estimation technique to detect keyframes and segment a video into sequences containing a single slide. Potential gestures were tracked using active contours, found by computing the absolute difference between the keyframe and images in the warped sequence. By successfully recognising all pointing gestures, presentations could be fully annotated per slide. This automatic video analysis system helped users to access presentation videos intelligently by providing access using specific slides and gestures.

Prosodic information from the audio stream to identify speaker emphasis during presentations was used in [6], in addition to pause information to avoid selecting segments for summaries which start mid-phrase. They also garnered information from slide transition points to indicate the introduction of a new topic or sub-topic. They developed three summary algorithms: a slide transition based summary, a pitch activity based summary and a summary based on slide, pitch and user-access information. They found that computer generated summaries were rated poorly on coherence, in which participants complained that summaries jumped topics. No significant difference between users' preferences for the three methods was found, leading to the conclusion that the simpler methods may be preferable. Audio-visual presentations were found to be less susceptible to pitch-based emphasis analysis than the audio-only stream, meaning emphasis is more easily analysed from pitch in the audio-only stream.

The user's facial expressions were captured and analysed in [7] for the generation of perception based summaries which exploit the viewer's affective state, perceived excitement and attention. They found it unlikely that a single summary could generally be seen as highlighting the key features of a video by all viewers. Results suggested that there were at least two or three distinguished parts of videos that can be seen as the highlight by different viewers.

A set of tools for creating video digests of informational videos was developed in [8]. These tools included text summarisation, chapter and section segmentation, and had a video digest authoring interface. Informal evaluation suggested that these tools made it easier for authors of informational talks to create video digests. They also found that crowdsourced experiments suggested that video digests afford browsing and skimming better than alternative video presentation techniques.

We aim to extend this earlier work by classifying the most engaging and comprehensible parts of presentations and identifying emphasised regions within them, before summarising them. This will enable summaries to include highly rated regions of such high-level concepts, in addition to keywords taken from the transcript of the presentation.

2.2 High-Level Concept Classification

The novel video summarisation method reported in this study incorporates the high level concepts of audience engagement, emphasised speech and the speakers potential to be comprehended. In this section we overview our previous work on the development of these high-level concept detectors.

Classification of Audience Engagement. Prediction of audience engagement levels and ratings for 'good' speaking techniques was performed in [9]. Human annotators were first employed to watch video segments of presentations and provide a rating of how good each speaker was at presenting the material. Audience engagement levels were measured in a similar manner by having annotators watch video segments of the audience to academic presentations, and providing estimates of just how engaged the audience appeared to be as a whole. Classifiers were trained on extracted audio-visual features using an Ordinal Class Classifier.

It was demonstrated that the qualities of a 'good' speaker can be predicted to an accuracy of 73% over a 4-class scale. Using speaker-based techniques alone, audience engagement levels can be predicted to an accuracy of 68% over the same scale. By combining with basic visual features from the audience as whole, this can be improved to 70% accuracy.

Identification of Emphasised Speech. Identification of emphasised speech was performed in [10]. Human annotators labelled areas of perceived emphasised speech. Annotators were asked to watch 5-minute presentation video clips and to mark areas where they considered the speech to be emphasised. Basic audio-visual features of audio pitch and visual motion were extracted from the data. From analysis of this data, it was clear that speaker emphasis occurred in areas of high visual motion coinciding with areas of high pitch.

Candidate emphasised regions were marked from extracted areas of pitch within the top 1, 5, and 20 percentile of pitch values, in addition to the top 20 percentile of gesticulation down to the top 40 percentile of values respectively. All annotated areas of emphasis contained significant gesturing in addition to pitch within the top 20 percentile. Gesturing was also found to take place in non-emphasised parts of speech, however this was much more casual and was not accompanied by pitch in the top 20 percentile.

Predicting the Speaker's Potential to Be Comprehended. Prediction of audience comprehension was performed in [11]. In this work, human annotators were recruited through the use of crowdsourcing. Annotators were asked to watch each section of a presentation and to first provide a textual summary of the contents of that section of the presentation, and following this to provide an estimate of how much they comprehended the material during that section. Audio-visual features were extracted from video of the presenter in addition to visual features extracted from video of the audience, and OCR over the slides for each presentation. Additional fluency features were also extracted from the speaker audio. Using the above described extracted features, a classifier was trained to predict the speaker's potential to be comprehended.

It was demonstrated that it is possible to build a classifier to predict potential audience comprehension levels, obtaining accuracy over a 7-class range of 52.9%, and over a binary classification problem to 85.4%.

3   Multimodal Corpus

Since no standard publicly available dataset exists for work of this nature, we developed a suitable corpus for our study. To do this, we recorded parallel video of the audience and of the speaker for academic presentations at an international conference on research in speech technology [12]. Our dataset contains 31 academic presentations totalling 520 min of video, with high quality 1080p parallel video recordings of both the speaker and the audience to each presentation. Four individual videos were chosen from this dataset for evaluation of video summaries to ensure good coverage but to avoid too much evaluations. These four videos were chosen on the basis of them having being found by our classifiers to be: the most engaging, the least engaging, the most comprehensible video, and the video with highest presentation ratings from this dataset.

4   Creation of Presentation Summaries

This section describes the steps involved in our generation of presentation summaries. Presentations had been processed by *SpokenData*[1], who extracted ASR transcripts and extracted significant keywords from these transcripts. Summaries were generated using these ASR transcripts, the significant keywords extracted from them, and annotated values for 'good' public speaking techniques, audience engagement, speaker emphasis and the speaker's potential to be comprehended.

1. ASR outputs were segmented using the pause information in the transcripts, which indicate start and end times for each spoken phrase. These segments provided a basis for the segmentation of presentations at the phrase-level, with significant phrases selected for inclusion in the summary.
2. We first applied a ranking for each phrase based on the number of keywords, or words of significance, contained within it. For the first set of baseline summaries, we generated summaries by using the highest ranking phrases.
3. Speaker Rating's were halved before applying this ranking to each phrase. We halved the values for speaker ratings so as not to overvalue this feature, as these values were already encompassed for classification of audience engagement levels.
4. Following this, audience engagement annotations were also applied to phrases. We took the final annotated engagement level and applied this value to each phrase contained within each segment throughout the presentation.
5. As emphasis was not annotated for all videos, we used automatic classifications for intentional or unintentional speaker emphasis. For each classification of emphasis, we applied an additional value of 1 to the phrase containing that emphasised part of speech.
6. Finally, we used the human annotated values for audience comprehension throughout the dataset, in order to evaluate summaries from best scenarios. Once again the final comprehension value for each segment was also applied

---

[1] https://spokendata.com/.

to each phrase within that segment. For weightings of paralinguistic feature values, we chose to half the Speaker Rating annotation, while choosing to keep the original for the other annotations for engagement, emphasis and comprehension. This is because Speaker Ratings were already used for classification of engagement. Points of emphasis received a value of 1, while keywords received a value of two, in order to give importance to the role of keywords in the summary generation process.

To generate the final set of video summaries, the highest scoring phrases in the set were selected. To achieve this, the final ranking for each phrase is normalised to between 0 and 1.

7. By then assigning an initial threshold value of 0.9, and reducing this by 0.03 on each iteration, we selected each sentence with a rank above this threshold. By calculating the length of each selected sentence, we then applied a minimum size to our generated video summaries. Using this method we chose a minimum summary length, allowing us to avoid summaries which were too detailed or not sufficiently detailed. Final selected segments were then joined together to generate small, medium and large summaries of each presentation. The temporal order of segments within summaries was preserved. Algorithm 1 below is taken from the conference paper [4].

Algorithm 1. Generate Summaries (from [4]).

> **for all** $_1 Sentence \rightarrow S$ **do**
>> **if** $S\_contains\_Keyword$ **then**
>>> $_2 S \leftarrow S + 2$
>>
>> **end if**
>> $Engagement \rightarrow E$
>> $Speaker Rating \rightarrow SR$
>> $Emphasis \rightarrow Es$
>> $Comprehenson \rightarrow C$
>> $_3 S \leftarrow S + E$
>> $_4 S \leftarrow S + SR/2$
>> $_5 S \leftarrow S + Es$
>> $_6 S \leftarrow S + C$
>
> **end for**
> **while** $Summary < length$ **do**
>> **if** $S \geq Threshold$ **then**
>>> $_7 Summary \leftarrow S$
>>
>> **end if**
>
> **end while**

---

5   Evaluation of Video Summaries

We evaluated the effectiveness of the summarisation strategy described in this paper through the use eye-tracking. In this regard, we carried out our study using an eye-tracking system in which participants watched full presentations and separate presentation summaries. From studying the eye-movements and focus of participants we can make inferences as to how engaged participants were as they watched presentations and summaries. Half of the participants watched full presentations first, while the other half watched summaries first in order to avoid any issues of bias from affecting results.

Eye-tracking was performed for this evaluation because, as shown in previous work, an increased number of shorter fixations is consistent with higher cognitive activity (attention), while a reduced number of longer fixations is consistent with lower attention [13]. This allows us to understand clearly whether generated summaries have any impact on participants attention/engagement levels as they watch presentation summaries compared to full presentations.

Questionnaires were provided to eye-tracking participants in order to discover how useful and effective the participants considered the presentation summaries to be. Also, by summarising using only a subset of all available features, we aimed to discover how effective the individual features are by crowdsourcing a separate questionnaire on presentation summaries generated using subsets of available features. Features used for this further evaluation were: full feature classifications, visual only classifications, audio only classifications, and full feature classifications with no keywords.

5.1 Gaze-Detection Evaluation

During eye-tracking the participants watched one full presentation whilst having their eye-movements tracked. Participants also watched a separate presentation summary, again whilst having their eye-movements tracked. The question being addressed here was whether or not participants retained attention for longer periods of the presentations for summaries than for full presentations, to test the hypothesis that summaries were more engaging and comprehensible.

24 separate participants completed the eye-tracking study. As there were 4 videos to be evaluated in total, eight different test condition were developed, with 4 participants per test. This allowed for full variation of the order in which participants watched the videos. Therefore, half of all participants began by watching a full presentation and finished by watching a summary of a separate presentation. The other half began by watching a presentation summary and finished by watching a full, separate presentation.

Table 1 is taken from the conference paper [4], and shows the core values for eye-tracking results per video, version and scene. The videos are listed 1 to 4, with plen2 as video 1, prp1 as video 2, prp5 as video 3, and speechRT6 as video 4. Version is listed 1 to 2, where version 1 corresponds to the video summary, and version 2 to the full video. The overall scene is 1 and the attention scene - the area around the slides and the speaker is 2. Measurements obtained include: number of fixations, mean length of fixations, total sum of fixation lengths, percentage of time fixated per scene, fixation count and number of fixations per second.

From Table 1, we can see that participants consistently spend a higher proportion of time fixating on the attention scene for summaries than for the full presentation video. This is repeated to an even greater extent for Fixation Counts, where this figure is consistently higher for summaries than for full presentations.

Table 1. Totals per video, version, scene (from [4]).

Vid	Version	Scene	Fixations	mean fixation	fixated	% fixated	fixations	F.P.S.
1	Summ	Whole	432.5	0.492	203.986	94.438	432.625	2.003
1	Summ	Atten	417.37	0.495	199.17	92.208	417.375	1.932
1	Full	Whole	1580	0.582	889.486	92.079	1580	1.636
1	Full	Atten	1523	0.587	865.952	89.643	1523	1.577
2	Summ	Whole	311.87	0.695	209.284	95.129	311.875	1.418
2	Summ	Atten	293.25	0.71	201.996	91.816	293.25	1.333
2	Full	Whole	1153.12	0.709	780.864	89.446	1153.125	1.321
2	Full	Atten	1091.12	0.724	761.826	87.265	1091.125	1.250
3	Summ	Whole	224.37	0.62	135.407	91.491	224.375	1.516
3	Summ	Atten	193.87	0.694	130.091	87.899	193.875	1.310
3	Full	Whole	1076.75	0.641	643.995	83.963	1076.75	1.404
3	Full	Atten	891.37	0.8	656.5	85.593	891.375	1.162
4	Summ	Whole	406.37	0.431	169.388	89.624	406.375	2.150
4	Summ	Atten	385.5	0.466	174.105	92.119	385.5	2.040
4	Full	Whole	1591.25	0.536	832.177	88.908	1591.25	1.700
4	Full	Atten	1414.37	0.561	775.37	82.839	1414.375	1.511

Again, this is evidence of increased levels of participant engagement for video summaries than for full presentation videos.

The number of fixations per second is consistently higher for video summaries, while the mean fixation length is consistently shorter for summaries. As previous work has shown, an increased number of shorter fixations is consistent with higher cognitive activity (attention). This shows that video summaries attract higher attention levels for summaries than for full presentations. As can be seen from inspecting the results tables below, this is more intense for presentations which were less engaging to begin with. Tables 2, 4, 6 and 8 come from the paper [4], these are supplemented with additional attention scene results in Tables 3, 5, 7 and 9.

Table 2. Eye-tracking Video 1 - full scene by **version** (from [4]).

I	J	Variable	Measure	Diff	Error	Sig
Summ	Full	FD.M	Scheffe	−0.09	0.06	0.163
Summ	Full	Percent	Scheffe	2.36	1.68	0.181
Summ	**Full**	**FCp100**	**Scheffe**	**36.73**	**17.12**	**0.050**

Table 3. Eye-tracking Video 1 - attention scene by **version**.

I	J	Variable	Measure	Diff	Error	Sig
Summ	Full	FD.M	Scheffe	−0.09	0.06	0.159
Summ	Full	Percent	Scheffe	2.57	2.05	0.232
Summ	**Full**	**FCp100**	**Scheffe**	**35.57**	**16.13**	**0.045**

Tables 2 and 3 shows a statistically significant difference between the summary and full versions, for the number of fixations per 100 s. Taking these results in conjunction with the overall core figures in Table 1 show that video 1 summary is more engaging than the overall presentation video for video 1.

Table 4. Eye-tracking Video 2 - full scene by **version** (from [4]).

I	J	Variable	Measure	Diff	Error	Sig
Summ	Full	FD.M	Scheffe	−0.01	0.08	0.865
Summ	**Full**	**Percent**	**Scheffe**	**5.68**	**2.41**	**0.033**
Summ	Full	FCp100	Scheffe	7.04	14.51	0.516

Table 5. Eye-tracking Video 2 - attention scene by **version**.

I	J	Variable	Measure	Diff	Error	Sig
Summ	Full	FD.M	Scheffe	−0.01	0.08	0.862
Summ	Full	Percent	Scheffe	4.55	2.89	0.138
Summ	Full	FCp100	Scheffe	8.31	11.59	0.485

Again in Tables 4 and 5, key differences are observed in the average fixation duration per scene, and to a lesser extent in the fixation count per 100 s, more clearly visible from the figures in Table 1, neither of these differences are statistically significant. Participants spent a statistically significant higher proportion of their time fixating on the attention scene for video summaries than for full video presentations.

Table 6. Eye-tracking Video 3 - full scene by **version** (from [4]).

I	J	Variable	Measure	Diff	Error	Sig
Summ	Full	FD.M	Scheffe	−0.02	0.09	0.813
Summ	Full	Percent	Scheffe	7.53	3.63	0.057
Summ	Full	FCper100	Scheffe	11.22	15.24	0.474

Table 7. Eye-tracking Video 3 - attention scene by **version**.

I	J	Variable	Measure	Diff	Error	Sig
Summ	Full	FD.M	Scheffe	−0.11	0.11	0.333
Summ	Full	Percent	Scheffe	2.31	3.24	0.488
Summ	Full	FCper100	Scheffe	14.78	15.23	0.348

Tables 6 and 7 shows that there is no statistically significant difference between the two scene's of the video, however, there is a large, but not significant difference in the percentage of time spent fixating on the attention scene during the video summary compared with during the full video presentation.

Table 8. Eye-tracking Video 4 - full scene by **version** (from [4]).

I	J	Variable	Measure	Diff	Error	Sig
Summ	Full	FD.M	Scheffe	−0.11	0.06	0.080
Summ	Full	Percent	Scheffe	0.72	3.62	0.846
Summ	**Full**	**FCp100**	**Scheffe**	**45.01**	**15.27**	**0.011**

Table 9. Eye-tracking Video 4 attention scene by **version**.

I	J	Variable	Measure	Diff	Error	Sig
Summ	Full	FD.M	Scheffe	−0.10	0.05	0.099
Summ	**Full**	**Percent**	**Scheffe**	**9.28**	**3.84**	**0.030**
Summ	**Full**	**FCp100**	**Scheffe**	**52.86**	**16.14**	**0.006**

Tables 8 and 9, shows a statistically significant ($p < 0.05$) difference between the summary and full versions for the number of fixations per 100 s. There is also a big difference between versions for the mean fixation duration. As engagement and focus has been found to be consistent with a high number of short fixations, this indicates that users found the summary of this video to be much more engaging than the full presentation. Further, this video had previously been found to be least engaging by our classifiers before summarisation, indicating that the affect of summarisation may be increased for non-engaging full presentations.

5.2 Gaze Plots

We now present gaze plots from the eye-tracking studies undertaken. These are data visualisations which can communicate important aspects of visual behaviour clearly. By looking carefully at plots for full and summary videos, the difference in attention and focus for different video types becomes more clearly defined. For each video, 4 representative gaze plots are chosen, 2 from full presentations above, and 2 from presentation summaries below. The gaze plots presented below come directly from the conference paper [4].

From the representative gaze plots in Fig. 1 we see that participants hold much higher levels of attention during summaries than for full presentations, with far less instances of them losing focus or looking around the scene, instead focusing entirely on the slides and speaker. The many small circles over the slides area represent a large number of smaller fixations - indicating high cognitive involvement/engagement.

From the representative plots in Fig. 2 we see improvements in summaries over full presentations. While participants still lose focus on occasion, and improvements from full presentations is not as refined as for the previous video, improvements are still gained, with the vast majority of fixations taking place over the presentation slides and the speaker. For comparison, gaze plots for the full video shows that fixations tended to be quite dispersed.

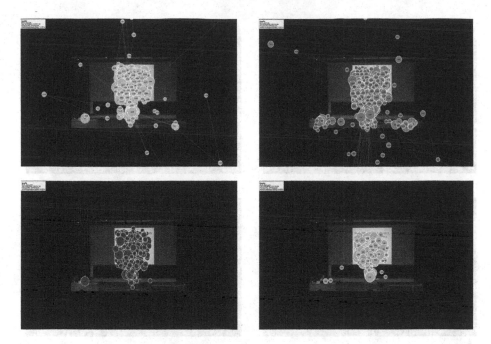

Fig. 1. Plen 2 - representative gaze plots (from [4]).

From the representative gaze plots presented in Fig. 3 we see how the number of occasions on which participants lose focus is reduced, with big improvements on full presentations. Gaze plots show the difference for this video much better than the statistical tests in the previous section do. For full presentations, fixations are dispersed with large numbers of fixations away from the slides and speakers. Summaries show a large improvement with a much reduced number of instances of participants losing focus.

From the representative gaze plots in presented Fig. 4 we can see that while summaries are imperfect, with instances of participants losing attention, huge improvements in attention and focus are made, although this may depend on how engaging the videos were in the first place. While summaries for Video 4 (speechRT6) still show some instances of participants losing focus, the original full presentation was found to be the least engaging video of the dataset. This is also noticeable from gaze plots. The plots show a high number of fixations away from the slides and presenters. Plots of summaries also show smaller fixations than full presentation gaze plots, which indicates higher levels of engagement for presentation summaries, in addition to the obvious position of these fixations taking place predominantly over the slides and speakers.

Overall, gaze plots show many fewer instances of participants losing focus from the presentation. Gaze during summaries is primarily focused on the presentation slides as users gain more new information, with deviations from this usually reverting back to the speaker. Also visible from gaze plots of Video

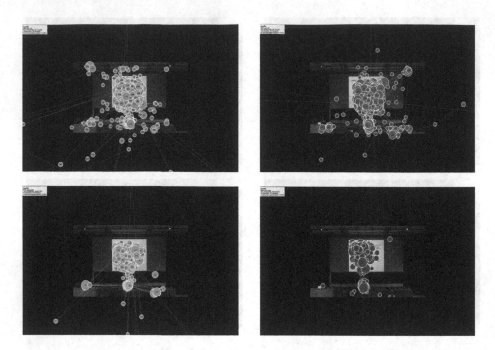

Fig. 2. prp 1 - representative gaze plots (from [4]).

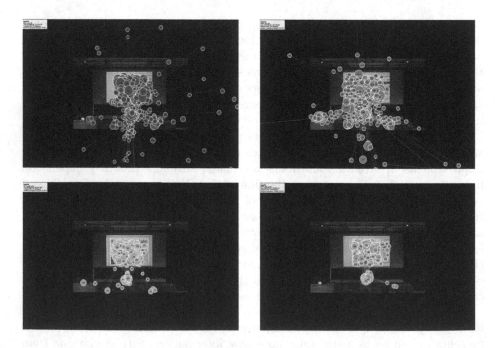

Fig. 3. prp 5 - representative gaze plots (from [4]).

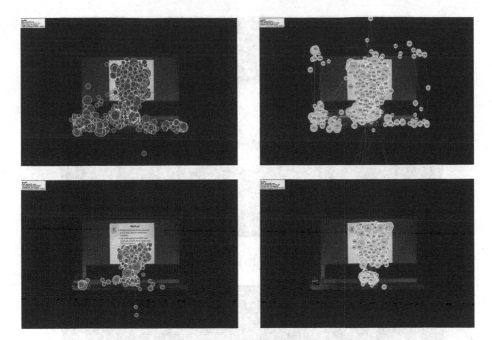

Fig. 4. speechRT6 - representative gaze plots (from [4]).

1 (plen2) and particularly Video 4 (speechRT6), are the shorter fixations (smaller circles) for summaries than for full presentations. This can be seen more clearly by looking back to the figures reported in Table 1.

5.3   Heat Maps

We now demonstrate heat maps generated automatically from eye-tracking outputs. These show consistently more focus on the speaker for full presentations and slightly more focus on slides for presentation summaries. While there are periods in which participants lose focus from the attention scene, this happens for too little time to show as significant in the heat maps. The higher focus on slides for presentation summaries demonstrates that participants spent a higher proportion of time reading through the slides for summaries than for full presentations, and also spent a higher proportion of time focusing on the speaker themselves during full presentations than for presentation summaries. This indicates that presentation summaries contain a higher concentration of new information than full presentations.

Figures 5 and 6 show heat maps for plenaryoral2 full version, with high intensity over the speaker and not too much intensity over the presentation slides. Figure 6 shows slightly more intensity over slides than Fig. 5, both maps however show far more intensity over the speaker than over slides. Intensity on these maps indicates where eye-tracking participants have focused their gaze. This

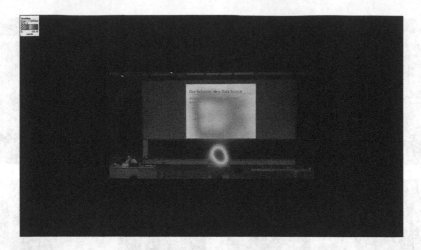

Fig. 5. Pleanaryoral2 full - heat map 1.

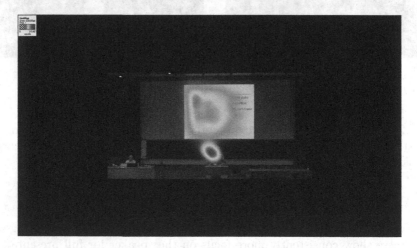

Fig. 6. Pleanaryoral2 full - heat map 2.

shows that participants held their gaze on the speaker for far longer periods than they spent reading the slides.

Figures 7 and 8 show heat maps from plenaryoral2 summary version, these show higher intensity over the presentation slides than heat maps for the full version. These maps do not show reduced intensity over the speaker, however with far more intensity over slides, almost equalling intensity over the speaker, this indicates that participants spend far more of their time reading the slides during the summaries than during full presentations. This indicates that participants were consuming new information for a higher proportion of the time when they were watching summaries than for full presentations.

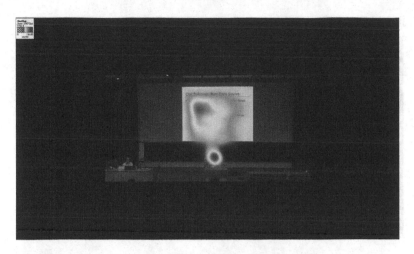

Fig. 7. Plenaryoral2 summary - heat map 1.

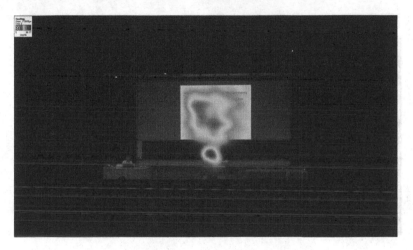

Fig. 8. Plenaryoral2 summary - heat map 2.

Figures 9 and 10 show heat maps from prp1 full version, and shows near equal intensity between speaker and presentation slides, indicating that participants spent near equal time focusing on slides and on the speaker. Figure 10 however shows slightly less intensity over slides than for speaker. This map also shows a slight tinge of intensity over the table to the speakers left, indicating that they have lost focus entirely over the attention area for small sections during these full presentations.

Not too much difference is noticeable in the heat maps of prp1, shown in Figs. 11 and 12, compared to the previous heat maps of the full version of the same video, Figs. 9 and 10. In Fig. 11 however there are noticeable light blobs of heat around the edges of the stage, indicating some participants had a tendency

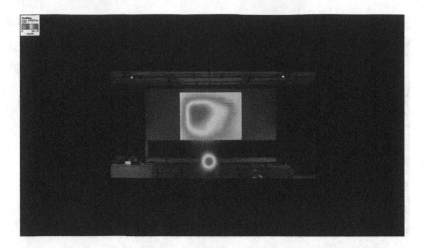

Fig. 9. prp1 full - heat map 1.

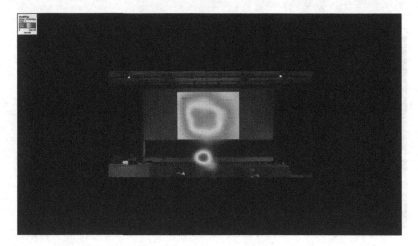

Fig. 10. prp1 full - heat map 2.

to lose focus for short periods of time during these summaries, which suggests that these summaries were perhaps not as engaging as we would wish. In Fig. 11 there is a noticeable increase in intensity over the presentation slides than for the corresponding image for the full version, indicating that participants spend more time reading the slides and taking in new information during the summary.

The heat maps from prp5 full version, shown in Figs. 13 and 14, show that participants spent most of the time during this presentation focused on the speaker. Little intensity over the slides for these two maps indicates that little time was spent reading the slides for these presentations. It should be noted that this full presentation scored very highly for engagement.

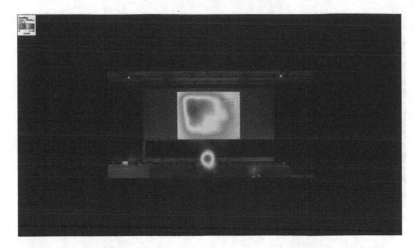

Fig. 11. prp1 summary - heat map 1.

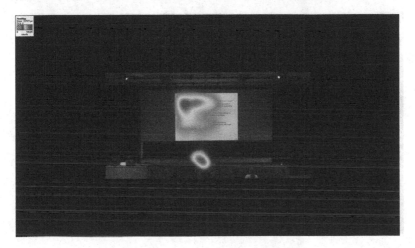

Fig. 12. prp1 summary - heat map 2.

Heat maps for prp5 summary version, Figs. 15 and 16, show much higher intensity over the area of the presentation slides, indicating that participants spent a much higher proportion of time reading the slides during summaries than for the full presentation. Also noticeable is that this area of high intensity appears over the same part of the slides for both maps, Figs. 15 and 16, with little covering the rest of the slides. It should be noted too that slides for this presentation were designed more like newspaper clippings than a typical set of presentation slides. This presentation also scored very highly for audience engagement.

Heat maps above for speechRT6 full version, as shown in Figs. 17 and 18, show that participants spent a very high proportion of the time looking at the

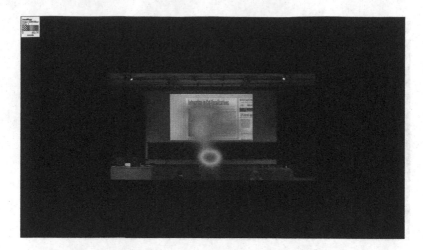

Fig. 13. prp5 full - heat map 1.

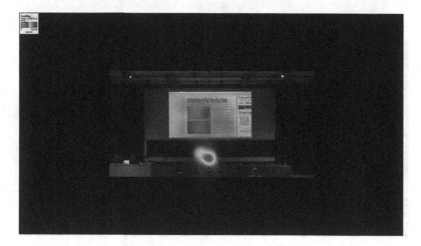

Fig. 14. prp5 full - heat map 2.

presentation slides. In Fig. 17, very little intensity appears over the speakers, indicating that participants spent the vast majority of their time looking at the slides. In Fig. 18, light blobs are noticeable around the edges of the stage indicating that their were times during these full presentations in which participants lost focus. It should be noted that this presentation was found to be the least engaging presentation of the full dataset.

Heat maps for speechRT6 summary version are shown in Figs. 19 and 20, and show an even higher intensity over presentation slides, and even less intensity over the speakers. Intensity in Fig. 20 is also much more spread around the whole area of the slides, indicating that participants spend almost the entire time during these summaries reading the slides to consume the new information.

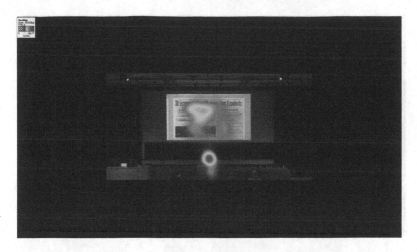

Fig. 15. prp5 summary - heat map 1.

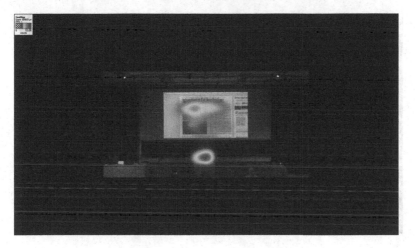

Fig. 16. prp5 summary - heat map 2.

There are also less blobs around the edges indicating that participants lost focus less frequently during summaries than for full presentations.

5.4 Questionnaire Evaluation of Summary Types

We now present questionnaire responses from crowdsourcing participants who watched summaries generated using all available features or just a subset of available features. Summaries were generated using all available features, audio features only, visual features only, or audio-visual features with no keywords used. The goal of this evaluation was to discover the importance of different features in presentation summaries. A total of 48 participants watched the various summaries and answered a questionnaire on each summary. Each was evaluated

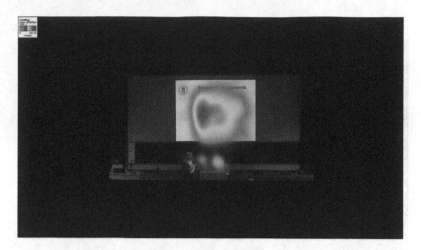

Fig. 17. speechRT6 full - heat map 1.

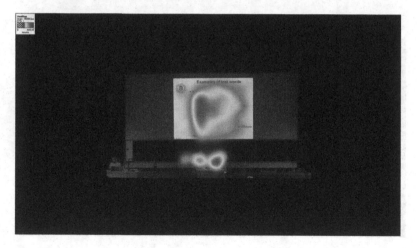

Fig. 18. speechRT6 full - heat map 2.

by 12 participants in total. The order in which participants watched summaries was also alternated to avoid issues of bias affecting results.

Table 10 shows further evaluations between summaries built using all available features, and summaries built using just a subset of features. For audio-only summaries, classification of the paralinguistic features of Speaker Ratings, Audience Engagement, Emphasis, and Comprehension was performed as described in the earlier chapters but by using only audio features, with visual features not being considered. Similarly, for visual only summaries, classification of these features was performed using only visual features, with audio features not being considered. For no keyword summaries, classification of these features is performed and the only information excluded were keywords. For Classify summaries, all available information was used to generate summaries. For this evaluation actual

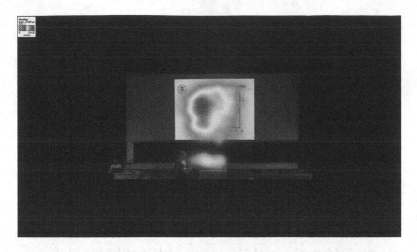

Fig. 19. speechRT6 summary - heat map 1.

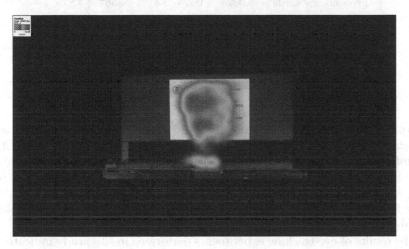

Fig. 20. speechRT6 summary - heat map 2.

classification outputs were used rather than the ground truth of human annotations for most engaging, comprehensible parts of presentations. Results in this table reflect Likert scale rankings of participants' level of agreement with each statement. Tables 10 and 11 below come directly from [4]. The following is the list of statements for which participants were asked to rate their level of agreement for each video.

1. This summary is easy to understand.
2. This summary is informative.
3. This summary is enjoyable.
4. This summary is coherent.
5. This summary would aid me in deciding whether to watch the full video.

Table 10. Questionnaire results - likert scale (from [4]).

Video	Q1	Q2	Q3	Q4	Q5
plen2_Classify	2.625	3.75	3.125	3.4375	4.625
plen2_audio_only	2.3125	3.5	2.4375	3.8125	4.8125
plen2_video_only	3	4.625	2.4375	4.0625	4.75
plen2_no_keywords	3.5625	4.8125	3.75	4.25	5.0625
prp1_Classify	2.875	4.3125	2.3125	3.8125	4.5
prp1_audio_only	2.25	3.875	2.4375	2.9375	4.9375
prp1_video_only	2.375	3.25	2	2.875	4.0625
prp1_no_keywords	2.5625	3.8125	2.8125	3.875	5.0625
prp5_Classify	4.25	4.875	4.5	4.4375	4.8125
prp5_audio_only	3.625	4.25	3.375	3.625	5.125
prp5_video_only	4.25	4.5	4.4375	4.125	5.3125
prp5_no_keywords	5.0625	5.0625	3.8125	4.5625	4.875
spRT6_Classify	2.875	4.125	2.625	3.875	5.4375
spRT6_audio_only	2.8125	4.5625	2.5	4	5.0625
spRT6_video_only	2	3.5	2.5	3.0625	5.125
spRT6_no_keywords	2.6875	3.9375	2.4375	3.3125	4.5

From Table 10, we see that the results of audio-only classifications and visual-only classifications result in summaries which are rated less easy to understand and informative than summaries built using full information and with no key words. Summaries built using no keywords lack coherence, while summaries built using all available features score highly on helping users decide if they wished to see full presentations. The purpose of these summaries built using a subset of available features was to evaluate the effectiveness of individual features.

The results of eye-tracking experiments performed in this study indicate that generated summaries tend to contain a higher concentration of relevant information than full presentations, as indicated by the higher proportion of time participants spend carefully reading slides during summaries than during full presentations, and also by the lower proportion of time spent fixating on areas outside of the attention zone during summaries than during full presentations. This can be seen from Tables 2, 3, 4, 5, 6, 7, 8 and 9, and Figs. 1, 2, 3 and 4.

Table 11. Levels of agreement (from [4]).

#	Level of agreement
1	Very much disagree
2	Disagree
3	Disagree somewhat
4	Neutral
5	Agree somewhat
6	Agree
7	Very much agree

6 Conclusions

In this paper we describe an investigation into the automatic generation of academic presentation summaries using linguistic and paralinguistic features. We report on the comprehensive evaluation of presentation summaries, including eye-tracking evaluation of participants as they watch full presentations and automatically generated presentation summaries. Separate presentation summaries were also developed using subsets of available audio-visual features and questionnaire evaluations performed to discover the effects of individual classification features on final summaries.

We have shown that classification of speaker ratings, audience engagement, emphasised speech and audience comprehension is useful for summarisation of academic presentations. Though effectiveness has been shown to be dependent of how engaging and comprehensible presentations were to begin with. Presentations which have been rated as not very engaging see much bigger improvements in engagement after summarisation than highly engaging presentations.

Heat maps and gaze plots also show big improvements for presentation summaries. Heat maps consistently show increased intensity over presentation slides as users focussed their attention on the slides during presentations, and much reduced intensity over the speakers. Gaze plots show increased fixation counts with reduced fixation durations for summaries, confirming that users are more attentive for presentation summaries. This difference is more pronounced for videos not already classified as highly engaging videos. Earlier studies conducted on this summarisation strategy in [14] support the results reported in this paper.

Additional Questionnaire evaluations on summaries built from a subset of features show that audio-only classifications and visual-only classifications result in summaries which are rated less easy to understand and less informative than summaries built using full information and with no keywords. Summaries built using no keywords also lack coherence. These additional questionnaire evaluations show the importance of using all available features including keywords for generation of presentation summaries.

One possible future work direction of this research is the development of a conference portal where user's can view presentation summaries developed on the fly using the features described in this paper. Such a portal could allow for further evaluation of the effectiveness of these features over a greater pool of participants. Another possible future work direction is the use of Natural Language Processing techniques to develop more content dependant summaries.

Acknowledgments. This research is supported by Science Foundation Ireland through the CNGL Programme (Grant 12/CE/I2267) in the ADAPT Centre (www.adaptcentre.ie) at Dublin City University. The authors would like to thank all participants who took part in these evaluations. We would further like to express our gratitude to all participants who took part in previous experiments for classification of the high-level paralinguistic features discussed in this paper.

References

1. Huiskes, M.J., Thomee, B., Lew, M.S.: New trends and ideas in visual concept detection: the MIR flickr retrieval evaluation initiative. In: Proceedings of the International Conference on Multimedia Information Retrieval, pp. 527–536. ACM (2010)
2. Chechik, G., Ie, E., Rehn, M., Bengio, S., Lyon, D.: Large-scale content-based audio retrieval from text queries. In: Proceedings of the 1st ACM International Conference on Multimedia Information Retrieval, pp. 105–112. ACM (2008)
3. Lew, M.S., Sebe, N., Djeraba, C., Jain, R.: Content-based multimedia information retrieval: State of the art and challenges. ACM Trans. Multimed. Comput. Commun. Appl. (TOMM) **2**, 1–19 (2006)
4. Curtis, K., Jones, G.J.F., Campbell, N.: Summarising academic presentations using linguistic and paralinguistic features. In: Proceedings of the 13th International Joint Conference on Computer Vision, Imaging and Computer Graphics Theory and Applications - Volume 2: HUCAPP, INSTICC, pp. 64–73. SciTePress (2018)
5. Ju, S.X., Black, M.J., Minneman, S., Kimber, D.: Summarization of videotaped presentations: automatic analysis of motion and gesture. IEEE Trans. Circuits Syst. Video Technol. **8**, 686–696 (1998)
6. He, L., Sanocki, E., Gupta, A., Grudin, J.: Auto-summarization of audio-video presentations. In: Proceedings of the Seventh ACM International Conference on Multimedia (Part 1), pp. 489–498. ACM (1999)
7. Joho, H., Jose, J.M., Valenti, R., Sebe, N.: Exploiting facial expressions for affective video summarisation. In: Proceedings of the ACM International Conference on Image and Video Retrieval, p. 31. ACM (2009)
8. Pavel, A., Reed, C., Hartmann, B., Agrawala, M.: Video digests: a browsable, skimmable format for informational lecture videos. In: UIST, pp. 573–582 (2014)
9. Curtis, K., Jones, G.J.F., Campbell, N.: Effects of good speaking techniques on audience engagement. In: Proceedings of the 2015 ACM on International Conference on Multimodal Interaction, pp. 35–42. ACM (2015)
10. Curtis, K., Jones, G.J.F., Campbell, N.: Identification of emphasised regions in audio-visual presentations. In: Proceedings of the 4th European and 7th Nordic Symposium on Multimodal Communication (MMSYM 2016), Copenhagen, 29–30 September 2016, Number 141, pp. 37–42. Linköping University Electronic Press (2017)
11. Curtis, K., Jones, G.J.F., Campbell, N.: Speaker impact on audience comprehension for academic presentations. In: Proceedings of the 18th ACM International Conference on Multimodal Interaction, pp. 129–136. ACM (2016)

12. Curtis, K., Campbell, N., Jones, G.J.F.: Development of an annotated multimodal dataset for the investigation of classification and summarisation of presentations using high-level paralinguistic features. In: Proceedings of the Eleventh International Conference on Language Resources and Evaluation (LREC 2018). European Language Resources Association (ELRA) (2018)
13. Rayner, K., Sereno, S.C.: Eye movements in reading: psycholinguistic studies. In: Handbook of Psycholinguistics, pp. 57–81 (1994)
14. Curtis, K., Jones, G.J.F., Campbell, N.: Utilising high-level features in summarisation of academic presentations. In: Proceedings of the 2017 ACM on International Conference on Multimedia Retrieval, pp. 315–321. ACM (2017)

Information Visualization Theory and Applications

An ROI Visual-Analytical Approach for Exploring Uncertainty in Reservoir Models

Zahra Sahaf[1(✉)], Roberta Cabral Mota[1], Hamidreza Hamdi[2],
Mario Costa Sousa[1], and Frank Maurer[1]

[1] Department of Computer Science, University of Calgary, Calgary, Canada
{zahras,roberta.cabralmota,smcosta,fmaurer}@ucalgary.ca
[2] Department of Geoscience, University of Calgary, Calgary, Canada
hhamdi@ucalgary.ca

Abstract. Uncertainty in reservoir geological properties has a major impact on reservoir modeling and operations decision-making, and it leads to the generation of a large set of stochastic models, called geological realizations. Flow simulations are then used to quantify the uncertainty in predicting the hydrocarbon production. However, reservoir flow simulation is a computationally intensive task. In a recent paper, we proposed a visual based analytical framework to select a few models from a large ensemble of geological realizations. In this paper, we extend our prior framework by introducing the region of interest concept, that helps to perform the entire analysis only based on a specific portion of the reservoir. The effectiveness of region of interest selection techniques is shown on two case studies. We also performed a complete user study with the engineers. User feedback suggests that usefulness, usability and visual interactivity are the key strengths of our approach.

Keywords: Visual analysis · Region of interest · Clustering · Mutual information · Volumetric ensembles reservoir models · Flow simulation

1 Introduction

Geological properties are important parameters used in the oil extraction processes from reservoirs. These parameters influence the production performance of the reservoirs. Geological uncertainty exists because of the lack of knowledge to exactly describe the geological properties of every section of the reservoir. Techniques such as well logging and core analysis can give some ideas about the local geological properties of interest areas of the reservoir. However, the inter-well geological properties of many uncored areas will be yet unknown. As a result, the geological uncertainty will always exist in reservoir description workflows [1].

Reservoir performance can be quantified by the flow simulation, which provides the production time series such as the cumulative oil production (COP)

© Springer Nature Switzerland AG 2019
D. Bechmann et al. (Eds.): VISIGRAPP 2018, CCIS 997, pp. 121–142, 2019.
https://doi.org/10.1007/978-3-030-26756-8_6

rate and the net present value (NPV). The flow production parameters strongly depend on the underlying geological properties of the reservoir. It is very important to quantify the impact of geological uncertainty on reservoir modeling procedures. Otherwise, the model may give an unreliable assessment of production capacity of the reservoir. To represent the geological uncertainty, multiple geological realizations are usually generated using geostatistical tools [2] (called geological realizations) so as to obtain a broad range of possible geological properties for a subject reservoir. However, reservoir flow simulations cannot be run for all of the possible realizations due to the significant computer processing time. Therefore, in practice, only a small number of geological realizations are chosen to perform reservoir simulations to describe the geological uncertainty [3]. However, all the current selection techniques [4,5] are the one-time automated processes, that lack any visualization prospective and more importantly they do not incorporate the user's knowledge into the selection process.

In a recent paper [6], we proposed an analytical process for selection of geological models. Our approach relies on a pair-wise distance based clustering technique that groups the geological realizations based on their similarities. There are limited comprehensive distances defined in the domain for the geological models. Therefore, we proposed a block based distance calculation method, which employs the mutual information concept [33,34]. Thereafter, dimensionality reduction techniques are employed to calculate the distances required for mapping the reservoir models into lower spaces (like a point in a 2D or 3D space). Clustering would be then performed on the lower space. Each cluster contains similar geological realizations, and cluster center is the representative of that cluster. In order to have more accurate results (in terms of distance calculation between the reservoir models and clustering of the models) and better performance (in terms of time), three interactive region of interest (ROI) selection techniques are added to our existent framework to let the users perform the analysis on particular areas of the reservoir model. The entire process has been designed in a visual interactive process and has been developed in a virtual reality environment, which can enhance the incorporation of the user's knowledge in the entire process.

The reminder of the paper is organized as follows: Sect. 2 provides an overview of geological realization techniques in the engineering domain and also the current visual interactive processes for similar datasets, Sect. 3 provides an overview of the proposed framework, Sect. 4 provides the details of variance model calculation and the proposed selection techniques, Sect. 5 provides the details of distance calculation, Sect. 6 explains about the clustering technique, Sect. 7 explains how the variance model is interacted with the clustering results, Sect. 8 provides case studies and the results, Sect. 9 provides the user study evaluations and finally conclusions are presented in Sect. 10.

2   Related Work

2.1   Current Approaches for Selection of Geological Realizations

Various methods are available for selecting geological realizations. Random selection of realizations is one of the easiest methods; however, it can not give a correct measure of geological uncertainty [7]. Ranking [4] is the most common method for selecting geological realizations, that arranges the geostatistical models based on an easily computable measure in an ascending/descending order and then selects the ones with low, medium, and high values of that measurement. Ranking methods suffer from a major drawback, that they rely greatly on the type of the measure that is used. Distance based methods have been recently investigated by some researchers [5,8], that they try to select few representative models using the similarity distances between the models.

The need of petroleum industry to address the geological uncertainty using a limited number of geological realizations necessitates designing an analytical framework that is computationally less expensive that is dependent on the static properties of geological models rather than flow simulation results. In addition to enhance the exploration of the geological model and perform some specific engineering tasks on the model, It is also highly favorable to create a visual and interactive environment capable of showing differences and similarities between the models.

2.2   Visual Analytics Techniques for Multi-run Data

The most similar dataset in computer science domain to the geological models in petroleum engineering is multirun data. In general, multirun data stems from a type of process (like geostatistical algorithms in our case) that is repeated multiple times with different parameter settings, leading to a large number of collocated data volumes [9]. Since multirun data consists of a superset of volumetric models, their representation and analysis are challenging [10].

Accordingly, one of the common ways for visualization of such datasets is to aggregate the distributions of multirun data, by computing statistical summaries [11] and representing them mainly by box plot [12], line chart [13], glyphs [14], or InfoVis techniques such as parallel coordinates or scatterplot matrices [15]. For the analysis of multirun data, statistical methods (such as mean, variance, skewness, and kurtosis) are vastly used to reduce the data dimensionality [16]. Alternatively, mathematical and procedural operators are also used to transform the multirun data into some compact forms (e.g. streamlines, isosurfaces, or pseudocoloring) where existing visualization techniques are applicable [11,17]. Data mining techniques such as clustering are also among the recent methods being used to explore the multirun data [18–20], that try to identify similar behavior across different simulation runs. Most of these analytics researches are on the 2D ensembles such as 2D images. For the 3D ensembles, their aggregations are usually used for the analysis tasks, which we want to avoid in this research, due to the importance of 3D structures in the reservoir models.

3   Analytical Framework

An overview of our extended process is represented in Fig. 1. Initially, we have a set of 3D geological models (a). Variance is calculated per cell for a specific geological property that is called "variance model" in this study. (b). Different selection techniques are used with the variance model to select the ROIs (c). The proposed block based similarity metric is calculated for all pairs of models considering only the user selected ROIs (d). The similarity values are then utilized to project models into a 2D space using multidimensional scaling techniques (e). Each point in the 2D space corresponds to a 3D model. The distance between points in the projected space represents the similarity between the models; the closer the points, the more similar the 3D models are. Cluster centers are selected by default and considered as the representative models for each cluster. These models are the candidates for running the flow simulations and uncertainty assessment (f). Cluster centers are expected to be very different from each other. However, it is very important to show how models are different spatially (i.e. in terms of which areas model are different). This is because the spatial variation of the properties can have a large impact on the flow simulation results. On the other hand, users might want to select other models than the cluster centers. To leverage these requirements, an ROI analysis method is proposed. As such, the variance is calculated only for the selected models and is projected on the cells that are within the ROI. If the selection of a new model increases the variance, it is indicative of a very distinct model. However, if only minimal changes are observed in the variance model, it is inferred that the selected model is potentially similar to the other models in the cluster. More importantly, the visual inspection of variance changes on the cells of ROI helps the users to easily observe if a different model has been selected. The entire process has been designed and developed in a virtual reality environment. Each of these stages are explained in more detail in the subsequent sections which can also be inspected visually in the prepared video[1].

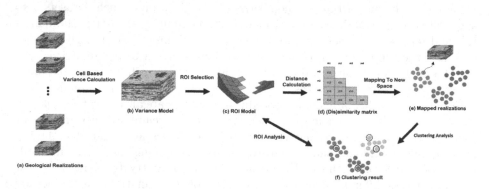

Fig. 1. An overview of our extended visual analytical framework.

[1] https://vimeo.com/251921649.

4   Variance Model and ROI Selection

Reservoir models are usually very large and consist of millions of cells. The models often embed complicated structures with non-uniform layers. In many circumstances, the engineers need to only focus on specific areas of the models for particular studies such as local history matching (i.e., calibration). The calibration processes are aimed to find a geological model that can best match the dynamic data. However, very often, the outcome of this process is not entirely satisfactory as the dynamic production of data of certain wells might not match the observed data. Another example is the 4D seismic history matching where the local discontinuities (e.g. faults or permeability variations) can cause the spatial measured seismic response not to match the simulated seismic data. In all these examples, the lack of large conditioning data is meant to having a large number of models that can equally produce the same response (i.e. non-uniqueness). As such, the focus of the engineer would be on specific spatial areas (e.g. around wells, aquifer, anticline, etc.) across many equiprobales models to fine tune the local unknown to achieve a reasonable match. Depending on the type of the reservoir, these regions of interest can be different. To facilitate the improvement of this local investigation processes, we provide three different selection methods: filtering, group selection, and single cell selection. They all help particular requirements of the users by interactive and visual selection of ROIs for a subject reservoir model. All these selection techniques are performed on the calculated variance model. In this variance model, variance is calculated per cell over all ensemble of geological models as shown in Fig. 2. Figure 3 shows a sample of variance model for one of our case studies. Red and blue areas illustrates high and low variance areas subsequently, that shows the realizations are more different in red areas (lack of certainty).

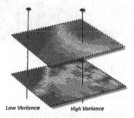

Fig. 2. Variance calculation between geological realizations.

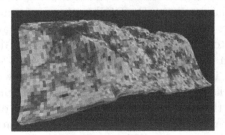

Fig. 3. A sample of calculated variance model. (Color figure online)

Fig. 4. Interactive filtering of the variance model.

In the filtering selection technique, the user specifies a variance threshold interactively. As a result, the cells below the specified threshold are filtered out (Fig. 4). As mentioned in the previous section, the areas with large variability indicate the lack of knowledge, that is resulted from the lack of enough spatial constraining data. In contrast to the low variance areas, these high variance areas contribute more in detecting differences between models. Therefore, it is very important to inspect these areas by filtering out low variance areas, as shown in Fig. 5.

Fig. 5. Filtered out variance model.

In the group selection technique, a group of cells can be selected using a visual and interactive box widget. This box can be created dynamically in any size, in any location and as many times as needed. Using this technique, users can select multiple collocated cells (as the ROI) with one operation. As an example, in Fig. 6 the user tries to create a box in a high variance area. Consequently, a large box is selected to cover the area as shown in Fig. 7. Multiple boxes can be also created as shown in Fig. 8.

Last but not least, is the single cell selection technique, where a cross sectional view is provided to the users, where they can select individual cells. Using the cross sectional view, the users can observe internal areas of the reservoirs, and select important cells with high variance. Figure 9 shows an example where that user tries to select cells around a subject well.

Fig. 6. Interactive creation of box for the group selection.

Fig. 7. A sample representation of group selection using the interactive box.

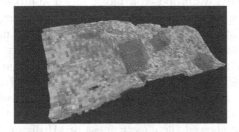

Fig. 8. Multiple creation of boxes for selection of the ROIs.

Fig. 9. Single cell selection around a well.

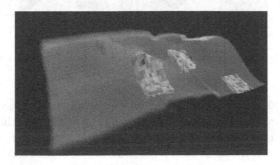

Fig. 10. A sample ROI selection.

The final ROI is the union of all the user selected areas (group selection and filtering) and cells (single selection), that can be subsequently used for the calculation of distance between the realizations. A sample ROI is shown in Fig. 10.

5   Distance Calculation

Many of reservoir engineering tasks are usually performed on a single geological model. Therefore, "distance" between reservoir models is rather a new concept in that domain [21] and it is important to define a distance that reflects the requirement of the engineering tasks. Two models are called similar, when they have similar dynamic result (reservoir performance).

In our recent study, we proposed a block based approach for calculation of distance between geological realizations [6]. In this technique, we use a 3D block as the moving template, where each block consists of a few number of grid cells. This 3D block sweeps the entire reservoir model (as shown in Fig. 11), and at each step, the (dis)similarity distance is calculated between the corresponding blocks in two models. Finally, we take the average of the (dis)similarity values between all the corresponding blocks. The distance metric which is used in this study is Mutual Information (MI). In [6], we performed a thorough evaluation study on the MI and showed the effectiveness of MI distance on the geological realization in comparison to the other well-known distance (e.g. Euclidean and Hausdorff distances). More importantly, our proposed distance metric was successfully applied to a number of specific reservoir engineering problems [22,23]. Figure 12 shows a summary of our distance calculation between two different models.

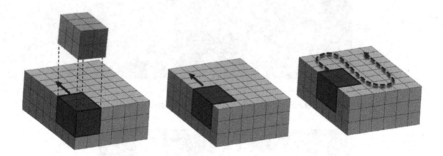

Fig. 11. Block based approach for calculating distance between realizations.

Block size is an essential component of our proposed distance measurement. We use the concept of entropy, as suggested in [24], to base the optimal block size. This optimal value is provided as a suggestion to the users in our designed application; however, the users can change the size of block based on their knowledge such as the use of correlation length [25] as it is used in generating some geological patterns.

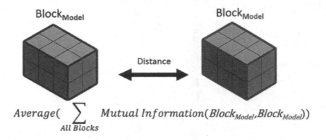

$$Average(\sum_{All\ Blocks} Mutual\ Information(Block_{Model}, Block_{Model}))$$

Fig. 12. Calculation of distance between two blocks.

6   Projection with Clustering

The calculated distances are utilized within a clustering algorithm in order to group similar models. Each cluster center is a default representative member of the containing cluster, which leads to our main requirement - that is to reduce the number of models needed to be simulated. The K-Means Clustering (KMC) algorithm [18] is employed in this step because of its computational efficiency on large data sets. However, KMC suffers from a noticeable drawback. In the case where the data embeds a complex structure (e.g. data are non-linearly separable), a direct application of KMC is not suitable because of its tendency to split data into globe-shaped clusters [26]. In order to solve this problem, as suggested in [27], data will be mapped by a kernel transformation [28] to a new space where samples become linearly separable. The crucial aspect in the new space is the relative distance between projected points. The closer points are to each other, the more similar they are based on the original defined distance. Other than having a better and simpler visualization of the projected models using kernel transformation, it has also a great benefit for clustering algorithm that is providing more accurate results [29]. This technique is called kernel k-means in the literature [30, 31].

The efficiency of kernel KMC in clustering the geological models is shown in Figs. 13 and 14. They both show how the representation of data and clustering is different in two scenarios: projection with and without kernel transformation, one in 2D view and the other one in 3D view. In both views, it can be seen that the representation of data looks better and more importantly clustering results are more representative when a kernel transformation has been applied. Without kernel transformation, projected points are very close to each other, and that makes separation of clusters complicated. However, with kernel transformation, a well-organized and linear structure can be seen in the results, and clusters are better represented and separated.

Fig. 13. 2D view of clustering results of projected models with (b) and without (a) kernel transformation.

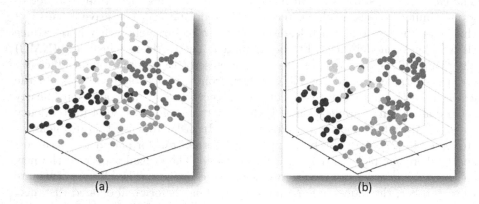

Fig. 14. 3D view of clustering results of projected models with (b) and without (a) kernel transformation.

7   ROI Analysis

As mentioned in the previous section, cluster centers are the default selected models that represent the variability in the entire set of subject ensemble of reservoir models. These representative models would be different in terms of simulation result, and tend to cover the entire range of the production variability. However, users might want to run additional simulations for other different models to have a better understanding of the estimated uncertainty range by the cluster members. The first potential candidates are the outlier models. For instance, in Fig. 15, although the clusters centers are well calculated (annotated with stars), there are some models that are located very far from the cluster centers and look different (highlighted with black circles). Generally, ROI analysis is a proposed component that helps users explore other different models. In this analysis, initially users see the variance model calculated only between the centers for the ROI (Fig. 15). In the next step, users can interactively select other different models (can be outliers), and the variance model is re-calculated to include the additional selected models. If the calculated variance increases (in the areas that user prefers) (Fig. 16 - (b)), it shows that the selected model is a different model (comparing to the previous selected ones). However, if the variance decreases (Fig. 16 - (a)), it shows that the selected model is similar to the previous ones, and there is no benefit in running an additional simulation for this model, because it is likely that the production uncertainty rage would not be changed.

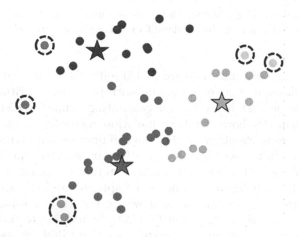

Fig. 15. Representation of some outsider models in each cluster that can be considered as potential different models.

8   Results (with Case Studies)

For evaluation of our proposed extended analytical framework, we first compare our results with the current alternative process in the industry, i.e. to run flow simulation for all the models individually. We run the complete flow simulation for all the models using the CMG reservoir simulator package [35], and plot the simulation results for the 'oil recovery factor'. The plotted results show a range of uncertainty on the oil production and we expect that our cluster centers cover this range adequately. In the second phase of evaluation, our engineer colleagues select an ROI on the reservoir model. The pair-wise distances are then calculated between the reservoir models only considering the ROI regions. According to our framework, models are then clustered into similar groups. Finally, effectiveness of ROI selection is shown by comparing clustering results with and without the ROI selection. In terms of the datasets, our industry partner generated different datasets for us using different geostatistical algorithms and scenarios. The idea is to cover almost all different types of datasets in the domain. In the first case study, our engineer colleagues generate 20 realizations by changing the seed in the variogram of permeability property. Other geological properties are remained

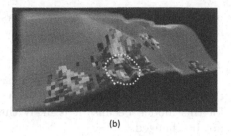

(a)   (b)

Fig. 16. ROI analysis with selection of the most outsider model (a) and the second most outsider model (b), and observation of variance changes in each scenario.

unchanged. The size of realizations are 26,000 cells. All the realizations were conditioned with the same well log data. Our entropy based algorithm [6] suggests 15 * 10 * 3 as the best block size for calculating similarity distance between realizations. Figure 18 shows the flow simulation curves for all the 20 models. A good clustering result should cover this range of uncertainty. Figure 17 shows the clustering results in the scenario that no ROIs are selected, and the clustering is performed on the entire model. It can be seen that the range of uncertainty is not covered completely. However, when some appropriate ROIs are selected (like high variance areas and well areas) as shown in Fig. 21, clustering results cover the entire range of uncertainty better (Fig. 20). In addition to that, the clusters are more coherent (see how clusters are spread without ROI selection) and better reflect the distances of models (Fig. 19). On the other hand, the whole process is much quicker with the ROI selections. The reason is that less number of cells are involved and hence the calculations is naturally faster. In this specific example, without ROI selection, the entire process takes around 3 min, while with the ROI selections, only 30 s takes to generate the clustering results.

In the second case study, 100 models are generated as a result of changing the variogram of all the available geological properties (porosity, permeability, net-to-gross and water saturation). Each realizations consists of 60,000 cells. Figure 23 shows the flow simulation curves for all 100 models which represent a more diverse range of uncertainty in this case study. Similar to the previous example, clustering results are calculated with (Fig. 22) and without (Fig. 24) ROI selection scenarios (ROI is shown on Fig. 26), and similar results are received. The highlighted cluster centers on the actual simulation plots show that the range of uncertainty is better covered with the ROI selection (Fig. 25). In addition to that, without ROI selection, many models are detected to be very similar to each other and collocated in the projected view. However, with the ROI selection, the differences of models are better represented. In terms of the time-wise performance, with the ROI selection, the entire process took around 3 min, while without the ROI selection, it took around 2 h to produce the clustering result for 100 models.

Fig. 17. Clustering result without the ROI selection (20 models).

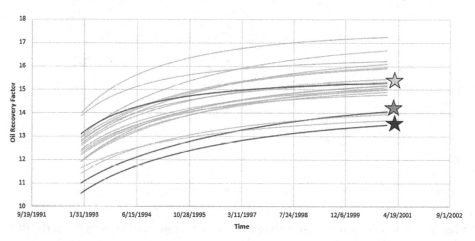

Fig. 18. Representation of cluster centers on the actual simulation plots (20 models and without the ROI selection).

9   User Evaluations (Result of User Studies)

We evaluated our proposed visual interactive analytical framework in a series of formal user evaluations. We conducted 12 sessions with external (industry) and internal (graduate students with experience at the industry) reservoir engineering experts. Each of these evaluation sessions lasted around 90 min.

Sessions started with a brief introduction to the goals of the study - the subjective and qualitative evaluation of the visual interactive framework for the selection of geological realization - and the workflow of our proposed framework and also a brief interview to better delineate the participant's fields of expertise, as well as previous experience within the domain. Two specific tasks were

Fig. 19. Clustering result with the ROI Selection (20 models).

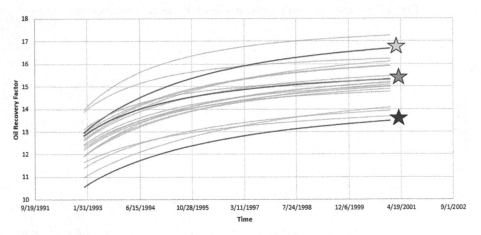

Fig. 20. Representation of cluster centers on the actual simulation plots (with the ROI selection and 20 models).

designed for each session. Each task was started with a demo session, in which we introduced the goal of the task followed by the required interactions and steps needed for accomplishing the task. We then invited the participants to try the task out to be familiar with the VR environment, in order to be able to perform the task independently. After this, users were informed to accomplish the specified task. After each task, participants were asked to express their ideas about the task, reflecting the usefulness of task, potential problems and suggestions for improvement. Sessions were recorded, for posterior qualitative analysis. Figure 27 shows screenshots from some of our user study evaluation sessions, while users are performing the mentioned tasks. A short video is also prepared to show a summary of user studies.

Fig. 21. ROI selection for the reservoir (20 models).

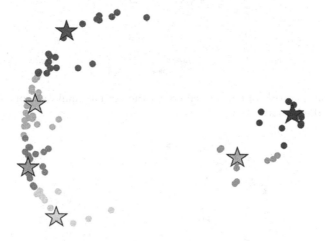

Fig. 22. Clustering result without the ROI selection (100 models).

9.1 Participants

Four females and eight males participated in this study. Participants' ages were ranged from 25 to 50 years old. All participants had at least a bachelor's degree in petroleum related areas. In addition, they were either working in the related industry or having some past industry experience in their field as interns or full time employees.

Although all participants were familiar with the specific reservoir models, they had slightly different backgrounds (such as specializations in reservoir simulation, oil production history matching, drilling engineering, geophysics, and so on [32]). We believe that factor did not compound our evaluation but rather contributed in allowing reflections on different point of views, and helped in diversifying and enriching the possible usage perspectives of our proposed framework. Despite this variety, we were still able to perceive many common opinions, which we collected and analyzed for each of the components in our proposed framework. In the next subsections, we explain each task in detail and discuss some of the results.

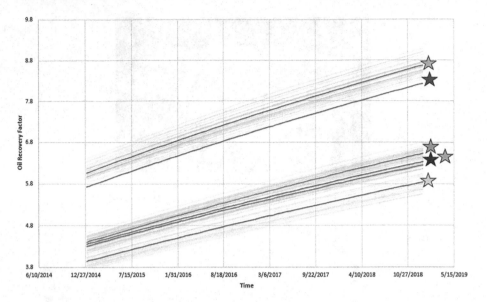

Fig. 23. Representation of cluster centers on the actual simulation plots (100 models and without the ROI selection).

Fig. 24. Clustering result with the ROI Selection (100 models).

9.2   ROI Selection Task

In this task, the three proposed selection techniques were introduced to the users: filtering, group selection and single cell selection. Users were requested to select ROI for a reservoir model using the three selection techniques. The main goals of this task were to recognize which regions of a reservoir model are important and to find out the usefulness of the selection techniques. As stated in the previous sections, ROI selection is performed on the variance model, which

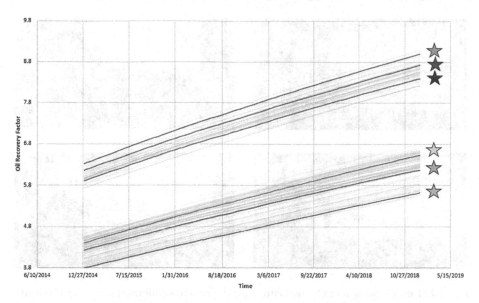

Fig. 25. Representation of cluster centers on the actual simulation plots (with the ROI selection and 100 models).

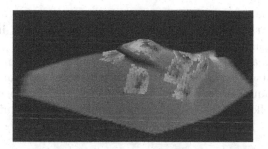

Fig. 26. ROI selection for the reservoir (100 models).

is calculated based on the realizations in a reservoir ensemble. When inquired about the common ROIs of a reservoir model, we received a list of common opinions, as the following:

– High variance areas. Almost all the participants selected the high variance areas (that are shown in colors that are more reddish). The main reason was that they believed that these areas can contribute more in different simulation results. Some of the participants tended to select all the high variance areas, while some others focused more on the centered areas. Centered areas or areas around wells are believed to be more important, since they have more impact on the oil production results.

Fig. 27. Representation of cluster centers on the actual simulation plots (with the ROI selection and 100 models).

- Well areas. The second common selected areas were areas around wells. The reason is that they believe that well areas have the most impact on the oil production results.
- Heterogeneous areas. Other than the two mentioned common areas, some of the participants (6 out 12) focused on other heterogeneous areas like fractures, faults, hills, aquifers, etc. They believed that the heterogeneous areas can effect on the flow paths and therefore could generate different simulation results.

Among the three selection methods that participants had for the selection of ROI, they preferred the filtering and group selection options. Single cell selection was pointed out to be less usable, since *"Reservoir models are usually very large, and they contain very thin cells. And that makes single cell selection time consuming and tedious"*. However, few of them believed that single cell selection is helpful for selection of cells in the well paths and other cells in upscaled reservoir models. The improvement suggestions that we received for each section are as follows:

- Filtering. Filtering was the most familiar component in our framework, therefore, not very important improvement comments received for this section, except one: *"sometimes I need to specify a range of variance to show the cells only within that range. It would be good if I can edit the range of variance on the filtering widget"*.

- Group selection. Although it was a new way of selection for many participants, they liked this type of interaction with the box. They found it very smooth, user friendly, and useful for selection of a group of cells. We also received some additional improvement comments, like *"instead of square shape, maybe other form of widgets can be used like circles or hexahedron"* or *"free form sketches on the 2D cross sections can be very useful"*.
- Single cell selection. We designed a dynamic cross sectional view for single cell selection. This dynamic view follows the participants head movements, wherever user moves or looks, that part of the reservoir cuts and user can perform the single selection with the hand controllers. If user has many head movements, that view changes a lot and makes the view confusing. Therefore, one improvement comment that we received was: *"it's better to fix the view and then do the single cell selection"*. Due to the large number of cells, one of the good comments that we received for faster single cell selection was: *"an idea of brushing can be used for single cell selection, that user can quickly sweep several cells and perform the selection"*.

9.3 Analysis Task

In this task, mapping and clustering are performed for a specific ROI. Both the ROI and the clustering results are then represented to the users in a single view. Cluster centers are selected by default in the initial view and the ROI shows the variance calculation only for the centers. Users were then inquired to make decisions about the selection of other different models for each cluster. For each cluster, they were asked to first find and select the outlier of the cluster (the farthest node from the center of cluster). Then, they have to visually inspect if the selected model is different enough or not. If not, they would inspect the second most outsider, and they continue this process until they find different models in each cluster.

Generally, most of the participants were found the application more enjoyable and useful in this second task, since they believed that they get used to the application environment. Using the distance and visual inspection of models, most of them selected the right different models. Therefore, they found the whole idea of interactive model selection with ROI and distance inspection, important and usable: *"It is very beneficial that I can visually inspect if a different model is selected or not"* or *"the visual inspection of changes is very important, since I can better focus on changes in particular areas. For instance, changes in the surrounding of the reservoir is not important to me, but changes around wells are important"* or *"it's very good that I can see where the changes happen"*. Some of the common issues and improvement tasks that we received for this task were: *"Interior changes cannot be seen immediately like the changes on the surface"*, *"reduce the amount of information that are shown in inspection of model distance in the node diagram"* and *"size of spheres in the node diagram can be changed according to the distance, that I can inspect the distances easier"*.

10   Conclusion

In this paper, we extended our previously proposed visual analytics framework, that is used for selecting a few representative models from an ensemble of geostatistical models that represents the overall production uncertainty. The framework is extended to include ROI selection concept, and the entire selection process can be applied only on particular areas of the reservoir models. To achieve this purpose, first a variance model is calculated based on the entire ensemble, then three selection methods are proposed for the selection of ROIs: filtering, group selection and single cell selection. Then, models are grouped based on their similarity distances. Center of each group is selected by default, as the suggested models for reservoir simulations. ROI analysis, in the next step, would help users to select more different models. The proposed workflow was first evaluated with one case study to show the importance of RQI selection. In the second round of evaluation, we performed formal user studies with the domain experts. Many improvement ideas were received in the evaluation sessions, and in the future studies, we are going to work on those ideas to enhance our framework and address the weaknesses, such as providing more selection techniques to give users more options for selecting ROIs, designing analytical visual tasks to be able to better see the interior areas of the reservoir models, and providing special views for comparison of clustering results for different ROIs.

References

1. Caers, J.: Modeling Uncertainty in the Earth Sciences. Wiley, Hoboken (2011)
2. Goovaerts, P.: Geostatistical tools for characterizing the spatial variability of micro-biological and physico-chemical soil properties. Biol. Fertil. Soils **27**(4), 315–334 (1998)
3. Idrobo, E.A., Choudhary, M.K., Datta-Gupta, A.: Swept volume calculations and ranking of geostatistical reservoir models using streamline simulation. In: SPE/AAPG Western Regional Meeting. Society of Petroleum Engineers, January 2000
4. Ballin, P.R., Journel, A.G., Aziz, K.: Prediction of uncertainty in reservoir performance forecast. J. Can. Petrol. Technol. **31**(04), 52–62 (1992)
5. Scheidt, C., Caers, J.: Bootstrap confidence intervals for reservoir model selection techniques. Comput. Geosci. **14**(2), 369–382 (2010)
6. Sahaf, Z., Hamdi, H., Cabral Ramos Mota, R., Costa Sousa, M., Maurer, F.: A visual analytics framework for exploring uncertainties in reservoir models. In: Proceedings of the 13th International Joint Conference on Computer Vision, Imaging and Computer Graphics Theory and Applications - Volume 3: IVAPP, pp. 74–84 (2018). https://doi.org/10.5220/0006608500740084, ISBN 978-989-758-289-9
7. Yazdi, M.M., Jensen, J.L.: Fast screening of geostatistical realizations for SAGD reservoir simulation. J. Petrol. Sci. Eng. **124**, 264–274 (2014)
8. Rahim, S., Li, Z.: Reservoir geological uncertainty reduction: an optimization-based method using multiple static measures. Math. Geosci. **47**(4), 373–396 (2015)
9. Wilson, A.T., Potter, K.C.: Toward visual analysis of ensemble data sets. In: Proceedings of the 2009 Workshop on Ultrascale Visualization, pp. 48–53. ACM, November 2009

10. Kehrer, J., Hauser, H.: Visualization and visual analysis of multifaceted scientific data: a survey. IEEE Trans. Visual Comput. Graphics **19**(3), 495–513 (2013)
11. Love, A.L., Pang, A., Kao, D.L.: Visualizing spatial multivalue data. IEEE Comput. Graphics Appl. **25**(3), 69–79 (2005)
12. Kao, D., Luo, A., Dungan, J.L., Pang, A.: Visualizing spatially varying distribution data. In: Proceedings of the Sixth International Conference on Information Visualisation, pp. 219–225. IEEE (2002)
13. Demir, I., Dick, C., Westermann, R.: Multi-charts for comparative 3D ensemble visualization. IEEE Trans. Visual Comput. Graphics **20**(12), 2694–2703 (2014)
14. Kehrer, J., Muigg, P., Doleisch, H., Hauser, H.: Interactive visual analysis of heterogeneous scientific data across an interface. IEEE Trans. Visual Comput. Graphics **17**(7), 934–946 (2011)
15. Nocke, T., Flechsig, M., Böhm, U.: Visual exploration and evaluation of climate-related simulation data. In: Proceedings of the 39th Conference on Winter Simulation: 40 years! The Best is Yet to Come, pp. 703–711. IEEE Press, December 2007
16. Kehrer, J., Filzmoser, P., Hauser, H.: Brushing moments in interactive visual analysis. Comput. Graph. Forum **29**(3), 813–822 (2010)
17. Fofonov, A., Molchanov, V., Linsen, L.: Visual analysis of multi-run spatio-temporal simulations using isocontour similarity for projected views. IEEE Trans. Visual Comput. Graphics **22**(8), 2037–2050 (2016)
18. Correa, C.D., Chan, Y.H., Ma, K.L.: A framework for uncertainty-aware visual analytics. In: IEEE Symposium on Visual Analytics Science and Technology, VAST 2009, pp. 51–58. IEEE, October 2009
19. Bordoloi, U.D., Kao, D.L., Shen, H.W.: Visualization techniques for spatial probability density function data. Data Sci. J. **3**, 153–162 (2004)
20. Bruckner, S., Moller, T.: Result-driven exploration of simulation parameter spaces for visual effects design. IEEE Trans. Visual Comput. Graphics **16**(6), 1468–1476 (2010)
21. Fenwick, D.H., Batycky, R.P.: Using metric space methods to analyse reservoir uncertainty. In: Proceedings of the 2011 Gussow Conference, Banff, Alberta, Canada (2011)
22. Sahaf, Z., Hamdi, H., Maurer, F., Nghiem, L., Sousa, M.C.: Clustering of geological models for reservoir simulation studies in a visual analytics framework. In: 78th EAGE Conference and Exhibition 2016, May 2016
23. Sahaf, Z., Hamdi, H., Maurer, F., Nghiem, L., Chen, Z., Sousa, M.C.: Filtering geological realizations for SAGD. In: 79th EAGE Conference and Exhibition 2017, June 2017
24. Honarkhah, M., Caers, J.: Stochastic simulation of patterns using distance-based pattern modeling. Math. Geosci. **42**(5), 487–517 (2010)
25. Mela, K., Louie, J.N.: Correlation length and fractal dimension interpretation from seismic data using variograms and power spectra. Geophysics **66**(5), 1372–1378 (2001)
26. MacKay, D.J., Mac Kay, D.J.: Information Theory, Inference and Learning Algorithms. Cambridge University Press, Cambridge (2003)
27. Shawe-Taylor, J., Cristianini, N.: Kernel Methods for Pattern Analysis. Cambridge University Press, Cambridge (2004)
28. Schölkopf, B., Smola, A., Müller, K.R.: Nonlinear component analysis as a kernel eigenvalue problem. Neural Comput. **10**(5), 1299–1319 (1998)
29. Schölkopf, B., Smola, A.J.: Learning with Kernels: Support Vector Machines, Regularization, Optimization, and Beyond. MIT Press, Cambridge (2002)

30. Williams, C.K.: On a connection between kernel PCA and metric multidimensional scaling. Mach. Learn. **46**(1–3), 11–19 (2002)
31. Dhillon, I.S., Guan, Y., Kulis, B.: Kernel k-means: spectral clustering and normalized cuts. In: Proceedings of the Tenth ACM SIGKDD International Conference on Knowledge Discovery and Data Mining, pp. 551–556. ACM, August 2004
32. Cosentino, L.: Integrated reservoir studies. Editions Technip (2001)
33. Goshtasby, A.A.: Image Registration: Principles, Tools and Methods. Springer Science & Business Media (2012)
34. Lin, D.: An information-theoretic definition of similarity. In: ICML, vol. 98, pp. 296–304. Citeseer (1998)
35. Computer Modelling Group Ltd.: Imex, black oil reservoir simulator (1980). cmgl.ca/imex

A Descriptive Attribute-Based Framework for Annotations in Data Visualization

Pierre Vanhulst[1(✉)], Florian Evequoz[1,2], Raphael Tuor[1], and Denis Lalanne[1]

[1] Human-IST Institute, University of Fribourg,
Boulevard de Pérolles 90, Fribourg, Switzerland
{pierre.vanhulst,florian.evequoz,raphael.tuor,denis.lalanne}@unifr.ch
[2] HES-SO Valais-Wallis, IIG, University of Applied Sciences Western Switzerland,
Technopole 3, Sierre, Switzerland
florian.evequoz@hes-so.ch

Abstract. Annotations are observations made during the exploration of a specific data visualization, which can be recorded as text or visual data selection. This article introduces a classification framework that allows a systematic description of annotations. To create the framework, a real dataset of 302 annotations authored by 16 analysts was collected. Then, three coders independently described the annotations by eliciting categories that emerged from the data. This process was repeated for several iterative phases, until a high inter-coder agreement was reached. The final descriptive attribute-based framework comprises the following dimensions: insight on data, multiple observations, data units, level of interpretation, co-references and detected patterns. This framework has the potential to provide a common ground to assess the expressiveness of different types of visualization over the same data. This potential is further illustrated in a concrete use case.

Keywords: Data visualization · Collaboration ·
User-authored annotations · Classification

1 Introduction

Visualization makes it easier to understand data: it empowers users with visual cues allowing to identify characteristics of the data such as trends, correlations, and outliers. Identification of such patterns results in the creation of knowledge, and is thus an important goal for data analysis. Visualization systems often provide tools to create annotations. They are a way to materialize insights, share knowledge with collaborators, and store them permanently for further reference. Although annotations have been implemented in previous collaborative data visualization systems [1–3], annotations per se have never been a subject of research. Different types of annotations may be formed as a result of interpreting data visualization. Therefore, a formal classification of the types of annotations

© Springer Nature Switzerland AG 2019
D. Bechmann et al. (Eds.): VISIGRAPP 2018, CCIS 997, pp. 143–166, 2019.
https://doi.org/10.1007/978-3-030-26756-8_7

has yet to be formed. For example, such a classification would allow to compare different visual encodings or visualization idioms with respect to the type of annotations that they support. This could allow to recommend visualization idioms best suited to certain specific tasks or questions.

In this paper, we introduce a descriptive attribute-based framework for visualization annotations. We created this framework with a bottom-up approach. 300 annotations recorded by 16 participants were collected, and we derived various dimensions from them in an iterative fashion taking inspiration from Grounded Theory. We ended up with a system that comprises 6 orthogonal dimensions. We were able to link some of those dimensions to previous work investigating the types of questions and tasks supported by data visualization. The validity of our framework was evaluated iteratively: the annotations were classified by three coders and by computing Inter-Coder Reliability scores.

The notion of "classification" can be interpreted in various ways. In our understanding and for the rest of this article, a classification is considered as a set of attributes - also called "dimensions" - that can help differentiate elements of similar nature (in our case, the annotations of data visualizations). However, this definition will not match all domains' expectations. For instance, certain practitioners in the field of Big Data would regard a classification as several sets of elements characterized by their common attributes: these sets form the classes themselves. For instance, a class could be named "students", with its elements being characterized by their age (between 16 and 19 years old) and their occupation (school).

In the remainder of this article, we first introduce a formal definition of annotations (Sect. 2). Next, we present a literature review of conceptual work related to annotations (Sect. 3). Next, we describe how we collected a dataset of annotations (Sect. 4). The classification itself is presented (Sect. 5), followed by a description of the iterative process that led to both its inception and evaluation (Sect. 6). At the end of the paper, we describe a use case for this classification system as a tool to qualitatively compare different visualization idioms (Sect. 7). This paper is an extended version of a paper initially published in the *Proceedings of 9th International Conference on Information Visualization Theory and Applications (IVAPP)* [4]. Among some minor clarifications of the notions we use in this study, we extended the analysis of our case in Sect. 7, offering an insight on the sequence used by our analysts while taking annotations, along with a concrete proposal to improve the framework we tested during the experiment.

2   Defining Annotations

The concept of "annotation" appears with different meanings in previous research. Visualization authoring tools and languages like Lyra [5], ChartAccent [2] or Vega [6] consider annotations as blocks of texts, sometimes completed by overlaid visual elements (arrows, closures, highlighting) that are part of the visualization itself and serve an explanatory purpose. In this article, we propose another definition, closer to Zhao et al. [3] and Munzner [7]'s versions that are informed by the traditional acceptation of annotations in the Information Retrieval field. To the former, annotating is *"an essential activity when making sense of data during exploratory analysis"* and *"a key step performed by analysts"*. Annotations can be used to *"support the process of generating hypotheses, verifying conjectures, and deriving insights, where it is not only critical for analysts to document key observations, but also to communicate findings with others"* [3]. To the latter, annotating is *"the addition of graphical or textual annotations associated with one or more pre-existing visualization elements, typically as a manual action by the user. When an annotation is associated with data items, the annotation could be thought of as a new attribute for them"* [7]. Drawing inspiration from their work, we propose to define an annotation as follows. An annotation consists in an observation, made by exploring a visual representation of data, that is recorded either as text or visual data selection (or both). Annotations are metadata: they are not necessarily embodied in the visualization. An annotation can be either an insight about the data, or a comment left for others to see. Annotations generally concern the data itself, and are therefore relevant regardless of its visual representation.

3   State of the Art

Although the research community has yet to agree upon a formal classification system of visualization annotations, previous works have provided valuable elements for such a classification. In the following section, we first review conceptual work relevant to annotations classification systems. Then, we review collaborative platforms that have implemented their own model for annotations classification.

3.1   Conceptual Work Relevant for a Classification of Annotations

To the best of our knowledge, no formal annotations classification system in the research community has been proposed to this day. However, there has been some formalization of both the types of questions that can be asked about a visualization, and the tasks that can be carried out with the help of visualization. Since annotations can be considered as elements in the sensemaking process of visualization, they have strong links to questions and tasks. Jacques Bertin [8] does not explicitly cover annotations in his work. Nevertheless, he states that several types of questions can be asked on a graphical representation of data, one type of question for each type of data component. For example, if the data being represented is a time-series of stock values, date and value would be two components of the data. He states that questions can be of three different levels that he coins "levels of reading":

- elementary level: questions introduced by a single element of a component (e.g. "on a given date...")
- intermediate level: questions introduced by a group of elements in a component (e.g. "on the first three days, what is the trend of the price?")

– superior/overall level: questions introduced by the overall component (e.g. "on the whole period, what is the trend of the price?")

Based on this definition, questions can be described by their type (i.e. components of the data impacted) and level of reading, which suggests an implicit hierarchy (elementary-intermediate-superior). In a similar attempt to classify types of questions that can be asked on a graphical data representation, Frances Curcio [9] used tasks of three different types to evaluate graph comprehension by students:

– literal tasks, coined "read the data", where users literally read individual data from the graph, or from its title or axes labels;
– comparison tasks, coined "read between the data", where users "logically or pragmatically infer" an answer;
– extension tasks, involving e.g. inference, prediction, coined "read beyond the data", where users rely on preliminary knowledge to predict an outcome or infer a discovery that could not be derived by the visual representation of the data alone.

Susan et al. [10] summarize previous research on the topic and note that a consensus seems to emerge for the three levels of tasks defined by Curio [9], with minor differences between the researchers. They also note that while students make less errors with tasks consisting in "reading the data", they do experience more difficulty with "reading between the data". The tasks consisting in "reading beyond the data" are the most challenging. More recently, the concept of "Visualization Literacy" has received an increased interest from the visualization research community. Boy et al. [11] build partly upon the research described earlier, but also contribute to defining categories of tasks that are relevant in the context of interpreting a graph. Those categories of tasks are:

– Extrema: "finding maximum or minimum data points"
– Variation: "detecting trends, similarities or discrepancies in the data"
– Intersection: "finding the point at which the graph intersects with a given value"
– Average: "estimating an average value"
– Comparison: "comparing different values or trends"

Additionally, Boy et al. [11] expand the work of Susan et al. [10] and identify different levels of congruency of questions: perception questions refer to the visual aspect of a graph only (e.g. "what colour are the dots?"), while other questions exhibit a highly or lowly congruent relation between visual encoding and data. More precisely, they define those concepts as follows: "A highly congruent question translates into a perceptual query simply by replacing data terms by perceptual terms (e.g. what is the highest value/what is the highest bar?). A low-congruence question, in contrast, has no such correspondence (e.g. is A connected to B– in a matrix diagram?)".

Munzner [7] defines an overarching framework for analyzing and designing visualizations. It consists of three steps: "What-Why-How". The "Why" step is particularly relevant in our context. It defines the user's goals that are materialized into tasks. She defines a taxonomy of tasks, where an abstract task is a combination of an action and a target. Actions can be classified into three broad types (analyse, search, query) that can be later subdivided into specific subtypes (for example, the creation of annotations is one of the subtypes of the "analyse" action in this framework). Targets of tasks can be all data, one or several attributes of the data, topologies in case of a graph, or shapes in case of spatial visualization. We believe that this exhaustive taxonomy of tasks related to data visualization is a solid basis on which to build a taxonomy of annotations.

3.2 Annotations Classifications in Collaborative Visualization Systems

Several collaborative visualization systems have been developed over the years. Annotations play a crucial role in the collaborative data analysis process based on visualization. Therefore, it is no surprise that the designers of those systems came up with propositions to classify annotations.

ManyEyes [12] was a pioneering online collaborative visualization platform that allowed users to upload data, choose a visual representation and annotate it. Annotating visualizations was made possible by a web comments system similar to what is used on blogs or forums. Annotations were simply added to a visualization as a discussion thread and were not classified in categories.

Heer et al. [13] designed another platform – sense.us – allowing users to annotate visualizations through fours tools: "double linked discussion", "bookmark trails", "geometric annotations" and "comment listings". In their study, they found that these tools encourage richer discussion and globally improve the analysis process. CommentSpace [1] is an enhanced version of sense.us, in which analysts can use a set of predefined tags and links to categorize their annotations. Namely, analysts can define an annotation as a "hypothesis", a "question" or a "to-do", and link them to previous observations either as an "evidence-for" or "evidence-against". Therefore, this linking system is a way to keep trace of the hypothesis validity checking process, or more broadly speaking, of the sensemaking process. The authors found that participants were overall more efficient and consistent in their interactions with visualizations using CommentSpace. PathFinder [14], a collaboration environment for citizen scientists, offers similar annotation features. It is based on the concept of structured discussion that consists of background, questions, hypothesis, evidences, conclusions and to-dos.

Zhao et al. propose AnnotationGraph [3], a tool for collaborative analysis. A graph represents the user-authored annotations, and depicts the relations between annotations and data selections to explicit the annotation semantics. This empowers analysts with an overview of comments and insights, and the links between them in the analysis process. In particular, the authors rely on the ESDA Framework (Exploratory Sequential Data Analysis) to describe the cognitive process of analysts when they annotate the visualizations. The steps in this framework are called the "Eight C's (C8)" (Conversion, Constraints, Chunks, Computations, Comparisons, Comments, Codes, Connections). Three

Fig. 1. Graph representing the use case for this study. A single topic, 2 datasets and 4 visualizations. (Reproduced with permission from [4]).

of them are relevant in the context of annotations. Chunks (also referenced by Boy et al. [11]) are subsets of data on which analysts make an annotation. Comments are textual description for Chunks. Codes (tags) are labels applied to Comments. Unlike CommentSpace, AnnotationGraph does not use predefined Codes so that analysts can express a wider range of views. Authors note that their system improves the whole annotation process from the reading of data to the production of new annotations.

3.3 Conclusion

A limitation of the annotation taxonomies used in collaborative visualization systems is that they are purely functional. They characterize the role of the annotation, namely its purpose in the analysis process [1]. They do not attempt to classify annotations according to other characteristics that could be derived from the conceptual work presented earlier, like for example congruency (relevance to data/visualization), level of reading, target of tasks, etc. In the remainder of this article, we present a model that aims to bridge this gap. Furthermore, we expect our model to characterize visualizations themselves: knowing what visualizations foster the most annotations of a certain type would allow designers to build systems with complementary visual encodings. Also, to the best of our knowledge, no studies have been done on the reliability of empirically assessing the type of an annotation. This work also contributes several findings in this regard.

4 Annotations Gathering

Gathering annotations was the first step of our study. We developed a web platform featuring an annotation interface for various visualizations over Internet. We recruited 16 participants to provide as many annotations as possible during the analysis of 4 visualizations.

4.1 Web Platform

The platform developed for this study aimed to work with any visualizations developed with the "Data-Driven Document" (D3) JavaScript Library [15], including those relying on more recent systems built on the top of D3, such as Vega [6], Vega-Lite [16] and Voyager [17]. We configured it to display a concrete use case, the relationships between the characters in "Les Misérables", through 4 visualizations and 2 datasets. We used 2 popular examples of D3 visualizations: the graph from "Force-Directed Graph" [18] and the matrix from "Les Misérables Co-occurrence" [19]. These two examples allow to explore the co-occurrences of 77 characters across the book. Both visualizations are interactive: the graph allows to move nodes by drag-and-dropping them, while the matrix allows to sort characters depending on three parameters (name, number of co-occurrences and clusters). We then built a second dataset containing the occurrences of 7 characters across the 350 chapters of the story. These data were encoded into a Streamgraph and a Heatmap, both static D3 visualizations. Together, the four visualizations cover almost all of the cases mentioned in the "Why" step of Munzner's Framework [7], except for spatial visualization that was not considered for feasibility reasons. Figure 1 summarizes our use case.

4.2   Implementation

From an implementation perspective, the software stack used to develop the platform was NodeJS and the Framework Nuxt on the server side, along with a client library that allows visualizations to communicate with the server. Visualizations are "hooked" inside the platform via an iFrame. Communication is handled through the standardized window.postMessage method. This workflow requires only minimal adaptations from the visualization designer, and explains why we managed to adapt regular D3 visualizations easily.

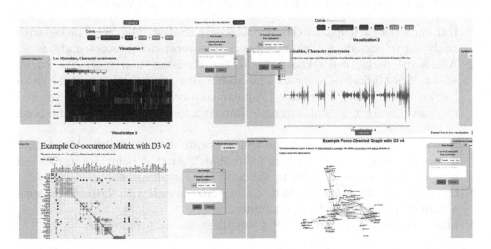

Fig. 2. Screenshots of the 4 visualizations. From up left to bottom right: heatmap, streamgraph, matrix and force-directed graph. Analysts write annotations in the floating window. (Reproduced with permission from [4]).

A prevalent feature of this platform is that annotations are "data-aware" even though visualizations are not specifically designed for it: users can select data from the visualization with a rectangle selection tool. When D3 inserts new DOM elements, it provides them with a __data__ property, which contains the datum used to create them. In this study, we call those elements "data units". When using the rectangle selection tool, the application sends its coordinates to the visualizations, which then identifies all data units whose positions lie within the said coordinates. It returns these data units to the platform that can finally record them along with the annotation. While this process is mature in terms of implementation, pilot tests showed that rectangle selection does not work well with all visualizations, especially Streamgraph with which users tried to select only parts of a single data unit. Figure 2 shows the interface and the 4 visualizations.

Interface. The interface of the platform is composed of a left-column which displays the selected data units, a right column which displays previously taken annotations by chronological order and a floating window where analysts can write their annotations and save them. At the top of the window, a timer indicates the time elapsed since the window.onload handler was fired.

The center of the window displays the visualization itself, that is overlaid by a "selection canvas" when analysts select the underlying data units, using the rectangle selection tool.

4.3   Annotation Production

16 participants were recruited for this study. The protocol was as follows:

1. Introduce the participant to her role as a data analyst. They were tasked with analysing relationships of characters across several visual representations.
2. Assess the participant's knowledge of the domain - how much she knows about "Les Misérables" - on a range from 1 (low) to 3 (high). 1 would mean "Never heard before", 2 means "Popular culture, read the book or watched the movie years ago" and 3 means "Robust knowledge, remember the book or the movie".
3. Instruct the participant that she will annotate 4 visualizations based on 2 different datasets related to "Les Misérables". At that point, we introduced the possibility to use a stylus to annotate the visualization.
4. Offer a chance for the participant to familiarize herself with the interface with a dummy visualization for five minutes.
5. Lead the participant through all 4 visualizations for 5 min each.

Participants were completely free in their annotation process: they could analyse data and find insights, as well as comment the visualization's relevance.

Table 1. Summary of the dimensions. (Reproduced with permission from [4]).

Dimension	Possible values	Examples
Insight on data	Boolean. Annotations that do not provide insight about data were sorted in three categories: positive comment, negative comment, or description	– "Valjean is the main character" provides an insight on the data
	They were then skipped for the rest of the process	– "It's hard to see relationships between more than three characters at once" is a negative comment about the visualization
Multiple observations	Boolean. Annotations featuring several observations were skipped for the rest of the process	– "Valjean is the main character, while Myriel is only a secondary character. Valjean seems related to Cosette in some ways"
		– "Myriel disappears at the beginning of the book. During the last chapters, almost all characters appear"
Data units	One or several mentions in the annotation. A data unit has a scale (single or aggregated) and a role (subject or complement)	– "Cosette appears strongly during a few successive chapters"."Cosette" is a single subject data unit, while "successive chapters" is an aggregated complement data unit
Level of interpretation	Non-exclusive choices: visual, data or meaning	– "The green group is the leftmost" only refers to visuals
		– "Valjean is the most connected character" starts to refer to the data, instead of visual shapes
		– "Valjean is the main character" is a hypothesis that gives meaning to the data
Co-references	Boolean	– "On the opposite, he appears the least often in the middle of the book" obviously refers to another annotation
Detected patterns	Non-exclusive choices: singularity, duality or plurality. Singularities can be either implicit or explicit	– "Valjean is the main character" is an implicit singularity
		–"Valjean is the most connected character" is an explicit singularity
		– "Valjean is more important than Javert" is a duality
		– "In average, all characters have three connections" is a plurality

Participants' Profiles. We selected 16 participants, of which 12 were male and 4 were females. All of them were between 20 and 35 years old. 6 participants held a Master degree (3 in Computer Science, 1 in Psychology, 1 in Physics, 1 in Biology), 3 held a Bachelor degree or equivalent (2 in Computer Science, 1 in Graphic Design), 3 left school after High School and 4 were Bachelor students

(3 in Computer Science, 1 in Law). 2 participants were knowledgeable of Data Visualization, while the other 14 had only common knowledge of the domain. Over the 16 participants, 2 assessed their knowledge of the domain as "high", 3 judged that their knowledge was low, and the 11 others had average knowledge of the story.

Variants. There were 8 variations of order for the 4 visualizations. We obtained these variations by inverting the order of each visualization within a single dataset, then by inverting the datasets themselves. Each variation was used with two participants.

Preliminary Remarks on the Results. In total, participants produced 323 annotations in French or English from which 21 were removed. Only 45 graphical annotations were taken during the experiment, of which 38 were spread over 4 participants. The other 12 preferred to focus on the analysis and thought the graphical annotation process was adding an unnecessary layer of complexity to their task.

5   Classification System of User-Authored Annotations

For the sake of clarity, we describe in this section the final classification system. The next section describes the iterative process that we followed to produce it. Our classification system has six dimensions, described below. These are summarized in Table 1.

5.1   Insight on Data (Abbreviated: Data)

The first dimension is used to distinguish annotations between those concerning the data and those concerning the visualization itself. During the annotation gathering process, most participants asked the permission to write their opinion regarding the visual representation, usually either to express disappointment or scepticism, or to compare with a visualization that they had analysed previously. These annotations are precious to understand the learning process of a visualization. We sorted them into three categories: positive (positive comment regarding the visualization), negative (negative comment regarding the visualization) and description (descriptive comment about the visualization's features). As the other dimensions of the classification could not apply for such annotations, we skipped annotations that did not target data for the rest of the classification process. Some examples:

– "On voit mieux les liens entre les différents groupes de couleurs" ("We see links between different groups of colors much better") is a positive comment.
– "On dirait un fichier audio" ("It looks like an audio file") is a descriptive comment.

5.2 Multiple Observations (Abbreviated: Multiple)

The second dimension concerns the number of insights within a single annotation. As each observation could be considered for the classification – a case that was not expected – we decided to skip multiple insights annotations for the rest of the process. Example: "Les pics d'apparition sont l' élément qui resort le plus, on voit l' apparition importante de Javet et Valjean vers le chapitre 115, Gavroche vers 245 et un pic particulier vers la fin de Cosette et Marius" ("The apparition peaks stand out the most, we can see the importance of Javet and Valjean near chapter 115, the importance of Gavroche near chapter 245 and a particular peak near the end for Cosette and Marius").

5.3 Data Units (Abbreviated: Units)

Typical annotations refer to one or several "units" in one dimension of the data – may it be characters, relationships or chapters in our use case. When no unit can be identified, it is generally possible to find references to aggregated groups of units. The third dimension of our classification thus concerns the "data units" mentioned in the annotation. The data units have two attributes: their role (subject or complement) and their scale (single or aggregated). A "subject data unit" is the emphasis of an annotation, while a "complement data unit" is usually another dimension of the visualization used to highlight a particularity of the subject data unit. Data units are best thought of as entries in a relational database. The conjunction of two tables is thus also a potential data unit. In our use case, a "frequency" results from both one or several characters and one or several chapters. In our literature, Munzner [7] uses the concept of "Target", Zhao et al. [3] use the terms "Chunks" to define the subsets of the whole data targeted by an annotation. Ren et al. [2] refer to this as "Annotation target type", considering whether it is aggregated not ("Data item" for what we call "single data unit", "set", "series" or "coordinate space target" for what we call "aggregated data unit"). Some examples:

- "Cosette, Valjean et Marius sont très présents à la fin de l'histoire" ("Cosette, Valjean and Marius are very present at the end of the Story"). The three characters mentioned are three subject single data units. They belong to the "Character" dimension of the data. The "end of the Story" is a complement aggregated data unit: it serves only to underline where the subjects have a common particularity (that is, being particularly present) and belongs to the "Time" dimension of the data.
- "Cosette is present during all scenes, but infrequently except for the chapter 95". "Cosette" is a subject single data unit, while "chapter 95" is a complement single data unit.
- "Très longs passages durant lesquels certains personnages n' apparaissent pas du tout". ("Very long passages where some characters do not appear at all"). "Very long passages" forms a subject aggregated data unit, while "some characters" forms a complement aggregated data unit.

5.4   Level of Interpretation (Abbreviated: LOI)

Some annotations propose hypotheses that go beyond the simple reading of the data, while others simply annotate visual phenomena. The fourth dimension of our classification tries to categorize the "level of interpretation" of the data in three levels.

1. Visual: references to purely visual elements. "the squares", "the frequency", "the violet cluster".
2. Data: reattribution of the visual elements toward the data that they represent. There is an attempt at contextualizing and making sense of the data.
3. Meaning: opinion or hypothesis going beyond the simple observation, usually requiring prior knowledge of the data.

These levels are non-exclusive, some annotations using several of them to reinforce their assertion. In our literature, Bertin [8] and Curcio [9] speak of three levels of reading: "elementary", "intermediate" and "superior" for the former; "data", "between data", "beyond data" for the latter. Other authors followed the same idea of "three steps" [10,20–22]. Some examples:

– Visual: "Valjean co-apparaît le plus souvent" ("Valjean co-appears the most").
– Data: "Valjean est lié à beaucoup de personnages" ("Valjean is linked to many characters").
– Meaning: "Valjean est le personnage principal" ("Valjean is the main character").

5.5   Co-references (Abbreviated: Ref)

Even though our interface did not allow users to see other analysts' annotations, some annotations still refer to others, previously written by the same analyst. The fifth dimension specifies whether an annotation is a reference to another, or if it is independent. In our literature, many previous works allow users to see and reply to others [1,3,12,13]. This dimension is inspired by their work. Example:

"En revanche, ils sont bien présents durant les derniers (225), sauf Myriel, Fantine et Javert" ("However, they are still present during the last (225), apart from Myriel, Fantine and Javert"). This annotation refers to another one, which states that no character is present at the very last chapter.

5.6   Detected Patterns (Abbreviated: Patterns)

The sixth and last dimension of our classification concerns the patterns detected by the analyst in her annotation. We used three categories to sort them:

– Singularity: the annotation concerns only one unit that stands out. Can be either implicit or explicit.
  • Implicit: specific property of a unit, such as its distribution along another dimension of the data. No reference to other units of the same dimension.

- Explicit: mention of one unit that stands out from either a larger group of similar units, or all similar data units present on the visualization.
- Duality: the annotation compares two data units or more. These data units are similar in scale and come from the same dimension. This category regroups correlations, similarities, dependencies and orderings.
- Plurality: concerns a common feature of all data units of the same dimension (or its majority).

In our literature, Munzner [7] uses a more complete set of patterns. In the context of this study, it was deemed too complex to find acceptable agreement score. Some examples:

- Singularity (implicit): "Gavroche appears a lot around chapter 245, then plays a minor role".
- Singularity (explicit): "Valjean is the most represented character, but he does not have a peak of occurrences, he plays his role overall well across the chapters".
- Duality: "Few chapters with Valjean without mention of Cosette".
- Plurality: "The chapters seem to switch from character to character rather than following everyone".

6   Design and Evaluation

In this section, we describe the iterative process that has led to the final classification presented in the previous section. To design the initial dimensions of our classification, we derived a set of dimensions by randomly selecting groups of three annotations and comparing them, without prior expectations. Our goal was to make dimensions emerge from the data, rather than sorting data through predefined filters. Figure 3 shows the web platform that we used to reach this goal. The validity of this classification system was then assessed in several iterations (or phases). During each, three experts (three of the authors of this article, also referenced to as "coders") independently categorized the same subsets of annotations. At the end of each iteration, we computed an Inter-Coder agreement (or Inter-Coder Reliability ICR) to validate each dimension. When the score was too low, the dimension was reworked and reassessed in another phase. In total, the validation of all dimensions required five phases.

The first two phases were pilots: two sets of 32 annotations – 8 for each visualization – were randomly selected for the experts to categorize. The initial weaknesses of the classification were thus identified and fixed. During the third phase, all 302 annotations were annotated for all dimensions: this process revealed new weaknesses that we addressed in a fourth phase. The outcome of the fourth phase was mostly satisfying, leading the experts to confront their opinion about the last stumbling blocks that resulted from insufficiently explained dimensions. This discussion is regarded as the fifth phase.

We computed both a classical Pairwise Percentage Agreement score, along with a Fleiss' kappa. The Pairwise Percentage Agreement measures the average agreement rate for all possible pairs of coders, its values ranging from 0%

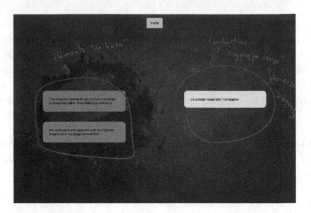

Fig. 3. This web platform shuffles all annotations and displayed three of them. Our purpose was to differentiate two of them from the other. (Reproduced with permission from [4]).

(perfect disagreement) to 100% (perfect agreement). In the domain of Human-Machine Interaction, a score superior to 80% is usually recommended to validate the coding model. For its part, the Fleiss' kappa [23] (an extension of Cohen's kappa [24] used with more than two coders) measures whether the perceived agreement is the result of chance or not. It scales from -1 to 1. Negative values implies that there is no agreement. A value of 0 represents an agreement level that can be achieved by chance alone, while a value of 1 means a perfect agreement between coders. Landis and Koch [25] propose the following interpretations for Fleiss' Kappa: from 0.01 to 0.20, the agreement is "slight". From 0.21 to 0.40, the agreement is "fair". From 0.41 to 0.60, the agreement is deemed "moderate". From 0.61 to 0.80, the agreement is "substantial", while it is "almost perfect" from 0.81 to 1. For this study, we deemed values superior to 0.21 as sufficient, since there exists no score recommendation in the domain of Human-Machine Interaction. We processed each possible choice of multiple choices dimensions independently from the others, in order to judge both the reliability of the whole dimension and each of its choices. The dimension "Data Unit" is a special case, since the coders had various ways of identifying the same element. Faced with the multitude of choices offered by this dimension, we only computed the Pairwise Percentage Agreement.

Table 2 summarizes the results that validated our classification as presented in the previous section. Tables 3 and 4 present the results for each choice of the two multiple choices dimensions. Figure 4 shows the evolution of the classification through all phases, along with the following comments.

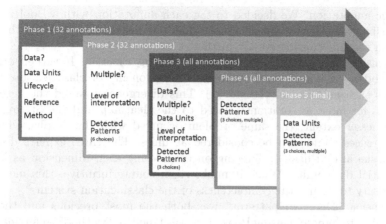

Fig. 4. The 5 phases necessary to build the classification. Dimensions that scored poorly are in red. (Reproduced with permission from [4]). (Color figure online)

Table 2. All dimensions, by phase, percentage agreement and Fleiss' Kappa. [4].

Dim	Phase	%	Kappa
Data	3	97.56%	0.935
LOI	3	82.43%	0.393
Ref	3	96.40%	0.549
Multiple	3	94.89%	0.232
Patterns	5	92.76%	0.778
Units	5	94.89%	NA

Table 3. "Level of interpretation" [4].

LOI	%	Kappa
Visual	82.99%	0.398
Data	78.23%	0.361
Meaning	86.05%	0.419

Table 4. "Detected patterns" [4].

Patterns	%	Kappa
Singularity	89.91%	0.702
Duality	92.66%	0.811
Plurality	95.72%	0.821

– Dimension "Level of interpretation" was initially labelled "Cognitive lifecycle" , because we believed that it represents a step within the sequential process of sensemaking when analysing a visualization, as described by Bertin [8]. This claim was hard to validate with this study, and the label was deemed too ambiguous; hence the change for a more comprehensible one.
– Dimension "Multiple observations" was not present in the first phase, but proved to be necessary during the computation of the first Inter-Coder agreement: several annotations unexpectedly contained more than one insight. This fact led to a dozen of disagreements, as coders did not classify the same part

of the annotation. We decided to tag each annotation with a Boolean value describing whether it contains more than one insight or not. If so, the annotation was not considered any further.

- Dimension "Data units" scored poorly during Phase 3. It turned out that one coder did not consider temporal dimension in her classification process (units such as "End of the story"). This divergence lowered the agreement to 2/3 for most annotations related to the Heatmap and the Streamgraph. To a lesser extent, the same problem occurred with the graphs, where co-occurrences could also be considered as units. The three experts discussed the issue after Phase 4, agreeing on considering each dimension as bearing potential data units. While it might seem counterintuitive, this measure is necessary to ensure the completeness of the classification system.
- Dimension "Detected patterns" was both the most precious and the most laborious to handle. During Phase 1, it was labelled "Method", referring to the method used by the annotator to formulate her insight. It also contained all the patterns proposed by Munzner [7]. The label changed for "Detected Patterns" in Phase 2, as it was deemed more self-explanatory. Moreover, coders did not agree on the definition of each pattern, as different patterns could be used to qualify a single insight. We thus reduced its values to three distinctive choices during Phase 3. These choices became non-exclusive in Phase 4, since several cases presented insights that belonged to more than one option.

7   Use Case

The classification of the 302 annotations provided by the participants offers a first idea of what to expect when the classification will be used in a large-scale study comparing the type of annotations made over different visualizations of the same datasets.

Of the 4 visualizations, participants generated the least annotations with the matrix, while the heatmap generated the most, as seen in Fig. 5a. Conversely, Fig. 5b shows that the visualization which generated the most non-data annotations was the matrix: more than a third of its annotations speak of the visualization itself, rather than the data. Finally, as seen in Fig. 6a, the matrix did not provoke the most negative reactions – the streamgraph did. One hypothesis is that the matrix was the most confusing for new users. If so, the "Data" dimension of our classification could be an indicator of the ease of learning of a visualization: the more it generates non-data related annotations, the harder it is to comprehend. However, this dimension alone does not translate the perceived quality of a visualization, since the participants complained significantly more about the streamgraph. Figure 6b shows that for both the heatmap and the streamgraph, participants have a median of data-related annotations of 100%, whereas both graphs are below. This would mean that both temporal visualizations were easier to handle for our participants.

As seen in Fig. 7, most annotations concern the "data" level of interpretation. However, the extent of this phenomenon varies importantly between each

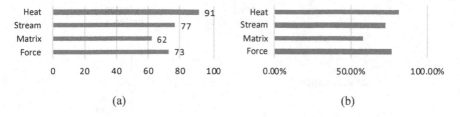

Fig. 5. (a) Annotations produced, by visualization. **(b)** Data-related annotations, by visualization and in percent. Heat: N = 17. Stream: N = 21. Matrix: N = 26. Force: N = 18. (Reproduced with permission from [4]).

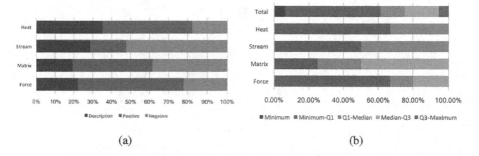

Fig. 6. (a) Types of non-data related annotations, by visualization and percent. Total: N = 215. Heat: N = 73. Stream: N = 55. Matrix: N = 35. Force: N = 56. **(b)** Distribution of data-related annotations by visualization amongst participants. The number of occurrences for each visualization is indicated to the right. (Reproduced with permission from [4]).

visualization. Graphs (matrix and force-directed graph) generate more annotations related to the visual elements: analysts speak of the position of nodes, of the opacity of the lines, etc. "Meaning" level of interpretation is mostly found in the force-directed graph: this finding should be tempered by the fact the dummy visualization was a force-directed graph as well. Two explanations are possible: either the knowledge of a visualization facilitates the interpretation of the data (this might sound trivial, but still worth validating), or the graphs and their "proximity" metaphor are easier to understand.

Overall, as seen in Fig. 7, a large majority of the annotations concern singularities. Analysts usually spotted a few units standing out, rather than comparing similar elements or qualifying of the entirety of the data. A trivial explanation is that there exists simply less to say about the entirety of the data, rather than by isolating specific units.

A qualitative review of the data unit dimension led us to believe there exists a distinction between annotations that mention a subject aggregated data unit ("the violet group", "the main characters") and several subject single data units ("Valjean, Cosette and Marius", "Fantine and Myriel"). In the latter, the purpose of the annotation is to highlight a common property of a set of single data

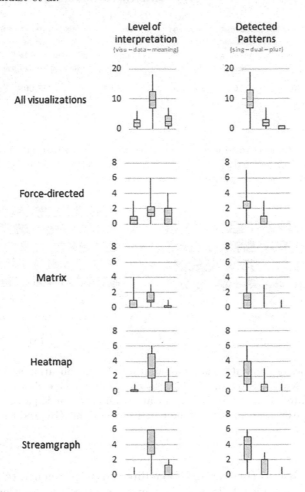

Fig. 7. Distribution of levels of interpretation and detected patterns, by visualization. (Reproduced with permission from [4]).

units. In the former, the annotation tends to point to a property that is not directly linked to their common characteristics. For instance, in the annotation "the violet cluster is denser than the others", the density of the cluster is not directly linked to the colour of its constituent single data units.

Finally, we performed an informal analysis of the sequence in which annotations were produced by analysts. Several initial observations can be made that give hints about how analysts proceed to explore a data visualization. First, it seems that annotations that do not relate to the data decrease significantly as the sequence progresses, as seen in Fig. 8a. This trend holds true for all four visualizations, analyzed independently. Less intuitive is the fact that analysts who start with annotations unrelated to the data are very likely to keep annotating that way two more times, before either dropping or moving on to data-related annotations. This is particularly visible with the Matrix (Fig. 8b). Moreover, contrary to our expectation, the number of annotations with a "meaning" level of interpretation (either alone or along with another level) seems to decrease, as shown in Fig. 9a. Interestingly, this analysis also highlights a trend for more "visual" levels of interpretation in the Matrix, while the opposite seems true for the Heatmap. The progression of the "detected patterns" shows that the plurality tends to gain importance along the way (Fig. 9b), something that can be found in all visualizations, except the Heatmap where combinations of singularities and dualities increase to the detriment of all other types of patterns.

7.1   Further Improving the Classification

Despite our best efforts, the classification struggles to encompass several annotations met during this study.

Its design raised many questions for more specific and ambiguous cases. Among them, textual references to an absence of data units remain to be classified properly. In the annotation "There was nobody at first", "nobody" is simultaneously an absence of data, but also the subject of the insight. As it stands now, we interpret "nobody" as "everybody" and thus regard it as a subject aggregated data unit. While this solution makes sense, it requires extensive pondering from the classifier and seems almost counter-intuitive.

This dimension also suffers from another ambiguity: the "role" of a data unit is not always objectively identifiable. While the agreement score for this dimension was acceptable, the three experts had long discussions for each disagreement regarding the role of a data unit; without clarifications from the analyst who authored the annotations, it might not be possible to find out which unit was the most prevalent for her. The relevance of this distinction is also debatable and should be either clarified in further studies, or simply given up. However, this last option would heavily impact the classification, since the identification of the subject is preliminary to the identification of the "detected pattern". Getting rid of this distinction could lead to a more complex classification, where each data unit would have different "Detected patterns". To illustrate this idea, consider the following annotation: "At the end of the book, the appearances of all characters raise drastically". A character-focused view would be to consider "the main characters" as the subject of the annotation. Following this, the pattern would be a plurality, as we specify how the whole set of characters works. However, if one considers the organization of the book instead of the characters, the subject would be "the end of the book". The end of the book distinguishes itself from the rest by the raise of the appearances of the characters - this is a "singularity" pattern.

The choice of the former example is not completely innocent, as it also pictures another challenge of the "data unit" dimension: is it possible to select a subject that is the result of the combination of two dimensions of the data? "The appearances of the characters at the end of the book" is a value assigned to the connection between characters and a set of chapters. Obviously, its raise is also the real phenomenon pointed by the author of the annotations. This value is

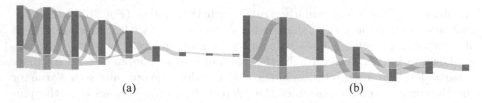

(a)   (b)

Fig. 8. (a) The sequence of annotations, as seen for the "data" dimension, shown as a Sankey diagram. Blue bars show data-related annotations, orange bars show non-data related annotations. The horizontal layout represents the annotation process (first stacked bars represent the first annotations of all analysts, the second stacked bars represent the second annotations, and so on). **(b)** Evolution of the dimension "data" during the sequence for the "Matrix" visualization (same meaning as a). Most analysts who start with annotations unrelated to the data keep doing so for at least two steps. (Color figure online)

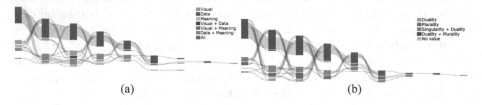

(a)   (b)

Fig. 9. (a) The sequence of annotations, as seen for the "level of interpretation" dimension. Bars representing "meaning" levels of interpretation are the red (data + meaning), the green (visual + meaning), the gray (all levels) and the pink (meaning only). There are no sign of a gain of importance of these bars along the sequence. **(b)** The sequence of annotations, as seen for the "detected patterns" dimension. Green bars represent the pluralities, which grow in importance as the sequence goes on. (Color figure online)

not attached to any of the two dimensions, but to their associative entity (as defined in the entity-relationship theory). Keeping in mind that one of the purposes of the framework presented in this paper is to explain which visualizations are best for different types of tasks, we believe necessary to consider references to associative entities as data units. However, it might be relevant to add one more attribute to the "data unit" dimension, to distinguish "raw" entities from "associative" ones. With this improvement, we would be able to find whether a visualization allows analysts to reflect upon the associations of several entities easily.

The "Multiple" dimension of this classification came as a surprise; we did not expect to meet such problems when classifying annotations. This issue arises because a single annotation can contain several observations, and it could be solved by differentiating between the dimensions relating to the annotation itself (the textual or graphical token) and those relating to the observations. Thus, a further step in improving the classification would be to further split our dimensions accordingly:

- The "data" dimension speaks of the annotation itself. Either it provides one or several insight(s) about the data, or not at all.
- The "co-references" dimension describes whether the whole annotation refers to another one, or not. It should remain attached to the whole annotation instead of each observation.
- The "multiple" dimension might simply be dropped, or be kept only as an informational dimension that counts the number of observations that were identified within the annotations.
- Each observation provides its own "data units", with their own roles.
- Each observation has its own "level of interpretation". This could help testing the seemingly preconceived notion that analysts would start their work with low-level observations, before concluding with a high-level interpretation.
- Each observation uses its own "detected patterns".

An annotation such as "Jean Valjean seems to be the main character. Javert appears only in a few chapters and is likely a supporting character" would be classified as a "data-relating" annotation, with no co-reference and two observations. The first observation, "Jean Valjean seems to be the main character", would have a single subject data unit (Jean Valjean), a "meaning" level of interpretation, and an implicit singularity pattern. The second observation, "Javert appears only in a few chapters and is likely a supporting character", would have a single subject data unit (Javert), a complement aggregated data unit ("a few chapters"), a "data" and a "meaning" levels of interpretation, and an implicit singularity pattern. Figure 10 shows a visual representation of both the proposed structure and this example.

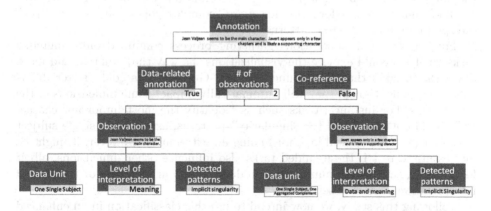

Fig. 10. Illustrated example of a possible improvement for the classification.

While this proposal solves the issue of annotations with multiple observations, it has yet to be tested through a robust intercoder agreement. Such a modification of the classification would increase its complexity, in addition to the fact that differentiating "duality" observations within an annotation from multiple observations that are not related is a delicate matter and requires some thinking. In our example, it is not easy to figure out if the analyst meant a comparison between Valjean and Javert (in which case the annotation would present a duality pattern between two data units) or if these observations are completely separate. Once again, it might simply not be possible to understand this simply by looking at the annotation without further explanations from its author.

7.2 Building on the Classification

Our initial study aimed to gather 300 annotations, but we did not have enough participants, datasets, use cases and visualizations to find out significant relationships between the knowledge of the domain and the different dimensions of our classification. As stated earlier, the profiles of our participants were also homogeneous, a fact that prevents us from asserting that our classification can be generalized to anyone, regardless of their demographic affiliation or level of expertise. Another problem is that our use case was not real: one might expect actual experts of a topic to produce different annotations than non-expert users. Further studies with a larger pool of participants will offer more reliable results, as well as proving the classification's completeness. Such studies will be able to either confirm or deny the correlation between several of our dimensions. For instance, while we believe a distinction is necessary between the detected patterns and the level of understanding, they seem to be tightly coupled, as hinted by Bertin [8] and many authors following his trail [10, 20–22]. To confirm or deny this hypothesis, a new study is necessary: one that would not simply require more participants, but also push further the analysis of the sequence of the annotations, so that it will be possible to find out whether users start with "simple" annotations before building more "complex" ones – both in terms of interpretation and detected patterns.

Furthermore, our annotations gathering process contained only unguided tasks: analysts could explore the visualizations the way they wanted, and mark down the insights that they found relevant. Guided tasks could foster different annotations, though they will automatically impact some dimensions of the annotations. For instance, tasks such as "identify the most important character" would obviously lead to "singularity" patterns, as well as a single subject data unit (as analysts will look for finding an extremum). However, it might be interesting to test if these guided tasks also influence other dimensions, albeit less directly, such as the number of non-data related annotations or the level of interpretation of each observation.

Following this study, we now intend to use this classification in an enhanced version of our annotation platform, as we believe that sorting and filtering through others' annotations might be improved by using it. Once enough annotations will be produced and classified, a further step will be to provide the Data Visualization community with a ground truth regarding which visualizations are most relevant for various tasks. Moreover, the possibility to bridge this definitional gap sketched at the beginning of this article will also become possible:

with a sufficient amount of annotations, we might derive "classes" of annotations that would match the common definition of "classification".

8   Conclusion

This article introduced a descriptive attribute-based framework for annotations in data visualization. The framework was created on the basis of a dataset of 302 annotations obtained from 16 analysts, that 3 coders have classified using a bottom-up approach informed by Grounded Theory until a high level of inter-coder agreement was attained. The final framework proposed has six dimensions, some of which reflect the types of questions and tasks supported by data visualization that were outlined in several previous conceptual works.

The contributions of this work to the field of data visualization are manifold. First, it establishes the prominent place of annotation in the process of understanding and analyzing data through visualization by providing a formal definition of annotations. In addition, it introduces a comprehensive framework for the systematic description of annotations using descriptive attributes along 6 complementary dimensions. Finally, it postulates that this framework can serve as a basis for a high-level qualitative comparison of different visualization idioms dealing with the same data. Indeed, taking this framework as a common reference system can allow experts to compare visualization idioms on the basis of the types of annotations that these idioms lend more naturally to produce.

This work also opens up a series of perspectives for research and practice in data visualization. Since this system could provide a framework for the qualitative assessment of visualization techniques, to measure how they facilitate the production of a certain type of annotations, this could further lead to guidelines for better design visualization depending on the tasks that need to be supported for a given application and data set. This framework also provides a better structure to highlight and understand potential patterns in the sequence of production of the annotations. We hope future research can build on our framework proposal and apply it to new cases, including larger scales and other types of data visualization, to evaluate and possibly improve its completeness and genericity.

Acknowledgements. We would like to thank all our supports during the design and the tenure of this study. In particular, many thanks go to the reviewers of this article, as well as to Professor Jaya Sreevalsan Nair for her precious advice and comments.

References

1. Willett, W., Heer, J., Hellerstein, J.M., Agrawala, M.: CommentSpace: structured support for collaborative visual analysis. In: Sigchi, pp. 3131–3140 (2011)
2. Ren, D., Brehmer, M., Lee, B., Hollerer, T., Choe, E.K.: ChartAccent: annotation for data-driven storytelling. IEEE, pp. 18–21 (2017)
3. Zhao, J., Glueck, M., Breslav, S., Chevalier, F., Khan, A.: Annotation graphs: a graph-based visualization for meta-analysis of data based on user-authored annotations. IEEE Trans. Visual Comput. Graphics **23**, 261–270 (2017)

4. Vanhulst, P., Evéquoz, F., Tuor, R., Lalanne, D.: Designing a classification for user-authored annotations in data visualization. In: Proceedings of 9th International Conference on Information Visualization Theory and Applications (IVAPP), Madeira (2018)
5. Satyanarayan, A., Heer, J.: Lyra: an interactive visualization design environment. Comput. Graph. Forum **33**, 351–360 (2014)
6. Satyanarayan, A., Russell, R., Hoffswell, J., Heer, J.: Reactive Vega: a streaming dataflow architecture for declarative interactive visualization. IEEE Trans. Visual Comput. Graphics **22**, 659–668 (2016)
7. Munzner, T.: Visualization Analysis and Design. CRC Press, Boca Raton (2014)
8. Bertin, J.: Sémiologie graphique: les diagrammes, les réseaux, les cartes (1967)
9. Curcio, F.R.: Comprehension of mathematical relationships expressed in graphs. J. Res. Math. Educ. **18**, 382–393 (1987)
10. Susan, N., Friel, F.R., Curcio, G.W.: Bright, source: making sense of graphs: critical factors influencing comprehension. J. Res. Math. Educ. **32**, 124–158 (2001)
11. Boy, J., Rensink, R.A., Bertini, E., Fekete, J.D.: A principled way of assessing visualization literacy. IEEE Trans. Visual Comput. Graphics **20**, 1963–1972 (2014)
12. Viegas, F.B., Wattenberg, M., Van Ham, F., Kriss, J., McKeon, M.: Many eyes: a site for visualization at internet scale. IEEE Trans. Visual Comput. Graphics **13**, 1121–1128 (2007)
13. Heer, J., Viégas, F.B., Wattenberg, M.: Voyagers and voyeurs: supporting asynchronous collaborative visualization. Commun. ACM **52**, 87–97 (2009)
14. Luther, K., Counts, S., Stecher, K.B., Hoff, A., Johns, P.: Pathfinder: an online collaboration environment for citizen scientists. In: Proceedings of the SIGCHI Conference on Human Factors in Computing Systems, pp. 239–248 (2009)
15. Bostock, M., Ogievetsky, V., Heer, J.: D3 data-driven documents. IEEE Trans. Visual Comput. Graphics **17**, 2301–2309 (2011)
16. Satyanarayan, A., Moritz, D., Wongsuphasawat, K., Heer, J.: Vega-lite: a grammar of interactive graphics. IEEE Trans. Visual Comput. Graphics **23**, 341–350 (2017)
17. Wongsuphasawat, K., Moritz, D., Anand, A., Mackinlay, J., Howe, B., Heer, J.: Voyager: exploratory analysis via faceted browsing of visualization recommendations. IEEE Trans. Visual Comput. Graphics **22**, 649–658 (2016)
18. Bostock, M.: Force-Directed Graph (2017). bl.ocks.org
19. Bostock, M.: Les Misérables Co-occurrence (2012)
20. McKnight, C.C.: Task Analyses of Critical Evaluations of Quantitative Arguments: First Steps in Critical Interpretation of Graphically Presented Data. Technical report, Boston (1990)
21. Carswell, C.M.: Choosing specifiers: an evaluation of the basic tasks model of graphical perception. Hum. Factors **34**, 535–554 (1992)
22. Wainer, H.: Understanding graphs and tables. Educ. Res. **21**, 14–23 (1992)
23. Fleiss, J.L.: Measuring nominal scale agreement among many raters (1971)
24. Cohen, J.: A coefficient of agreement for nominal scales. Educ. Psychol. Measur. **20**, 37–46 (1960)
25. Landis, J.R., Koch, G.G.: The measurement of observer agreement for categorical data. Biometrics **33**, 159–174 (1977)

TabularVis: An Interactive Relationship Visualization Tool Supported by Optimization and Search Algorithms

György Papp$^{(\boxtimes)}$ and Roland Kunkli

Department of Computer Graphics and Image Processing,
Faculty of Informatics, University of Debrecen, Debrecen, Hungary
{papp.gyorgy,kunkli.roland}@inf.unideb.hu

Abstract. Visualizing relationships is becoming more and more essential nowadays, so we need efficient visualization solutions to meet the requirements of the users. One of its forms is when we use tables to describe the relationships and their associated values. In this work, we present TabularVis, an interactive, web client based application for visualizing relationships based on tabular data. Our visualization technique was inspired by the Table Viewer web application of the popular genome visualization software called Circos. For our solution, we only kept its central idea, and we built our new extensions and features around it. We also propose an automatic sorting solution to reduce the number of intersections in the diagram along with an edge bundling technique to improve the clarity of it. In the paper, we present the features of our visualization, which mainly focuses on improving the readability of the diagram in those cases when the difference between the values of the table is extremely small or large. Also, we compared our solution with Circos in a survey to prove the effectiveness of our proposed features. Beside this, we compared the sorting method with the edge bundling technique as well to confirm their performance. The result of the surveys is also presented in the paper. Furthermore, we provide running time measurements as well to show the effectiveness of the presented methods.

Keywords: Data visualization · Circular layout · Sorting · Table · Diagram · Search algorithm · Hierarchical edge bundling

1 Introduction

Relationship visualization is one of the earliest problems in the field of information visualization. Both in the scientific and industrial fields, almost everything has an effect on something else. Therefore, it is necessary to realize and understand the information described by these relationships. Often, these connections are represented by values which can indicate the type or property of the related connections.

© Springer Nature Switzerland AG 2019
D. Bechmann et al. (Eds.): VISIGRAPP 2018, CCIS 997, pp. 167–192, 2019.
https://doi.org/10.1007/978-3-030-26756-8_8

If one would like to store information about these mentioned relationships, tables often provide a useful representation of them, and they have a very long history in computer science and data management. In this work, we deal only with those connections, where the values are represented by numbers. However, just organizing them into a table does not necessarily make them easier to understand. If the table contains lots of rows and columns, then it becomes harder to deal with the values and the described connections by them. Therefore, there is a great need for the visualization methods, with which we, the users, can identify previously hidden information, relationships, and patterns from the generated diagrams. For such purposes, the circular layout is one of the most helpful techniques, and it is often used in the field of graph drawing and in many applications, including the popular and highly cited software package called Circos [1].

In our previously published work [2], we introduced an improved approach to the main idea of Circos, by providing new tools for displaying the direction, the value, and the patterns of the relationships. Also in our mentioned work, we introduced a sorting method as well, with which we can reduce the number of intersections in the diagram. This way the diagram can become more clear, and the links can be much easier to follow. In this paper, we present the improved version of our previous method, by providing new results based on a redefined model for generating sorted diagrams and new features for making them more customizable with improved quality. Our newly generated diagrams can visualize such information which was not visible using the technique we published in [2]. We also provide the results of a short survey in which we asked the users to tell us their opinion about the usefulness of our approach. In the paper, we also present a performance comparison between the previously published approach and the new one.

The structure of the paper is the following. At first, we discuss the previous works which are relevant to our topic; then in Sect. 3, we present the method of Circos—which inspired us the most in our work—in more detail and highlight some of its shortcomings. In Sect. 4, we start to introduce our new method, and in Sect. 5, we introduce our newly developed algorithms for creating the diagrams more clear by using sorting and edge bundling. In Sect. 6, we draw the lessons of our survey made for validation purposes; then in Sect. 7, we provide a detailed discussion about the performance and the features of our self-developed application, which was implemented to present our results. Conclusion closes the paper in Sect. 8.

2   Previous Work

Circular layout is popular for visualizing connections, especially in the case of genomic data or graphs. Furthermore, its advantages—which come from its symmetry and simplicity—make it useful for visualizing general data as well. The ability to reduce the number of eye movements, the rotation invariant property, and weakening the reading order implications are just three of these mentioned advantages, which are discussed in the paper of Chuah and Eick [3] in detail.

In the literature, we can see several examples of the usage of circular layout for genomic [4–7], network [8–11], and general [12–15] data visualization tasks by researchers from different disciplines.

Here, we would like to discuss and highlight those works, whose primary purpose was not only to use circular layout for different tasks but also to provide useful tools and software for the scientific community. Circos [1] is a free and open-source application under GPL license, and it is widely used in the field of genome research because of its success in displaying a positional relationship between genomic intervals and variation in genome structure. With its help, different plot types can be shown inside the tracks of the diagram, to provide more information about genomes. However, even though Circos is a potent tool for visualization, unfortunately, it is not user-friendly enough yet. The software is a command line application that uses configuration files to create the diagrams. The learning phase may be very long for researchers having only basic IT skills, to be able to create demonstrative and customized diagrams. Several applications exist (e.g., *OmicCircos* [16], *RCircos* [17], or *ggbio* [18]) which provide a much more user-friendly and improved genome visualization based on circular layout. All of these applications are packages for the R statistical software environment, which ensures that the users can take the advantages of R while using them.

Unfortunately, users can generate only static images by using the software mentioned above, that makes the customization process significantly harder than in the case of dynamic software solutions. The circular layout combined with interactive data visualization techniques (e.g., in *J-Circos* [19] or *Mizbee* [20]) can help the users to understand the data faster and better. However, customizing the diagram by changing or removing elements in it is not possible with this two software; although, this functionality may help the users to make the diagram more personalized. Thus, we were inspired by both applications to extend the possibilities of visualizing the values of the connections.

As we mentioned, besides genomic data, there is a demand for solutions, with which the users can visualize relationship information and connections based on more general data. With the *circlize* R package [21], we can generate diagrams based on non-genomic data as well, owing to its low-level graphic functions. Circos can also visualize general data but only described in a required format. A similar visualization technique is the solution of Jen Lowe [22], with which she has won the WikiViz 2011 challenge.

There is a growing trend to create visualizations in web browsers and make them more and more interactive. Probably the most used solutions for this kind of purpose are the libraries called *WebGL* and *D3.js* [23]. In the website of Chrome Experiments, we can find lots of examples to them [24], and different scientific projects used WebGL for visualization tasks as well [25–28]. Circos has an online application too, but only for tabular data, and it has much less functionality than the desktop version of it.

A diagram can become crowded quickly in the case of too many connections, which can make it harder to understand the data. In the field of graph theory, decreasing the number of intersections between graph edges is a well-known problem, also in the case of circular layout. Baur et al. [29] published a heuristic algorithm, in which the first phase minimizes the total length of the edges, and the second one uses the shifting heuristic to optimize the result of the previous step locally. In the work of Gansner et al. [30], the authors tried to find the best node placement by the minimization of the length of the edges using a heuristic algorithm as well.

If we would like to reduce the number of intersecting links in a diagram, edge bundling [31] can be an efficient alternative. However, in the case of tables, it would be much harder to recognize specific row-column intersections. Another solution exists to avoid crowded diagrams, which is the exterior routing; we can see an example to it in the work of Gansner et al. [30]. Our solution is based on hierarchical edge bundling [32] which is another well-known technique.

3   Table Visualization with Circos

One of the central concepts in the visualization method of Circos is that we can interpret a cell in a table as a connection between its row and column. Based on a circular layout, Circos connects circularly arranged segments with so-called "ribbons", and the width of these elements represent the value (only non-negative numbers are allowed) of a table cell. If the value of a cell is zero, it indicates that there is no connection between the row and the column defined by the position of the cell. During the preprocessing step, Circos collects these relationships defined by the table to visualize them, as we can see in Fig. 1. The angular size of the segments is based on the sum of the values in the represented row or column.

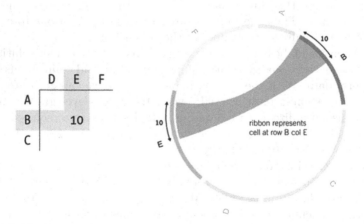

Fig. 1. The way how Circos visualize connections [33]. The ribbon on the right represents the value 10 of the cell at row B and column E. The value of the cell defines the thickness of the ribbon.

The smaller angular segments (so-called "ribbon caps") are located at both ends of a ribbon (see Fig. 2). These caps indicate the other participant in the relationship by using the color of the connected segment. However, they do not always appear in the diagram. In Circos, each connection has a direction: the starting position can be recognizable based on the property that the link reaches the segment completely. The so-called "contribution tracks" are positioned beyond the segments. As we go farther from the center of the circle, the first track shows the incoming relations and their represented values together, while the second one does the same but based on the outgoing ribbons. Both of these previously mentioned information are included in the outermost track.

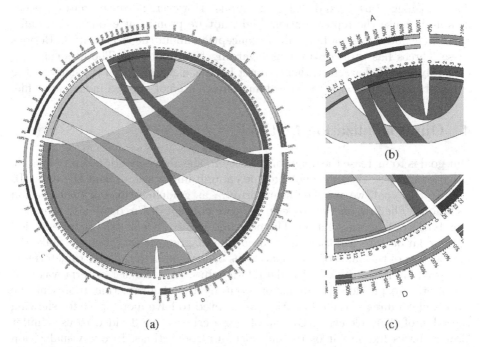

(a)   (b)   (c)

Fig. 2. In (a) we can see an exemplary diagram generated by Circos. We can see the contribution tracks outside the circle, the so-called tick marks and tick labels (the numbers and the percentage values). (b) shows that the red links start from a row segment and (c) displays the ending in the case of the segment which represents a column. (b) and (c) also provide a closer look at the ribbon caps between the segments and the ribbons. These images are from our previous work (Figure 2 in [2]). (Color figure online)

The visualization of Circos is well suited to highlight the relationships associated with larger values and to help the user perceive the values of these segments quickly. Also, it is useful for determining the segments that are connected with thick ribbons.

However, there are cases when Circos has shortcomings. One of them is that the users cannot read the exact value of the connections: they can only make assumptions based on the tick marks and the contribution tracks.

Another shortcoming is that the ribbons appear with very similar thickness when the difference between the values of the given table is minor. Therefore, it is much harder to distinguish the values of the relationships based on the thickness of the ribbons. Comparing two segments or two ribbons is even harder if they are placed far from each other. Furthermore, when the previously mentioned difference is significant, then thick ribbons could entirely cover the thin ones by default. Therefore, the user might not notice essential details in the diagram like the pattern formed by the connections and their directions.

As we mentioned above, Circos indicates the direction of a relationship by distinguishing starting and ending positions. However, it can be hardly recognizable because the representation might not be prominent enough; especially, when somebody does not have any preconception about the visualization. Besides these, Circos has three restrictions regarding the input files. The files can contain only ASCII characters, there cannot be space characters in the name of the segments, and duplicated row or column names are not allowed in the input file.

4   Our Visualization Method

Our goal is to increase the diagram's clarity in the above-mentioned problematic situations, where Circos cannot provide enough information about the data. To achieve this goal, we specified a few criteria as guidelines for our visualization technique. The first one was to keep the core concept of Circos by also using the circular layout in our solution. The next one was to redefine the representation of the relationships and their direction in the diagram. It was about to make the comparison of the value of the connections easier and help the user to determine the exact value associated with the relationship. And the last criteria was that we wanted to provide the ability of grouping the elements that represent the rows and columns of the table. Also, we wanted to have more space for showing the label of these elements. On top of these criteria, we decided to use similar Bézier curves like in Circos to construct our connections. In our visualization technique, we provide the different modifications based on the previously mentioned criteria. In our software these were implemented as optional features since they are suitable for different situations and use cases. Therefore the users can decide which one is the most appropriate for their purpose.

One of our main ideas was to remove the segments from Circos—which represent the rows and the columns—replace them with angular segments. The reason behind this decision is our first criteria, which is about to make the relationship value easier to compare and perceive. These newly defined angular segments serve as an extension of the connection in both directions, which determines both their thickness and height. These inherit the thickness of the connection, while their height is calculated based on the value associated with the connection (see Fig. 3). In the rest of the paper, these angular segments are called bars by reflecting their shapes.

The bars together represent the rows and the columns from the table, and we refer to these groups of bars as blocks in the rest of the paper. They are

Fig. 3. The extensions of the connections (the bars) together form a block, and they can be arranged into groups like *block B* and *block C*. The height and the angular length of a bar have the same meaning; they are both used for representing the value of a link. There are concentric circular arcs behind the blocks to make their values easier to read and compare, even if they are far from each other. Also, in *block E* we can see an example of a block which has been individually scaled.

created by placing the bars which belong to the same row or column next to each other and marking them with the same color. The user can filter the displayed bars and connection by defining number ranges to determine the visibility of a relationship. After the filtering, only those connections and bars are displayed, whose associated value was in one of the ranges defined by the user.

Additionally, our blocks can be arranged into groups to give more complexity to the diagram. Regarding our previous group concept, we made the following changes. Instead of attaching the blocks to represent a group, we added a new circular segment under the blocks with the name of the group inside of it (see in Fig. 3). We calculate their color by mixing the color of their blocks if there are at least two blocks in a group. Unlike in Circos, the user can define multiple rows

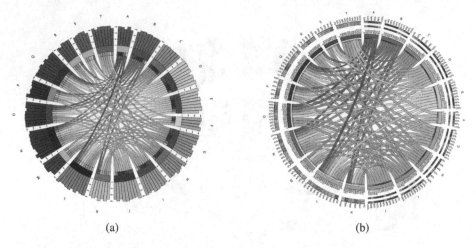

(a)   (b)

Fig. 4. The left image (a) shows how the bars can easily indicate the values with concentric circles, while in Circos (b) it is harder to read and compare the values of the connections.

or columns with the same name. In the diagram, by default, all blocks with the same label are merged to each other. However, the user can change this behavior of the blocks that have the same label by choosing to merge only those, which are in the same group. By changing the default behavior, the user can create diagrams with a more complex structure.

Behind the blocks, we placed dotted concentric circular arcs. All of these arcs have a number at one of their ends to indicate the value of the bars. These numbers and arcs together can help the users to determine the value of each bar and to make a comparison between them (see Fig. 4). The font sizes of these numbers are automatically calculated between the groups and blocks based on the size of the blank areas left out between them. They always fit in the space left between them. Furthermore, the users can display the exact value of each connection at the top of the bar. Therefore, they can decide to hide the value between the blocks and groups to gain more space for the connections. Also by replacing the concentric circles with circular arcs, we gained the possibility to individually scale the blocks based on their value (see Fig. 3). So in those cases when the relationships of a block have a different set of values than others, the user can display the height of the bars within the block correctly.

The blocks are not attached directly to the connections, because there are other shapes between them. These are additional tracks, that can show relevant information to the user. There are two kinds of tracks, based on whether they display information regarding the blocks or the bars. First (going from the center of the circle to the outer parts), there are the ones which are related to the blocks and then the ones related to the bars. Each track consists of multiple elements. The intensity of the color represents their value. The values that the elements can show are the following: it can represent the height of the bar; it can indicate

Fig. 5. The image shows the connections with unified thickness and our shapes with the arrow-style form to indicate the directions. For example, the shapes below *block E* indicate the source of the connections, and the ones below *block H* show their target.

the extremely small and large values; it can show the number of intersections of the connection of the bar; it can display the value of the block and the number of bars that were filtered out.

We intended to offer a different and more informative way to display the direction of the connections. Therefore, to indicate the direction of the link and also the other block of it, we added a new shape between the additional tracks and the links in a way that Fig. 5 shows us. That new shape can have three different forms based on the direction of the link. Two of these have arrow-style forms to indicate a direction. The last shape is a simple colored angular segment because it represents that a connection does not have a direction. Their color has a similar meaning as the ribbon caps have in Circos. These shapes are usually attached to the additional tracks, but when the user does not define them in the diagram, they are attached to the bars. With the shapes of the direction and the additional tracks, we increased the visibility of the bars. Therefore, we solved the problem of the barely perceptible bars, which occurred when the values of the relationships were too small.

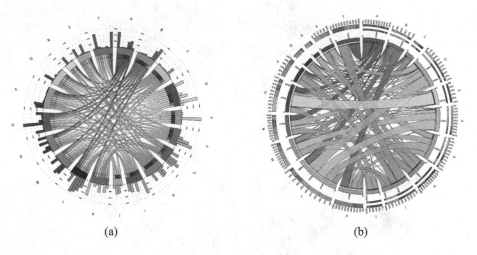

(a)   (b)

Fig. 6. The left image (a) shows our visualization with unified connection thickness, while in (b) we can see the visualization of Circos. We can recognize that the pattern of the connections is much more visible in the case of (a) than (b).

To increase the visibility of the thinner connections, we create all relationships equally visible by unifying the thickness of the links and the bars in the diagram. This modification results that the links are only representing the relationships from the table, and the height of the bars only represents the associated value of the relationships. Furthermore, the links with unified thickness make the pattern formed by the connections easier to perceive, instead of drawing our attention to a particular part of the diagram (see Fig. 6(a)). The usage of this feature also increases the visibility of the bars and the comparability of them, while it eliminates the redundancy mentioned at Fig. 3. Also, the unified connections help us to avoid the deformation problem of the arrow-style form.

5   Increasing the Clarity of Our Visualization

Our visualization method aims to help the users see the relationships and its properties described by tables. Therefore, it is crucial that in our visualization, we strive for increasing its clarity to support the users read our diagram. In our case, we determined two possible way to reduce the clutter in the diagram. The first one is to reduce the number of the intersections, and the second one is to bundle the connections. We propose a sorting method which searches the best position for the connections to eliminate the most intersections from the diagram, and we use a hierarchical edge bundling technique which can bundle the connections that represent a relationship between the same groups. In this section, we discuss each of our proposed solutions in more details separately.

5.1   Sorting the Connections

The high number of intersections in the diagram can significantly reduce the clarity because with each intersection the links are become much harder to follow from one block to another. Because the position of the groups and the blocks determines how we construct a link between them, it has a significant impact on how many intersections there are in the diagram. As a solution to this problem, we propose a sorting method. During the sorting, we search for the layout of the groups and the blocks which produce the least number of intersections in the diagram. In the rest of the paper, we reference this process as sorting of the connections.

By using this method, the user can automatically get a layout with reduced number of connections. In contrast, there is not any feature similar to this idea— to reduce the clutter in the diagram—in Circos. So in that visualization, the users have to find the best layout by themselves and then set it manually. Figure 7 shows an example where sorting can help to avoid the clutter.

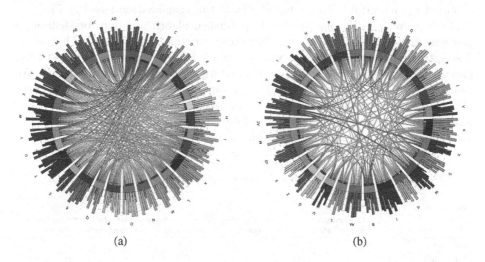

(a)   (b)

Fig. 7. Example of how the sorting of the connections increases the clarity in the diagram. The left image (a) shows the diagram without sorting, and the right image (b) shows the result that we get after applying it.

This sorting problem is known as the circular crossing minimization problem in the field of graph drawing, and it is NP-hard. To get a solution to it, usually, local search and optimization methods are used together with heuristics. In the work of Baur [29] and Gansner [30], we can see an example of how these methods can be used for a similar problem like ours. The purpose of our solution is to provide a fully automatic feature for reducing the number of intersections in the diagram, with the possibility of tweaking its result by setting specific starting position for blocks or groups before the sorting.

5.2   The Used Algorithms for Sorting

Our sorting method consists of different local search and optimization methods: two local search algorithms (hill climbing and min-conflicts) and three optimization methods (cross-entropy, simulated annealing, and bees algorithm). All of them are discussed in more detail in the work of Brownlee [34] and the book of Russell and Norvig [35].

These are used to find the best possible state in the search space which has the least number of intersections. However, it is not guaranteed that the results provided by the methods mentioned above will contain the best possible layout for the blocks and the groups. Since this is an NP-hard problem, by increasing the number of the blocks and the groups we drastically increase the number of layouts which we have to test to find the best possible solution. During this search, there is a high risk that the used algorithms stuck with the local best layout, instead of continuing the search to find the best global one. Therefore, due to the nature of the problem, our result will be just an approximation of the best "theoretical" solution. Despite that, in most cases, their results are good enough to remarkably increase the clarity of the visualization (see Fig. 7).

Because we modify our previously published algorithms only by defining a new search space, we do not write about them in details in this paper. Their short description can be found in our previous work [2]. However, we changed their parameters which controls their behavior, so we list these changes in Table 1. We can see that compared to the previous parameters of the algorithms, we were able to reduce some of the values and still achieve the same performance. Also, in another case, we can increase these values to get a better result, but we can avoid increasing the running time of the algorithms drastically.

Table 1. The predefined parameters for all of the used algorithms.

Algorithms	Parameters						
	Randomly changed state	Iteration	Generated states	Elite states	Acceptance ratio	Iteration per temperature	Groups for search
Hill climbing	10	10	-	-	-	-	-
Min-conflicts	-	10	-	-	-	-	-
Cross-entropy	-	20	20	5	-	-	-
Cross-entropy and Min-conflicts	-	20	20	5	-	-	-
Simulated annealing	-	100	-	-	0.8	10	-
Bees algorithm	-	10	10	2	-	-	2

The order of the bars is not changed directly by the search, since their position is determined by using the resulting layout of the blocks and the groups. We add the bars to a block, while we iterate over the elements of the layout. We start from the actual position, and we go back until we arrive to the actual element again. While we visit all elements, we add a bar to the actual block if there is a connection between the selected element of the layout and the actual block.

In our solution, the number of the connections defined by the table has a significant impact on the average running time of the algorithms. With the best-performing algorithm, the randomly generated tables with 20 rows and 20 columns have been sorted in $\approx 16\,$s. By considering the same tables, the fastest algorithms can provide a result within $\approx 3\,$s. More detailed information about the running time of the algorithms can be found in Table 2. A similar table can be found in our previous work (Table 1 in [2]) however, the values in it are different because of the improved algorithm. In the next subsections, we briefly introduce the methods and their time complexity.

Table 2. The running times given in seconds for all algorithms and table sizes.

Algorithms	5×5	10×10	15×15	20×20
Hill climbing	< 1	3	35	207
Min-conflicts	< 1	1	6	27
Cross-entropy	< 1	< 1	1	3
Cross-entropy and Min-conflicts	< 1	2	14	62
Simulated annealing	< 1	1	4	16
Bees algorithm	< 1	1	9	33

5.3   Search Space

The used local search and optimization methods require a search space that can be used while they are running because it consists of every possible outcome of the diagram. The model that describes the diagram in a way that the methods used for the sorting can operate on it is called state. In our previous paper, we defined the states as a representation of the diagram containing all required information by the sorting. This information was the position of the groups and the blocks, the relationships between them, and every operation that can be performed by any of our search or optimization algorithms. We built our newly defined state entirely around the connections by using a hierarchical data structure which contains the groups, the blocks, the bars, and the connections. This data structure stores every information about the previously mentioned elements and provides fast access to any element during the sorting. However, we kept a few things from the previous implementation of the model. For example, we still use the position of the groups and the blocks from the layout during the sorting. The reason behind this is that we do not want to change how the algorithms can go from one state to another one.

We made modifications on the neighborhood function of the state, but we kept the basic idea, which was that the algorithm changes states by replacing the indices of two elements which remained the same. The change in our new neighborhood function is about how we can select these two elements to swap their indices.

$$g\left(i,n\right) = \left\lfloor \frac{i}{\left(n-1\right)-1} \right\rfloor \tag{1}$$

$$f(i, n) = g(i, n) + i \bmod (n - 1) + 1 \tag{2}$$

Function (1) and (2) show how we define the selection of the groups. In both functions, i is the index of the selected neighbors by the sorting algorithms, and n is the number of the groups in the diagram. The return value of both functions is an index, that tells us which two groups of the layout we have to swap. The algorithms choose groups only to swap their indices, so they cannot change the position of the blocks directly inside a group. Their order is calculated independently every time the state goes into one of its neighbor states. During this calculation, we find the best order of the blocks in the same way as we do it for the group. However, the algorithms calculate the best layout of the blocks only for the group selected by the $g(i, n)$ function. With these modifications, we reduce the complexity of switching between the states, and in most cases, we completely avoid to copy or clone the data structure or the state. Also, we greatly reduce the number of how many times we copy or clone states when we cannot avoid that. Besides these, we can easily precalculate the numbers of intersections in the neighbors of the state to make a decision based on them, for example, which is the best neighbor of the actual state for continuing the search.

5.4 Goal Function

In our previous solution, we defined the optimization method by only using the indices of the blocks from a layout to calculate how many intersections there are in the diagram. We created ranges from these values, and then we tested whether they overlap. If they overlap with each other, then the connections represented by the range intersect as well. Therefore, this calculation is perfect for a goal function in an optimization method. However, the creation and the overlap test of the ranges required too much calculation. Therefore we simplified the test by transforming it into a geometric problem where we have to detect the overlap of circular arcs instead of ranges. To make this transformation possible, first, we have to define when two circular arcs overlap with each other. Two circular ranges k and l overlap with each other if k has at least one common point with l, but not all of their points are common. Our definition means that we exclude those cases when one of the circular arcs contains the other.

In our new goal function, we still depend on the actual layout of the sorting method, because we need to know where the blocks are precisely on the base circle. We can get this information by transforming the indices of the blocks and the groups from the layout into geometric information. Since we wanted to reduce the complexity of the optimization function, in our new function, the blocks are only represented by a point instead of a circular range. By turning the range of the block to a point, we can more easily test the intersection because our definition of the intersections says that there is no intersection between two connections if one of their endpoints is in the same block. So, we can reduce the complexity of the calculation of the goal function because it is easier to check whether the point of the blocks is the same or not, instead of checking this for the endpoints of the ranges.

The position of a block is stored as a polar coordinate because our method heavily relies on calculating the angle between two arbitrary points on the base circle. By using polar coordinates, we can quickly calculate any angle between two blocks as Function (3) shows for us. We call it as distance function in the rest of the paper.

$$d(a, b) = \pi - |\pi - |a - b|| \tag{3}$$

Our optimization method is based on this function, that is why we need to keep it simple. With this distance function, we can define the length of the connections by calculating the angle between the two blocks that it connects. Then we can see in Eq. (4) how we calculate the midpoint of the connections.

$$m(a, b) = b + \frac{1}{2}(-d(a, b)) \cdot sgn(a - b + \pi) \tag{4}$$

For the $m(a, b)$ function the two polar coordinates of the blocks must satisfy the following condition: $b > a$. By using the distance and midpoint functions, the optimization methods can calculate the necessary information to decide if there is intersection between two blocks (see Function (5)).

$$r(a, b, c, d) = \frac{d(m(a, b), m(c, d))^2 - \left(\frac{d(a,b)}{2} - \frac{d(c,d)}{2}\right)^2}{\left(\frac{d(a,b)}{2} + \frac{d(c,d)}{2}\right)^2 - \left(\frac{d(a,b)}{2} - \frac{d(c,d)}{2}\right)^2} \tag{5}$$

The method needs to know the distance of the connections defined as the distance between the midpoint of the connections. The method also needs the sum and the difference of the half of the lengths of the connections. From these, the final value is calculated as Function (6) shows for us. We denote the links by $c_1, \ldots, c_n$ where n is the number of the connections in the diagram. Their starting and ending points, which are calculated based on the positions of the blocks, are denoted with two functions: $s(c_i)$ and $e(c_i)$ respectively, where $i \in [1, n]$.

$$q(i, j) = \begin{cases} 1, & \text{if } 0 < r(s(c_i), e(c_i), s(c_j), e(c_j)) < 1 \\ 0, & \text{otherwise} \end{cases} \tag{6}$$

We use the square of the values in the function to avoid any negative value to occur, and because it is much faster than using the absolute value function of the used programming language. As the $q(i, j)$ function shows, when the ratio is between 0 and 1, then there is an overlap between the two circular arcs.

$$I = \sum_{i=1}^{n-1} \sum_{j=i+1}^{n} q(i, j). \tag{7}$$

By performing the $q(i, j)$ function on each combination of the connections, we can get the number of intersections in the diagram, as the summarized value shows in Eq. (7).

5.5   The Time Complexity of the Algorithms

To present the time complexity of the algorithms that we used during our sorting method, first, we have to define a few terms.

- b : number of blocks in the diagram
- g : number of groups in the diagram
- k : maximum number of iterations that the algorithm can take
- v : number of newly generated states
- o : time complexity of the built-in quick sort algorithm
- u : time complexity of updating the cross-entropy matrix $(b + g)(b + g)$
- p : maximum number of iterations to find the best starting temperature
- t : number of iterations allowed on each temperature
- c : maximum number of iterations to find the best reheat temperature
- w : number of random searches performed during an iteration
- l : number of best states stored in the algorithm

   We put all time complexity values in Table 3 to make the comparison between them more comfortable.

Table 3. The time complexities for all of the used algorithms. At the row of Cross-entropy and Min-conflicts methods, r_{mc} marks the time complexity of the Min-conflicts algorithm.

Algorithms	Time complexity without grouping	Time complexity with grouping
Hill climbing	$\mathcal{O}((k + 2v)\left(g^2 - g\right))$	$\mathcal{O}((k + 2v)\left(b^2 - b\right)\left(g^2 - g\right))$
Min-conflicts	$\mathcal{O}(kg - k)$	$\mathcal{O}(k\left(b^2 - b\right)(kg - k))$
Cross-entropy	$\mathcal{O}(kn + kq + ku)$	$\mathcal{O}(kn + kq + ku)$
Cross-entropy and Min-conflicts	$\mathcal{O}(kvr_{mc} + ko + ku)$	$\mathcal{O}(kvr_{mc} + ko + ku)$
Simulated annealing	$\mathcal{O}(p + kt + c)$	$\mathcal{O}(p + kt + c)$
Bees algorithm	$\mathcal{O}(kw + klg - kl)$	$\mathcal{O}(kw + klg - kl)$

5.6   The Result of the Algorithms

The performance of the previously mentioned methods was measured on tables with four different sizes (5×5, 10×10, 15×15, and 20×20). One hundred randomly filled tables were generated for each size. Our application was compiled into JavaScript, and after that, the tests were run in the latest Chrome Web Browser (Version 66.0.3359.181) on a system with an Intel Core i7-8550U Processor (8M Cache, up to 4.00 GHz) with 16 GB memory. The Dart language—with which we developed our previous application—evolved a lot in the few months, and the Dartium browser became deprecated. Dartium was the browser that we used for testing our previous methods because it has built-in native Dart support. Therefore, to provide a proper ground for the comparison, our previous solution was recompiled to JavaScript and were used in Google Chrome for the comparison. The running times of our previous algorithms are increased after this compared to the ones listed in our previous paper [2]. The reason of this is the conversion between the programming languages. We created similar diagrams like Figs. 9 and 10 from our previous work [2] to show the result of the above mentioned performance measurement. The comparison between the average performances and the running times of the new and the recompiled solutions are shown in Fig. 8.

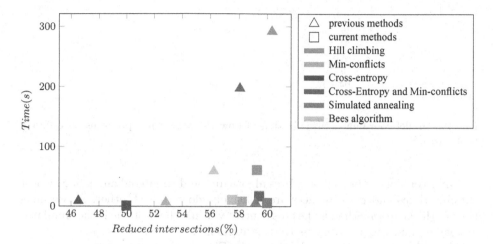

Fig. 8. Comparison of the average performances and average running times of our current and previous algorithms.

By using the newly defined search space and goal function, the algorithms became much faster in almost every cases, except the min-conflicts method, because the average running time of the previous one is faster by 2 s. Also, we can see that in most of the cases the new solution provides a better result than the previous one, except in the case of the hill climbing algorithm, because of the performance of the new method was worse by ≈ 1%. In some cases, our new solution has even better running time and performance than the Dart version of the previous one.

The overall result of the tests performed with only the algorithms of our new solution is shown in Fig. 9. Almost all of our method performed over 70% for the small tables, and with increased table sizes the performance stayed around 50%. Contrary to the previous solution, in this one, the user has an option to choose an algorithm that needs only seconds (1 s in average) to reduce the intersections in the diagram. However, the usage of the cross-entropy method requires compromise, because it is our worst performing algorithm (50% in average). The simulated annealing algorithm has the best performance in each table sizes (60% in average), and its running time is the second-best among the others (≈ 6 s).

When we grouped the results of the test by sizes, the difference between the tested methods became more apparent and more noticeable (see Fig. 10). As we can see in the diagram, there is a small group of algorithms (cross-entropy

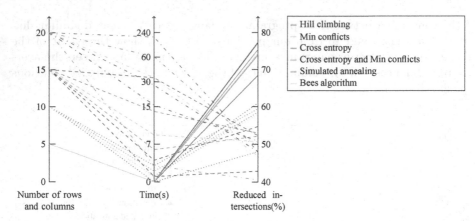

Fig. 9. Parallel coordinates visualization of how the algorithms performs on different table sizes.

and min-conflicts, min-conflicts, bees algorithm, and simulated annealing) whose running times and performances are relatively close to each other. As we mentioned, the fastest method is the cross-entropy, while the best one is the simulated annealing, and Fig. 10 supports these statements.

Regarding the groups of algorithms in Fig. 10, there are no significant differences between the performances of the methods ($\approx 5\%$). Therefore, when we choose an algorithm for our sorting process, we need to consider their running time and their effect on the clarity of the diagram.

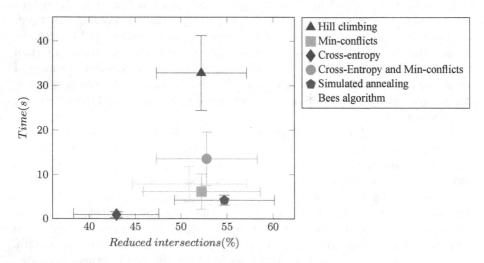

Fig. 10. Comparison of the execution times and the performances of the search algorithms on 100 tables with 15 rows and 15 columns.

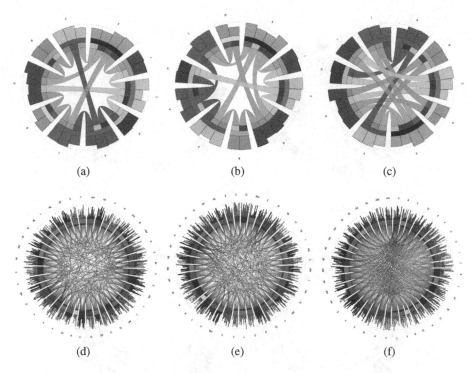

(a)   (b)   (c)

(d)   (e)   (f)

Fig. 11. Comparison of search algorithms based on two different table sizes. A 5 × 5 table was used for the upper set of images ((a), (b), and (c)) and one with 20 rows and 20 columns was used for creating the lower diagrams ((d), (e), and (f)). From the images above, (a) and (d) (sorted with simulated annealing) have the least number of intersections, (b) and (e) (sorted with min-conflicts) contain ≈ 5% more intersections, and the last two, (c) and (f) have not been sorted.

In Fig. 11, we can see an example of how much the difference is between the performance of the different sorting methods. We used two tables with different sizes to display this difference. The first table consists of 5 rows and 5 columns while the other one has 20 rows and 20 columns. The differences between the results are more clearly noticeable in the case of diagrams based on small tables, than in the case of the large ones. The difference is almost negligible in diagrams generated by using larges tables. Beside this, Fig. 11 shows us in both cases, that even a bit worse result is way better than the original diagram without applying any sorting on it.

The proposed algorithms have multiple parameters, and during their development, we focused on keeping a balance between their performance and their running time. The images in this paper were generated by using the previously mentioned parameters. Furthermore, they were used in our application as default parameter values for the sorting algorithms.

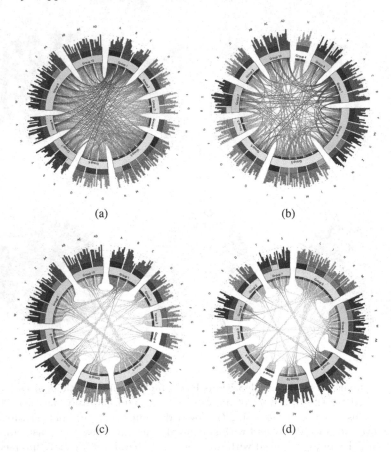

(a)   (b)

(c)   (d)

Fig. 12. Comparison of the sorting methods and the edge bundling. All diagrams were generated based on the same table. The first diagram (a) has not been modified, only the others. In the next two diagrams ((b) and (c)), we used our sorting and edge bundling solutions respectively. In the last diagram (d), we sorted and bundled the connections.

5.7   Edge Bundling

Another way of increasing the clarity of our visualization is to use an edge bundle technique. We intended to implement an edge bundling in a way that leaves the user with the ability to determine both segments of each link based on their shape after the bundling. Therefore, we decided to implement a hierarchical edge bundling where the connections are bundled based on their group information. It means that two links are bundled together if they both represent a relationship between blocks from the same two groups. To construct the links for the bundling, we used rational Bézier curves.

As we can see in the examples of Fig. 12, edge bundling is useful only in those cases when there is more than one connection between the two groups. Also, it shows us that the bundled links can be cluttered. However, by using the sorting algorithms with the edge bundling, the user can reduce this clutter between the links as Fig. 12 shows for us in the comparison. Besides this, edge bundling has the advantage in those cases when the size of the table is too large for the sorting algorithms because the edge bundling does not depend on the size of the table.

6   Survey

We created two surveys to evaluate our proposed visualization technique. In both of these, we intended to compare our visualization method with the technique of Circos and get feedback regarding our new features. The difference between the two surveys is that in the first one, the participants did not have any preconception about the visualization technique, while in the second one, we introduced both visualization method to the users at the beginning of the survey. We got 37 answers to the first and 24 answers to our second one. The surveys were written in Hungarian.

The results show that by unifying the links thickness in our visualization, we can display the pattern formed by the connections more clearly. However, this feature is not the most suitable for finding specific connections or values in the diagram, because the visualization of Circos achieved a better result in these cases. Although the users cannot read the exact value of the relationships based on only the thickness of the links, the height of the bars helped the users to read the connections values more accurately. Our solution to display the direction of the connections performed better (94%/5%) in the surveys than the solution of Circos.

More than half (52%) of the participants agreed that grouping the elements or filtering them can be beneficial in the visualization, and only 18% of them was against it. The remaining 30% was unable to decide whether it is useful. When we asked the participants to select the diagram that can be more easily read, they selected the result of the sorting methods over the edge bundling (84%/16%) when we grouped the blocks in the diagram. However, when we did not group any blocks in the diagram, the participants almost equally chose (53%/46%) the diagram that was only sorted and the diagram that was sorted and edge bundled at the same time. Also, based on the answers we can say that the sorting can not help in those cases when the diagram elements were already "well organized" before using our sorting method.

7   Application

A client-side web application was implemented in the Dart programming language to present our proposed visualization method and our solutions to avoid the clutter in the diagram. We used the AngularDart framework [36] for building the user interface of the application, and the ChronosGL [37] WebGL 2.0 engine is responsible for displaying our visualization. With the help of the AngularDart framework, we built a clear and straightforward interface by using the provided elements of Google's Material Design. The display area and the table editor got the primary focus in our application. Therefore those were positioned at the center, while we placed the settings around them. The sidebar can be hidden by the user to give more focus to the visualization and the editor. The visualization page of our application can be seen in Fig. 13.

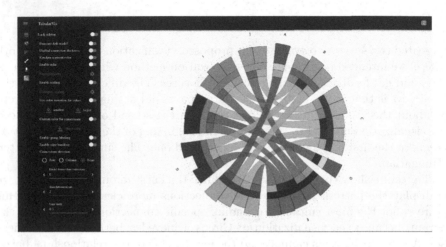

Fig. 13. The visualization page of our application, where the user can customize the diagram.

Our visualization technique provides many options to customize a diagram. Therefore, we built an interactive application which can offer the followings to the users: quickly apply any previously mentioned feature on the diagram through the UI; modify the diagram by changing the input data stored in the table or the properties (position, appearance) of a shape; change the default parameter of labeling the concentric circular arcs; individually scale the height of the blocks and the groups; change the control points of the Bézier curve used for the connections; and apply predefined coloring scheme for the visualization.

During the sorting of the connections, the application is not interactive since it is a computationally expensive task. However, after the result was provided by the algorithms, the user can continue to work with the diagram.

Our application can work with the data files of Circos and Excel spreadsheets as well. Also, our software implements a table editor used by the Handsontable Community Edition library [38]. These mentioned features allow easy data entry to the user.

The users can download the resulting diagram of the visualization in a PNG file, as well as they can export the input data in a simple text file. This file is created by following the formatting rules defined in the case of the input files of Circos. Also, the result of our sorting solution is also placed in this text file. Our new application supports the following browsers: Google Chrome, Mozilla Firefox, and Opera.

The URL for our previous application can be found in our earlier paper [2]. We plan to update the web-application with our new solutions in the near future.

8 Conclusion

In this paper we present a new visualization technique with which diagrams have increased clarity, especially in those cases when Circos has shortcomings. We proposed our modifications as different features, so the users can choose the most suitable ones regarding the data that they want to visualize. The first modification was that the segments were replaced by bars. These can represent the value of a relationship in a much more visible way when the scatter in the values of the table is almost negligible. To indicate the value represented by the height of the bars we added dotted concentric circular arcs behind them. By replacing the previous concentric circles to these, the user gains the ability to scale the blocks individually. It means that they can create a more complex diagram which can consist of relationships from the different set of values. Another modification was to unify the thickness of the connections. It helps the users to see the pattern formed by the connections more clearly. Moreover, it prevents the deformation of the shapes, that was proposed to represent the direction of the link in a more obvious way. Also, more space is available for the labeling by using this feature in those cases when the difference in the values of the table is significant. Furthermore, the users can group the blocks to create a hierarchy in the visualization. We redefined how the groups are displayed in the diagram to make the hierarchy represented by them more apparent to the reader. Under the blocks, additional tracks were added to display more information about the connections. One of these tracks shows information about our connection filtering feature. It helps the users to select the connections to be displayed by filtering their values. Therefore, they can display only a set of relationships in a more detailed view, instead of showing them all at once.

To improve the clarity of our diagram further, we proposed two different solutions. The first one tries to reduce the number of intersections in the diagram by using local search algorithms and global optimization methods to modify the order of the groups and the blocks. The other one is a hierarchical edge bundling technique which bundles the links based on their group information. We used rational Bézier curves for constructing the bundled connections.

We also created a survey for validation purposes, and it showed us that our proposed modifications help the user to perceive information from the diagram more efficiently in the targeted cases. However, in some other cases, the visualization technique of Circos was better than ours. This result supports our decision to keep these modifications as optional features, so the users can have connections with different thickness, while they can have the advantages of the rest of our modifications.

The limitations of our proposed visualization provide opportunities for further improvements. One of these is that our technique can only work on tables which do not contain negative numbers. Another one is that the center of the diagram can be too dense and the connections can become too crowded when we want to visualize too many connections. It mainly occurs when the table has more than twenty rows and twenty columns, and only a few of its cells contain zero. Our sorting methods also have similar limitations regarding its running time and performance. The required time for sorting the connections can significantly increase with each connection newly added to the diagram. However, while its running time is increasing, its performance is dropping in the case mentioned above. Based on these limitations, a possible future improvement can be ensuring the visualization method works with tables filled with rational numbers. Also, to detect and eliminate those intersections in the diagram which are not justified by the end position of the connection is another candidate for future improvement. Moreover, the optimization of the parameters of the Bézier curves to maximize the used area in the diagram can be another potential way of improving our work. We intend to create our visualization more interactive by displaying additional information about the elements of the visualization (e.g., statistical information) by hovering the mouse over them. Besides these, further investigation of using image-based edge bundling techniques also can be a viable option for future improvement.

Acknowledgement. Supported by the ÚNKP–17–4 New National Excellence Program Of The Ministry Of Human Capacities.

References

1. Krzywinski, M., et al.: Circos: an information aesthetic for comparative genomics. Genome Res. **19**, 1639–1645 (2009)
2. Papp, Gy., Kunkli, R.: TabularVis - a Circos-inspired interactive web client based tool for improving the clarity of tabular data visualization. In: Proceedings of the 13th International Joint Conference on Computer Vision, Imaging and Computer Graphics Theory and Applications - Volume 3: IVAPP, INSTICC, pp. 120–131. SciTePress (2018)
3. Chuah, M.C., Eick, S.G.: Information rich glyphs for software management data. IEEE Comput. Graph. Appl. **18**, 24–29 (1998)
4. Katapadi, V.K., Nambiar, M., Raghavan, S.C.: Potential G-quadruplex formation at breakpoint regions of chromosomal translocations in cancer may explain their fragility. Genomics **100**, 72–80 (2012)
5. Burkart-Waco, D., et al.: Hybrid incompatibility in Arabidopsis is determined by a multiple-locus genetic network. Plant Physiol. **158**, 801–812 (2012)
6. Schmutz, J., et al.: A reference genome for common bean and genome-wide analysis of dual domestications. Nat. Genet. **46**, 707–713 (2014)
7. Tine, M., et al.: European sea bass genome and its variation provide insights into adaptation to euryhalinity and speciation. Nat. Commun. **5**, 5770 (2014)
8. Lin, X., Dang, Q., Konar, M.: A network analysis of food flows within the United States of America. Environ. Sci. Technol. **48**, 5439–5447 (2014)
9. Dang, Q., Lin, X., Konar, M.: Agricultural virtual water flows within the United States. Water Resour. Res. **51**, 973–986 (2015)
10. Irimia, A., Horn, J.D.V.: The structural, connectomic and network covariance of the human brain. NeuroImage **66**, 489–499 (2013)

11. Irimia, A., Van Horn, J.: Systematic network lesioning reveals the core white matter scaffold of the human brain. Front. Hum. Neurosci. **8**, 51 (2014)
12. Blasco-Soplón, L., Grau-Valldosera, J., Minguillón, J.: Visualization of enrollment data using chord diagrams. In: Proceedings of the 10th International Conference on Computer Graphics Theory and Applications - Volume 1: GRAPP, (VISIGRAPP 2015), INSTICC, pp. 511–516. SciTePress (2015)
13. Pan, K.X., Zhu, H.X., Chang, Z., Wu, K.H., Shan, Y.L., Liu, Z.X.: Estimation of coal-related CO_2 emissions: the case of China. Energy Environ. **24**, 1309–1321 (2013)
14. Fujiwara, Y.: Visualizing open data of input-output tables in Kobe city. In: SIGGRAPH Asia 2015 Visualization in High Performance Computing SA 2015, pp. 18:1–18:1. ACM, New York (2015)
15. Nicholas, M., Archambault, D., Laramee, R.S.: Interactive visualisation of automotive warranty data using novel extensions of chord diagrams. In: Elmqvist, N., Hlawitschka, M., Kennedy, J. (eds): EuroVis - Short Papers, The Eurographics Association (2014)
16. Hu, Y., et al.: Omic-Circos: a simple-to-use R package for the circular visualization of multidimensional omics Data. Cancer Inform. **13**, 13–20 (2014)
17. Zhang, H., Meltzer, P., Davis, S.: RCircos: an R package for Circos 2D track plots. BMC Bioinform. **14**, 244 (2013)
18. Yin, T., Cook, D., Lawrence, M.: ggbio: an R package for extending the grammar of graphics for genomic data. Genome Biol. **13**, R77 (2012)
19. An, J., Lai, J., Sajjanhar, A., Batra, J., Wang, C., Nelson, C.C.: J-Circos: an interactive Circos plotter. Bioinformatics **31**, 1463–1465 (2015)
20. Meyer, M., Munzner, T., Pfister, H.: MizBee: a multiscale synteny browser. IEEE Trans. Vis. Comput. Graph. **15**, 897–904 (2009)
21. Gu, Z., Gu, L., Eils, R., Schlesner, M., Brors, B.: Circlize implements and enhances circular visualization in R. Bioinformatics **30**, 2811–2812 (2014)
22. Bayer, T.: A Thousand Fibers Connect Us - WikiViz 2011 winner visualizes Wikipedia's global reach (2011). https://blog.wikimedia.org/2011/10/06/a-thousand-fibers-connect-us-wikiviz-winner-visualize-wikipedias-global-reach/. Accessed 06 Mar 2018
23. Bostock, M., Ogievetsky, V., Heer, J.: $\mathbb{D}^3$: data-driven documents. IEEE Trans. Vis. Comput. Graph. **17**, 2301–2309 (2011)
24. Google: (Chrome Experiments—Experiments with Google). https://experiments.withgoogle.com/collection/chrome. Accessed 06 Mar 2018
25. Mwalongo, F., Krone, M., Becher, M., Reina, G., Ertl, T.: Remote visualization of dynamic molecular data using WebGL. In: Proceedings of the 20th International Conference on 3D Web Technology. Web3D 2015, pp. 115–122. ACM, New York (2015)
26. Andrews, K., Wright, B.: FluidDiagrams: web-based information visualisation using javascript and WebGL. In: Elmqvist, N., Hlawitschka, M., Kennedy, J. (eds): EuroVis - Short Papers, The Eurographics Association, pp. 43–47 (2014)
27. Bornelöv, S., Marillet, S., Komorowski, J.: Ciruvis: a web-based tool for rule networks and interaction detection using rule-based classifiers. BMC Bioinform. **15**, 139 (2014)
28. Cui, Y., et al.: BioCircos.js: an interactive Circos JavaScript library for biological data visualization on web applications. Bioinformatics **32**, 1740–1742 (2016)
29. Baur, M., Brandes, U.: Crossing reduction in circular layouts. In: Hromkovič, J., Nagl, M., Westfechtel, B. (eds.) WG 2004. LNCS, vol. 3353, pp. 332–343. Springer, Heidelberg (2004). https://doi.org/10.1007/978-3-540-30559-0_28

30. Gansner, E.R., Koren, Y.: Improved circular layouts. In: Kaufmann, M., Wagner, D. (eds.) GD 2006. LNCS, vol. 4372, pp. 386–398. Springer, Heidelberg (2007). https://doi.org/10.1007/978-3-540-70904-6_37

31. Lhuillier, A., Hurter, C., Telea, A.: State of the art in edge and trail bundling techniques. Comput. Graph. Forum **36**, 619–645 (2017)

32. Holten, D.: Hierarchical edge bundles: visualization of adjacency relations in hierarchical data. IEEE Trans. Vis. Comput. Graph. **12**, 741–748 (2006)

33. Krzywinski, M.: (Articles // CIRCOS Circular Genome Data Visualization). http://circos.ca/presentations/articles/vis_tables1/#tables. Accessed 06 Mar 2018

34. Brownlee, J.: Clever Algorithms: Nature-Inspired Programming Recipes, 1st edn. Lulu.com (2011)

35. Russell, S., Norvig, P.: Artificial Intelligence: A Modern Approach. Prentice Hall Series in Artificial Intelligence. Prentice Hall, Englewood (2010)

36. Google: (AngularDart). https://webdev.dartlang.org/angular. Accessed 24 Mar 2018

37. Robert, M., Ray, H.: ChronosGL A minimal WebGL2 3D Engine written in Dart. http://chronosteam.github.io/ChronosGL/. Accessed 18 May 2018

38. Handsoncode: (Handsontable Community Edition). https://github.com/handsontable/handsontable. Accessed 10 May 2018

Computer Vision Theory and Applications

Visual Computing Methods for Assessing the Well-Being of Older People

Chiara Martini[1]([✉]), Francesca Odone[1], Nicoletta Noceti[1], Manuela Chessa[1],
Annalisa Barla[1], Alessandro Verri[1], Alberto Cella[2], Alberto Pilotto[2],
and Gian Andrea Rollandi[2]

[1] Department of Informatics, Bioengineering, Robotics and System Engineering,
Università degli studi di Genova, Genova, Italy
chiara.martini@dibris.unige.it, {francesca.odone,nicoletta.noceti,
manuela.chessa,annalisa.barla,alessandro.verri}@unige.it
[2] E.O. Ospedali Galliera, Genova, Italy
{alberto.cella,alberto.pilotto,gianandrea.rollandi}@galliera.it

Abstract. With the increasing share of elderly population worldwide,
the necessity of assistive technologies to support clinicians in monitoring their health conditions is becoming more and more relevant. Recent
medical literature has proposed the notion of *frail elderly*, which rapidly
became a key element of clinical practices for the estimation of well-being
in aging population. The evaluation of frailty is commonly based on self
reported outcomes and occasional physicians evaluations, leading to possibly biased results. In this work we propose a data driven method to
automatically evaluate two of the main aspects contributing to the frailty
estimation, i.e. the *motility* of the subject and his *cognitive* status. The
first one is evaluated using visual computing tools, while the latter relies
on a virtual reality based system. We provide an extensive experimental
assessment performed on two sets of data acquired in a sensorised protected discharge facility located in a local hospital. Our results are in
good agreement with the assessment manually performed by physicians,
nicely showing the potential capability of our approach to complement
current protocols of evaluation.

Keywords: Visual computing · Frailty · Frailty index ·
Motility index · Aging · Skeleton data · Virtual reality ·
Cognitive assessment

1 Introduction

According to the World Bank, Italy has the second-highest share of population
aged over 65 worldwide, i.e., 23% in 2016, and statistics related to G20 countries
are becoming increasingly similar. Liguria, our region, is among the highest in
this ranking worldwide. Aging causes, in general, the reduction of the individual's potential, leading to a state of vulnerability and instability of the clinical

© Springer Nature Switzerland AG 2019
D. Bechmann et al. (Eds.): VISIGRAPP 2018, CCIS 997, pp. 195–211, 2019.
https://doi.org/10.1007/978-3-030-26756-8_9

condition. To highlight this condition, recent medical literature has proposed the notion of *frail elderly*, an individual with an elevated risk of complications that may result in loss of functional autonomy or death [1].

Hospitalization is the first cause of functional decline in the elderly: indeed, 30 to 60% of elderly patients lose some independence in basic Activities of Daily Living (ADL) in the course of a hospital stay [2]. In fact, beside the disabling effect of the acute event, hospitalization itself might represent an additional stressor in terms of environmental hazard, reduced caloric intake, low physical activity or prolonged bed-rest, depressed mood and social isolation. Prolonged hospital stays may increase the risk of infections and other iatrogenic complications, worsen the patient quality of life especially in the elderly, and imply a waste of economic and human resources [3,4]. In the worst case these complications may lead to mortality [2]. Recent studies conducted in various countries show that a significant proportion of hospital beds (about 8%) is indeed occupied by patients who experience a delayed hospital discharge (DHD) [5]. Among them, more than half (52.7%) spend extra time in hospital after recovery from acute condition waiting for the arrangement of either special assistance at home or the admission to long-term care facilities. A large amount of DHDs might thus be avoided in presence of smart home-like facilities, able to guarantee the appropriate level of assistance required for these typology of patients, but mitigating the human and financial efforts that a prolonged hospital stay would require. Technologies currently available offer now the possibility of putting in practice this concept.

In our work we propose a paradigm shift in assistance, in which intelligent environments act as personalized, social-aware and evolving cognitive prostheses to assisted people, which adaptively integrate their cognitive capabilities. We target elderly and people with mild cognitive impairments, partially autonomous, but in need of a light assistance, possibly in a post-hospitalization stage. This study is a part of a larger project whose aim is to design and implement a model of protected discharge, in which the patient, after being discharged from the hospital, is hosted for few days (about one week) in an apartment. The facility is located within the Galliera Hospital in Genova (Italy) and equipped as a comfortable apartment, where patients can be monitored by a system of sensors, while physicians and nurses have the possibility of monitoring them remotely. The system consists of a set of subsystems, each one developed to solve specific problems. Each part concurs to the core task, the estimation of the *frailty index* of the patient, providing integrated statistical tools to quantify *motility*, daily living activities and, in general, his quality of life.

One of the most commonly accepted operational definition of *frailty* is the classification proposed by Fried et al. [6]. In this study the authors define frailty as a clinical syndrome in which three or more of the following criteria are present: unintentional weight loss, exhaustion, decrease grip strength, slow gait speed, low physical activity. Inspired by this definition, several methods have been proposed in clinical practice and research to estimate the overall clinical and functional status of the hospitalized older subjects [7]. Among them, the Multidimensional

Prognostic Index (MPI), based on a standard Comprehensive Geriatric Assessment (CGA) [8] showed very good accuracy and excellent calibration in predicting several negative health status outcomes as well as institutionalization, re-hospitalization and mortality [9–11]. MPI score is based on the evaluation of the clinical, cognitive, functional, nutritional, and social domains, as defined in the International Classification of Functioning, Disability, and Health[1]. However, all these proposed evaluations are derived from self-reported questionnaires and sporadic medical evaluations, so the index is prone to bias and based on episodic and not quantitative assessments. An objective and continuous evaluation of different dimensions would complement such clinical evaluations, leading to a reduction in the medical assistance, and a positive overall benefit on public healthcare [12]. Recently, with the advent of assistive technologies, various approaches for the automatic estimation of frailty have been proposed [13–16]. On the same line, in this work we quantitatively evaluate the frailty of elderly considering the physical and cognitive dimension. In particular, we use visual computing tool to analyze patients *motility* and postural transfers, and we formulate a *motility index* to compare patient's performances. We perform this evaluation considering short time windows (few days), providing a significant advance with respect to current literature usually based on long observations of the patient (6–12 month) (see e.g. [17]). Moreover, we assess the *cognitive* status of patients, using a game-like approach based on virtual reality (VR) tool, that represents an alternative to traditional tests in which patients can be evaluated in ecological conditions [18]. In fact, VR allows to reproduce complex situations of daily living, where psychopathological reactions and cognitive functions of patients can be more reliably evaluated.

The structure of this work can be summarised as follows. Firstly, we describe the system, our research objectives and the sensors installed in the facility (Sect. 2). Then we present data analysis and the obtained results (Sects. 3 and 4). The paper is closed with conclusion and future works (Sect. 5).

2   The Concept

In this section we first describe the apartment, then we summarise the sensors installed in the facility and the corresponding measurements. The experimental set up is rich of sensors, we will briefly illustrate all the devices but, for the purpose of the study, we will use only a subset of them.

The aim of our project is the continuous monitoring of the patient's motility. In particular, we focus on the automatic estimation of the motility index (see Sect. 3.3) based on walking time and physical activity that, according to [6], are strongly related to the patients frailty.

As shown in Figs. 1 and 2, the apartment consists of two bedrooms, one with a bed and a sofa-bed (for an accompanying person) and one with two beds (patient and caregiver), a gym, and a common room with kitchenette and living room. To make the atmosphere homely, an architectural study was conducted to choose

---

[1] http://apps.who.int/classifications/icfbrowser/.

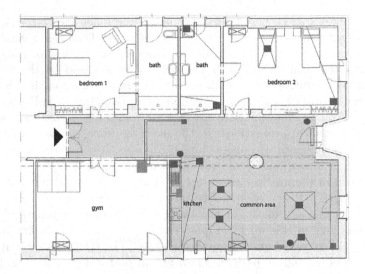

Fig. 1. Apartment plan. Blue rectangles represent the RGB-D sensors, the small red squares correspond to the cameras. Green circles represent the localisation tags, while purple rectangles indicate the Passive Infra-red (PIR) sensors and their field of view (through purple lines). They are all wired to the workstation (green square), placed in the gym. (This figure first appeared in [19]). (Color figure online)

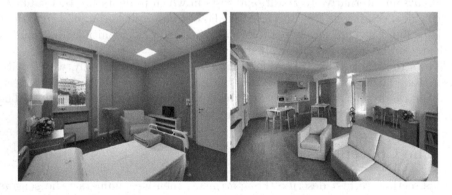

Fig. 2. Left panel shows one of the two bedrooms, right panel shows the common room. (This figure first appeared in [19]).

appropriate colors, arrangements and furniture, leading to an environment more similar to a regular apartment rather than a hospital room.

The common room, where most of the daily activities take place, hosts the majority of the sensors, including cameras and RGB-D sensors, localisation anchors, presence sensors, occupancy sensors for the chairs (pressure sensors), usage sensors on some cabinet door of the kitchenette (luminosity sensors). Health monitoring devices are located on a console table in the same area.

Bedrooms and bathrooms, for obvious privacy concerns, are only equipped with presence sensors, which detect whether there is any movement in the room.

Lastly, presence sensors have also been placed for monitoring specific meaningful disjointed locations, such as: the kitchen table, the desk, the bed and the shower. Similarly, an additional luminosity sensors has been installed to monitor the status of the TV set.

The redundancy of sensors and measures to monitor similar activities is a design choice that guarantee the robustness of the results.

2.1   Vision Sensors

Figure 3 shows the arrangement of visual sensors in the living room of the apartment, highlighting their fields of view and overlaps. The RGB-D sensors are Asus Xtion Pro, acquiring a depth stream with VGA resolution (640 × 480 pixels, at 30 fps). They cover a field of view of about 58° horizontal, 45° vertical and 70° diagonal, with a range of operation between 0.8 m and 3.5 m. The first RGB-D sensor ($RGBD_1$) is located over the kitchen's sink. Its Field Of View (FOV) is highlighted in blue in Fig. 3, right, and it covers all the kitchen and table area, i.e. where patients are supposed to have breakfast, lunch and dinner. The second one ($RGBD_2$) is located near the TV in front of the sofa, its field of view is highlighted in red in Fig. 3 right, and it covers the living room, i.e. the sofa, the armchair, the library, and the area of the vital monitoring devices. The cameras, henceforth referred to as CAM_1 and CAM_2, are high resolution mini-dome IP cameras acquiring 1920 × 1080 pixels frames at 25 fps. They are located in the two opposite corners of the room, indicated in green in Fig. 3 left. The mutual position of RGB-D sensors and cameras is intended to provide a partial overlap of the fields of view while covering complementary areas.

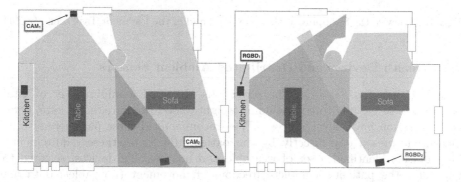

Fig. 3. A sketch of the visual sensors fields of view and their overlap. Left panel shows the field of view of the two cameras, while right panel shows the field of view of the two RGB-D sensors. (This figure first appeared in [19]). (Color figure online)

2.2   VR Based Device for Cognitive Assessment

Each patient is asked to perform a VR game, that runs on a standard tablet and consists of a virtual supermarket with two shelves and a fruit counter as shown in Fig. 4. The patient has to perform two tasks. The first one consists in buying all the items on a shopping list, the items are randomly chosen when the game starts; and the second task consists in paying the exact total amount. We designed the game in order to keep the interface as simple as possible. The patient cannot freely navigate the scene but he/she has to turn the camera toward the selected shelf using the arrows at the bottom of the screen. Only when he/she is in front of the desired shelf, he/she can interact with the items on it, for example by clicking or tapping on one of them a pop-up window with the product name is displayed and the player is asked if he/she wants to add that article to the cart or not. The VR game is developed on a standard tablet, which is used both to display the game itself and to compute some parameters to be used by the doctors to assess the cognitive status (see Sect. 4). In this way, the correctness of the required tasks (i.e. to select the elements starting from a given list, and to pay the correctly amount of money) is evaluated and correlated to the cognitive status of the patient. It is worth noting that this evaluation can be performed by using an ecological task inspired by common actions of every-day life (i.e. going to the supermarket).

Fig. 4. A view of the Shopping Task scene (left) and of the Payment Task scene (right)

2.3   Health Devices and Distributed Ambient Sensors

Health Monitoring Sensors. The physicians identified a minimal set of vital parameters to be monitored, including weight, blood pressure, heart rate, Oxygen saturation SpO2 level, glucose. They recommended these parameters to be measured twice a day directly by the patient. Based on these requirements, bioengineers identified a set of wearable and non-invasive devices, selected to guarantee the patient's complete freedom of movement (no cables, data are transmitted via wireless communication) and to allow for an automatic analysis on the acquired data (this involves the transmission of the collected data to a remote workstation running an appropriate management software). All the equipment is organized on a monitoring console table, to be used by the patients. The available devices are shown in Fig. 5 and they are all provided by iHealth

Labs[2]. This brand was preferred to competitors as all chosen instruments are CE marked medical devices, they are very user-friendly and all acquired raw data are available in .csv and .xls format, ready for further analysis. The collection of all measures is done via bluetooth by an LG G3 smart phone, which sends the data to the RiHealthy platform, which stores the data and also allows physicians and nurses to remotely monitor the parameters.

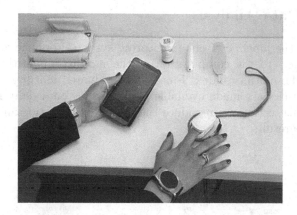

Fig. 5. Vital monitoring devices. From left to right, clockwise: blood pressure monitor, glucometer, oximeter and smart phone

Distributed Sensors. The localization system, Eliko KIO RTLS[3], is a Real Time Locating System (RTLS) based on the Ultra WideBand (UWB) technology, which allows for a positioning precision of about 30 cm. The system is based on the "tag and anchor" paradigm, which assumes the tag to be always attached to the person and the anchors to be in fixed, a-priori known locations in the environment (green dots in Fig. 1). Those sensors allow us to obtain localising information also out from the internal area delimited by the anchors (i.e.: the common area), but with less precision. The (X, Z) position of the tag is then estimated in real-time on the basis of its distance from the anchors. The system allows for a continuous and unambiguous tracking of the monitored person.

The presence sensors, Aeotek MultiSensor 6[4], are devices integrating six channels, among which we are currently exploiting the Passive Infra-Red (PIR) and the light sensors. Those have been placed in different locations (in purple in Fig. 1) and calibrated in such a way to monitor disjoined locations. Particular attention has been posed on the recognition of kitchen activities, with sensors placed in a cabinet of the kitchen and in the tables area, but also close to the sofa, in the bathroom, and in the bedroom.

Chair occupancy sensors, SparkFun Force Sensitive Resistor, detect whether there is a load or not on the chair by monitoring the pressure level measured

---

[2] https://ihealthlabs.com/.
[3] http://www.eliko.ee/products/kio-rtls/.
[4] http://aeotec.com/z-wave-sensor.

below its legs. The detection of the movement and the recognition of gestures performed by the patient can be improved by integrating information obtained from sensors distributed in the environment with measurements obtained by wearable accelerometers. So far, we have adopted a LG G Watch R5 equipped with a triaxial accelerometer.

3   Visual Data Analysis

Figure 6 shows the pipeline of our monitoring system, from the acquisition and processing stages, to the computation of the motility quantities, and to the estimation of the motility index. Finally, all evaluated motility quantities and associated statistics are made available to physicians on a daily report. In the remainder of this section we introduce the dataset, the motion analysis pipeline and discuss the results.

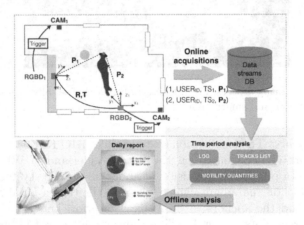

Fig. 6. A visual sketch of the pipeline of our system. Video acquisition is triggered by the RGB-D depth sensors which detect the presence of individuals in the common room. Acquired data are stored online in a Data Base that makes data available for offline analysis. (This figure first appeared in [19]).

3.1   Dataset

The dataset we consider in our experimental analysis is composed of two batches of data acquired with the help of 29 volunteers. The first batch is used for validating the system, the other to assess its performance. All the subjects had not constraints in the apartment, and spontaneously performed common daily-life activities.

The first batch includes 5 young volunteers (3 male and 2 female, mean age 27 ± 4) who spent at least 3 days in the facility, alone or in pairs, for a total of about 123 h of data. The collected data include simpler and more complex scenarios (single or multiple persons in the apartment), and they represent a suitable test-bed for the evaluation of our algorithms. To provide a quantitative evaluation of the proposed methods, we selected 5 sequences from the data set in which a single subject is observed, and we carefully annotated them by exploiting the available video sequences. Our current analysis considers three activities types: *walking, sitting, standing.*

The second batch of data, used to test the performance of the system, consists of 24 elder volunteers (10 male and 14 female, mean age 72.7 ± 5.4) who spent at least 2 h in the facility. For this second set of data, we integrated the dataset of 5 elder subjects presented at [19]. To simplify the experimental procedure, all volunteers are active and healthy aging over 65 years old, with $MPI \leq 0.25$ (MPI ranges from 0 to 1, where higher values corresponds to worst conditions). During their stay, volunteers were first interviewed by geriatricians, who estimated standard frailty tests and computed the Multidimensional Prognostic Index (MPI) [8], Short Physical Performance Battery (SPPB), and the Time Up and Go test (TUG). Then, the volunteers carried out the VR-based cognitive test which will be described in the next section. After that, they spent at most two hours in the facility, free to move, relax, read or watch TV, have a snack or a drink. This second batch of data has been very coarsely annotated. In this case the statistical analysis we performs reason on the correlation between the manual report provided by physicians and the automatic analysis obtained by our data analysis algorithms.

3.2 Localisation

The first task we need to address, prior higher level analysis, is localisation. The goal of localisation is to determine, at each time instant, the position of a person in the apartment. For this task we used the information coming from the RGB-D *depth* sensors providing (X, Y, Z) coordinates of the body joints.

Figure 7 provides an overall visual impression of the localisation obtained by RGB-D sensors installed in the common room, considering measures obtained on a temporal span of 30 min. The figure clearly shows the complexity of the trajectories collected in the environment by the RGB-D sensors. The maps are computed automatically and incorporate information from the two different sensors, one of which is considered as a reference frame (blue dots), while the other is related to the reference frame through a rigid roto-translation transformation which is learnt from data (red dots). As expected (see also Fig. 3 right), there are a few blind spots. This issue will be easily overcome by integrating data from the cameras.

Notice how from a simple analysis of these data it is immediate to identify regions of the common room where the volunteers spend most of the time, e.g. sitting at the bottom-right corner of the table, at the rightmost part of the sofa, or standing at the kitchen.

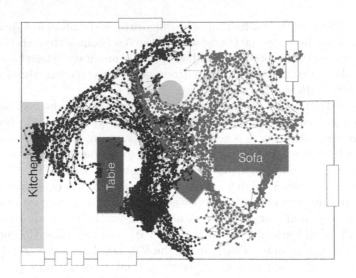

Fig. 7. A visual impression of the trajectories collected in the environment. A volunteer was asked to perform normal daily activities for 30 min (points are color-coded according to the acquisition sensor). (This figure first appeared in [19]). (Color figure online)

3.3 Motility Analysis

In this section we aim at automatically analyse patient's motility and postural transfers.

We first consider a low-level motion feature, i.e., an estimate of instantaneous velocity which we derive directly from localisation measurements. In Fig. 8 we provide an example of a velocity estimation in which a subject has been asked to walk at different speeds. As it can be noticed, the different dynamics are nicely estimated.

At a higher level, we compute the following motility quantities, identified with the help of geriatricians:

- Number of postural changes, i.e. from sitting to standing (TR_{2st}) and vice-versa (TR_{2sit}): this is done by looking at the variation in heights of the detected skeletons (through RGB-Ds) in the scene;
- The total time spent walking (TM), standing still (TS), and sitting (T_{sit}): this is done by checking the variation in the distribution of the velocity modulus;
- Number of instances of walk (W) – i.e. how many times, in a given observation period, people start walking – and stop (S) events;
- Longest walk distance;
- Longest walk time.

Such quantities are empirically estimated according to [20] analysing the instantaneous measures or series of temporally adjacent observations. More specifically we follow an approach based on thresholding the Y coordinate of

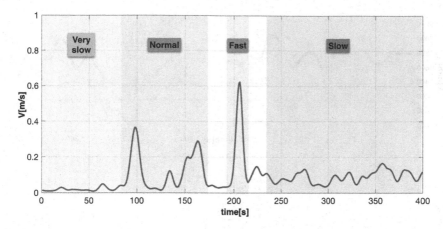

Fig. 8. Estimation of the velocity of a person moving at different speeds. (This figure first appeared in [19]).

the skeleton representation and the velocity (see Fig. 8). Then, some of them are used to compute the motility index which we see as a first quantitative continuous contribution to the frailty index.

Motility Index Estimation. We formalise the estimation of the *motility index* MI on the time period $\mathcal{T}$ as follows

$$MI(\mathcal{T}) = (1 - \alpha)\left(\frac{TM + TS}{TT}\right) + \alpha\left(C\frac{TR_{2sit} + TR_{2st} + W + S}{TT}\right)$$

where the first term quantifies the percentage of activity time, while the second determines the relative amount of postural and dynamic transitions with respect to the entire observation time (TT). The parameter α is a value to be chosen to weight the importance of the two terms of the equation, while C is a factor to make the second term numerically comparable with the first one. The motility index takes values between 0 and 1, approaching 1 when the motility of the subject is satisfactory.

3.4 Results

Tracks Detection and Analysis. A track is a continuous set of temporally adjacent observations where the dynamic and postural state of the user is unaltered. A new track is detected when the user is (re-)entering the scene, his posture is subject to a transition from sitting to standing or vice-versa, or the velocity rapidly grows from zero to a reference value, indicating that an instance of walking is starting, or the opposite.

The motility quantities are evaluated with statistics on the joints observations. More specifically, the estimation of the number of postural changes is based on the analysis of the Y coordinate of the head joint, and its temporal variations.

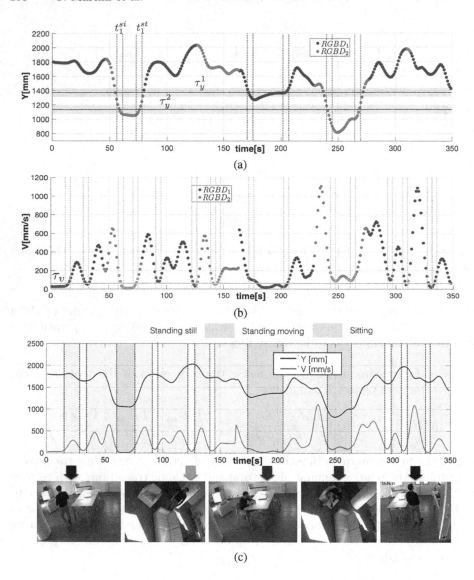

Fig. 9. An example of temporal analysis of the head height (a) and its velocity (b). Posture and velocity changes are detected on them and used to identify tracks (c).

More specifically, we fix a threshold (τ_y) and an interval around it, defining the range of values which identify a transition between sitting and standing posture. It is worth noting that such value strongly depends not only on the height of a person but also on the environmental elements and, from case to case, more than one value may be needed. For instance in our facility, we have to consider the presence of chairs and a sofa, for which the sitting postures are characterized by two different values of Y. For this reason we have two different value of (τ_y)

see Fig. 9(a). Considering the Number of walk and stop events, we aim here at identifying the time instants in which the magnitude of the velocity of the joint goes below or above a certain threshold (τ_v). Figure 9(b) clearly show an example of stop and walk events. When the velocity is below the threshold τ_v we have a stop event, and when it is over the threshold, an instance of walk begin. The plot in Fig. 9(c) reports an example of tracks detected and color-coded according to the reference class. We recognize global motility quantities, as follow:

- Walking is characterized by an high value of Y and V
- Standing still is characterized by an high value of Y but a low value of V
- Sitting is characterized by low value of Y and V.

Motility Index Estimation. Table 1 reports a detailed experimental analysis performed on the 5 fully annotated sequences of young volunteers. All the above mentioned measurements have been assessed – notice how the estimated values are always very close to the ground truth. The table also reports the estimated MI (we set $\alpha = 0.1$). The latter can not be associated with an objective ground truth, but we can comment on the appropriateness of the estimate with respect to a diary of activities maintained by the volunteers. Volunteer #$u2$ spent most of the time sitting (about the 83% of the total time of observation) and this corresponds to a lower value of MI. Conversely, the dynamism of subject #$u4$ is richer (the volunteer spent about the 64% of the total time walking around the apartment), thus the *motility index* is higher.

Table 1. A summary of the quantitative analysis on the motility quantities we performed on the first batch of (annotated) data. When appropriate, we report the ground truth value between brackets. The final column reports the estimates of the motility index.

Seq.	Age	Time [min]	T_{sit} [s]	TS [s]	TM [s]	TR_{2st}	TR_{2sit}	W	S	MI
#u1	23	90	496 (478)	74 (79)	283 (296)	10 (8)	8 (8)	6 (5)	13 (14)	0.433
#u2	22	150	5239 (5260)	752 (755)	1189 (1165)	20 (23)	21 (23)	37 (38)	57 (48)	0.324
#u3	24	120	202 (224)	164 (174)	213 (181)	5 (5)	5 (5)	11 (13)	10 (12)	0.632
#u4	36	30	128 (126)	84 (79)	377 (384)	9 (10)	8 (10)	9 (9)	18 (14)	0.730
#u5	40	30	92 (99)	81 (77)	167 (196)	3 (3)	3 (3)	7 (7)	7 (7)	0.635

On the second batch of data, acquired with the help of 24 over-65 volunteers, our experimental analysis is based on a series of correlation tests between the estimated MI and the indices computed by geriatricians in their standard daily practice. We first identify the set of observations that are above 20 min in duration. The reason for this pre-filtering is motivated by a simple empirical consideration—to behave in a natural way the volunteer needs some time to adjust to the unknown environment. The statistical analysis carried out through the Spearman correlation test highlighted the following results:

- MI and SPPB: Spearman coefficient = 0.85 p-val = 0.09
- MI and hand grip strength: Spearman coefficient = 0.417, p-val = 0.14
- MI and MPI: Spearman coefficient = 0.26 p-val = 0.18

We notice a very high correlation between our motility index and the aggregate measurement SPPB; we also notice a significant correlation with one specific dimension (hand grip strength). We also observe a low correlation with MPI; this is not surprising, as MPI incorporates a wider class of dimensions which are not directly related with motility like the Mini Nutritional Assessment (MNA) and the Cumulative Illness Rating Scale (CIRS).

It is more difficult to assess the reliability of our estimated velocities, as they are computed over a very heterogeneous and highly subjective set of activities, while the ones carried out by physicians are clearly associated with a specific request (e.g., walk along a line from a starting point to an end point). We report a correlation coefficient between the velocity associated with the TUG test and our estimated average velocity of about 0.71, p-val = 0.07.

The obtained results confirm the automatic measurements are meaningful, nicely correlated with medical tests, and can thus be used to assess motility between the sporadic medical evaluations.

4 VR-Based Cognitive Assessment

In order to understand whether the VR game, we have designed, can be successfully used for the *cognitive* assessment of patients, we conducted a set of experiments with a subset of 6 subjects in the second batch of the dataset (ages 72.8 ± 5.8). Before starting the evaluation of cognitive assessment by using the developed system, a doctor filled out the Short Portable Mental Status Questionnaire (SPMQ) questionnaire, and the General Practitioner Cognitive Assessment of Cognition (GPCog). We have used the final scores of SPMQ and GPCog in order to understand whether a useful correlation with the scores provide by our system exists.

The performance of the patients with the proposed VR-based cognitive assessment has been evaluated through several parameters. The ShoppingScore (SS) takes into account the number of the bought items that are (CI) and are not (WI) in the list and also the number of items deleted from the cart (DI). SS can vary between 0 and 10 and it is obtained thanks to the following equation:

$$SS = CI - \alpha * WI - \beta * DI$$

Different weights (α and β) are associated with different errors: if a patient selects an incorrect item it is a mistake, but if he/she realizes it and corrects it he/she will be less penalized. The PaymentScore (PS) is set to 0 if the payed amount is incorrect and 10 if it is correct, otherwise it is computed, taking into account the number of times the patient has reset the total, which is considered an error (E), as:

$$PS = 10 - 0.5 * E$$

In both cases, a low score can be related to an impairment in solving the task, and a high score means that the user completed it easily. Another evaluated parameter is the number of remembered items (RememberedItems): at the end of the game the subject was asked to write down all the items he/she remember he/she had bought. A manual comparison with the correct item list is performed by the physician. Moreover we compute the time to complete the shopping task (ShoppingtTime) and the payments task (PaymentTime).

We then computed the correlation coefficient among the scores computed with the proposed VR game and the two standard test. The GPCog test has an moderate correlation (more than 0.6) with the parameters ShoppingScore, PaymentScore, ShoppingtTime, and an high correlation (more than 0.8) with PaymentTime and RememberedItems.

5 Conclusion and Future Work

In this paper we presented a visual computing approach to estimate the overall well-being of older people. Specifically, the methods presented evaluate motility and the cognitive status of patients. The method is a part of a larger research project whose general goal is to design and implement a model of a protected discharge residence, a smart environment where people may spend a few hours or a day, while a multi-modal sensor network acquires and processes data of their overall well-being. The experimental setup considered in this paper includes visual sensors (cameras and RGBD sensors) and a VR interactive tool. The system continuously assesses patient's motility while medical staff have the opportunity to monitor them remotely. Physicians and nurses can also evaluate patient's cognitive status through manual and virtual reality (VR) based tool.

The system was first quantitatively validated with the help of 5 volunteers and then tested on 24 active and healthy aging over 65 subjects. The results are very encouraging, as they show correlation between the automatic motility evaluation, the VR based assessment of the cognitive status of the patient and the corresponding clinical analysis performed by physicians. These empirical observations encourage us to proceed with our research towards a continuous and automatic evaluation of the patient's health status that may cover, in principle, other aspects—emotion and stress level, socialization predisposition, as well as more complex analysis on the quality of Activity of Daily Living.

References

1. Fried, L.P., Ferrucci, L., Darer, J., Williamson, J.D., Anderson, G.: Untangling the concepts of disability, frailty, and comorbidity: implications for improved targeting and care. J. Gerontol. A Biol. Sci. Med. Sci. **59**(3), M255–M263 (2004)
2. Volpato, S., Daragjati, J., Simonato, M., Fontana, A., Ferrucci, L., Pilotto, A.: Change in the multidimensional prognostic index score during hospitalization in older patients. Rejuvenation Res. **19**(3), 244–251 (2016)

3. Lafont, C., Gérard, S., Voisin, T., Pahor, M., Vellas, B., et al.: Reducing "iatrogenic disability" in the hospitalized frail elderly. J. Nutr. Health Aging 15(8), 645–660 (2011)
4. Volpato, S., et al.: Italian Group of Pharmacoepidemiology in the Elderly Study (GIFA) Characteristics of nondisabled older patients developing new disability associated with medical illnesses and hospitalization. J. Gen. Intern. Med. 22(5), 668–674 (2007)
5. Lenzi, J., et al.: Sociodemographic, clinical and organisational factors associated with delayed hospital discharges: a cross-sectional study. BMC Health Serv. Res. 14, 128 (2014)
6. Fried, L.P., et al.: Frailty in older adults: evidence for a phenotype. J. Gerontol. A Biol. Sci. Med. Sci. 56, M146–M157 (2001)
7. Dent, E., Kowal, P., Hoogendijk, E.O.: Frailty measurement in research and clinical practice: a review. Eur. J. Intern. Med. 31, 3–10 (2016)
8. Pilotto, A., et al.: Development and validation of a multidimensional prognostic index for one-year mortality from comprehensive geriatric assessment in hospitalized older patients. Rejuvenation Res. 11, 151–161 (2008)
9. Volpato, S., Bazzano, S., Fontana, A., Ferrucci, L., Pilotto, A.: Multidimensional prognostic index predicts mortality and length of stay during hospitalization in the older patients: a multicenter prospective study. J. Gerontol. A: Biomed. Sci. Med. Sci. 70(3), 325–331 (2014)
10. Angleman, S.B., Santoni, G., Pilotto, A., Fratiglioni, L., Welmer, A.-K.: MPI_AGE Project Investigators, et al. Multidimensional prognostic index in association with future mortality and number of hospital days in a population-based sample of older adults: results of the EU funded MPI_AGE project. PloS One 10(7), e0133789 (2015)
11. Warnier, R.M.J., Van Rossum, E., Van Velthuijsen, E., Mulder, W.J., Schols, J.M.G.A., Kempen, G.I.J.M.: Validity, reliability and feasibility of tools to identify frail older patients in inpatient hospital care: a systematic review. J. Nutr. Health Aging 20(2), 218–230 (2016)
12. Martini, C., Barla, A., Odone, F.O., Verri, A., Rollandi, G.A., Pilotto, A.: Data-driven continuous assessment of frailty in older people. Front. Digital Humanit. 5, 6 (2018)
13. Cao, Y., Tao, L., Xu, G.: An event-driven context model in elderly health monitoring. In: 2009 Symposia and Workshops on Ubiquitous, Autonomic and Trusted Computing. UIC-ATC 2009, pp. 120–124. IEEE (2009)
14. Zouba, N., Bremond, F., Thonnat, M.: An activity monitoring system for real elderly at home: validation study. In: 2010 Seventh IEEE International Conference on Advanced Video and Signal Based Surveillance (AVSS), pp. 278–285. IEEE (2010)
15. Liu, R., Liu, M.: Recognizing human activities based on multi-sensors fusion. In: 2010 4th International Conference on Bioinformatics and Biomedical Engineering (iCBBE), pp. 1–4. IEEE (2010)
16. Bathrinarayanan, V., et al.: Evaluation of a monitoring system for event recognition of older people. In: 2013 10th IEEE International Conference on Advanced Video and Signal Based Surveillance (AVSS), pp. 165–170 (2013)
17. Scanaill, C.N., Carew, S., Barralon, P., Noury, N., Lyons, D., Lyons, G.M.: A review of approaches to mobility telemonitoring of the elderly in their living environment. Ann. Biomed. Eng. 34(4), 547–563 (2006)

18. Spooner, D.M., Pachan, N.A.: Ecological validity in neuropsychological assessment: a case for greater consideration in research with neurologically intact populations. Arch. Clin. Neuropsychol. **21**(4), 327–337 (2006)
19. Martini, C., et al.: La visual computing approach for estimating the motility index in the frail elder. In: 13th International Joint Conference on Computer Vision, Imaging and Computer Graphics Theory and Applications (2018)
20. Chessa, M., Noceti, N., Martini, C., Solari, F., Odone, F.: Design of assistive tools for the market. In: Leo, M., Farinella, G.M. (eds) Assistive Computer Vision. Elsevier (2017)

Pedestrian Detection and Trajectory Estimation in the Compressed Domain Using Thermal Images

Ichraf Lahouli[1,2,3]($\boxtimes$), Zied Chtourou[2], Mohamed Ali Ben Ayed[4], Robby Haelterman[1], Geert De Cubber[1], and Rabah Attia[3]

[1] Royal Military Academy, Brussels, Belgium
`ichraf.lahouli@rma.ac.be`
[2] VRIT Lab, Military Academy of Tunisia, Nabeul, Tunisia
[3] SERCOM Lab, Tunisia Polytechnic School, La Marsa, Tunisia
[4] High Institute of Electronics and Communication, University of Sfax, Sfax, Tunisia

Abstract. Since a few decades, the Unmanned Aerial Vehicles (UAVs) are considered precious tools for different military applications such as the automatic surveillance in outdoor environments. Nevertheless, the onboard implementation of image and video processing techniques poses many challenges like the high computational cost and the high bandwidth requirements, especially on low-performance processing platforms like small or medium UAVs. A fast and efficient framework for pedestrian detection and trajectory estimation for outdoor surveillance using thermal images is presented in this paper. First, the detection process is based on a conjunction between contrast enhancement techniques and saliency maps as a hotspot detector, on Discrete Chebychev Moments (DCM) as a global image content descriptor and on a linear Support Vector Machine (SVM) as a classifier. Second, raw H.264/AVC compressed video streams with limited computational overhead are exploited to estimate the trajectories of the detected pedestrians. In order to simulate suspicious events, six different scenarios were carried out and filmed using a thermal camera. The obtained results show the effectiveness and the low computational requirements of the proposed framework which make it suitable for real-time applications and onboard implementation.

1 Introduction

Thermal imagery is widely used for pedestrian detection and tracking especially in driver assistance and surveillance applications. Indeed, thermal images are considered a powerful tool despite the lack of color and texture information because they allow working on both day and night-time. For decades, video surveillance has mainly been ensured by stationary cameras and powerful back-end computers on which the heavy processing is done. Recently, UAVs have started to be used for surveillance applications due to their mobility and their ability to stream videos captured by optical or thermal sensors in real time. However, the amount of information transmitted to the ground is huge causing more

© Springer Nature Switzerland AG 2019
D. Bechmann et al. (Eds.): VISIGRAPP 2018, CCIS 997, pp. 212–227, 2019.
https://doi.org/10.1007/978-3-030-26756-8_10

power consumption which affects the mission duration and also causing problems with analysis and storage mostly because of unimportant and redundant information.

This paper proposes a fast and efficient framework to detect and estimate the trajectories of the pedestrians in thermal images with a low computational cost for automatic surveillance purposes. The ROI detection process is based on saliency maps in conjunction with a contrast enhancement technique as a first step to extract Regions Of Interest (ROI)s. Then, a global image content descriptor based on the Discrete Chebychev Moments (DCMs) [1] is used. Finally, a linear SVM is applied to distinguish between pedestrians and non-pedestrians. In order to evaluate the proposed ROI detector, two public thermal pedestrian datasets were used: the OTCBVS benchmark -OSU Thermal Pedestrian Database [2] and the thermal videos of the LITIV2012 dataset [3]. The choice is driven by the fact that the humans are taken from a relatively high altitude which can simulate images taken from a low altitude UAV. The performance of the proposed ROI detector is compared to the Maximally Stable Extremal Regions (MSER) detector [4] in terms of true and false positives rates and calculation time. MSER is a fast and widely used region based detector, introduced in 2004 but still up to date and used in recent works like in [5–13]. The popularity of MSER is due to its low complexity and its efficiency to extract salient regions which makes it adequate for real-time applications and low-cost embedded systems. The obtained results of comparison between MSER and the proposed ROI detector prove the robustness of the proposed method in terms of true detection rate and its superiority in terms of reducing false alarms and processing time. Furthermore, in order to simulate suspicious events in an outdoor surveillance context, we have generated our own dataset by carrying out six different scenarios and recorded videos using a thermal camera. The trajectory estimation process is based on the MPEG Motion Vectors (MVs) corresponding to the extracted ROIs. In fact, the algorithm keeps tracking these ROIs through time by computing their intermediate estimated positions. However, the codec H.264/AVC generates some estimation errors which can not be avoided. Consequently, we can not rely exclusively on the MPEG MVs. In order to compensate for these errors, each time that the codec updates its reference frame, the proposed ROI detector is launched to update the positions of the ROIs and correct the small drifts. The proposed framework does not need frame by frame, either pixel by pixel processing like in [14]. It relies on some frames for the ROI detection and on some MVs already computed for trajectory estimation, which makes it suitable for real-time applications with low-end computational platforms.

The paper is organized as follows: In Sect. 2 we review the related state of the art works in motion-based segmentation and tracking. In Sect. 3, we explain the proposed framework in detail, composed of the ROI detector and the ROI trajectory estimation and briefly explain the utility of the video compression. Section 4 is dedicated to the experiments and the obtained results: First, we present the different datasets. Then, the effectiveness of the proposed framework is shown by presenting the results of comparison between the proposed detector and MSER and by the performance of the trajectory estimation process. Finally, Sect. 5 summarizes the present work and exposes some perspectives for the future steps.

2   Related Works

The motion-based detection and trajectory estimation research works mainly use Optical Flow (OF) and local feature descriptors such as SIFT [15] or SURF [16] like in [5,17,18]. Improved trajectories for action recognition were used by Wang and Schmid in [19]. Camera motion was estimated by matching feature points using dense OF and SURF descriptors and then compensated. In [20], Wu et al. used OF to compute the dense particle trajectories of the objects and then proposed an optimisation method to distinguish between the trajectories due to the camera motion and those of moving objects. Nevertheless, OF, whether sparse or dense, is time-consuming and computationally heavy which limits its applicability for real-time applications and challenges the mission autonomy (duration of the UAV flight). Some researchers exploited the use of MPEG MVs as an alternative to OF for tracking, trajectory estimation and action recognition. In 2003, Park et al. proposed a tracking scheme of an object in the MPEG compressed domain [21]. They used a generalised Hough transform to estimate the camera motion and then tracked the centre of the ROI based on the spatial distribution of colours. In 2004, Babu et al. used MVs of compressed MPEG video for segmentation [22] then proposed MPEG MV based features along with a Hidden Markov Model (HMM) and motion history information for action recognition [23]. In 2006, Yeo et al. captured the salient features of actions which have independent appearances based on MV information. Then, they computed frame-to-frame motion similarity based on both MV's orientation and magnitude [24]. Aggarwal et al. presented a scheme for object tracking using motion estimation in MPEG videos and background subtraction [25]. However, their method is mainly concerned with stationary cameras, which makes it not suitable for a moving camera onboard a UAV. The second drawback is that the selection of the targets is not automatic but selected by the user manually. In 2013, Biswas et al. captured the orientation information from the motion vectors to classify H.264/AVC compressed videos [26]. Histogram of Oriented Motion Vectors (HOMV) was computed as the motion characteristics of space-time cubes which partially overlap. Then, they used Bag of Features approach (BOF) for classification. Käs and Nicolas presented an approach to trajectory estimation of moving objects using the H.264/AVC MVs [27]. Their method consists on performing a Global Motion Estimation (GME) based on the MVs extracted from the compressed stream. The generated outlier masks are the input for an object detection stage, followed by an object matching stage in order to estimate the trajectories in the scene. However, the main drawback of their method is that it can not deal with non-moving people since the first step of their flowchart is the GME.

In 2014, Kantorov et al. focused on activity recognition using MPEG MVs. They computed Histograms of Optical Flow (HOF) and Motion Boundary Histograms (MBH) using the MPEG MVs as local descriptors and Support Vector Machine (SVM) for classification [28]. A comparison with the OF showed that the use of MPEG MVs leads to a significant computational speedup ($\simeq$66%) with a small reduction of recognition accuracy. More recently, Zhang et al. proposed a real-time action recognition method using MVs extracted directly from the decoded video stream as an alternative to the OF. In order to boost the recognition performance, they adapted the models of OF Convolutional Neural Network (CNN) to MV CNN [29]. Poularakis et al. proposed a motion-based method for fast recognition of activities of daily living. They replaced OF calculation with block matching randomly initialized or based on the pre-computed MPEG MV [30]. The processing is limited to the data within the Motion Boundary Activity Area (MBAA) [31]. In other words, the full video decoding is not necessary. These works are mostly dedicated to activity recognition by describing short actions and not to tracking people in long videos. In addition, none of them worked with thermal images.

In this paper, we consider the detection and the trajectory estimation of the pedestrians in UAV videos taken by a thermal camera for day and night surveillance applications. Our main focus is the efficiency and the reduction of the computational cost in order to present an approach suitable for low-performance processing algorithms and real-time applications.

3   Proposed Methodology

The proposed framework can mainly be split into two different algorithms: the ROI detector and the ROI trajectory estimation process. The first algorithm is a human detector that determines the pedestrians in the scene. It is based on a conjunction between saliency maps and contrast enhancement techniques, while the DCMs are used as a global image content descriptor and a linear SVM is used as a classifier. The second algorithm aims to extract the MVs of the ROIs, drawn directly from the MPEG compressed video. The aforementioned algorithms are combined to offer an efficient framework for pedestrian detection and tracking with low computational cost. It can be integrated within an H.264/AVC codec as it relies on the intermediary data that is used to produce the output stream. We will consecutively present the two algorithms in detail in the following paragraphs.

3.1   Proposed ROI Detector

Once we plan to work on outdoor scenes, pedestrians could be considered as Hot Spots assuming that they are brighter than their background. We detect ROIs taking into account certain restrictions regarding brightness and target size. The pedestrian detection part is composed of the following three steps:

1. ROI extraction: A fusion between a saliency map (produced on the basis of Lab colour space) [32] and a wavelet-based contrast enhancement technique [33],
2. Shape description: A global region content descriptor based on the DCMs [1] up to order $4*4$,
3. Classification: SVM in order to distinguish between human and non-human hotspots.

Initially, a Gaussian filter is applied to the input image. The resulting output is fed to the saliency map module and to the contrast enhancement module. Then, the two outputs are normalized and fused together using the geometric mean. Finally, the result is converted into a binary image by keeping only hot spot areas, which are further filtered using a size threshold to discard very small/large ROIs.

In this work, the saliency-based map is created fast enough and successfully highlights the included hot spots. The proposed method is kept intentionally simple enough in order to combine efficiency and calculation speed. We further enhance the results of the saliency map by fusing its output with a contrast-enhanced image. Another advantage of the proposed method for ROI selection is that it darkens the surrounding background of hot spots and at the same time highlights them, perfectly preserving their shape. This is very important, since, the shape of objects is used by the Discrete Chebyshev Moment-based descriptor in order to further recognize human objects using a linear SVM. In Subsect. 4.3, we will present the results obtained after applying this algorithm to the OSU Thermal Pedestrian Database [2] and the LITIV2012 dataset [3]. More details and results could be found in [34].

3.2 Proposed Trajectory Estimation Process Using MPEG MVs

The algorithms of ROI detection and MPEG MV extraction are combined together to detect pedestrians in thermal images, estimate their trajectories while ensuring a low computational overhead.

Video Compression. A brief explanation of how the video compression standards work is needed. The video compression has as purpose to reduce the bits required to store and transmit a video stream while ensuring a certain quality. Mainly an MPEG video can be seen as a sequence of frames. Two successive frames often have small differences (except in scene changes). Indeed, the background is still almost the same. Only the foreground objects or precisely the moving objects show the difference between these frames. The similarities are present in both temporal and spatial directions. Spatial redundancy is compensated by the use of the Discrete Cosine Transform (DCT), while the temporal redundancy is compensated by the block matching method. Only the parts of the image that do change significantly are coded/predicted and the rest is simply copied from some "'reference'" frames.

It is important to mention that the MPEG image/video coding techniques are not pixel-level techniques but employ what is called a macroblock (MB).

It is a block of pixels usually 8 * 8 or 16 * 16 pixels on which they apply the DCT to code the intensity information. MBs are also used to generate the motion information by computing the displacements between them in two consecutive frames. In other words, the MPEG stream simultaneously carries the intensity and motion information. Motion information is represented by the motion vectors (MV)s which correspond to the displacements of the MBs and the intensity is represented by a set of DCT coefficients.

One of the most famous and widely used video compression standards is the H.264/AVC or commonly called MPEG-4. It aims to reduce the spatial and temporal redundancy by using three types of frames:

- I-frame: or "'key-frames'". They have no reference to other frames. They are also called the reference frames. They are not highly compressed. Only an Intra correlation is computed to remove the spatial redundancy.
- P-frame: Predicted Frames. They can be predicted from an earlier I-frame or P-frame. P-frames cannot be reconstructed without their referencing frame. Only the differences are stored so they need less space than the I-frames.
- B-frame: Bi-directional Predicted Frames. They are a two-directional version of the P-frame, referring to both directions (one forward frame and one backward frame).

An I-frame is sent whenever there is a scene change, so the reference frame must be updated in order to allow the decoder to restore the background. In addition, the I-frame is sent in a cyclic way even if there is no scene change. This periodicity parameter is called the Group Of Pictures (GOP). Usually it is set to 16 and 32 frames. The order of transmitting the I, P and B frames in the compressed video stream might differ but always start with an I-frame and ends also with an I-frame.

Proposed Algorithm for Trajectory Estimation. Initially, the first I-frame is selected as an input image (I-$Frame_{init}$). The detection algorithm is applied to extract the ROIs (pedestrians) in this initial frame. The resulting outputs are fed to the MPEG MV extractor module which extracts the MPEG MVs corresponding to the initial ROIs' bounding boxes. Actually, it starts by finding the MBs that cover each ROI (MB's size is 16 * 16 pixels in our case). Then, the algorithm keeps tracking these MBs by extracting their relative MPEG MVs and computing the intermediate estimated positions until a new I-frame is detected by the decoder.

Driven by the fact that MVs are already computed as an integral part of the H.264/AVC codec, the computational cost is reduced considerably compared to any approach that relies on a frame by frame process. Indeed, we do not require the image processing techniques (contrast enhancement + saliency map) to detect the pedestrians in all the P- and B-frames. However, we cannot rely exclusively on the MPEG MVs due to the errors generated by the estimation steps in the H.264/AVC video coding standard. The proposed solution is to call the aforementioned ROI detector at a certain rate in order to compensate these errors before pursuing the tracking.

The main difference between this work and our previous work presented in [35] is that an adaptive approach to recall the ROI detector was introduced in order to further reduce the computational cost of the proposed framework. Indeed, what has been changed is the way we call the detection process to update the ROIs positions. Before, it was called at a re-detection rate that we computed somehow empirically. In this paper, the call of the detection process is synchronized with the H.264/AVC codec. Each time an I-frame is detected, the ROI detection process is launched which leads to more robustness and less computational overhead.

4   Experiments and Results

4.1   Presentation of the Different Datasets

In order to validate the proposed ROI detector, we used two different public datasets in an outdoor urban environment. Firstly, the OSU Thermal Pedestrian Database [2], acquired by the Raytheon 300D thermal sensor. It is composed of 10 test collections with a total of 284 frames taken within one minute but not temporally uniformly sampled. The OSU thermal dataset covers a panoply of environmental conditions such as sunny, rainy and cloudy days. Secondly, the nine thermal sequences were taken from the LITIV2012 dataset [3]. Actually, the dataset is composed of nine pairs of visual/thermal sequences.

The public datasets, used to validate the proposed ROI detector, are collections of frames that are not temporally uniformly sampled and don't provide H.264 encoding data which make these datasets not adequate to validate the proposed ROI tracker. In addition, they present pedestrians walking 'normally' in the street. However, our main purpose is to detect suspicious events of pedestrians taken from a thermal sensor on-board of an aerial platform and thus based on the analysis of their trajectories and velocities. Therefore, we have generated our own dataset by carrying out some specific scenarios of suspicious events in an outdoor environment. Video sequences were shot using an MPEG thermal camera.

The different scenarios of abnormal events could be described as follow:

1. *Brutal Turn Back*: two people move slowly in one direction simulating two policemen. A suspicious person walks in the opposite direction and will quickly turn back as soon as he sees them.
2. *Convergence/Divergence*: three people converge at a specific point. They quickly exchange a suspicious object and then diverge and quit the scene.
3. *Velocity Changes*: one person alternates between walking and running.
4. *Occlusion/Non-occlusion*: one person tries to hide behind a car.
5. *Circular Trajectory*: one person moves around a car while focusing on it as if he has some robbery intention.
6. *Rapid Dump of Suspicious Object*: one person is walking and carrying a backpack. When he reached a specific vehicle, he quickly throws his backpack down and continues walking.

The thermal videos were shot using a stationary camera from a relatively high altitude (to simulate an oblique view of a UAV) with a frame rate of 25 frames per second (fps) and an image resolution of 576 * 704 pixels.

4.2 Synchronization Between the ROI-Detection Process and the I-Frame Update

Like mentioned before, in our previous work in [35], the ROI detector was launched at a specific re-detection rate N to avoid the propagation of the estimation errors caused by the extracted MPEG MVs. Choosing this rate was a trade-off between guaranteeing good tracking accuracy and keeping low computational requirements. This parameter was set empirically after some tests and was equal to the fps of the video (25). In this paper, we decided to propose an adaptive way to set the re-detection rate. We found out that the logical idea is to synchronise the call of the ROI detector with the update of the reference frame by the codec. The codec efficiently knows when there is a need to resend an I-frame.

The remainder of this section is organized as follows. We will present the performance of the proposed ROI detector including the results of the comparison between the proposed ROI extractor and MSER. After that, we will present some results of the proposed ROI trajectory estimation process using examples that illustrate how the trajectories are computed and how the positions are estimated.

4.3 Results of the Proposed ROI Detector

Figure 1 illustrates the outputs of the different modules that compose the proposed ROI detector including SVM. The input is an image from the LITIV2012 dataset. Figure 1(a) presents the corresponding saliency map and Fig. 1(b) the result of the contrast enhancement technique. These two outputs are combined together based on their geometric mean to obtain Fig. 1(c). At this step, a brightness threshold is applied to obtain the binary image Fig. 1(d) where the Hot Spots are highlighted. After applying a size filter to discard very small/large areas, ROIs are extracted like shown Fig. 1(e). The green bounding boxes correspond to the ground truth presented within the dataset. The blue bounding boxes correspond to the true positives while the red ones clearly represent the false positives. The DCMs of the detected ROIs are computed as features vectors and fed to the SVM classifier. Figure 1(f) shows how the SVM kept only the true positives.

First, we begin by validating the proposed ROI extractor by comparing its performance to the one of the MSER detector [4] which is a fast and widely used region based detector. The implementation is done in Matlab. Thus, we used the *DetectMSERFeatures* function available within the *Computer Vision System Toolbox*. For a reliable comparison, we kept the same set of parameters as for the proposed ROI extractor. The obtained results, shown in Table 1, prove its robustness in terms of true detection with approximately 96% for the OSU Thermal Pedestrian Database and 95% for the LITIV2012 dataset. Furthermore, the proposed ROI extractor presents the advantage of reducing the number of false alarms compared to the MSER detector which is a significant gain and a relevant criterion for surveillance purposes. In addition, it runs about two to three times faster. At this point, the proposed method has not yet been computationally optimized, which means that further gains are possible if it is tweaked accordingly. These two improvements are very important regarding the final purpose which is a real-time implementation on a low-performance processing platform. The UAV should select and then send only pertinent information to the central control station, that does require human attention.

Table 1. Proposed ROI extractor vs MSER.

Criterion	Proposed ROI extractor	MSER
OSU thermal		
True detection rate	96.93%	**96.04%**
False alarms rate	**35.14%**	59.33%
CPU-time per image	**0.17 s**	0.46 s
LITIV2012		
True detection rate	**95.13%**	85.28%
False alarms rate	**26.25%**	39.76%
CPU-time per image	**0.098 s**	0.151 s

Once the ROIs are extracted, we resize all of them at their mean size. Then they are described using DCMs up to order $4*4$ in order to obtain a feature vector of 25 elements for each sample. Half of the feature vectors are assigned for training and the second half for testing the performance of the classifier. Using the OSU Thermal Pedestrian Database, we obtained 851 human samples and 491 non human samples. We used different kernels of SVM and we found out that the results are quite similar so we keep using a linear SVM. The maximum percentage of true positives is 88%. Concerning the true negatives, all the kernels present rates approaching 100% but this is explainable due to their small number and nature as they are static objects such as a public lighting pole or parked cars. Using the thermal videos from the LITIV2012 dataset, we obtained 6237 human samples and 9997 non human samples. The increased number of samples leads to a better training and thus better classification. For all the kernels, SVM gives a quite similar true positives rate approaching 98%. More results can be found in [34].

Figure 2 illustrates the difference between the outputs of MSER and the proposed ROI detector. It is shown how the number of false alarms is reduced using the proposed method while keeping a good true detection rate [35].

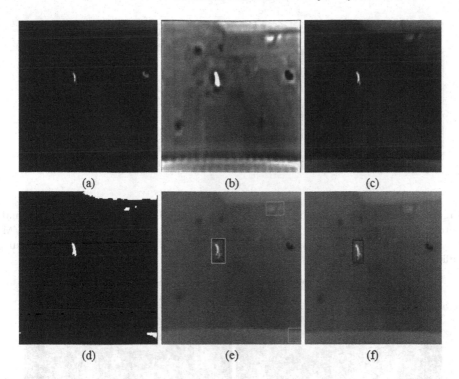

Fig. 1. Examples of the different outputs of the proposed ROI detector (LITIV2012 dataset) [35]. (a): Saliency Map (b): Contrast Enhancement (c): geometric mean of SM & CE (d): Binary image (e): Proposed ROI extractor (f): SVM (*green*: Ground Truth ROIs. *blue*: true detections, *red*: false positives). (Color figure online)

4.4   Results of the Proposed ROI Trajectory Estimation Process

First of all, we will present how the algorithm of ROI detection and MEPG MV extraction work. Thus, we start by showing in Fig. 3 the estimated trajectories of the different ROIs between two re-detection times (I-$Frame_{init}$ & I-$Frame_{second}$). The Fig. 3(a) shows how the ROI detection algorithm is able to detect the three pedestrians and trace their bounding boxes around them (blue) while the Fig. 3(b) shows the ROIs detected at I-$Frame_{second}$ (green). The blue boxes define the initial positions for the rest of the framework. The MBs (here blocs of 16 * 16 pixels) that cover each ROI are determined, then their relative MPEG MVs are extracted. After that, we follow these MBs through time during one cycle (or until a scene change occurs) in order to construct the estimated trajectory for each one of them. The estimated positions are then computed based only on the resulting MPEG MVs. Figure 3(c) presents how the proposed algorithm traces the different estimated trajectories of each ROI, by connecting the intermediate positions and traces the final estimated trajectories. At this stage, the ROI re-detection process is called in order to avoid the propagation

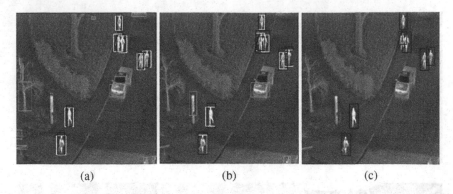

     (a)   (b)   (c)

Fig. 2. Example of different outputs from the ROI detector (OSU thermal database) [35]. (a): MSER detector (b): Proposed ROI extractor (c): SVM (*green*: Ground Truth ROIs, *blue*: true detections, *red*: false positives). (Color figure online)

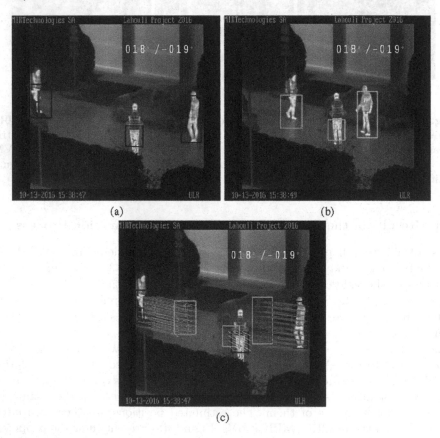

Fig. 3. ROI detection and trajectory estimation between **two** successive I-Frames. (a): ROI detection results at I-$Frame_{init}$. (b): ROI detection results at I-$Frame_{second}$. (c): Trajectory estimation between I-$Frame_{init}$ and I-$Frame_{second}$. (Color figure online)

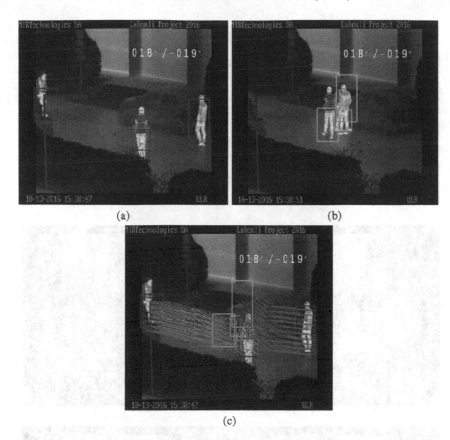

(a)   (b)

(c)

Fig. 4. ROI detection and trajectory estimation between **three** successive I-Frames. (a): ROI detection results at I-$Frame_{init}$. (b): ROI detection results at I-$Frame_{third}$. (c): Trajectory estimation between I-$Frame_{init}$ and I-$Frame_{third}$. (Color figure online)

of the estimation errors in the rest of the framework. Indeed, the final estimated position at I-$Frame_{second}$ is updated by the real position obtained by the ROI detection algorithm.

Figure 4 is similar to what is presented in Fig. 3 but this time we keep tracking the MBs until a third I-frame is detected (I-$Frame_{third}$). Despite the unavoidable estimation errors generated by the codec, Fig. 4(c) shows how the proposed framework was able to track the pedestrians after two cycles of I-frame updates in a quite complicate scenario of convergence where we could see the occlusion between the ROIs.

In Fig. 5, we tried to show in a clearer sub-figures how each ROI is detected and tracked after respectively one and two updates of the I-frame. It shows the effectiveness of the proposed framework to predict the trajectories of three different people in the convergence scenario. Blue boxes always represent the output of the ROI extractor at the initial I-$Frameinit$. Red lines present the

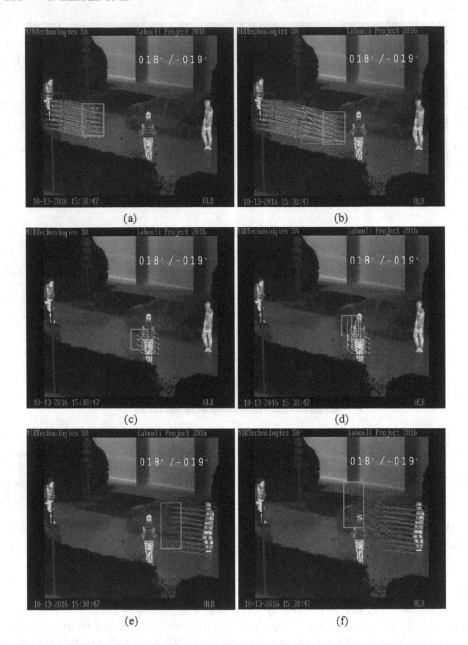

(a)   (b)

(c)   (d)

(e)   (f)

Fig. 5. Example of trajectory estimation for each ROI. (a): Estimated trajectories of ROI_1 between I-$Frame_{init}$ and I-$Frame_{second}$. (b): Estimated trajectories of ROI_1 between I-$Frame_{init}$ and I-$Frame_{third}$. (c): Estimated trajectories of ROI_2 between I-$Frame_{init}$ and I-$Frame_{second}$. (d): Estimated trajectories of ROI_2 between I-$Frame_{init}$ and I-$Frame_{third}$. (e): Estimated trajectories of ROI_3 between I-$Frame_{init}$ and I-$Frame_{second}$. (f): Estimated trajectories of ROI_3 between I-$Frame_{init}$ and I-$Frame_{third}$. (Color figure online)

estimated trajectories of each MB. The green boxes are the output of the ROI extractor at respectively the I-$Frame_{second}$ and the I-$Frame_{third}$. It shows how the framework is able to detect the trajectories of the three people.

5   Conclusion and Future Works

This paper proposed an efficient framework for pedestrian detection and trajectory estimation in thermal images. An adaptive approach to recall the ROI detector module was introduced by the synchronization with the H.264/AVC codec. Indeed, each time an I-frame is detected, the ROI detector is relaunched to adjust the positions of the pedestrians in the scene and to compensate the estimation errors. Due to its efficiency and its low computational requirements, the proposed approach is properly amenable for integration into real-time applications and is suitable for automatic surveillance purposes like the detection of suspicious behaviour based on trajectory analysis. In the future, we will aim to extract not only trajectories but velocity and acceleration information from MPEG MVs. The combination of these features would lead to a robust framework for action recognition and suspicious event detection.

References

1. Karakasis, E., Bampis, L., Amanatiadis, A., Gasteratos, A., Tsalides, P.: Digital elevation model fusion using spectral methods. In: 2014 IEEE International Conference on Imaging Systems and Techniques (IST) Proceedings, pp. 340–345. IEEE (2014)
2. Davis, J.W., Keck, M.A.: A two-stage template approach to person detection in thermal imagery. In: Seventh IEEE Workshops on Application of Computer Vision, 2005, WACV/MOTIONS 2005, vol. 1, pp. 364–369, January 2005
3. Torabi, A., Massé, G., Bilodeau, G.-A.: An iterative integrated framework for thermal-visible image registration, sensor fusion, and people tracking for video surveillance applications. Comput. Vis. Image Underst. **116**, 210–221 (2012)
4. Matas, J., Chum, O., Urban, M., Pajdla, T.: Robust wide-baseline stereo from maximally stable extremal regions (MSER). Image Vis. Comput. **22**(10), 761–767 (2004)
5. Tun, W.N., Tyan, M., Kim, S., Nah, S.-H., Lee, J.-W.: Marker tracking with AR.Drone for visual-based navigation using SURF and MSER algorithms. In: Korean Society for Aeronautical & Space Sciences Conference, pp. 124–125 (2017)
6. Sun, X., Ding, J., Dalla Chiara, G., Cheah, L., Cheung, N.-M.: A generic framework for monitoring local freight traffic movements using computer vision-based techniques. In: 2017 5th IEEE International Conference on Models and Technologies for Intelligent Transportation Systems (MT-ITS), pp. 63–68. IEEE (2017)
7. Kumar, A., Gupta, S.: Detection and recognition of text from image using contrast and edge enhanced MSER segmentation and OCR. IJOSCIENCE (Int. J. Online Sci.) **3**(3), 07 (2017)
8. Khosravi, M., Hassanpour, H.: A novel image structural similarity index considering image content detectability using maximally stable extremal region descriptor. Int. J. Eng. Trans. B Appl. **30**(2), 172 (2017)

9. Alyammahi, S.M.R., Salahat, E.N., Saleh, H.H.M., Sluzek, A.S., Elnaggar, M.I.: Hardware architecture for linear-time extraction of maximally stable extremal regions (MSERs), 22 August 2017. US Patent 9,740,947

10. Śluzek, A.: MSER and SIMSER regions: a link between local features and image segmentation. In: Proceedings of the 2017 International Conference on Computer Graphics and Digital Image Processing, p. 15. ACM (2017)

11. Lu, T., Liu, R.: Detecting text in natural scenes with multi-level MSER and SWT. In: Ninth International Conference on Graphic and Image Processing (ICGIP 2017), vol. 10615, p. 106150G. International Society for Optics and Photonics (2018)

12. Zhang, X., Gao, X., Tian, C.: Text detection in natural scene images basedon color prior guided MSER. Neurocomputing **307**, 61–71 (2018)

13. Karim, S., Halepoto, I.A., Manzoor, A., Phulpoto, N.H., Laghari, A.A.: Vehicle detection in satellite imagery using maximally stable extremal regions. IJCSNS **18**(4), 75 (2018)

14. Ma, Y., Wu, X., Yu, G., Xu, Y., Wang, Y.: Pedestrian detection and tracking from low-resolution unmanned aerial vehicle thermal imagery. Sensors **16**(4), 446 (2016)

15. Uemura, H., Ishikawa, S., Mikolajczyk, K.: Feature tracking and motion compensation for action recognition. In: BMVC, pp. 1–10 (2008)

16. Bay, H., Ess, A., Tuytelaars, T., Van Gool, L.: Speeded-up robust features (SURF). Comput. Vis. Image Underst. **110**(3), 346–359 (2008)

17. Zhang, S., Zhang, L., Gao, R., Liu, C.: Mobile robot moving target detection and tracking system. In: Proceedings of the 2017 The 7th International Conference on Computer Engineering and Networks CENet2017), 22–23 July 2017, Shanghai, China (2017)

18. Sundari, V.K., Manikandan, M.: Real time implementation of surf based target tracking algorithm. Int. J. Intell. Electron. Syst. 11(1) (2017)

19. Wang, H., Schmid, C.: Action recognition with improved trajectories. In: Proceedings of the IEEE International Conference on Computer Vision, pp. 3551–3558 (2013)

20. Wu, S., Oreifej, O., Shah, M.: Action recognition in videos acquired by a moving camera using motion decomposition of lagrangian particle trajectories. In: 2011 IEEE International Conference on Computer Vision (ICCV), pp. 1419–1426. IEEE (2011)

21. Park, S.-M., Lee, J.: Object tracking in MPEG compressed video using mean-shift algorithm. In: Proceedings of the 2003 Joint Conference of the Fourth International Conference on Information, Communications and Signal Processing, 2003 and Fourth Pacific Rim Conference on Multimedia, vol. 2, pp. 748–752. IEEE (2003)

22. Babu, R.V., Ramakrishnan, K., Srinivasan, S.: Video object segmentation: a compressed domain approach. IEEE Trans. Circ. Syst. Video Technol. **14**(4), 462–474 (2004)

23. Babu, R.V., Ramakrishnan, K.: Recognition of human actions using motion history information extracted from the compressed video. Image Vis. Comput. **22**(8), 597–607 (2004)

24. Yeo, C., Ahammad, P., Ramchandran, K., Sastry, S.S.: Compressed domain real-time action recognition. In: 2006 IEEE 8th Workshop on Multimedia Signal Processing, pp. 33–36, IEEE (2006)

25. Aggarwal, A., Biswas, S., Singh, S., Sural, S., Majumdar, A.K.: Object tracking using background subtraction and motion estimation in MPEG videos. In: Narayanan, P.J., Nayar, S.K., Shum, H.-Y. (eds.) ACCV 2006. LNCS, vol. 3852, pp. 121–130. Springer, Heidelberg (2006). https://doi.org/10.1007/11612704_13
26. Biswas, S., Babu, R.V.: H.264 compressed video classification using histogram of oriented motion vectors (HOMV). In: 2013 IEEE International Conference on Acoustics, Speech and Signal Processing (ICASSP), pp. 2040–2044. IEEE (2013)
27. Käs, C., Nicolas, H.: An Approach to trajectory estimation of moving objects in the H.264 compressed domain. In: Wada, T., Huang, F., Lin, S. (eds.) PSIVT 2009. LNCS, vol. 5414, pp. 318–329. Springer, Heidelberg (2009). https://doi.org/10.1007/978-3-540-92957-4_28
28. Kantorov, V., Laptev, I.: Efficient feature extraction, encoding and classification for action recognition. In: Proceedings of the IEEE Conference on Computer Vision and Pattern Recognition, pp. 2593–2600 (2014)
29. Zhang, B., Wang, L., Wang, Z., Qiao, Y., Wang, H.: Real-time action recognition with enhanced motion vector CNNs. In: Proceedings of the IEEE Conference on Computer Vision and Pattern Recognition, pp. 2718–2726 (2016)
30. Poularakis, S., Avgerinakis, K., Briassouli, A., Kompatsiaris, I.: Efficient motion estimation methods for fast recognition of activities of daily living. Signal Process. Image Commun. **53**, 1–12 (2017)
31. Avgerinakis, K., Briassouli, A., Kompatsiaris, I.: Recognition of activities of daily living for smart home environments. In: 2013 9th International Conference on Intelligent Environments (IE), pp. 173–180. IEEE (2013)
32. Achanta, R., Hemami, S., Estrada, F., Susstrunk, S.: Frequency-tuned salient region detection. In: IEEE International Conference on Computer Vision and Pattern Recognition (CVPR 2009), pp. 1597–1604 (2009)
33. Arodź, T., Kurdziel, M., Popiela, T.J., Sevre, E.O., Yuen, D.A.: Detection of clustered microcalcifications in small field digital mammography. Comput. Methods Programs Biomed. **81**(1), 56–65 (2006)
34. Lahouli, I., et al.: Hot spot method for pedestrian detection using saliency maps, discrete chebyshev moments and support vector machine. IET Image Process. **12**, 1284–1291 (2018)
35. Lahouli, I., Haelterman, R., Chtourou, Z., Cubber, G.D., Attia, R.: Pedestrian detection and tracking in thermal images from aerial mpeg videos. In: Proceedings of the 13th International Joint Conference on Computer Vision, Imaging and Computer Graphics Theory and Applications, VISAPP, vol. 5, pp. 487–495. INSTICC, SciTePress (2018)

Flash, Storm, and Mistral: Hardware-Friendly and High Quality Tone Mapping

Nikola Banić[(✉)] and Sven Lončarić

Image Processing Group, Department of Electronic Systems and Information Processing, Faculty of Electrical Engineering and Computing, University of Zagreb, 10000 Zagreb, Croatia
{nikola.banic,sven.loncaric}@fer.hr
https://ipg.fer.hr/

Abstract. While high dynamic range (HDR) images are being used ever more widely, the majority of display devices are able to properly handle only low dynamic range (LDR) images. Tone mapping operators (TMOs) solve this problem by compressing the dynamic range of HDR images so that they can be displayed as LDR images. The problem with many state-of-the-art TMOs is that despite giving high quality results they are often too complex to be used for simple hardware implementations. In this paper several new TMOs formed around the perceptually based Naka-Rushton equation are proposed with the main goal being hardware-friendliness. The proposed TMOs are of gradually increasing complexity, which allows choosing the most appropriate trade-off between quality and complexity, and all of them are designed to have $O(1)$ per-pixel complexity. The results are presented and discussed and it is shown that the proposed TMOs outperform most well-known publicly available TMOs in terms of quality and speed. The source codes of the proposed TMOs written in C++, Matlab, Python, Java, and HTML+JavaScript are available at http://www.fer.unizg.hr/ipg/resources/color_constancy/.

Keywords: HDR · Image compression · Image enhancement · LDR · Naka-Rushton equation · Retinex · Tone mapping operator

1 Introduction

The dynamic range of an image is the ratio between its largest and smallest non-zero intensity. Although the use of high dynamic range (HDR) images is on the rise [1], most display devices are still limited to work properly only with low dynamic range (LDR) images. A HDR image can be displayed on such devices only if its dynamic range is compressed in the process called tone mapping by applying methods called tone mapping operators (TMOs). TMOs usually work on the image luminance channel, often calculated as the Y channel of the YUV

© Springer Nature Switzerland AG 2019
D. Bechmann et al. (Eds.): VISIGRAPP 2018, CCIS 997, pp. 228–242, 2019.
https://doi.org/10.1007/978-3-030-26756-8_11

colorspace. For a pixel with a given RGB representation $\mathbf{p} = (R, G, B)^T$, its value of Y channel is obtained by using the following equation [2]:

$$Y = 0.299R + 0.587G + 0.114B. \tag{1}$$

Besides the regular grayscale, other alternative luminance channels can be found in HSV, HSL, and Lab colorspaces as well as in custom definitions [3,4]. If the luminance value L of $\mathbf{p}$ is tone mapped to L', then $\mathbf{p}$ is changed to

$$\mathbf{p}' = \frac{L'}{L}\mathbf{p} = \left(\frac{L'}{L}R, \frac{L'}{L}G, \frac{L'}{L}B\right)^T. \tag{2}$$

Global TMOs process intensities based only on their value and regardless of their locations, while local TMOs also take into account the local neighborhood when processing individual pixels. Some of the better know examples of global TMOs are application of Steven's law [5–7], imitation of human response to light [8–11], histogram adjustment [12], and sigmoidal contrast enhancement [13]. Examples of local TMOs include application of anisotropic diffusion [14], bilateral filtering of the image base layer [15], photographic practice [16], luminance gradient field manipulation [17,18], Retinex theory [19–21]. The main advantage of global TMOs is their higher speed and simplicity when compared to local ones, while on the other hand local TMOs can give results of higher quality [22–24]. However, the problem with many TMOs that produce high-quality results is that they are too slow to be used in real-time applications and additionally they can be too complex for a simple and effective hardware implementation. In this paper several new TMOs are proposed whose steps are primarily designed to achieve high speed and to be practically implementable i.e. hardware-friendly. The secondary goal during the designing was that the TMOs produce low dynamic range (LDR) images of high quality. The proposed TMOs are based on Naka-Rushton equation used in combination with techniques for additional image quality improvement and they have $O(1)$ per-pixel complexity. The presented and discussed results show that, beside being faster and potentially more practical, the proposed TMO outperforms many well known publicly available TMOs in terms of resulting LDR image quality. To further demonstrate its practicality, the publicly available source code of the proposed TMOs is written in several programming languages including JavaScript with an HTML interface that can be used even with only a browser with no special libraries. This paper is an extension of a conference paper published as VISAPP 2018 [25].

The paper is structured as follows: in Sect. 2 the foundations for the new TMOs are laid, in Sects. 3 the first local TMO is proposed, Sect. 4 makes another proposal for a more hardware-friendly local TMO, in Sect. 5 experimental results are presented and discussed, and Sect. 6 concludes the paper.

2   Flash - Starting Globally

2.1   Initial Tone Compression

Recently a high quality two-phase TMO called Puma with $O(1)$ per-pixel complexity has been proposed [21]. It first performs global tone mapping by means of a method called Flash, which is fast and efficient since it uses a curve that is simply calculated. Since the resulting LDR image is crude and of low quality, its appearance is enhanced by applying Smart Light Random Memory Sprays Retinex (SLRMSR) [26, 27], a brightness adjustment method, whose parameter values are specifically adjusted for this purpose. SLRMSR produces the final high quality LDR image and it has $O(1)$ per-pixel complexity. Although Puma has a $O(1)$ per-pixel complexity, it is not especially fast due to a large constant number of steps per pixel used in SLRMSR. Another problem is that several of SLRMSR's parameters have to be tuned for various tone mapping effects. Because of that, Puma does not fully abide by the constraints laid out in the introduction. Nevertheless, if SLRMSR is left out, Flash can still be used as a good foundation for a desired new TMO because of its effectiveness, while for the enhancement of its results a more efficient method has to be found. The core of Flash is the Naka-Rushton equation [28], which can also be given in the form

$$L' = \frac{\frac{L}{L_w}}{\frac{L}{L_w} + a} = \frac{L}{L + aL_w} \tag{3}$$

where L is the initial luminance, a is a scaling parameter, and L_w is the image key usually approximated by calculating the geometric luminance mean [7, 16]

$$L_w = \exp\left(\frac{1}{N}\sum_i \ln\left(L\left(i\right) + \epsilon\right)\right) \tag{4}$$

where N is the number of pixels, $L(i)$ is the i-th pixel luminance, and ϵ is a small value to avoid logarithm of zero. The Naka-Rushton equation is a special case of the perceptually based Michaelis-Menten equation [29] and therefore it is to some degree inherently also perceptually based. All this makes Flash theoretically sound and even more attractive than some other curve-based methods. $Flash_a$ denotes the application of Flash for a given value of a. To obtain high quality results, Flash uses the V channel of the HSV colorspace as the luminance channel instead of the Y channel where V is calculated as $V = \max\{R, G, B\}$. The beneficial effect of using the V channel was already shown in [3]. Consider the example given in Fig. 1: both green and blue patch have the same channel intensities, and the image key is the same as the blue grayscale value. After applying Eq. (3) with $a = 1$ the green patch becomes darker although the ratio of their brightnesses should intuitively have stayed the same. It may be argued that using grayscale values during tone mapping is needless since the human visual system afterwards anyway calculates grayscale i.e. luminance values by itself. To avoid similar problems, in some image processing areas other luminance definitions are used, e.g. the sum of channel values as in [30]. Another example of the difference between using Y and V during tone mapping is shown in Fig. 2.

(a)   (b)

Fig. 1. Grayscale as luminance: (a) a linearly scaled HDR image and (b) result of applying Eq. (3) to its grayscale.

(a)   (b)

Fig. 2. The same scene tone mapped by applying Eq. (3) to (a) the grayscale and (b) V image channel. If needed, the results of multiplication in (2) were linearly scaled to preserve the colors from the effects of clipping.

2.2 Leap - Simple Image Enhancement

After Flash has been applied, the next step is to enhance its crude results in a way that abides by the constraints laid out in the introduction. A good starting point in designing such an enhancement procedure motivated to some degree by [31] is to look for simple properties common to many tone mapped LDR images of high quality. Once such properties are found, they can be incorporated into the initial results of Flash and theoretically perhaps increase their quality.

The set of high quality tone mapped LDR images required to look for such properties was obtained by tone mapping the HDR images available at [32] and [33] into LDR images. The tone mapping was performed by applying the procedure described in [34]. This procedure takes an initial LDR version of a given HDR image and changes it iteratively in order to increase the value of TMQI-II [34], an adapted version of Tone Mapped image Quality Index (TMQI) [35] that evaluates structural fidelity and statistical naturalness of a tone mapped image by using the initial HDR image as a reference. The procedure is too slow to be used in practical real-time systems, but its final results are by definition of high quality. To create the set of mentioned set of high quality LDR images required to look for interesting properties, the procedure was iteratively applied to individual HDR images until the TMQI-II value of an each of them was very close to the maximum of 1 or the number of iterations reached 500.

The analysis of different properties across all of the obtained high quality LDR images has shown that the arithmetic mean of the grayscale image values is very similar for all images and that when all these means for all images are combined, they have a low standard deviation. For the first dataset [32] the mean of the images' grayscale means was 100.57 with a standard deviation 3.85 and for the second dataset [33] these values were 100.04 and 5.12, respectively. This suggests that an appropriate mean grayscale value could maybe also assure a higher quality. One of the simplest ways to make an image have a given mean grayscale value is to multiply it by a scalar i.e. to jump from the initial mean grayscale to a given one. In Sect. 5.2 it is shown that such a procedure may indeed significantly increase the image quality of a given LDR image. For easier notation this procedure is named $Leap_g$ with g being the target mean grayscale to which an image is adjusted. In case of some low key images their already bright pixels may appear "burned" after their brightness is increased even further when Leap is applied, but as explained in [16], this can actually be desirable. As a matter of fact, in [16] an extension of Eq. (3) has been proposed for exactly that purpose. The pseudocode for Leap is given in Algorithm 1. In the Sect. 5.2 it is shown that Flash combined with Leap is a fast and high quality global TMO.

In order to get some default values for parameters a and g, the subjective assessment of a large number of LDR images obtained by Flash and Leap was carried out. It was concluded that round default values for parameters a and g that already produce visually appealing results are 10 and 110, respectively.

Algorithm 1. Leap.

Input: image $\mathbf{I}$, target mean grayscale g, upper bound U
1: $m = CalculateMeanGrayscale(\mathbf{I})$
2: **for all** pixel i in $\mathbf{I}$ **do**
3:     $\mathbf{p} = \mathbf{I}(i)$
4:     $p'_R = \max\left(\frac{g}{m}p_R, U\right)$
5:     $p'_G = \max\left(\frac{g}{m}p_G, U\right)$
6:     $p'_B = \max\left(\frac{g}{m}p_B, U\right)$
7:     $\mathbf{R}(i) = \mathbf{p}'$
8: **end for**
Output: image $\mathbf{R}$

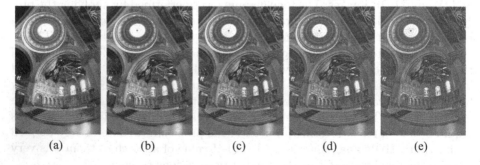

(a)   (b)   (c)   (d)   (e)

Fig. 3. Applications of Storm with different kernels followed by and $Leap_{110}$ and gamma correction: (a) $Storm_{20}^{(1)}$, (b) $Storm_{20}^{(1,\frac{1}{4})}$, (c) $Storm_{20}^{(1,\frac{1}{4},\frac{1}{16})}$, (d) $Storm_{20}^{(1,\frac{1}{4},\frac{1}{16},\frac{1}{64})}$, and (e) $Storm_{20}^{(1,\frac{1}{4},\frac{1}{16},\frac{1}{64},\frac{1}{256})}$. Images are taken from [25].

3   Storm - Continuing Locally

3.1   Extension to a Local TMO

While global TMOs are fast and simple, when results of highest quality are needed, local TMOs are used [22,23]. For this reason a natural direction of further Flash improvement is to try to extend it to a local TMO. One of the simple ways to do this is to use the same global operation but with different parameters for each pixel. This parameters are determined by looking only at the local area surrounding a given pixel instead of at the whole image [1]. With respecte to that, it is useful to consider the fact that there is evidence that early stages of visual processing can be modelled by filtering of retinal image using filters of different scales [36] and similar approaches have been used in various tone mapping and image enhancement methods [37–39]. Therefore, the local extension of Flash proposed here does the same thing. If R and C are the number of image rows and columns, respectively, then let d be the smaller of these two i.e. $d = \min\{R, C\}$. For a pixel i Flash is applied to M squares of size $s_j d \times s_j d$ with pixel i in their center where s_j is the scaling factor for the j-th square. If k_j is the j-th square and $F_a^{(k_j)}(i)$ the value of luminance of pixel i after applying Flash$_a$ to k_j with i in its center, then the final luminance value for i is

$$S(i) = \frac{1}{M} \sum_{j=1}^{M} F_a^{(k_j)}(i). \tag{5}$$

The main computation cost of Eq. (5) consists of calculating Eq. (4) for each i and k_j. Nevertheless, this can be efficiently done by means of convolution over the luminance logarithms. Such an approach was motivated by the multiscale Retinex (MSR) algorithm [38], but with two differences. First, while MSR uses Gaussian kernels, having square kernels in Eq. (5) is much faster if an integral image [40] is used. Because of this the per-pixel complexity of Eq. (5) is $O(M)$. Second, unlike in MSR, there are no weights in Eq. (5) for individual kernels

---

Algorithm 2. Storm.

Input: image $\mathbf{I}$, brightening parameter a, M kernel sizes s_j, upper bound U
  1: **for all** pixel i in $\mathbf{I}$ **do**
  2:     $\mathbf{p} = \mathbf{I}(i)$
  3:     $L = \max\{p_R, p_G, p_B\}$
  4:     $L' = 0$
  5:     **for** $j = 1$ **to** M **do**
  6:        $L' = L' + F_a^{(k_j)}(i)$
  7:     **end for**
  8:     $\mathbf{R}(i) = \frac{L'}{L}\mathbf{p}$
  9: **end for**
 10: $\mathbf{R} = U \cdot \mathbf{R} / \max(\mathbf{R}(:))$
Output: image $\mathbf{R}$

---

234 N. Banić and S. Lončarić

because using them has shown no significant benefit in terms of quality. Since the proposed local TMO applies Flash multiple times and multiple flashes often occur during storms, it is named Storm for easier notation, while its application with n specified scaling factors and value of a for the underlying Flash is denoted $\text{Storm}_a^{(s_1,\ldots,s_n)}$. The pseudocode for Storm is given in Algorithm 2. The contribution of kernels of various size is shown in Fig. 3. It can be seen that using smaller kernels has a significant effect on brightening smaller dark regions. This is because these kernels can adjust to such confined local conditions much easier that larger kernels that take into account wider surrounding parts that are bright and thus increase the local key. Like with Flash, higher values of a for Storm also give better contrast in the final resulting image as shown in Fig. 4.

(a)   (b)

Fig. 4. Results of application of (a) $\text{Storm}_1^{\left(1,\frac{1}{4},\frac{1}{16}\right)}$ and (b) $\text{Storm}_{20}^{\left(1,\frac{1}{4},\frac{1}{16}\right)}$ to the same image. Images are taken from [25].

3.2 Properties

Figure 3 shows how more kernels make more details visible. With well chosen kernels Storm outperforms Flash in terms of quality, but at the cost of using additional memory that is required to store the integral image.

In terms of complexity, Storm is more complex than Flash. Firstly, Storm calculates the integral image in $O(1)$ per-pixel complexity. Next, to each pixel

Eq. (3) is applied M times and each time in $O(1)$ per-pixel complexity by using the previously calculated integral image. Together this gives $O(M)$ per-pixel complexity, which seemingly violates the $O(1)$ per-pixel complexity constraint set up in the introduction. However, M is supposed to be very small because already for $M \in \{2, 3, 4\}$ the results are of high quality as shown in Fig. 3. Additionally, since M is practically a hyperparameter, its value is not changed that often so it is effectively a constant. Taking all this into account, Storm can also be regarded as having $O(1)$ per-pixel complexity. Speed tests in Sect. 5.2 corroborate such reasoning since the difference between Flash and Storm is minimal.

Based on subjective assessment of a large number of LDR images obtained by applying Storm and Leap with various parameters, it was found that the combination with round default values that already produce visually appealing results without showing unrealistically too much details is $\text{Storm}_{20}^{\left(1, \frac{1}{4}, \frac{1}{16}\right)} + \text{Leap}_{110}$.

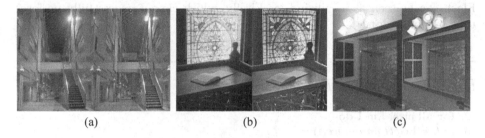

(a)   (b)   (c)

Fig. 5. Pairwise comparison between the results of Reinhard's local TMO [16] on the left and Storm + Leap on the right; for Reinhard's TMO its Luminance HDR implementation with default parameter values was used. Images are taken from [25].

4 Mistral - Local and Hardware-Friendly

The problem with Storm TMO is that in cases where using significant amounts of additional memory like for Storm's integral image is problematic, e.g. in hardware implementations, Storm cannot be considered fully hardware-friendly. To obtain a local TMO that is more hardware-friendly, its filtering and any other used technique have to be designed so that it does not consume significant amounts of memory nor carry out too complex steps that would significantly slow it down or be too complicated for a simple hardware-implementation. One of the solutions to this problem is not to design such a method for direct tone mapping, but like in the case of the earlier mentioned Puma TMO [21], the initial compression could first be performed by Flash and then additional image enhancement could follow by applying an appropriate i.c. hardware-friendly brightness adjustment method. A suitable candidate that meets all required criteria is the Firefly method [41], whose steps are summarized in Algorithm 3.

Its input is a given LDR image and its output is the enhanced version of this image with adjusted brightness. The first step of Firefly is to calculate approximated local mean brightness for the subsampled original image of size $r \times r$ by repeating box filtering on it s times thus bringing the complexity of the whole step to $O(r \times r \times s)$. Since the values of r are supposed to be around 32 and the values of s up to 5 [41], the product $r \times r \times s$ is several orders of magnitude smaller than the number of pixels in contemporary images. This means that the complexity of the calculation of approximated local mean brightness can be disregarded in further complexity analysis. What follows is the brightness adjustment of every pixel in the original image. First, its local neighborhood mean brightness is approximated from the closest points of the $r \times r$ subsampled mean brightness by means of bilinear interpolation. Then both the current brightness and the approximated local mean brightness are used as the input to a previously learned two-dimensional look-up table (LUT), which gives as the result the final brightness of the initial pixel based on its surround. Reading from the LUT is done in $O(1)$ so there is no complicated calculation included. The combination $Flash_a + Firefly$ is named $Mistral_a$ because the application of Flash can be seen as a tailwind for Firefly, which cannot successfully perform tone mapping alone.

Algorithm 3. Firefly.

Input: image **I**, fitted LUT, mean parameters r, k, s
 1: $\mathbf{R} = \mathbf{I}$
 2: **for all** pixel i in **I** **do**
 3:    $L = \mathbf{I}.GetLuminance(i)$
 4:    $m = \mathbf{I}.CalculateInterpolatedMean(i, r, k, s)$
 5:    $L' = LUT(L, m)$
 6:    $\mathbf{R}.SetLuminance(i, L')$
 7: **end for**
Output: image **R**

The main advantage of Mistral over Storm is that the memory used for calculation of the approximated local mean brightness is much smaller. On the other hand, Mistral's handling of smaller dark regions highly depends on the subsampling parameter r, while in Storm such regions can easily be handled by simply adding a smaller kernel. Another useful thing with Mistral is that Firefly already takes care of the brightness adjustment so that applying Leap is not as important as in the case of Flash and Storm. For this reason it is also easier to use higher values of a for Mistral since Firefly will compensate for eventual local brightness losses. Because of that, combinations $Mistral_{50}$ and optionally $Mistral_{50} + Leap_{110}$ were chosen as the default Mistral parameter settings.

A direct comparison between Flash, Storm, and Mistral is given in Fig. 6. It can be seen that Mistral produces effects in between of those produced by Flash and Storm since its applications leaves neither dark nor overenhanced regions.

Fig. 6. Comparison of tone mapping results of the proposed TMOs: (a) $\text{Flash}_{10} + \text{Leap}_{110}$, (b) $\text{Storm}_{20}^{(1, \frac{1}{4}, \frac{1}{16})}$, and (c) Mistral_{50}.

Table 1. Mean TMQI and FSITM^G-TMQI obtained on images from [42] with cumulative execution time.

TMO	TMQI	FSITM^G-TMQI	t (s)
Ashikhmin [43]	0.6620	0.7338	225.23
Drago [10]	0.7719	0.8158	30.69
Durand [15]	0.8354	0.8405	225.14
Fattal [17]	0.7198	0.7810	64.78
Mantiuk [18]	0.8225	0.8266	88.03
Mantiuk [44]	0.8443	0.8494	36.20
Pattanaik [9]	0.6813	0.7635	46.91
Reinhard [16]	0.8695	0.8581	33.41
Reinhard [11]	0.6968	0.7679	30.01
Flash$_{10}$	0.8072	0.8315	**21.19**
Flash$_{10}$ + Leap$_{110}$	0.8755	**0.8625**	21.26
Storm$_{20}^{(1, \frac{1}{4}, \frac{1}{16})}$	0.7675	0.8004	24.35
Storm$_{20}^{(1, \frac{1}{4}, \frac{1}{16})}$ + Leap$_{110}$	**0.8782**	0.8551	24.59
Mistral$_{50}$	0.8568	0.8497	24.04
Mistral$_{50}$ + Leap$_{110}$	0.8681	0.8551	24.52

5   Experimental Results

5.1   Image Quality Metrics

The best way to the assess the quality of tone mapped images would be to carry out subjective perceptual experiments. However, such experiments have been omitted here because they are time-consuming, they require special environment and carefully calibrated equipment, they are not easy to reproduce, and they are available only at certain given times. Instead of that, two objective measures wre used to compare the quality of the proposed TMOs to the one of other well-known publicy available ones: Feature Similarity Index For Tone-Mapped images (FSITM) [45] and the already mentioned TMQI. TMQI-II was not used here because while images with a high TMQI-II are usually of high quality, a lot of images with a low TMQI-II are actually of high quality as well. This is because TMQI-II is too susceptible to mean grayscale value as shown in [46]. FSITM is based on local phase information of images and it was shown to give better results than TMQI. If combined with TMQI, it performs a better assessment than both TMQI and TMQI-II and this combination is denoted as FSITM^C-TMQI where C is a color channel. The green (G) color channel is used here since it was shown to be a good choice [45]. Both FSITM and TMQI are in range $[0, 1]$ with a higher number meaning higher quality. These metrics are well established, easy to reproduce in a fact and automatic way, they have a sound theoretical background, and they were shown to be well correlated with subjective measures.

5.2   Tone Mapping Quality and Speed

The quality of the results of the proposed TMO was evaluated by applying them to images in the HDR dataset given at [42]. For TMOs with fixed parameters this dataset is challenging because it contains HDR images from various sources including artificially generated ones. Table 1 shows the obtained values of previously described objective quality measures for the proposed and existing TMOs with default parameter values. For results of other TMOs the open source Luminance HDR software was used like in [34] in order to compare the proposed TMOs to easily available implementations of other well-known TMOs. While they are certainly much newer TMOs that have been proposed, their implementations can rarely be publicly found. The results for Flash differ from the ones given in [21] because here the gamma correction was carried out after tone mapping as it is supposed to be done. The values of objective metrics are higher for Flash, Storm, and Mistral than for all other tested TMOs and while the differences are small, they still demonstrate the quality of the proposed TMOs. It can be seen that Mistral is some kind of an intermediate between Flash and Storm. In this way the proposed TMOs form a series of TMOs with gradual changes in complexity and quality so they can be used in various kinds of trade-offs between simplicity and quality. Since Reinhard's local TMO [16] is considered to be among the best, in Fig. 5 its results are compared to the results of Storm.

As for speed, Table 1 also shows that Flash, Storm, and Mistral are faster than other TMOs, which makes them good candidates for real-time applications.

6   Conclusions

A group of hardware-friendly TMOs centered around the perceptually based Naka-Rushton equation have been proposed with one of them being global and the other two local. All of them were shown to outperform most well-known TMOs with publicly available implementations in terms of speed and quality. The main difference between the proposed TMOs is the complexity of their design, which effectively means that they represent good choices for various levels of required trade-offs between the simplicity of a used design and the quality of its final result. Additionally, the proposed TMOs serve as a successful proof-of-concept that having hardware-friendliness as the primary goal can still result in TMOs that produce state-of-the-art results in a computationally inexpensive way. Future work will focus on finding additional ways of simplifying structures such as integral images to the level where they do not consume as much resources as in their original form in order to create even better hardware-friendly TMOs.

References

1. Reinhard, E., Heidrich, W., Debevec, P., Pattanaik, S., Ward, G., Myszkowski, K.: High Dynamic Range Imaging: Acquisition, Display, and Image-Basedlighting. Morgan Kaufmann, Burlington (2010)

2. Koschan, A., Abidi, M.: Digital Color Image Processing. Wiley, Hoboken (2008)
3. Banić, N., Lončarić, S.: Improving the Tone Mapping Operators by Using a Redefined Version of the Luminance Channel. In: Image and Signal Processing. Springer (2014) 392–399
4. Nguyen, R.M., Brown, M.S.: Why you should forget luminance conversion and do something better. In: Proceedings of the IEEE Conference on Computer Vision and Pattern Recognition, pp. 6750–6758 (2017)
5. Tumblin, J., Rushmeier, H.: Tone reproduction for realistic images. IEEE Comput. Graph. Appl. **13**, 42–48 (1993)
6. Chiu, K., et al.: Spatially nonuniform scaling functions for high contrast images. In: Graphics Interface, Canadian Information Processing Society, p. 245 (1993)
7. Ward, G.: A contrast-based scalefactor for luminance display. In: Graphics gems IV, pp. 415–421 (1994)
8. Schlick, C.: Quantization techniques for visualization of high dynamic range pictures. In: Sakas, G., Müller, S., Shirley, P. (eds.) Photorealistic Rendering Techniques, pp. 7–20. Springer, Heidelberg (1995). https://doi.org/10.1007/978-3-642-87825-1_2
9. Pattanaik, S.N., Tumblin, J., Yee, H., Greenberg, D.P.: Time-dependent visual adaptation for fast realistic image display. In: Proceedings of the 27th Annual Conference on Computer Graphics and Interactive Techniques, pp. 47–54. ACM Press/Addison-Wesley Publishing Co. (2000)
10. Drago, F., Myszkowski, K., Annen, T., Chiba, N.: Adaptive logarithmic mapping for displaying high contrast scenes. In: Computer Graphics Forum, vol. 22, pp. 419–426. Wiley Online Library (2003)
11. Reinhard, E., Devlin, K.: Dynamic range reduction inspired by photoreceptor physiology. IEEE Trans. Visual Comput. Graphics **11**, 13–24 (2005)
12. Larson, G.W., Rushmeier, H., Piatko, C.: A visibility matching tone reproduction operator for high dynamic range scenes. IEEE Trans. Visual Comput. Graphics **3**, 291–306 (1997)
13. Braun, G.J., Fairchild, M.D.: Image lightness rescaling using sigmoidal contrast enhancement functions. J. Electron. Imaging **8**, 380–393 (1999)
14. Tumblin, J., Turk, G.: LCIS: A boundary hierarchy for detail-preserving contrast reduction. In: Proceedings of the 26th Annual Conference on Computer Graphics and Interactive Techniques, pp. 83–90. ACM Press/Addison-Wesley Publishing Co. (1999)
15. Durand, F., Dorsey, J.: Fast bilateral filtering for the display of high-dynamic-range images. In: ACM Transactions on Graphics (TOG), vol. 21, pp. 257–266 (2002)
16. Reinhard, E., Stark, M., Shirley, P., Ferwerda, J.: Photographic tone reproduction for digital images. In: ACM Transactions on Graphics (TOG), vol. 21, pp. 267–276. ACM (2002)
17. Fattal, R., Lischinski, D., Werman, M.: Gradient domain high dynamic range compression. In: ACM Transactions on Graphics (TOG), vol. 21, pp. 249–256. ACM (2002)
18. Mantiuk, R., Myszkowski, K., Seidel, H.P.: A perceptual framework for contrast processing of high dynamic range images. ACM Trans. Appl. Percept. (TAP) **3**, 286–308 (2006)
19. Meylan, L., Susstrunk, S.: High dynamic range image rendering with a retinex-based adaptive filter. IEEE Trans. Image Process. **15**, 2820–2830 (2006)
20. Banić, N., Lončarić, S.: Color badger: a novel retinex-based local tone mapping operator. In: Elmoataz, A., Lezoray, O., Nouboud, F., Mammass, D. (eds.) ICISP

2014. LNCS, vol. 8509, pp. 400–408. Springer, Cham (2014). https://doi.org/10. 1007/978-3-319-07998-1_46

21. Banić, N., Lončarić, S.: Puma: a high-quality retinex-based tone mapping operator. In: Signal Processing Conference (EUSIPCO), 2016 24rd European, pp. 943–947. IEEE (2016)

22. Kuang, J., Yamaguchi, H., Johnson, G.M., Fairchild, M.D.: Testing HDR image rendering algorithms. In: Color and Imaging Conference, vol. 2004, pp. 315–320. Society for Imaging Science and Technology (2004)

23. Kuang, J., Yamaguchi, H., Liu, C., Johnson, G.M., Fairchild, M.D.: Evaluating HDR rendering algorithms. ACM Trans. Appl. Percept. (TAP) **4**, 9 (2007)

24. Urbano, C., Magalhães, L., Moura, J., Bessa, M., Marcos, A., Chalmers, A.: Tone mapping operators on small screen devices: an evaluation study. In: Computer Graphics Forum, vol. 29, pp. 2469–2478. Wiley Online Library (2010)

25. Banić, N., Lončarić, S.: Flash and storm: fast and highly practical tone mapping based on Naka-Rushton equation. In: International Conference on Computer Vision Theory and Applications (VISAPP), pp. 47–53 (2018)

26. Banić, N., Lončarić, S.: Smart light random memory sprays retinex: a fast retinex implementation for high-quality brightness adjustment and color correction. JOSA A **32**, 2136–2147 (2015)

27. Banić, N., Lončarić, S.: Towards hardware-friendly Retinex algorithms. In: 2017 10th International Symposium on Image and Signal Processing and Analysis (ISPA), pp. 104–108. IEEE (2017)

28. Shapley, R., Enroth-Cugell, C.: Visual adaptation and retinal gain controls. Prog. Retinal Res. **3**, 263–346 (1984)

29. Dowling, J.E.: The Retina: An Approachable Part of the Brain. Harvard University Press, Cambridge (1987)

30. Joze, H.R.V., Drew, M.S., Finlayson, G.D., Rey, P.A.T.: The role of bright pixels in illumination estimation. In: Color and Imaging Conference, vol. 2012, pp. 41–46. Society for Imaging Science and Technology (2012)

31. Huang, J., Mumford, D.: Statistics of natural images and models. In: IEEE Computer Society Conference on Computer Vision and Pattern Recognition, 1999, vol. 1. IEEE (1999)

32. NTUST, C.G.G.: http://graphics.csie.ntust.edu.tw/pub/hdr/ (2015)

33. Fairchild, M.D.: http://rit-mcsl.org/fairchild/hdrps/hdrthumbs.html (2015)

34. Ma, K., Yeganeh, H., Zeng, K., Wang, Z.: High dynamic range image compression by optimizing tone mapped image quality index. IEEE Trans. Image Process. **24**, 3086–3097 (2015)

35. Yeganeh, H., Zhou, W.: Objective quality assessment of tone mapped images. IEEE Trans. Image Process. **22**, 657–667 (2013)

36. Wilson, H.R.: Psychophysical models of spatial vision and hyperacuity. Spat. Vis. **10**, 64–81 (1991)

37. Peli, E.: Contrast in complex images. JOSA A **7**, 2032–2040 (1990)

38. Jobson, D.J., Rahman, Z.U., Woodell, G., et al.: A multiscale retinex for bridging the gap between color images and the human observation of scenes. IEEE Trans. Image Process. **6**, 965–976 (1997)

39. Pattanaik, S.N., Ferwerda, J.A., Fairchild, M.D., Greenberg, D.P.: A multiscale model of adaptation and spatial vision for realistic image display. In: Proceedings of the 25th annual conference on Computer graphics and interactive techniques, pp. 287–298. ACM (1998)

40. Crow, F.C.: Summed-area tables for texture mapping. ACM SIGGRAPH Comput. Graph. **18**, 207–212 (1984)

41. Banić, N., Lončarić, S.: Firefly: a hardware-friendly real-time local brightness adjustment method. In: 2015 22nd IEEE International Conference on Image Processing (ICIP), pp. 3951–3955. IEEE (2015)
42. Ward, G.: http://www.anyhere.com/gward/hdrenc/pages/originals.html (2015)
43. Ashikhmin, M.: A tone mapping algorithm for high contrast images. In: Proceedings of the 13th Eurographics Workshop on Rendering, pp. 145–156. Eurographics Association (2002)
44. Mantiuk, R., Daly, S., Kerofsky, L.: Display adaptive tone mapping. In: ACM Transactions on Graphics (TOG), vol. 27, p. 68. ACM (2008)
45. Ziaei Nafchi, H., Shahkolaei, A., Farrahi Moghaddam, R., Cheriet, M.: FSITM: a feature similarity index for tone-mapped images. IEEE Signal Process. Lett. **22**, 1026–1029 (2015)
46. Banić, N., Lončarić, S.: Sensitivity of tone mapped image quality metrics to perceptually hardly noticeable differences. In: Proceedings of The Fifth Croatian Computer Vision Workshop (CCVW 2013), no. 1, pp. 15–18. University of Zagreb Faculty of Electrical Engineering and Computing (2016)

A Simple and Exact Algorithm to Solve Linear Problems with ℓ^1-Based Regularizers

Yohann Tendero[1]($\boxtimes$), Igor Ciril[2], and Jérôme Darbon[3]

[1] LTCI, Télécom-ParisTech, Université Paris-Saclay, 75013 Paris, France
`yohann.tendero@telecom-paristech.fr`
[2] DR2I, Institut Polytechnique des Sciences Avances, 94200 Ivry-sur-Seine, France
[3] Division of Applied Mathematics, Brown University, Providence, RI 02912, USA

Abstract. This paper considers ℓ^1-based regularized signal estimation that are often used in applications. The estimated signal is obtained as the solution of an optimization problem and the quality of the recovered signal directly depends on the quality of the solver. This paper describes a simple algorithm that computes an exact minimizer of $\|D \cdot \|_1$ under the constraints $A\mathbf{x} = \mathbf{y}$. A comparative evaluation of the algorithm is presented. An illustrative application to real signals of bacterial flagellar motor is also presented.

Keywords: Compressive sensing · ℓ^1 minimization ·
Total variation minimization · Inverse scale space · Sparsity ·
Non-smooth optimization · Bacterial flagellar motor

1 Introduction

Compressive sensing and methods that rely on sparsity have gained a significant interest. These methods are used in many areas: inverse problems, data analysis, signal/image processing and their applications. Indeed, these methods can be used to estimate signals (or images) from few (or partial) measurements in the noisy or noiseless cases. In their simplest form, namely in the noiseless (or exact) case, they amount to find a suitable $\mathbf{x}$ that satisfies

$$A\mathbf{x} = \mathbf{y} \tag{1}$$

where $\mathbf{y}$ can be thought as some observed data, $A \in \mathcal{M}_{m \times n}(\mathbb{R})$ (or $\mathcal{M}_{m \times n}(\mathbb{C})$) and usually $m \ll n$. (In the sequel we just assume that $m \leqslant n$). The matrix A usually models a degradation, such as a blur, a re-sampling or may model an acquisition device like a camera for instance. The columns of A can also represent some frame, dictionary or some kind of over-complete basis used to efficiently encode $\mathbf{x}$. The number of unknowns n in (1) is usually large. Indeed, if $\mathbf{x}$ represents an image then n is equal to the number of pixels. Furthermore,

© Springer Nature Switzerland AG 2019
D. Bechmann et al. (Eds.): VISIGRAPP 2018, CCIS 997, pp. 243–261, 2019.
https://doi.org/10.1007/978-3-030-26756-8_12

in general problem (1) is ill-posed: it has too many solutions and it is usually impossible to compute all of them. Hence, more information is needed to turn the estimation problem (1) into a well-posed and tractable problem. Consequently, one usually assumes that $\mathbf{x}$ is "simple enough". This simplicity assumption often translates into assuming that $\mathbf{x}$ has minimal support in the cardinality sense. This yields to replace (1) by the following optimization problem

$$\begin{cases} \inf_{\mathbf{x} \in \mathbb{R}^n} & \|\mathbf{x}\|_0 \\ \text{s.t.} & A\mathbf{x} = \mathbf{y}. \end{cases} \tag{P_{ℓ^0}}$$

Indeed, the ℓ^0 pseudo-norm measures the support, in the cardinality sense, of the solution $\bar{\mathbf{x}}$. However, finding a solution to (P_{ℓ^0}) is difficult: not only the problem is high-dimensional but also non-smooth and non-convex. Hence, methods [2, 10, 13, 17–19, 26, 28] that aim at solving (P_{ℓ^0}) usually only guarantee an optimal solution with high probability and, to the best of our knowledge, for specific classes of matrices A. The second class of methods propose to replace (P_{ℓ^0}) by

$$\begin{cases} \inf_{\mathbf{x} \in \mathbb{R}^n} & \|\mathbf{x}\|_1 \\ \text{s.t.} & A\mathbf{x} = \mathbf{y}. \end{cases} \tag{P_{ℓ^1}}$$

Problem (P_{ℓ^1}) is known in the literature as the "basis pursuit problem", see, e.g., [8]. Problem (P_{ℓ^1}) is non-smooth since it involves the ℓ^1-norm but is convex and more tractable than (P_{ℓ^0}) as we shall see.

In short, one often solves the convex program (P_{ℓ^1}) instead of (1). Indeed, under various assumptions, the minimizers remain the same if one replaces the ℓ^0 pseudo-norm by the ℓ^1-norm (see, e.g., [6, 7, 11, 12] and the references therein). In addition, the convex program (P_{ℓ^1}) enjoys strong uniform guarantees for sparse signal recovery, see, e.g. [22].

The derivative of a piecewise constant signal is sparse. It follows that a piecewise constant or a piecewise smooth signal can be estimated by replacing (P') with

$$\begin{cases} \inf_{\mathbf{x} \in \mathbb{R}^n} & \|D\mathbf{x}\|_{\ell^1} \\ \text{s.t.} & A\mathbf{x} = \mathbf{y}, \end{cases} \tag{P}$$

where D is often the matrix of a discretized differential operator. For instance, if $D \in \mathcal{M}_{n \times n}(\mathbb{R})$ is chosen as the bi-diagonal matrix given by

$$D_{i,j}^D = \begin{cases} -1 \text{ if } i = j \\ 1 \text{ if } j = i+1 \\ 0 \text{ otherwise} \end{cases} \quad \text{or} \quad D_{i,j}^N = \begin{cases} -1 \text{ if } i = j, \ \forall i \in \{1, \ldots, n-1\} \\ 1 \text{ if } j = i+1, \ \forall i \in \{1, \ldots, n-1\} \\ 0 \text{ otherwise}, \end{cases} \tag{2}$$

then (P) is a discrete total variation with Dirichlet (respectively Neumann) boundary conditions if $D := D^D$ (respectively $D := D^N$). We shall see in the experiments section (Sect. 3) that a discrete total variation is a suitable choice when estimating piecewise constant signals. The particular case of problem (P_{ℓ^1})

is more suitable for sparse signals. For more general classes of piecewise smooth signals D must be replaced by the discrete derivative of appropriate order.

In the noisy case, it may be impossible to find some $\mathbf{x}$ that satisfies $A\mathbf{x} = \mathbf{y}$. Hence, this equality constraint is often replaced by (e.g.) $\|A\mathbf{x} - \mathbf{y}\|_2^2 \leqslant \sigma^2$. Henceforth, the problem becomes

$$\begin{cases} \inf_{\mathbf{x} \in \mathbb{R}^n} & \|D\mathbf{x}\|_{\ell^1} \\ \text{s.t.} & \|A\mathbf{x} - \mathbf{y}\|_2^2 \leqslant \sigma^2, \end{cases} \tag{P'}$$

where $\sigma^2 \geqslant 0$ is related to the variance of the observed data. If D in (P') is chosen as the identity then (P') formalizes that we look for a sparse vector that approximately fits the observed data in the quadratic sense. Similarly, if D is chosen as one of the operator given in (2) then the solution to (P') will be a piecewise constant signal.

The aforementioned problems, namely (P_{ℓ^1}), (P) and (P'), are convex but high-dimensional and non-smooth. Indeed, their dimensions n, or number of unknowns, are the signal length or the number of pixels of an image and developing effective algorithms is still challenging. For instance, the standard CVX solver is not a suitable choice [14, Sect. 1.3] for very large problems that commonly arise from signal or image processing applications. Many methods have been proposed to solve (P_{ℓ^1}), see, e.g. [1,15,20,24,29]. For instance, a new simple and exact algorithm to solve the noiseless problem (P_{ℓ^1}) was proposed in [9]. Theoretical studies predict a sharp phase transition for the exact recovery of sparse signals. The algorithm given in [9] allows to observe very accurately this phase transition. Yet, the algorithm proposed in [9] only allows to solve (P_{ℓ^1}).

This paper proposes a new algorithm that computes an exact solution to (P). This algorithm can be employed to solve many problems that can be formally written as (P). Indeed, we mainly assume that A is full row rank. Examples on real data of bacterial flagellar motor show that the algorithm proposed in this paper is robust. This paper also presents numerical comparisons with standard algorithms of the literature for the particular case (P_{ℓ^1}). These comparisons illustrate that our algorithm compares advantageously to standard algorithms available in the literature.

Outline of this Paper. The paper is organized as follows. Section 2 describes the algorithm proposed in this paper. This algorithm generalizes the one given in [9]: not only it can solve (P_{ℓ^1}) but also the more general problem (P). It is given by Algorithm 1 on page 6. Section 3 presents an illustrative example of the performances of Algorithm 1 for simulated and real signals of bacterial flagellar motor. Section 3 also describes a numerical comparison of this algorithm proposed in this paper with some other state-of-the-art methods solving (P_{ℓ^1}). Discussions and conclusions are summarized in Sect. 4. The Appendix A.1 on page 18 contains a glossary of notations and definitions. In the sequel, Latin numerals refer to the glossary of notations on page 18.

2 An Exact Algorithm Solving (P)

This section presents the methodology proposed in this paper to solve (P). This methodology yields to Algorithm 1 on page 6. We would like to use the fact that $m \leqslant n$ and that, very often, we even have $m \ll n$. To do so, we use a two steps method. The first step involves a descent method to compute, after finitely many iterations, an exact solution $\bar{\lambda}$ to a dual problem. The second step computes a solution $\bar{\mathbf{x}}$ to (P) from $\bar{\lambda}$ and relies on a constrained least square problem. Hereinafter, we assume that $A \in \mathcal{M}_{m \times n}(\mathbb{R})$ is full row rank. We present the calculations for (P) with Dirichlet boundary conditions. Similar calculations can be carried out for (P) with Neumann boundary conditions. If we use the particular case "$D = I_n$" (see (vi)) one can retrieve the method and algorithm given in [9]. (We recall that hereinafter Latin numerals refer to the glossary of notations and definitions given on page 18).
Let

$$\forall\, \mathbf{x} \in \mathbb{R}^n, \qquad J(\mathbf{x}) := \|D\mathbf{x}\|_1 \tag{3}$$

and $\mathbf{y} \in \mathbb{R}^m$ be some given vector. Consider the Lagrangian $\mathcal{L} : \mathbb{R}^n \times \mathbb{R}^m \to \mathbb{R}$ associated with (P_{ℓ^1}), namely

$$\forall (\mathbf{x}, \lambda) \in \mathbb{R}^n \times \mathbb{R}^m, \quad \mathcal{L}(\mathbf{x}, \lambda) := J(\mathbf{x}) + \langle \lambda, A\mathbf{x} \rangle + \langle \lambda, -\mathbf{y} \rangle. \tag{4}$$

The Lagrangian dual function $g : \mathbb{R}^m \to \mathbb{R} \cup \{+\infty\}$ associated with (4) is

$$g(\lambda) := -\inf_{\mathbf{x} \in \mathbb{R}^n} \mathcal{L}(\mathbf{x}, \lambda) = -\inf_{\mathbf{x} \in \mathbb{R}^n} \left\{ J(\mathbf{x}) - \left\langle -A^\dagger \lambda, \mathbf{x} \right\rangle \right\} - \langle \lambda, -\mathbf{y} \rangle$$

$$= J^* \left(-A^\dagger \lambda \right) + \langle \lambda, \mathbf{y} \rangle. \tag{5}$$

In (5), J^* denotes the convex dual or Legendre-Fenchel transform (see (xii)) of the convex function $J \in \Gamma_0(\mathbb{R}^n)$ (see (ix)-(x)) defined in (3) and $A^\dagger$ denotes the transpose of the matrix A (see (vii)). The Lagrangian dual problem associated with (P) is

$$\inf_{\lambda \in \mathbb{R}^m} \quad g(\lambda). \tag{D}$$

As we can see, the problem (D) is a $m \ll n$ dimensional problem. It turns out that one can obtain a solution to (P) from a solution to (D). This means that one can obtain an efficient and exact algorithm to solve (P) that performs most computations with low dimensional vectors.

Computation of an Exact Solution to (P). Given some $\bar{\lambda} \in \mathbb{R}^m$ solution to (D), one can compute a solution $\bar{\mathbf{x}}$ to (P) by solving the following constrained least squares problem

$$\begin{cases} \min_{\mathbf{x} \in \mathbb{R}^n} & \|A\mathbf{x} - \mathbf{y}\|_2 \\ \text{s.t.} & x_i \geqslant 0 \text{ if } \langle \bar{\lambda}, M\mathbf{e}_i \rangle = -1, \quad \text{and} \quad M := -A \left(D^D \right)^{-1}. \\ & x_i \leqslant 0 \text{ if } \langle \bar{\lambda}, M\mathbf{e}_i \rangle = 1, \\ & x_i = 0 \text{ otherwise,} \end{cases} \tag{6}$$

In (6) and everywhere $\mathbf{e}_i$ denotes the i-th canonical vector of $\mathbb{R}^n$ (see (**iv**)), and $\left(D^D\right)^{-1}$ is the lower triangular matrix given by

$$\forall (i,j) \in [\![1,n]\!] \times [\![1,n]\!], \quad \left(D^D\right)^{-1}_{i,j} := \begin{cases} -1 & \text{if } i \leqslant j \\ 0 & \text{if } i > j. \end{cases} \tag{7}$$

where and everywhere $[\![1,n]\!] := \{1,\ldots,n\}$ (see (**i**)). We now detail how to compute a solution to (D).

Computation of an Exact Solution to (D). We consider an Euclidean steepest descent method (see, e.g., [3, Chap. 9]). Without loss of generality, we always initialize it with $\boldsymbol{\lambda}_0 := \mathbf{0}$. The algorithm proceeds as follows: (1) direction $\mathbf{d}_k$ computation, (2) step-size $\overline{\Delta t}_k$ computation and (3) update the iterate. As usual with descent algorithms, the couple direction/step-size is chosen so that for every $k \geqslant 0$, we have $g\left(\boldsymbol{\lambda}_k + \overline{\Delta t}_k \mathbf{d}_k\right) < g\left(\boldsymbol{\lambda}_k\right)$. We now give the methods to compute the direction $\mathbf{d}_k$ and then the step-size $\overline{\Delta t}_k$.

For any $\boldsymbol{\lambda}_k \in \mathbb{R}^m$, we define the binary set $S\left(\boldsymbol{\lambda}_k\right)$ of active indexes by

$$S\left(\boldsymbol{\lambda}_k\right) := \left\{ i \in [\![1,2n]\!] : \left\langle \boldsymbol{\lambda}_k, \widetilde{M}\tilde{\mathbf{e}}_i \right\rangle = 1 \right\}. \tag{8}$$

In (8) and everywhere $\tilde{\mathbf{e}}_i$ denotes the i-th canonical vector of $\mathbb{R}^{2n}$ (see (**iv**)). The matrix $\widetilde{M}$ is defined by the column-wise concatenation $\widetilde{M} := [M \mid -M]$ of M defined by (6)–(7).

The steepest descent direction $\mathbf{d}_k$ for g at $\boldsymbol{\lambda}_k$ is given by

$$\mathbf{d}_k := -\mathbf{y} - \underset{\mathbf{d} \in G(\boldsymbol{\lambda}_k)}{\arg\min}\|\mathbf{d}+\mathbf{y}\|_2^2 \quad \text{with} \quad G(\boldsymbol{\lambda}_k) := \left\{ \sum_{i \in S(\boldsymbol{\lambda}_k)} \eta_i \widetilde{M}\tilde{\mathbf{e}}_i : \eta_i \geqslant 0 \right\}. \tag{9}$$

Note that formula (9) can be computed by a constrained least squares similar to the one in (6). The step-size $\overline{\Delta t}_k > 0$ is given by

$$\overline{\Delta t}_k := \min_{i \in S^+(\mathbf{d}_k)} \left\{ \frac{1 - \left\langle \widetilde{M}\tilde{\mathbf{e}}_i, \boldsymbol{\lambda}_k \right\rangle}{\left\langle \widetilde{M}\tilde{\mathbf{e}}_i, \mathbf{d}_k \right\rangle} \right\} \quad \text{with} \quad S^+(\mathbf{d}_k) := \left\{ i \in [\![1,2n]\!] : \left\langle \mathbf{d}_k, \widetilde{M}\tilde{\mathbf{e}}_i \right\rangle > 0 \right\}. \tag{10}$$

The update rule is

$$\boldsymbol{\lambda}_{k+1} := \boldsymbol{\lambda}_k + \overline{\Delta t}_k \mathbf{d}_k.$$

As we have argued, the same methodology applies to (P_{ℓ^1}) and (P) with D chosen to use Neumann or Dirichlet boundary conditions. Some easy calculations shows that we need to use

- $M := A$, $S\left(\boldsymbol{\lambda}_k\right)$ defined by (8) and the reconstruction formula (6) to solve (P_{ℓ^1});
- $M := -A(D^D)^{-1}$, $S\left(\boldsymbol{\lambda}_k\right)$ defined by (8) and the reconstruction formula (6) to solve (P) with Dirichlet boundary conditions;

– $M := -A(D^D)^{-1}$, $\mathrm{S}(\boldsymbol{\lambda}_k)$ defined by

$$\mathrm{S}(\boldsymbol{\lambda}_k) := \left\{ i \in [\![1, 2n]\!] : \left\langle \boldsymbol{\lambda}_k, \widetilde{M}\tilde{\mathbf{e}}_i \right\rangle = 1 \right\} \cup \{n, 2n\} \tag{11}$$

and the reconstruction formula given by

$$\begin{cases} \min_{\mathbf{x} \in \mathbb{R}^n} & \|A\mathbf{x} - \mathbf{y}\|_2 \\ \text{s.t.} & x_n \in \mathbb{R} \ (\text{unconstrained}), \\ & \forall i \neq n, \ x_i \geqslant 0 \text{ if } \langle \bar{\boldsymbol{\lambda}}, M\mathbf{e}_i \rangle = -1, \\ & x_i \leqslant 0 \text{ if } \langle \bar{\boldsymbol{\lambda}}, M\mathbf{e}_i \rangle = 1, \\ & x_i = 0 \text{ otherwise,} \end{cases} \tag{12}$$

to solve (P) with Neumann boundary conditions.

> **Input:** Matrix M (see remark 1) and $\mathbf{y}$
> **Output:** $\bar{\mathbf{x}}$ solution to (P)
> Set $k = 0$ and $\boldsymbol{\lambda}_k = \mathbf{0} \in \mathbb{R}^m$
> **repeat**
> 1. Compute $\mathrm{S}(\boldsymbol{\lambda}_k)$
>   Use (8) for (P_{ℓ^1}) and (P)-Dirichlet or (11) for (P)-Neumann;
> 2. Compute $\mathbf{d}_k$ (see (9));
> 3. Compute $\mathrm{S}^+(\mathbf{d}_k)$ then $\overline{\Delta t}_k$ (see (10));
> 4. Update current point $\boldsymbol{\lambda}_{k+1} := \boldsymbol{\lambda}_k + \overline{\Delta t}_k \mathbf{d}_k$;
> 5. Set $k = k + 1$ and set $\boldsymbol{\lambda} := \frac{\boldsymbol{\lambda}}{\|M^\dagger \boldsymbol{\lambda}\|_\infty}$ if $\|M^\dagger \boldsymbol{\lambda}\|_\infty > 1$;
>
> **until** $\mathbf{d}_k = \mathbf{0}$ *(see remark 2)*;
> Compute $\bar{\mathbf{x}}$ using (6) for (P_{ℓ^1}) and (P)-Dirichlet or (12) for (P)-Neumann.

Algorithm 1. Algorithm computing $\bar{\mathbf{x}}$ solution to (P).

We now state Algorithm 1 that computes a solution to (D). This algorithm requires to evaluate inner products and to solve constrained least squares problems. To implement Algorithm 1 one can easily adapt the pseudo-code given in [9] with the modifications given above.

Remark 1 (Computation of the matrix M). To solve (P) with Algorithm 1 we need to compute the matrix $M := -A(D^D)^{-1}$. An easy calculation shows that M is made with cumulative sums, namely $\forall i \in [\![1, n]\!]$, $col(M, i) = \sum_{k=1}^{i} col(A, k)$, where and everywhere $col(M, i)$ denotes the i-th column of matrix M (see **(viii)**).

Remark 2 (Stopping condition [9]). The stopping condition, namely $\mathbf{d}_k = \mathbf{0}$, was replaced by $\|\mathbf{d}_k\|_2 \vee \|\overline{\Delta t}_k \mathbf{d}_k\|_2 < 10^{-10}$ in all of our experiments. In step 3, to prevent numerical issues, we test if the computed $\overline{\Delta t}_k$ satisfies $\overline{\Delta t}_k \geqslant 0$. If $\overline{\Delta t}_k < 0$ we set $\overline{\Delta t}_k := 0$ which ends the while loop at the current position.

Claim: Algorithm 1 converges after finitely many iterations to $\bar{\mathbf{x}}$ solution to (P).

For problem (P_{ℓ^1}), the claim was briefly justified in [9]. For problem (P) the claim is still valid since the matrices D considered in this paper are invertible. We now give an useful variant of Algorithm 1 for noisy signals.

Variant of Algorithm 1 for noisy signals. Following an idea used in, e.g., [4,5,25], for noisy signals estimation, one can use an early stopping rule. This rule is based on the following remark. Let $\mathbf{x}_k$ be the estimated signal obtained by applying one of the reconstruction formula, namely (6) or (12), with the current iterate $\boldsymbol{\lambda}_k$. It can be proved that $\|\mathbf{d}_k\|_2 = \|A\mathbf{x}_k - \mathbf{y}\|_2$ and that $k \mapsto \|\mathbf{d}_k\|_2$ is decreasing. As we have seen in Sect. 1, for noisy signals, one usually replaces the constraints $A\mathbf{x} = \mathbf{y}$ by $\|A\mathbf{x}_k - \mathbf{y}\|_2 \leqslant \sigma^2$. Here, this just means that we need to replace the stopping criterion of Algorithm 1, namely $\mathbf{d}_k = \mathbf{0}$, by $\|\mathbf{d}_k\|_2 \leqslant \sigma^2$.

3   Numerical Experiments

This section gives two kinds of experiments to evaluate the behavior of Algorithm 1. In a first paragraph, we evaluate it on real and simulated piecewise constant signals. For this first evaluation, we used the variant of Algorithm 1 with a total variation with Neumann boundary conditions. In a second paragraph we give an empirical evaluation of OMP [26], CoSamp [21], AISS [4], GISS [20], and Algorithm 1 for compressive sensing signal recovery, namely problem (P_{ℓ^1}).

Piecewise Constant Signals Denoising. Piecewise constant (PWC) signals arise in many application and we therefore illustrate the denoising behavior of Algorithm 1 on a simulated signal and on real signals of bacterial flagellar motors. Obviously, the matrix A is chosen as the identity matrix since we would like to denoise signals. For instance, if we wished to simultaneously denoise and upsample the signal we would deduce A from the positions of known entries in the observed data. For these denoising experiments with PWC signals, the variant of Algorithm 1 with Neumann boundary conditions is used. Figure 1 gives an examples of a PWC and of a noisy PWC signals. The difficulty of denoising PWC signals is that one usually want to avoid to introduce to much smoothness in the estimated signal contrarily to what a low pass filter would do. Figure 2 shows the estimated (or denoised) signal computed by Algorithm 1 from the noisy signal depicted on the right panel of Fig. 1. The estimated signal is close to the original one as expected. Figure 2 also shows that the sequence $k \mapsto \|\mathbf{d}_k\|_2$, where k is the number of iterations of Algorithm 1, is decreasing (see also last paragraph of Sect. 2). We now turn to the experiments on real signals of bacterial flagellar motor.

A flagellar motor plays the role of an electric motor for many bacteria. This motor allows a propellor-like structure called a flagellum to turn and enables the bacterium to swim. Signals related to the angular velocity are obtained by high-speed video recording of fluorescent beads attached to sticky flagellar filaments [27]. To analyze these signals one usually replaces them by PWC approximation as done in e.g., [27], see also [23]. To illustrate the behavior of Algorithm 1 on real noisy signals we used signals of *Escherichia coli* flagellum bacteria from [27]. For real signals the noise variance and distribution is often unknown and to apply Algorithm 1 two methods can be employed. One can store the entire sequence $\boldsymbol{\lambda}_k$ computed by Algorithm 1 and chose the adequate denoising parameter, or equivalently k, by visual inspection of restored signals $\mathbf{x}_k$ obtained by applying (12) with several (or every) $\boldsymbol{\lambda}_k$. An alternate strategy would be to chose the value of the residual $\sigma^2 := \|A\mathbf{x}_k - \mathbf{y}\|_2$ as we did for the experiments below. Indeed, it can be proven that $\|A\mathbf{x}_k - \mathbf{y}\|_2 = \|\mathbf{d}_k\|_2$ and that $k \mapsto \|\mathbf{d}_k\|_2$ is decreasing (see also Fig. 2). The adequate stopping criterion for Algorithm 1 becomes $\|\mathbf{d}_k\|_2 \leqslant \sigma^2$ instead of $\|\mathbf{d}_k\|_2 = 0$. Figures 3 and 4 show estimated (denoised) signals. As we have argued, the difficulty of denoising PWC signals is to avoid producing too smooth results. As can be seen on Figs. 3 and 4 Algorithm 1 succeeded at this task. We now turn to the compressive sensing signals recovery experiments.

Compressive Sensing Signal Recovery. Compressive sensing consists of solving problem (P_{ℓ^1}). Briefly, one would like to recover an unknown sparse vector $\mathbf{x}$

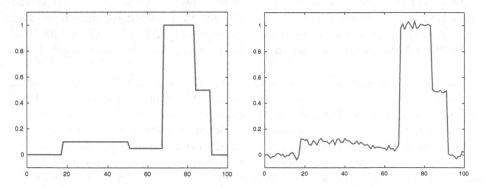

Fig. 1. Left panel: a piecewise constant signal. Right panel: the same signal corrupted by 2% additive white Gaussian noise.

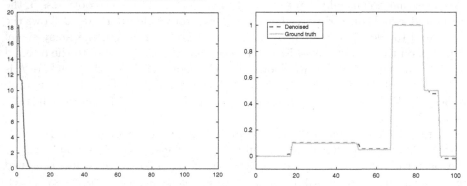

Fig. 2. Experiment on a simulated signal. Left panel: plot of $k \mapsto \|\mathbf{d}_k\|_2$ where k is the number of iterations of Algorithm 1 to verify that the sequence is decreasing. At (around) iteration $k = 11$, the residual $\|\mathbf{d}_k\|_2$ is of the order of the noise level and Algorithm 1 can be stopped. Right panel: estimated signal at iteration 11 (dashed line) from the noisy signal given on the right panel of Fig. 1 and ground-truth signal (solid line).

from a few inner products of $\mathbf{x}$ against the columns of a known measurement matrix A. We empirically evaluate the performance of OMP [26], CoSamp [21], AISS [4] GISS [20], and Algorithm 1. For these experiments, the matrix A has 1000 columns. The entries of A are drawn from i.i.d. realizations of a centered Gaussian distribution. Without loss of generality, we normalize the columns of A so that $\forall\, i$, $\|col(A, i)\|_2 = 1$. The number of rows of A, i.e., the number of measurements p, lives in $P := \{50, \ldots, 325\}$ with steps of 25. For $p \in P$, the *sparsity level* s varies between 5% and 40% with steps of 5%. The sparsity level is related to the ℓ^0 pseudo-norm of $\mathbf{x}$ by "$\|\mathbf{x}\|_0 = \text{round}\,(s \times p)$". The positions of

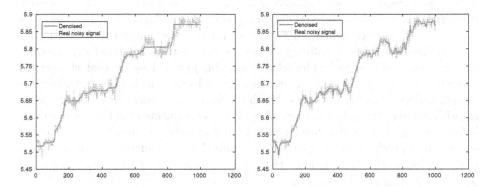

Fig. 3. Experiment with a real recorded signal of a bacteria flagellar motor corrupted by an unknown noise. The x-axis represents the time and the y-axis represents an angle. The left and right panels show two estimated signals (solid lines) from the observed noisy signal (dotted lines) using Algorithm 1. Left panel: after $k = 20$ iterations. Right panel: $k = 55$ iterations. The estimated signal fits better the observed signal when the number of iterations k increases but also becomes noisier.

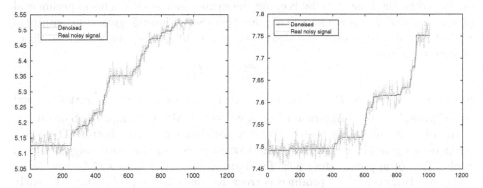

Fig. 4. Experiment with real recorded signals of a bacteria flagellar motor corrupted by an unknown noise. The x-axis represents the time and the y-axis represents an angle. The left and right panels show two estimated signals (solid lines) from the two observed noisy signals (dotted lines). Algorithm 1 was stopped based on the value of the residue $\|\mathbf{d}_k\|_2$ (see text).

the non-zero entries of $\mathbf{x}$ are chosen randomly, with uniform probability. The non-zero entries of $\mathbf{x}$ are drawn from i.i.d. realizations of a uniform random variable on $[-1, 1]$. To compute accurate statistics for each $s \in S := \{0.05, \ldots, 0.4\}$ and $p \in P$ we repeated the experiments $1,000$ times. For CoSamp and OMP we used the code of S. Becker (code updated on Dec 12th, 2012) that can be found online[1]. For AISS and GISS we used codes given by the authors of [4,20]. The implementation of CoSamp requires an estimate of the sparsity and we used an oracle for CoSamp, i.e., provided the exact ℓ^0 pseudo-norm of the source element.

For the comparison in terms of quality, we need to define when an experiment is a "success". Two natural options can be considered. A first choice would be to define the *success* as "the estimated signal $\mathbf{x}_{est}$ is a solution to (P_{ℓ^1})". However, this criterion would be verified for every output for Algorithm 1. Thus, this choice seems too much in favor of Algorithm 1 and rather uninformative. Another natural choice consists of defining *success* as "the estimated signal $\mathbf{x}_{est}$ is equal to the source element $\mathbf{x}$". This choice can be justified by several theoretical studies, see, e.g., [6,7,11,12]. Thus, this second criterion is chosen thereafter. This criterion is slightly in favor of methods designed to solve (P_{ℓ^0}) compared to algorithms, like Algorithm 1, that solve (P_{ℓ^1}). This means that the comparisons below are slightly biased in favor of [21,26]. Obviously, computations are carried out at finite precision and we therefore define that a reconstruction is *a success* if $\frac{\|\mathbf{x}-\mathbf{x}_{est}\|_2}{\|\mathbf{x}\|_2} < 10^{-10}$. It follows that, for any $(p, s) \in P \times S$, the empirical probability of success is given by

$$P_{(p,s)} := \frac{1}{\# \text{ of tests}} \sum_i \mathbb{1}_{\left\{ \frac{\|\mathbf{x}^i - \mathbf{x}^i_{est}\|_2}{\|\mathbf{x}^i\|_2} < 10^{-10} \right\}}(i), \tag{13}$$

where $\mathbf{x}^i_{est}$ (respectively $\mathbf{x}^i$) is the estimated signal (respectively source signal) of the i-th experiment. (We recall that "# of tests = 1000"). Every methods are evaluated on the same data by keeping the same random seed. This experimental setup was also considered in [9,17] for instance. Figure 5 gives the empirical probability of success (13). We also consider the difference between probabilities of success, namely

$$D_{(m,s)} := P^{algo\ 1}_{(m,s)} - P_{(m,s)}, \tag{14}$$

where $m \in M$, $s \in S$, $P^{algo\ 1}_{(m,s)}$ (respectively $P_{(m,s)}$) denotes the quantity defined by (13) obtained with Algorithm 1 (respectively OMP, CoSamp, AISS or GISS). If the quantity in (14) is positive then Algorithm 1 performs better. These differences are given in Fig. 6. OMP and CoSamp recover the source signal with a probability of approximately 80% for many more $p \in P$ and $s \in S$ than other methods. However, they produce correct results with a probability of nearly 100% for a much smaller set of parameters $p \in P$ and $s \in S$ than AISS, GISS, or Algorithm 1. Table 1 summarizes the main similarities and differences between OMP [26], CoSamp [21], AISS [4], GISS [20] and Algorithm 1. Table 1 also gives

---

[1] https://fr.mathworks.com/matlabcentral/fileexchange/32402-cosamp-and-omp-for-sparse-recovery.

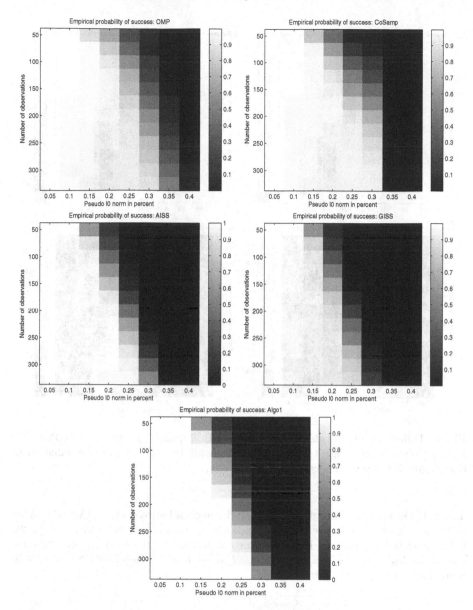

Fig. 5. Empirical probability of success (13). Panels (a)–(e): OMP [26], CoSamp [21], AISS [4], GISS [20] and Algorithm 1.

the empirical probability that a least $\alpha\%$ of signals are successfully estimated. This statistical indicator is defined by

$$P_{\geqslant \alpha} = \frac{\#\left\{(p, s) \in P \times S \,:\, P_{(m,s)} \geqslant \alpha\right\}}{\#P \cdot \#S}, \tag{15}$$

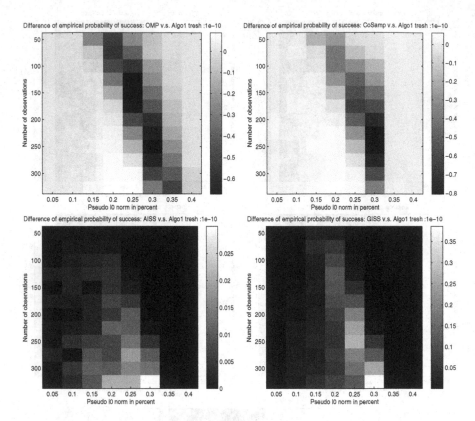

Fig. 6. Difference of probability of success (14). Panels (a)–(d): Algo 1-OMP [26], Algo 1-CoSamp [21], Algo 1-AISS [4] and Algo 1-GISS [20]. A positive value means that Algorithm 1 performs better.

Table 1. Overview of main similarities and differences between OMP, CoSaMP, AISS, GISS and algorithm 1. Below, E.R.C. stands for exact recovery condition see, e.g., [26], R.I.C. stands for restricted isometry constant see, e.g., [21], l.s. (respectively c.l.s.) stands for least squares (respectively constrained least squares) and h.t. stands for hard thresholding. Table taken from [9].

Algorithm	OMP [26]	CoSamp [21]	AISS [4]	GISS [20]	Algorithm 1
Assumptions: A/y	E.R.C	R.I.C	$\exists \mathbf{x} : A\mathbf{x} = \mathbf{y}$	E.R.C	full row rank
Variable(s)	$\mathbf{x}_k \in \mathbb{R}^n$	$\mathbf{x}_k \in \mathbb{R}^n$	$\mathbf{x}_k \in \mathbb{R}^n, \mathbf{p}_k \in \mathbb{R}^m$	$\mathbf{x}_k \in \mathbb{R}^n, \mathbf{p}_k \in \mathbb{R}^m$	$\lambda_k \in \mathbb{R}^m$
Update rule(s)	l.s. in $\mathbb{R}^n$	l.s., h.t. in $\mathbb{R}^n$	c.l.s. in $\mathbb{R}^n$	l.s. in $\mathbb{R}^n$	c.l.s. in $\mathbb{R}^m$
Convergence type	Probabilistic	Probabilistic	Exact	Exact	Exact
$P_{\geqslant 0.9}$ (15)	0.5104	**0.5521**	0.4688	0.4063	0.4688
$P_{\geqslant 0.95}$ (15)	0.3854	**0.4583**	0.4375	0.3333	0.4479
$P_{\geqslant 0.99}$ (15)	0.1042	0.1250	0.3438	0.1042	**0.4271**
$P_{\geqslant 0.999}$ (15)	0	0	0.1250	0	**0.3958**
$P_{\geqslant 1}$ (15)	0	0	0.0521	0	**0.3958**

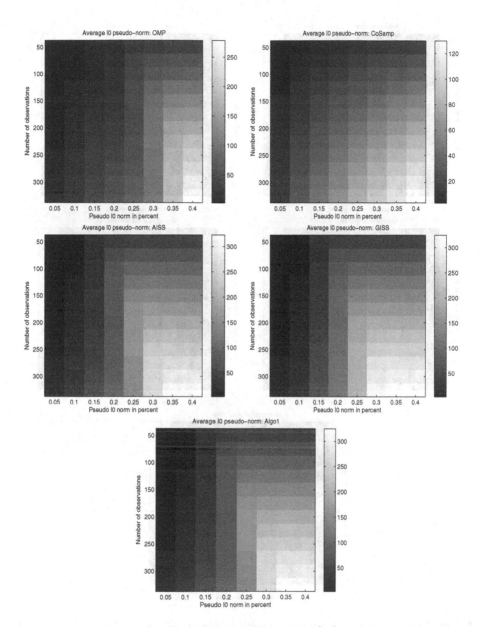

Fig. 7. Average ℓ_0 pseudo-norm. Panels (a)–(e): OMP [26], CoSamp [21], AISS [4], GISS [20] and Algorithm 1.

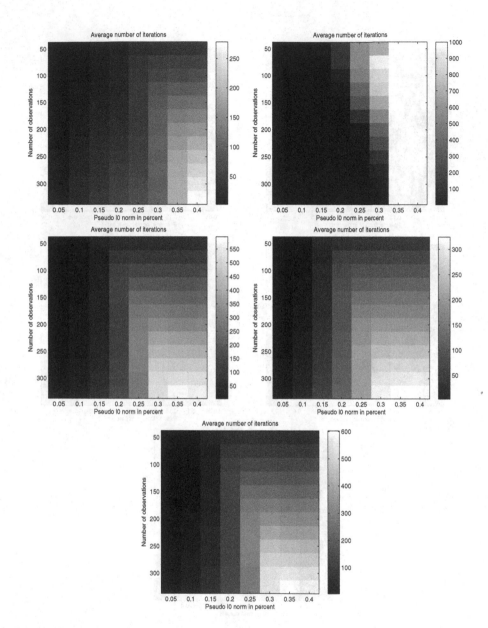

Fig. 8. Average number of iterations. Panels (a)–(e): OMP [26], CoSamp [21], AISS [4], GISS [20] and Algorithm 1. Greedy methods converge faster than AISS [4] or Algorithm 1.

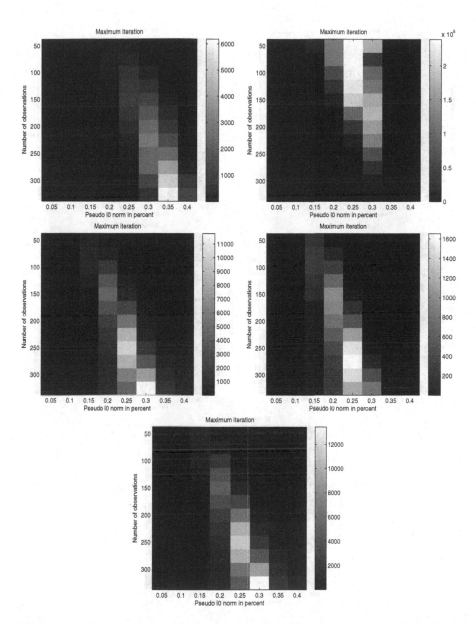

Fig. 9. Maximal number of iterations. Panels (a)–(e): OMP [26], CoSamp [21], AISS [4], GISS [20] and Algorithm 1.

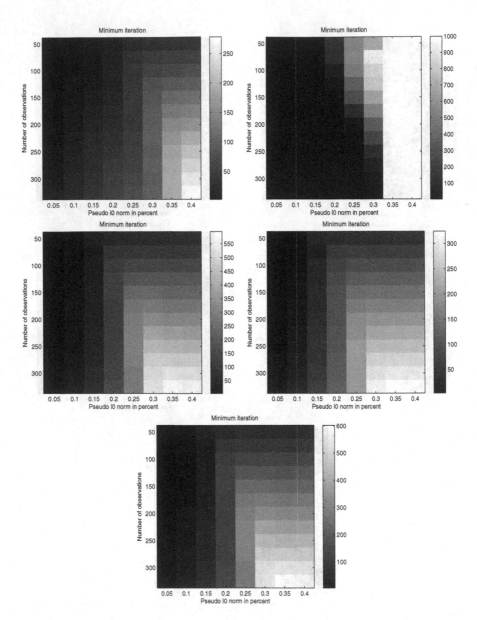

Fig. 10. Minimal number of iterations. Panels (a)–(e): OMP [26], CoSamp [21], AISS [4], GISS [20] and Algorithm 1.

where $P_{(m,s)}$ is defined by (13) and # denotes the cardinality of a set. Figure 7 gives the average ℓ^0 pseudo-norm of the estimated signals. Figure 8 gives the average number of iterations needed by the considered algorithms. Figures 9 and 10 give the maximal and minimal number of iterations needed by the considered algorithms.

4   Conclusion

In this paper, a new algorithm for signal estimation with ℓ^1-based *priors* was given. The algorithm is exact: it computes an exact minimizer of functionals of the form $\|\cdot\|_1 + \chi_{\{\mathbf{y}\}}(A\cdot)$ after finitely many iterations. This algorithm is simple to program. Indeed, it involves the evaluation of inner products and constrained least squares problems. This new algorithm just assumes that A has full row rank and can therefore be used in many situations. Compressive sensing signal estimation was considered and comparisons of this new algorithm with several standard methods of the literature were presented. Experiments on real noisy signals of bacterial flagellar motor were performed. These examples on real data show that the algorithm proposed in this paper is robust.

Acknowledgments. We would like to thank Y. Sowa for the flagellar motor data used in our experiments. We also would like to thank M. Möller for providing the implementation of the AISS and GISS algorithms.

Appendix

A.1   Notations and Definitions

(i) (n first integers) $\{1, \ldots, n\} := [\![1, n]\!]$

(ii) (Vectors) Vectors of, e.g., $\mathbb{R}^n$ are denoted in bold typeface, e.g., $\mathbf{x}$. Other objects like scalars or functions are denoted in non-bold typeface. Entries of $\mathbf{x}$ are denoted, e.g., x_i

(iii) (Norms) $\|\mathbf{x}\|_1 := \sum_i |x_i|$, $\|\mathbf{x}\|_2 := \sqrt{\sum_i |x_i|^2}$ and $\|\mathbf{x}\|_\infty := \max_i |x_i|$

(iv) (Canonical basis) $\mathbf{e}_i$ denotes the i-th canonical vector of $\mathbb{R}^n$, and $\tilde{\mathbf{e}}_i$ denotes the i-th canonical vector of $\mathbb{R}^{2n}$

(v) (Inner product) $\langle \mathbf{x}, \mathbf{y} \rangle = \sum_i x_i y_i$

(vi) (Identity matrix) I_n denotes de identity matrix of size $n \times n$

(vii) (Transpose operator) $M^\dagger$ denotes the transpose of a matrix M

(viii) (Column of matrix) $col(M, i)$ denotes the i-th column of matrix M

(ix) (Convex function) A function $f : \mathbb{R}^n \to \mathbb{R} \cup \{+\infty\}$ is said to be convex if $\forall (\mathbf{x}, \mathbf{y}) \in \mathbb{R}^n \times \mathbb{R}^n$ and $\forall \alpha \in (0, 1)$ $f(\alpha \mathbf{x} + (1-\alpha)\mathbf{y}) \leqslant \alpha f(\mathbf{x}) + (1-\alpha)f(\mathbf{y})$ holds true (in $\mathbb{R} \cup \{+\infty\}$)

(x) (Set $\Gamma_0(\mathbb{R}^n)$) The set of lower semi-continuous, convex functions with dom $f \neq \emptyset$ is denoted by $\Gamma_0(\mathbb{R}^n)$

(xi) (Characteristic function of a set) $\chi_E(\mathbf{x}) = 0$ if $\mathbf{x} \in E$ and $\chi_E(\mathbf{x}) = +\infty$ otherwise

(xii) (Convex conjugate) For any f convex that satisfies dom $f \neq \emptyset$, the function f^* defined by $\mathbb{R}^n \ni \mathbf{s} \mapsto f^*(\mathbf{s}) := \sup_{\mathbf{x} \in \text{dom } f} \{\langle \mathbf{s}, \mathbf{x} \rangle - f(\mathbf{x})\}$. (See, e.g., [16, Def. 1.1.1, p. 37])

References

1. Beck, A., Teboulle, M.: A fast iterative shrinkage-thresholding algorithm for linear inverse problems. SIAM J. Imaging Sci. **2**(1), 183–202 (2009)
2. Blumensath, T., Davies, M.E.: Iterative hard thresholding for compressed sensing. Appl. Comput. Harmonic Anal. **27**(3), 265–274 (2009)
3. Bonnans, J.F., Gilbert, J.C., Lemaréchal, C., Sagastizábal, C.A.: Numerical Optimization: Theoretical and Practical Aspects. Springer, Heidelberg (2006). https://doi.org/10.1007/978-3-540-35447-5
4. Burger, M., Möller, M., Benning, M., Osher, S.: An adaptive inverse scale space method for compressed sensing. Math. Comput. **82**(281), 269–299 (2013)
5. Cai, J.F., Osher, S., Shen, Z.: Linearized bregman iterations for compressed sensing. Math. Comput. **78**(267), 1515–1536 (2009)
6. Candes, E.J., Tao, T.: Decoding by linear programming. IEEE Trans. Inform. Theory **51**(12), 4203–4215 (2005)
7. Candes, E.J., Tao, T.: Near-optimal signal recovery from random projections: universal encoding strategies? IEEE Trans. Inform. Theory **52**(12), 5406–5425 (2006)
8. Chen, S.S., Donoho, D.L., Saunders, M.A.: Atomic decomposition by basis pursuit. SIAM Rev. **43**(1), 129–159 (2001)
9. Ciril, I., Darbon, J., Tendero, Y.: A simple and exact algorithm to solve l1 linear problems - application to the compressive sensing method. In: Proceedings of the 13th International Joint Conference on Computer Vision, Imaging and Computer Graphics Theory and Applications - Volume 4: VISAPP, pp. 54–62. INSTICC, SciTePress (2018)
10. Dai, W., Milenkovic, O.: Subspace pursuit for compressive sensing signal reconstruction. IEEE Trans. Inform. Theory **55**(5), 2230–2249 (2009)
11. Donoho, D.L.: Compressed sensing. IEEE Trans. Inform. Theory **52**(4), 1289–1306 (2006)
12. Donoho, D.L., Elad, M.: Optimally sparse representation in general (nonorthogonal) dictionaries via $\ell 1$ minimization. Proc. Natl. Acad. Sci. **100**(5), 2197–2202 (2003)
13. Foucart, S.: Stability and robustness of weak orthogonal matching pursuits. In: Bilyk, D., De Carli, L., Petukhov, A., Stokolos, A., Wick, B. (eds.) Recent Advances in Harmonic Analysis and Applications, vol. 25, pp. 395–405. Springer, New York (2013). https://doi.org/10.1007/978-1-4614-4565-4_30
14. Grant, M.C., Boyd, S.P.: The CVX Users' Guide, Release 2.1
15. Hale, E.T., Yin, W., Zhang, Y.: A fixed-point continuation method for l1-Regularized minimization with applications to compressed sensing. CAAM Technical Report TR07-07 (2007)
16. Hiriart-Urruty, J.B., Lemarechal, C.: Convex Analysis and Minimization Algorithms II: Advanced Theory and Bundle Methods. Grundlehren der mathematischen Wissenschaften. Springer, Heidelberg (1996)
17. Jain, P., Tewari, A., Dhillon, I.S.: Orthogonal matching pursuit with replacement. In: Advances in Neural Information Processing Systems, pp. 1215–1223 (2011)
18. Maleki, A.: Coherence analysis of iterative thresholding algorithms. In: 47th Annual Allerton Conference on Communication, Control, and Computing, Allerton, pp. 236–243. IEEE (2009)
19. Mallat, S., Zhang, Z.: Matching pursuits with time-frequency dictionaries. IEEE Trans. Signal Process. **41**(12), 3397–3415 (1993)

20. Moeller, M., Zhang, X.: Fast sparse reconstruction: greedy inverse scale space flows. Math. Comput. **85**(297), 179–208 (2016)
21. Needell, D., Tropp, J.A.: CoSaMP: iterative signal recovery from incomplete and inaccurate samples. Appl. Comput. Harmonic Anal. **26**(3), 301–321 (2009)
22. Needell, D., Vershynin, R.: Uniform uncertainty principle and signal recovery via regularized orthogonal matching pursuit. Found. Comput. Math. **9**(3), 317–334 (2009)
23. Nirody, J.A., Sun, Y.R., Lo, C.J.: The biophysicist's guide to the bacterial flagellar motor. Adv. Phys.: X **2**(2), 324–343 (2017)
24. Osher, S., Burger, M., Goldfarb, D., Xu, J., Yin, W.: An iterative regularization method for total variation-based image restoration. Multiscale Model. Simul. **4**(2), 460–489 (2005)
25. Osher, S., Mao, Y., Dong, B., Yin, W.: Fast linearized bregman iteration for compressive sensing and sparse denoising. arXiv preprint arXiv:1104.0262 (2011)
26. Pati, Y.C., Rezaiifar, R., Krishnaprasad, P.: Orthogonal matching pursuit: recursive function approximation with applications to wavelet decomposition. In: Conference Record of The Twenty-Seventh Asilomar Conference on Signals, Systems and Computers, pp. 40–44. IEEE (1993)
27. Sowa, Y., et al.: Direct observation of steps in rotation of the bacterial flagellar motor. Nature **437**(7060), 916 (2005)
28. Tropp, J.A., Gilbert, A.C.: Signal recovery from random measurements via orthogonal matching pursuit. IEEE Trans. Inform. Theory **53**(12), 4655–4666 (2007)
29. Zhang, X., Burger, M., Osher, S.: A unified primal-dual algorithm framework based on bregman iteration. J. Sci. Comput. **46**(1), 20–46 (2011)

Spatial and Spectral Calibration of a Multispectral-Augmented Endoscopic Prototype

Omar Zenteno[1]([✉]), Alexandre Krebs[2], Sylvie Treuillet[1], Yves Lucas[1], Yannick Benezeth[2], and Franck Marzani[2]

[1] PRISME, Université d'Orléans, 45072 Orléans, France
{omar.zenteno,sylvie.treuillet,yves.lucas}@univ-orleans.fr
[2] Le2i EA 7508, Univ. Bourgogne Franche-Comté, allée Alain Savary, BP47870, 21078 Dijon Cedex, France
{alexandre.krebs,yannick.benezeth,franck.marzani}@u-bourgogne.fr

Abstract. We developed a multispectral-augmented endoscopic prototype which increases the common number of bands under analysis, allowing exploration in the visible and near infrared range (400–1000 nm). The prototype combines endoscopy with spectroscopy using white light (WL) or Narrow Band Imaging light (NBI) endoscope and two multispectral cameras connected to a twin-cam splitter. The splitter is then connected to an optical fiber and introduced in the endoscope instrument channel.

In this work, we introduce a spectral calibration and an axial displacement correction function to register both modalities. The former is based on a multi-linear transformation of multispectral bands and its performance is assessed using a Digital SG ColorChecker® pattern to report an RMSE of 6.78%. The latter relates the insertion depth of the fiberscope with the required geometric transformation. The performance was assessed using a chessboard pattern and its corner coordinates as ground truth. The mean RMSE error for the registration using our method was 2.3 ± 0.7 pixels, whereas the RMSE error using a frame by frame homographic registration was 1.2 ± 0.4 pixels. Finally, the technique was tested on mouth exploration samples to simulate in-vivo acquisition and display complete spectra for single points of analysis. The results reveal that our method provides similar performance when compared to a homographic transformation which would be impossible to perform in-vivo.

Keywords: Gastroendoscopy · Multispectral imaging · Image registration

1 Introduction

Gastric inflammation is an invariable finding in patients infected with *Helicobacter pylori* and represents the host immune response to the organism. Gastric

D. Bechmann et al. (Eds.): VISIGRAPP 2018, CCIS 997, pp. 262–280, 2019.
https://doi.org/10.1007/978-3-030-26756-8_13

tissue is prone to a variety of affections. It produces surface epithelial degeneration and infiltration of the gastric mucosa by acute and chronic inflammatory cells which typically manifest with a limited set of symptomatology on early stages. Current endoscopic systems capability on these early stages are limited. However, spectral measurements and analysis, which provide accurate quantifications of morphology and microvascularity, can outperform them by detecting and monitoring the progression of these pathologies on time.

Several commercial multispectral imaging approaches have been proposed to improve gastric exploration. Typical examples are Fuji Intelligent Chromo Endoscopy (FICE), proposed by Fuji and Narrow Band Imaging (NBI), proposed by Olympus [21]. NBI uses specific emission wavelengths (415 nm and 540 nm) which correspond to the peaks of absorption of hemoglobin and has proved its efficiency for the detection of diseases like Barrett's esophagus [9]. These techniques have shown the benefits of using multiple wavelengths for diagnosis. However they are limited in the number of wavelengths processed. We believe that using a larger number of bands in the visible and near infrared range (400–1000 nm) could improve gastro-endoscopic exploration and diagnosis.

The standard for in- and ex-vivo multispectral exploration is the use of filter wheels or push broom systems [13]. However, both systems are ineffective for mapping moving tissue due to the temporal lag between wavelengths. In contrast, snapshot multispectral cameras can easily acquire reflectance data from the same area in all wavelengths simultaneously. Their downside is the low spatial resolution which extends into small scanning areas.

The majority of endoscopic systems are built-in with an instrument channel into which different tools (i.e., biopsy sampler, clamp tool, etc.) can be inserted. This makes possible to insert a fiberscope, connected to multispectral cameras into this instrument channel, working as a localized multispectral probe. However, both modalities must be registered to provide medically relevant information. This is not a trivial task, since due to the aseptic practices during medical and surgical procedures, the fiberscope must be sterilized between exams, forcing the physician to remove and reintroduce it into the instrument channel on each examination. This procedure leads to different relative positions between the fiberscope and endoscope for each new video. In addition, it is impossible to estimate the relation between coordinate systems using calibration patterns before the insertion of the fiberscope because, during the medical examination, the physician introduces first the endoscope into the patient for exploration and then the fiberscope into the instrument channel for localized screening. Thus, registration cannot be performed with conventional approaches (e.g., by matching singular points).

During exploration, two sources of relative movement are present: rotation and insertion. Rotation can be neglected if the introduction of the fiberscope into the endoscope is controlled so as to be performed always in the same position. However, the physician continuously inserts and retracts the fiberscope making it necessary to estimate a real time relation between the two sensors. Fortunately the end-tip of the fiberscope is visible throughout the endoscopic exploration, it can then be used as a feature for probe tracking if it is properly tracked. By maintaining the relation between the two modalities, the prototype provides physicians with multispectral information in small regions of interest overlaid to endoscopic images.

The present manuscript is an extension of the results presented in [24]. In the previous work, the images were registered effectively and single bands were overlaid to the endoscopic images. However, visualization enhancement was limited since the monitor of a classical screen is not able to render multispectral images for more than three channels. The real value of multispectral imaging resides in the information obtained from multiple wavelengths. Therefore, the possibility to create a linear combination of these wavelengths which can be shown simultaneously in the screen would be of high relevance in the medical context.

Therefore, we present an axial displacement correction function for a multi-spectral-augmented endoscopic system based on the relative position between fiberscope and endoscope which is complemented with an spectral calibration and transformation to improve the multispectral information visualization.

The remainder of this document is organized as follow: Sect. 2 summarizes current related work, Sect. 3 describes the system setup and its components, Section 4 the spectral correction, Sect. 5 presents the spatial registration, Sect. 6 the results obtained and finally Sects. 7 and 8 the discussion and conclusion respectively.

2   Related Work

In the gastrointestinal field, most multispectral (MS) and hyperspectral (HS) imaging studies have involved ex-vivo biopsies, resected tumor tissues, or organs such as the skin, tongue, or larynx. Clancy et al. [4] developed a laparoscopic HS system based on a liquid-crystal tunable filter (LCTF). In [14] and [15] an HS system with fluorescence for imaging of the larynx was developed. Also [6], used a micro Fabry-Perot interference filter placed at the tip of a flexible endoscope to create a wavelength-adjustable spectral endoscope. Nevertheless, this has not been used clinically yet. In addition [7] and [11], reported certain differences observed between healthy and pre-cancerous ex-vivo colon tissues. However, the color of the resected sampling tissues differed from what is normally observed in vivo, which suggests that the spectral properties of tissue may change after the resection process. In a recent study, [16] assessed the difference in the in vivo spectral response of malignant colorectal tumors and normal mucosa. Nevertheless, the acquisition systems used a color filter wheel, which makes temporal registration in different wavelengths a non-trivial task. Therefore, the main challenge we face is the registration between the different modalities (i.e., endoscopic and MS images). Although some solutions for similar problems have been implemented in the past, they do not necessarily aim at quantitative measurements but rather to improve the visual perception of the surgeon to facilitate handling of the endoscope. For example: a non-tracked calibrated endoscope for 3D reconstruction and motion estimation from endo-nasal images was used in [3] to register computerized tomography (CT) scans to the endoscopic video. Another navigation aid using photogrammetry during endoscopic surgery was studied in [12]. Here, structural information was used to prevent the endoscope image from flipping when the camera rotates. In [23], the position of a marked tool inside the surgical scene was determined from laparoscopic images and used to create 3D renderings from different views for the surgeon. In addition, the wide wavelength range makes difficult to directly use data for classification. Different methods have been used for dimensional reduction from the hyperspectral cube. This methods can be classified into two main categories: the band transformation also called feature extraction methods and the band selection methods [2,22]. In [5,18,19] externally tracked cameras were used to augment the surgeon's view by fusing preoperative data with the actual endoscopic view. As mentioned before, none of them enhance the endoscopic image with MS information.

3 Multispectral Imaging Prototype

3.1 Experimental Setup

Figure 1 depicts a diagram of the flexible multispectral gastro-intestinal prototype, which can be used to obtain a serie of reflected MS images in a contactless manner in the wavelength range of 470 to 975 nm.

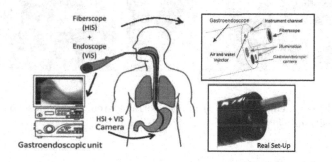

Fig. 1. Concept diagram of the multispectral prototype.

The system comprises six units: a mercury (Xenon) light source, an endoscope imaging unit, a visible (VIS) range MS camera, a Near Infrared (NIR) range MS camera, a fiberscope and a twin-cam camera splitter. It was implemented as a modification of the commercialized Olympus (Tokyo, Japan) EVIS EXERA III endoscopic system by introducing an ITConcepts (Lahnau, Germany) microflex m2.5-2500 fiberscope in the instrument channel for dual simultaneous exploration. The fiberscope is connected at one side to a Cairn research (Kent, UK) TwinCam® camera splitter by an optical adaptor and at the other to a mercury (Xenon) light source unit from Oriel Instruments® (California, USA). Finally, the VIS range camera MQ022HG-IM-SM4X4-VIS and the NIR camera model MQ022HG-IM-SM5X5-NIR from Ximea (Munster, Germany) are connected to both ends of the splitter respectively. Figure 2 depicts the multispectral system including the light source, TwinCam® system and fiberscope (left), the endoscopic system including the light source, processing system and endoscope (center) and an example of data acquisition using the prototype (right). The detailed specifications of the three cameras are presented in Table 1.

Table 1. [24] Camera specification.

Camera	Resolution	Bands
XIMEA SM5X5-NIR	409 × 216	25
XIMEA SM4X4-VIS	512 × 256	16
OLYMPUS EXERA III	720 × 576	3

a)   b)   c)

Fig. 2. [24] Experimental setup: (a) multispectral system, (b) endoscopic system, (c) in-vivo acquisition.

3.2 Acquisition Interface

A custom user interface for data acquisition was developed using C♯ programming language. The interface allows the user to capture raw MS images and gastroendoscopic video stream simultaneously while the three cameras are connected to the computer. The endoscope is connected through a firewire interface and the MS cameras are connected via USB 3.0 interface. The interface captures up to two images per second due to the high exposure time required for the MS system. All frames are timestamped to be able to associate each MS images to its closest endoscopic image. The association of both modalities allows the combination of textural information in endoscopic images and the spectral signature in MS images. The complete processing pipeline of the images is currently done off-line (i.e., image matching, filtering, spectral analysis).

4   Multispectral Preprocessing

The multispectral cameras do not directly give a reflectance spectra, they measure the radiance of the observed object. Thus a correction must be applied to remove sensor characteristics (i.e., quantum efficiency, transmission efficiency) and illumination. The spectral correction is divided in two parts. The first step is to remove the dark reference image b and divide by the exposure time τ as shown in Eq. 1. Where b represents what the camera captures while completely in the dark during the same exposure time τ as the measure. Secondly, the reflectance is obtained by a linear combination of the camera's bands. More formally, let x be a raw pixel of a MS image, represented as a row matrix of 41 values (16 in the visible and 25 in the NIR) and y the corresponding reflectance row matrix obtained trough an spectrometer. Then, there exist a transformation matrix W such that

$$\frac{(x - b)}{\tau} W = x'W = y. \tag{1}$$

Finding W can be done by imaging patches from a Digital ColorChecker® SG with MS cameras (x vectors). In practice, 96 patches were used for calibration and corrected to get x' vectors. The true reflectance y is acquired with a AvaSpec-ULS2048XL-EVO spectrometer from Avantes (Apeldoorn, Netherlands) and is able to acquire spectra between 200 nm and 1160 nm with non-constant spectral resolution. To provide a diffuse illumination on patches, an integrating sphere combined with an halogen light source AvaSphere-50-LS-HAL-12V, both from the same manufacturer as the spectrometer, are used.

W can then be obtained by classical least square method by minimizing

$$W^* = argmin \sum_i (x_i'W - y_i)^t (x_i'W - y_i). \tag{2}$$

To asses the performance of the spectral calibration, the aforementioned technique is used to simulate NBI and white light (WL) modes of an endoscope and compare them to the actual RGB endoscopic data. As for Eq. (1), there exist a transformation matrix W_{NBI} and a transformation matrix W_{WL} such that:

$$x'W_{NBI} = y_{NBI}. \tag{3}$$

$$and$$

$$x'W_{WL} = y_{WL}. \tag{4}$$

where y_{NBI} is a vector of three components corresponding to the color of a patch under NBI light and y_{WL} is a vector of three components corresponding to the R,G,B channels of a patch taken under white light. As NBI's wavelengths are 415 nm and 540 nm, the visible multispectral camera is enough to simulate NBI but for WL simulation, both cameras are used.

5   Spatial Registration

To calibrate all the cameras at the same time, we used a common chessboard pattern of 17×15 squares of 1 mm with an isosceles triangle in its center. The pattern allowed us to establish a relation between the geometrical coordinates of the two systems through a discrete measurement of how the triangle and its surroundings translate and expand in the image at different insertion depths.

The method is divided in two phases. An initial training phase which includes camera calibration and the estimation of the parametric correction model and an application phase that can be executed independently at any time using the images acquired by the physician. Both phases include a pre-processing initial stage. The overall process is illustrated in Fig. 3.

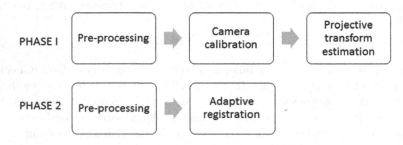

Fig. 3. Spatial registration: phase I (training) and Phase II (application).

5.1   Data Preprocessing

Noise reduction, contrast enhancement and illumination normalization were performed in the acquired raw images using common homomorphic filtering and devignetting techniques [8] and [17]. This procedure is necessary to remove noise and unwanted artifacts (i.e., the moiré effect or honeycomb patterns) produced by the disposition of fibers.

5.2   Cameras Calibration

Camera calibration was performed using MATLAB®'s built-in camera calibration toolbox which is a modified version of the method presented in [1] and uses the pin-hole camera model. The initial estimation of the planar homographies is based on the method presented in [25] and the closed-form estimation of the internal parameters was performed using orthogonality of vanishing points. The intrinsic model was similar to the one presented in [10] and includes radial distortion.

A set of endoscopic and multispectral (fiberscope) images before and after geometrical correction are presented in Fig. 4.

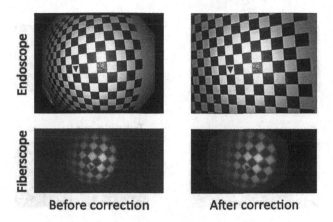

Before correction   **After correction**

Fig. 4. [24] Endoscopic and fiberscopic images: before (left) and after (right) radial distortion correction.

5.3   Projective Transform Estimation

The projective transformation (C_n) where n is the current frame can be formalized as a sequential transformation (as shown in Eq. 5) composed by homographic (H_0), scaling (S_n) and translation (T_n) transformations. H_0 is calculated only once during the training stage and is continuously used as the initial transformation at any depth. S_n and T_n are estimated for each frame and are linearly dependent on the detected insertion distance.

$$C_n = T_n * S_n * H_0 \qquad (5)$$

$$C_n = \begin{bmatrix} 1 & 0 & t_{x_n} \\ 0 & 1 & t_{y_n} \\ 0 & 0 & 1 \end{bmatrix} \begin{bmatrix} s_n & 0 & 0 \\ 0 & s_n & 0 \\ 0 & 0 & 1 \end{bmatrix} \begin{bmatrix} h_{11} & h_{12} & h_{13} \\ h_{21} & h_{22} & h_{23} \\ h_{31} & h_{32} & h_{33} \end{bmatrix}$$

The initial projective transformation matrix H_0 is calculated by matching similar control points in the two images under analysis. First, an adaptive histogram equalization is applied on the pattern's image to enhance the dynamic range. Then, automatic thresholding and morphological operations are performed to differentiate between triangles and rectangles (Number of vertices, extrema distribution and area relations). Then, the four proximate corners surrounding the triangle are used to define a new image reference frame to facilitate the control point matching (as shown in Fig. 5).

The scaling and translation matrix S_n and T_n are then estimated by relating the insertion measurement with the mean measured distance between points and the X and Y axis central displacement.

S_n is calculated based on the mean of the distances from the center of the triangle to 8 points in the borders of the central 2×2 pattern on all the images

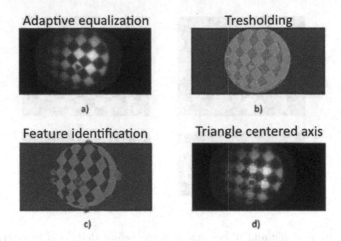

Fig. 5. Pattern identification and creation of new axis on fiberscopic images. (a) Histogram equalization, (b) Thresholding, (c) BO analysis, (d) New reference axis centered in the triangle vertex.

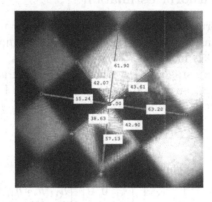

Fig. 6. [24] Measurement of distances to the center of the 2×2 central pattern.

in the data base. Figure 6 depicts the eight corners, the center of the pattern and the distance between each of them on a sample fiberscopic frame. We used this information to evaluate the relation between the insertion depth and how the mean distance between corners and center scales through different frames. To estimate the scaling factor, a normalization of the measured distance based on the first sampling frame was performed.

Similarly, the central displacement T_n is analyzed frame by frame based on the location of the center on the triangle from the pattern.

These measurements (i.e., scaling and translation) have to be correlated to the insertion depth. The depth measurement procedure is depicted in Fig. 7. After manual segmentation of the fiberscope the depth is measured by the

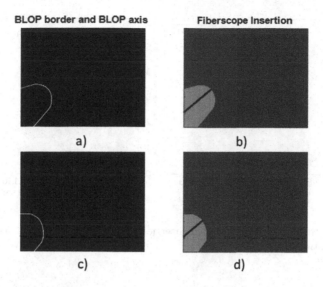

Fig. 7. [24] (a), (c): segmentation of the fiberscope tip and (b), (d): BLOP's axis intersection measurement.

Euclidean distance between the pixels intersecting the principal axis and the ellipsoidal boundaries.

Scaling and translation correction: s_n, t_{x_n} and t_{y_n} are formalized as a function of the insertion depth (d_n) as shown in Figs. 8 and 9. We used a training set consisting of 15 endoscopic and 15 multispectral images, each one with the fiberscope at a different insertion depth. Finally, a quadratic polynomial model is fitted to provide Eqs. 6, 7 and 8.

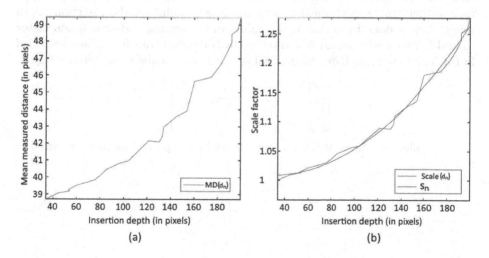

Fig. 8. [24] Relation graphs between insertion depth and: (a) mean measured distance, (b) normalized scaling factor.

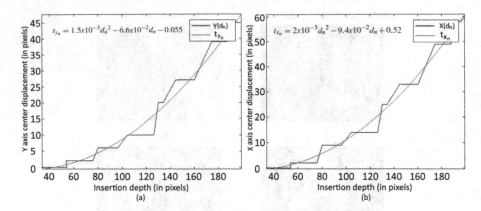

Fig. 9. [24] Relation graph between insertion depth and: (a) x-axis translation, (b) y-axis translation.

These two functions (i.e., scaling and translation correction functions: s_n, t_{x_n} and t_{y_n}) are formalized as a function of the insertion depth (d_n) as shown in Eqs. 6, 7 and 8.

$$s_n = 8.8 x 10^{-6} d_n^2 - 5 x 10^{-4} d_n + 1 \tag{6}$$

$$t_{x_n} = 2 x 10^{-3} d_n^2 - 9.4 x 10^{-2} d_n + 0.52 \tag{7}$$

$$t_{y_n} = 1.5 x 10^{-3} d_n^2 - 6.6 x 10^{-2} d_n - 0.055 \tag{8}$$

5.4   Adaptive Registration

Once the correction functions have been estimated, the fiberscope-to-endoscope registration can be performed at any continuous point on the insertion depth range. This is done by replacing the values of the scaling and translation factor s_n and t_n obtained from Eq. 6, 7 and 8 in the correction transformation described in Eq. 5 and applying it to the original image I_o to calculate registered image I_r as follows:

$$\begin{bmatrix} x' \\ y' \\ 1 \end{bmatrix}_{I_r} = T_n * S_n * H_0 * \begin{bmatrix} x \\ y \\ 1 \end{bmatrix}_{I_o} \tag{9}$$

The different stages of the adaptive registration procedure are presented in Fig. 10.

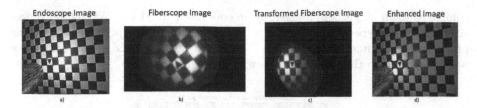

Fig. 10. Adaptive registration pipeline: (a) Pattern detection in original endoscope image, (b) Pattern detection in original fiberscope image, (c) Undistorted and transformed image and (d) Enhanced image.

6   Results

6.1   Spectral Calibration Validation

The spectral calibration was assessed using a Digital ColorChecker® SG for a total of 96 different color patches. These patches are acquired using both, the multispectral cameras and a spectrometer. After the transformation matrix W is computed. Each of the 96 acquisitions are multiplied by W and compared to the ground truth obtained by the spectrometer. The root mean square error (RMSE) for each wavelength is depicted on Fig. 11.

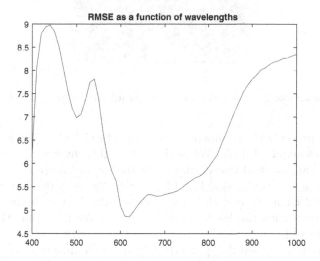

Fig. 11. RMSE as a function of wavelengths.

The RMSE is between 5% and 9% of error (mean 6.78%).In addition, we observe that the range between 600 nm and 650 nm is the range with the lowest error.

To measure how a change in a spectra affects the color we perceive we simulated NBI-like and WL-like images derived from the multispectral images and compared them 96 patches imaged by an endoscope in NBI or WL mode respectively. The multispectral images were transformed by multiplying them by the previously computed W_{NBI} or W_{WL} matrices. Finally, this simulated images were compared to the ones obtained with the endoscope.

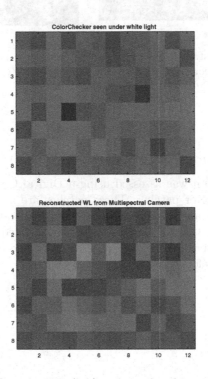

Fig. 12. Color checker® under WL (left) and simulated image from MS data (right).

Figure 12 presents the results obtained from the ColorChecker®. On the left, the 96 patches acquired under WL and on the right, the same patches acquired with the MS cameras and transformed with the learned matrix W_{WL} are shown respectively. In the same way, Fig. 13 presents the results obtained with the endoscope in NBI mode and the same patches acquired with the MS cameras and transformed with the learned matrix W_{NBI}. We note that the colors are well reconstructed.

For evaluation we used ΔE_{ab}^* metric, which is well known to compare colored images. This metric is the classical euclidean distance but it is applied on the CIE L*a*b* color space instead of the RGB color space. CIE L*a*b* was designed to be perceptually uniform with respect to human color vision, meaning that the same amount of numerical change in these values corresponds to about the same amount of visually perceived change [20]. The mean ΔE_{ab}^* value between the two images on Fig. 12 is 8.6. The mean ΔE_{ab}^* value between the two images on Fig. 13 is 17.5. These means that the difference between colors is perceptible but still similar in both cases.

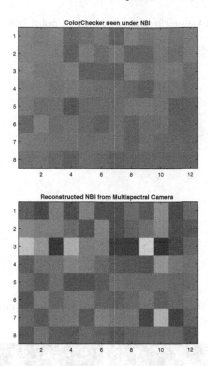

Fig. 13. Color checker under NBI (left) and simulated image from MS data (right).

6.2 Spatial Registration Assessment

The performance test was executed using a chessboard pattern as sample and the coordinates of its corners as ground truth. The test sample comprised 25 MS and endoscopic frames in which the fiberscope is at different insertion depths. The fiberscope is always observable in the endoscopic image. For evaluation, the mean and the standard deviation of the root mean square error (RMSE) (when compared to the ground truth coordinates) on each corner of the pattern after registration with our method were compared to those obtained when using a frame-by-frame homographic registration. This comparison is shown on Fig. 14. In addition, the registration was also tested on mouth exploration samples to simulate in-vivo acquisition. In all cases, the acquisition on all cameras was performed simultaneously.

An example of the registration results is depicted on Fig. 15. Four different registered fiberscope and endoscope image overlays at a different position of the fiberscope for each frame are shown. The endoscopic image appears in the background in a darker tone, while the transformed fiberscopic image appears highlighted. While observing the images it is easy to recognize the progressive transformation of the fiberscopic image at different depths.

Table 2. Comparison of the performance of control point homography vs the proposed method.

Frame	MEAN
H_n RMSE	1.2 ± 0.4
C_n RMSE	2.3 ± 0.7

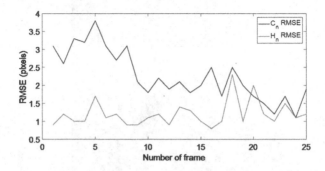

Fig. 14. Comparison of the performance of control point homography vs the proposed method for each different frame.

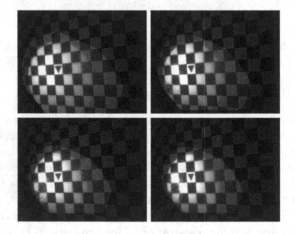

Fig. 15. Examples of registered images where the fiberscope is at different depths.

Performance statistics for each set of images are presented in Fig. 14 and Table 2. We observe that the highest errors are present in the frames were the tip position is close to the camera plane. In addition, the mean RMSE error between ground-truth coordinate points and the resulting transformed coordinates using frame-by-frame homography and our correction transformation matrix were 1.2 ± 0.4 and 2.3 ± 0.7 respectively.

In addition, the qualitative performance of the proposed method on mouth samples revealed a high level of coherence between the registered images and explored the ability to analyze the normalized spectrum for a selected point in the registered image. Figure 16 depicts a sample frame of the resulting video. The registered spectral information of a single wavelength and a frame of a mouth exploration endoscopic video are presented on the top left and right of the image respectively. The data of a single band is not enough to characterize the tissue, so the full corrected spectra is shown in the bottom part for the area inside the red square of Fig. 16.

7   Discussion

The spectral calibration effectively transform a multispectral image into reflectance spectra. This technique can be used to present the multispectral registered image in a simulated WL or NBI colorspace. However, the real potential of this technique could reside in the creation of new color spaces which can better represent textural or spectral features or highlight hypervascularity in the gastric mucosa. The exploration of these new spaces or possible combinations must be explored including in-vivo medical samples.

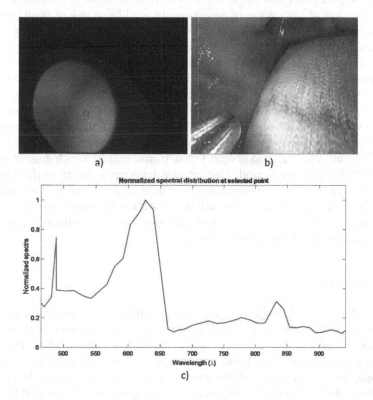

Fig. 16. Common grid creation on the new axis on (a) endoscopic images, (b) fiberscopic images.

While performing WL simulation, the biggest RME where related to the patches on the upper right corner of the ColorChecker® which were not perfectly reconstructed. For the NBI simulation, all the green patches (in WL) appeared red in NBI which was expected as the red channel is centered at 540 nm and green colors are approximately between 495 and 570 nm.

The spatial registration results are also encouraging, the registered pattern fits into the endoscopic image at different insertion depths. Statistically, the error in all cases was lower than 4 pixels. As the resolution of the endoscopic images is 726×576p, a 2–3 pixels error is less than 1% on each direction. Moreover, the simplicity of the proposed method and the use of common image processing tools make it ideal for future real-time implementations.

However, although the spatial registration function has proven to effectively correct the difference between the relative position of the two camera axes, some limitations are still present. First, in the current implementation the insertion of the endoscope was controlled to ensure that it was always performed in the same position. Even though it is a trivial task, it would be ideal to relieve the physician of this constraint. Secondly, we detected a third source of movement which we call precession that is produced by the circular movement of the fiberscope through the small surrounding space between the endoscope and the fiber. Further exploration of the effects of precession in a wider range of positions should be carried out. Thirdly, the correction function will always be system dependent, this means that the initial discrete homography process should always be executed if the physician changes the endoscope or video system. However, if the video system is modified, a camera calibration is always required and the two processes (i.e., calibration and correction) can be performed simultaneously with similar data. Finally, the current frame rate of the multispectral system is two images per second. This may produce motion artifacts introduced by either the probe operator or target movement and is not ideal to perform in-vivo acquisitions. In contrast, the endoscopic video frame rate is much higher with the standard 25 images per second. Further development is being performed in the interface on a real-time implementation of these steps, which will not only overlaid single endoscope images but will also be able to show real time spectral information to physicians. Also, a real gastro-endoscopic sample is required for further exploration of the spectral data.

8   Conclusion

A method for spectral calibration and compensation of the insertion and retraction motion of a fiberscope inserted in the instrument channel of an endoscope have been presented. The method relies on applying a linear affine transformation over a one-time control point homography. Experimental results using real endoscopic images showed that the method can track the camera insertion and retraction motion. The incorporation of more degrees of freedom and the combination of different spectral signatures may enable us to achieve real-time robust tracking and enhanced visualization in the future.

Acknowledgements. The authors would like to thank M.D. Dominique Lamarque for his expertise in gastro-enterology and his precious help in the project. This work was supported by the EMMIE (Endoscopie MultiModale pour les lésions Inflammatoires de l'Estomac) project funded by the ANR-15-CE17-0015 grant.

References

1. Bouguet, J.Y.: Matlab camera calibration toolbox. Caltech Technical report (2000)
2. Burgers, K., Fessehatsion, Y., Rahmani, S., Seo, J., Wittman, T.: A comparative analysis of dimension reduction algorithms on hyperspectral data. LAMDA Research Group, August 2009
3. Burschka, D., Li, M., Ishii, M., Taylor, R.H., Hager, G.D.: Scale-invariant registration of monocular endoscopic images to ct-scans for sinus surgery. Med. Image Anal. **9**(5), 413–426 (2005)
4. Clancy, N.T., et al.: Multispectral image alignment using a three channel endoscope in vivo during minimally invasive surgery. Biomed. Opt. Express **3**(10), 2567–2578 (2012)
5. Deligianni, F.: Visual augmentation for virtual enviromnents in surgical training. Ph.D. thesis, Imperial College London (2006)
6. Dohi, T., Matsumoto, K., Shimoyama, I.: The micro fabry-perot interferometer for the spectral endoscope. In: 18th IEEE International Conference on Micro Electro Mechanical Systems, MEMS 2005, pp. 830–833. IEEE (2005)
7. Galeano, J., Jolivot, R., Benezeth, Y., Marzani, F., Emile, J.F., Lamarque, D.: Analysis of multispectral images of excised colon tissue samples based on genetic algorithms. In: 2012 Eighth International Conference on Signal Image Technology and Internet Based Systems (SITIS), pp. 833–838. IEEE (2012)
8. Georgieva, V.: Homomorphic filtering approach for narrowband images enhancement. J. Appl. Electromagn. (JAE), in print (2015)
9. Hamamoto, Y., Endo, T., Nosho, K., Arimura, Y., Sato, M., Imai, K.: Usefulness of narrow-band imaging endoscopy for diagnosis of Barrett's esophagus. J. Gastroenterol. **39**(1), 14–20 (2004)
10. Heikkila, J., Silven, O.: A four-step camera calibration procedure with implicit image correction. In: Proceedings of the 1997 IEEE Computer Society Conference on Computer Vision and Pattern Recognition, 1997, pp. 1106–1112. IEEE (1997)
11. Kiyotoki, S., et al.: New method for detection of gastric cancer by hyperspectral imaging: a pilot study. J. Biomed. Opt. **18**(2), 026010–026010 (2013)
12. Koppel, D., Wang, Y.F., Lee, H.: Image-based rendering and modeling in video-endoscopy. In: IEEE International Symposium on Biomedical Imaging: Nano to Macro, pp. 269–272. IEEE (2004)
13. Lu, G., Fei, B.: Medical hyperspectral imaging: a review. J. Biomed. Opt. **19**(1), 010901 (2014)
14. Martin, M.E., et al.: Development of an advanced hyperspectral imaging (HSI) system with applications for cancer detection. Ann. Biomed. Eng. **34**(6), 1061–1068 (2006)
15. Martin, R., Thies, B., Gerstner, A.O.: Hyperspectral hybrid method classification for detecting altered mucosa of the human larynx. Int. J. Health Geogr. **11**(1), 21 (2012)
16. Martinez-Herrera, S.E., et al.: Identification of precancerous lesions by multispectral gastroendoscopy. Signal Image Video Process. **10**(3), 455–462 (2016)

17. Nair, J.J., Govindan, V.: Intensity inhomogeneity correction using modified homomorphic unsharp masking. J. Med. Imaging Health Inform. **4**(2), 285–290 (2014)
18. Sauer, F., Khamene, A., Vogt, S.: An augmented reality navigation system with a single-camera tracker: system design and needle biopsy phantom trial. In: Dohi, Takeyoshi, Kikinis, Ron (eds.) MICCAI 2002. LNCS, vol. 2489, pp. 116–124. Springer, Heidelberg (2002). https://doi.org/10.1007/3-540-45787-9_15
19. Scholz, M., et al.: Development of an endoscopic navigation system based on digital image processing. Comput. Aided Surg. **3**(3), 134–143 (1998)
20. Sharma, G., Bala, R.: Digital Color Imaging Handbook. CRC Press, Boca Raton (2002)
21. Song, L.M.W.K., et al.: Narrow band imaging and multiband imaging. Gastrointest. Endosc. **67**(4), 581–589 (2008)
22. Van Der Maaten, L., Postma, E., Van den Herik, J.: Dimensionality reduction: a comparative. J. Mach. Learn. Res. **10**, 66–71 (2009)
23. Westwood, J., et al.: Reconstruction and enhancement in monocular laparoscopic imagery. Medicine Meets Virtual Reality 12: Building a Better You: the Next Tools for Medical Education, Diagnosis, and Care, vol. 98, p. 37 (2004)
24. Zenteno, O., Krebs, A., Treuillet, S., Lucas, Y., Benezeth, Y., Marzani, F.: Dual-channel geometric registration of a multispectral-augmented endoscopic prototype. In: Proceedings of the 13th International Joint Conference on Computer Vision, Imaging and Computer Graphics Theory and Applications - Volume 4: VISAPP, pp. 75–82. INSTICC, SciTePress (2018). https://doi.org/10.5220/0006721200750082
25. Zhang, Z.: Flexible camera calibration by viewing a plane from unknown orientations. In: Proceedings of the Seventh IEEE International Conference on Computer Vision, vol. 1, pp. 666–673. IEEE (1999)

Random Forests Based Image Colorization

Helge Mohn, Mark Gaebelein, Ronny Hänsch$^{(\boxtimes)}$, and Olaf Hellwich

Computer Vision and Remote Sensing, Technische Universität Berlin,
Berlin, Germany
{r.haensch,olaf.hellwich}@tu-berlin.de
http://www.cv.tu-berlin.de

Abstract. The task of image colorization, i.e. assigninging color values
to grayscale images, is usually addressed by either exploiting explicit user
input or very large training data sets. In contrast, the proposed method
is fully automatic and uses several orders of magnitude less training
images. To this aim, a Random Forest is tailored to the task of regressing
plausible color value given a patch of the grayscale image. In order to
improve the colorization performance, the Random Forests also includes
a simple position prior. The proposed approach leads to satisfying results
over various colorization tasks and compares favorably with the state of
the art based on convolutional networks.

Keywords: Image colorization · Random forests · Regression

1 Introduction

From the first stable grayscale photo in history taken in 1826 by Joseph N.
Niépce, it took more than 60 years until photography was available for the mass
market with the introduction of Kodak Nr. 1 in 1888. Color films, however, would
not been available for another 50 years. Even after the release of color films by
Agfa and Kodak in 1936, grayscale films remained in common use - for specific
use cases even until today [1].

The century, when grayscale films have been the only possibility to take pho-
tographs, leaves a tremendous amount of pictures that would potentially benefit
from a robust and automatic colorization method [2,3]. Possible applications
of colorization, however, go beyond grayscale photography and include the colorization of night vision images or the production of pseudo-color images to
emphasize certain image structures such as structural damage in X-ray images.

Assigning plausible color values to a grayscale image is a very sophisticated
task and in general an ill-posed problem since several colors in the real world
would result in the same grayscale intensity [4]. Thus, prior knowledge needs
to be included, which helps to overcome these ambiguities. Existing work for
colorization of grayscale images can be coarsely divided based on the source of
this prior knowledge.

© Springer Nature Switzerland AG 2019
D. Bechmann et al. (Eds.): VISIGRAPP 2018, CCIS 997, pp. 281–297, 2019.
https://doi.org/10.1007/978-3-030-26756-8_14

Color embedding is an applicational area, which is only loosely related to colorization. Corresponding methods aim at saving the chrominance information within a given grayscale image. One example is [5], which maps color values to high-frequency textures of low visibility and adds them to the grayscale image. As this process is reversible, it allows a color-to-grayscale conversion as well as the "recolorization" of the obtained grayscale image. However, it requires the availability of the corresponding color image so that the correct information can be encoded into the grayscale image.

Fig. 1. A Random Forest (RF) is trained with color images that have a similar scenery as the query grayscale image. The trained RF is able to determine a plausible color version of a given grayscale image. Image taken from our previous work [6] with identical general workflow.

Another related field is the color transfer between frames of a grayscale video. Certain keyframes are colorized by a given method, e.g. manually, and the given color values are subsequently transferred from one frame of the video to the next. Corresponding methods rely on matches between the image content which can be established either manually as in [7] or automatically as in [8]. Due to the high similarity of adjacent frames, this process provides highly accurate and reliable results. The question how the keyframe can be colored is left unanswered, though.

A large group of colorization approaches involve a human operator to exploit the vast knowledge of humans about objects in the real world. Users label a few pixels within the image with corresponding colors, which are then propagated to neighboring pixels with similar intensity or textural patterns [8–11]. The strength of these approaches is certainly the user. On the one hand, humans are naturally well trained to match colors from memory. On the other hand, colors will be selected that are plausible on the object-or semantic level instead of being based on low-level image information such as texture or intensity alone. While these approaches result in a visually pleasing color version, the involvement of a human operator is time consuming and hinders the application to a large amount of images.

A second group of colorization approaches aims at limiting user interaction by using a (single) reference color image of high similarity [2,12–15]. Colors are then transferred from the reference to the target image by matching image areas based on characteristics such as local intensity and standard deviation [2] as well as more sophisticated features such as Gabor and SURF descriptors [15]. These approaches limit the amount of user interaction, but often require careful parameter tuning and rely on reference images of high similarity to enable a correct region matching.

The last group consists of fully automatic approaches which do not rely on any kind of manual interaction. Instead, they are based on a set of training images where additional to the grayscale data the corresponding color information is known. These methods derive a statistical model of the relationship between intensity and textural patterns on the one side and realistic colors on the other side. Recent examples are [16–18] which are based on Convolutional Networks (ConvNets) that are trained on millions of color images. The resulting networks are able to colorize general images and often lead to visually pleasing results.

While approaches such as [17] are based on millions of training images, our approach operates with 10–20 images with the additional constraint that these images show a similar scene (see Fig. 1). Due to the smaller amount of images, training is very efficient and can be easily tailored to specific scenes for various applications.

The here proposed method is an extension of our earlier work published in [6] and applies a Random Forest (RF, [19]) for the regression task of estimating plausible color information when provided with a local grayscale image patch. Color information is stored as 2D histograms over chrominance values within the CIE L*a*b* color space. Although the RF is trained on only a few images of a similar scene, the usage of local image patches as well as comparatively large histograms would lead to a large memory footprint if naively implemented. Two solutions are proposed to cope with this problem. First, the color histograms at the leafs are usually sparse and can thus be stored in a memory-efficient manner. The second solution is based on the observation, that only tree creation needs to hold all training samples in the memory (see Sect. 2.2), while tree training can be executed on training batches (see Sect. 2.3). Instead of pre-computing any kind of low-level features, the RF is applied to the grayscale images directly. Corresponding node tests compute several implicit features on the fly (as for example in [20]), which allow memory- and time-efficient processing and are furthermore highly adaptable to the specific colorization task. Observed color values are rebalanced similar to [17] to account for the fact that pastel colors occur more frequently than saturated colors.

The contribution of the proposed method is therefore seven-fold, where the last three points are extensions of this work over [6]:

- Decoupling tree creation and tree training to make full use of a large amount of training samples during the estimation of the target variable.
- Implicit feature learning makes the computation of predefined features obsolete.
- A sparse representation of the target variables leads to memory-efficient RFs.
- Color rebalancing leads to realistically saturated colors.
- Segmentation-based sampling increases diversity of training pixels.
- Weighted counting in leaf histograms eases quantization problems.
- Variable patch size allows to automatically learn the appropriate feature scale.

2   Colorization Algorithm

2.1   Preprocessing

The proposed colorization method is based on a RF (see Sects. 2.2–2.4) as regression method. As supervised approach, it relies on training data which - additionally to the grayscale images - provides the corresponding color information. While ground truth data is difficult to obtain in many other supervised machine learning problems such as semantic segmentation, it basically comes for free for colorization tasks. Any kind of color image can be transformed into a grayscale version where the latter is used as training data and the former as reference image. The proposed method uses the CIE L*a*b* color space to perform regression, since it decouples luminance from color information. Thus, training images are converted from RGB to CIE L*a*b*, where the luminance L* is used as training input and the a*b* components as target variable. During prediction, the luminance is provided by the query image itself, which is then fused by the estimated chrominance information to obtain a color image.

2.2   Creation of a Random Forest

A RF is a set of binary decision trees, where each tree is a hierarchical structure of split- and leaf-nodes. All trees are created independently from each other and should be as diverse as possible in order to benefit from averaging their results during prediction. Diversity is usually achieved by introducing randomization processes during tree creation. A first source of randomization is bagging, i.e. creating individual training sets for each tree by randomly sampling data from the training set.

During tree creation, split nodes are subsequently added to a tree starting at the root node. Every split node partitions the data, that is propagated to this node, based on a simple binary test Ψ. Depending on the outcome of this test, the corresponding subsets are propagated further to the left or right child node. The performance of each tree and thus of the whole forest depends strongly on the definition and selection of reasonable node tests. Vanilla RF implementations usually simply split along one randomly selected feature dimension, which in our application scenario corresponds to test whether the luminance L of a certain pixel $(x + \Delta x, y + \Delta y)$ within the patch at (x, y) is higher or lower than a threshold T. Equation 1 shows this first luminance feature (Ψ_1), which basically determines whether a pixel lies within a bright or a dark region. This work additionally applies node test variants that are more tailored towards the analysis of images (as for example proposed in [20]). Equation 2 shows a second luminance feature Ψ_2 which compares the luminance difference of two pixels $(x + \Delta x_i, y + \Delta y_i), i \in \{1, 2\}$ located in a patch at (x, y) to a threshold T. This feature is an approximation of the local gradient and thus analyses the local texture. Figure 2 visualizes these two features.

$$\Psi_1 : L(x + \Delta x, y + \Delta y) \geq T \tag{1}$$

$$\Psi_2 : L(x + \Delta x_1, y + \Delta y_1) - L(x + \Delta x_2, y + \Delta y_2) \geq T \tag{2}$$

In contrast to [6], we modell the offset vector $(\Delta x, \Delta y)$ as $r(\cos \theta, \sin \theta)$ where θ is drawn from a uniform distribution $U(0, 2\pi)$ and r from a Normal distribution $N(2, 5)$. For larger offset vectors, we use the average grayvalue over a small region as luminance value in Eqs. 1–2, i.e. regions of size 1×1 if $r \in [0, 3)$, 2×2 if $r \in [3, 5)$ and 3×3 if $r > 5$.

A second group of node tests aims at including a prior model on the positions that different colors take within an image. Depending on the application scenario, i.e. the nature of the query image, some colors are more likely to occur at certain image positions. Simple examples are landscape images, which often show blue pixels at the top (i.e. the sky) or portraits that show pixels of skin color rather in the center.

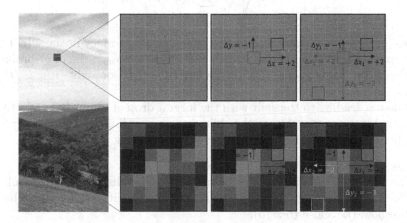

Fig. 2. From left to right: Part of a grayscale image; Example patches taken from marked pixel positions; Luminance feature Ψ_1; Luminance difference feature Ψ_2. The two rows show a homogeneous patch at the top and a textured patch at the bottom. Image taken from our previous work [6], that applies the same type of node tests. (Color figure online)

Three different node tests are used to enable the RF to learn the color prior from the training data. The first variant tests whether the pixel coordinates of a patch are within a circular area, whose position and size are randomly determined. The other two variants simply split either on the x- or on the y-coordinate of the patch position (very similar to test type Ψ_1) and thus divide the image into axis-aligned blocks.

Nearly all of the used node tests involve the comparison of a scalar value (either luminance or pixel coordinate) with a threshold. There are many ways to define this threshold ranging from random sampling to a completely optimized selection. We define the threshold as the median of the projected values as this splits the data into two equally large parts (if possible). This leads to trees that are most balanced. Thus, they apply a maximum amount of node tests to the data and achieve a fine-grained partition of the feature space. However, this threshold definition depends on the data only and is independent of the reference data.

In order to optimize the node tests with respect to the target variable, each newly created split node generates multiple different test candidates during tree creation. These different test instances are created by randomly sampling test parameters, e.g. which of the five different test types is applied, which pixel positions are to be used, etc. Each of these tests splits the local data into two subsets. While [6] computes the drop of impurity (Eq. 3) based on the Gini index, we use the mean deviation from the mean (Eq. 4) of the local sample as impurity measure which is better suited for regression problems.

$$\Gamma = I_{node} - (P_{left} \cdot I_{left} + P_{right} \cdot I_{right}) \tag{3}$$

$$I_n = \sqrt{\frac{1}{N_n} \sum_{i=1}^{N_n} ||(a,b)_i - \overline{(a,b)}_n||_2^2} \tag{4}$$

where $\overline{(a,b)}_n$ is the mean value of the reference a*b* values in the CIE L*a*b* color space of all N_n samples at node n and $P_n = N_n/N_{node}$ the prior probability whether a sample is propagated to the left ($n = left$) or right ($n = left$) child node.

The test leading to the split with the largest drop of impurity is selected and the samples are propagated to the child nodes accordingly.

The recursive splitting stops, if one of the following criteria is met:

- The maximum tree height is reached.
- The minimum number of samples within a node falls below a threshold.
- The largest drop of impurity of all generated split candidates is below a threshold (i.e. close to zero).

2.3   Training of a Random Forest

As colorization is an inherently ill-posed problem, it benefits from the virtually unlimited amount of training data. The creation of the random decision trees, however, relies on the availability of all data samples in order to perform node test optimization (see Sect. 2.2). Thus, only a certain fraction of available training samples is used to define the tree structure. While our previous work [6] samples those pixels randomly from all available training pictures, we extended this approach by performing a coarse segmentation of the images beforehand and draw a fixed amount of samples from each segment. This ensures that large homogeneous regions do not lead to a domination of certain color or textures in the training samples. Thus, the creation of the RF is based on a more diverse set of samples.

Once the trees are created, they have to be trained, i.e. an estimate of the target variable has to be assigned to the corresponding leaf nodes. This process does not require all samples to be present at once. Thus, to train the trees all samples from all training images are used.

Training patches are propagated through the tree based on the node tests as defined during tree creation. Once a patch reaches a leaf node, it is used to update the estimate of the target variable, i.e. the corresponding color. To this purpose the color information is quantized and stored in two-dimensional histograms representing the local posterior of the a*b* part of the CIE L*a*b* color space. To ease problems due to this quantization, a given color value is distributed to neighboring bins if its specific value lies close to the bin boundaries. Due to the nature of the decision trees, these histograms tend to be very sparse and can thus be saved in an efficient manner in order to minimize the memory footprint of the trees.

At the end of the training process all histograms are normalized according to the hue occurrence within the training data. This rebalancing is a typical processing step to ensure that samples that are underrepresented within the training data are treated with similar importance as more frequent samples. This is especially important in colorization tasks, since rather weak colors appear significantly more often than strongly saturated colors. Colors with a high occurrence in the training images would then dominate numerous hue histograms.

Figure 3 shows an input image on the left. The top of the right side shows a detail of the colorization result without normalization after the training process, while the bottom right illustrates the colorization result with normalization. In this example green is the dominant color which clearly dominates brown. Without proper normalization the brown tip of the tomato is falsely colorized in green. After performing a normalization the tomato point is correctly colorized in brown.

2.4   RF Application

During prediction, patches around all pixels of the query image are propagated through the trees in the same way as during tree training. A patch x will reach exactly one leaf n_t in each individual tree t. Let $p_{n_t}(a, b|x)$ be the a*b* histogram of the particular leaf n_t in tree t that had been reached by patch x. The a*b*-histograms of these leafs are averaged over all N_T trees and the maximal

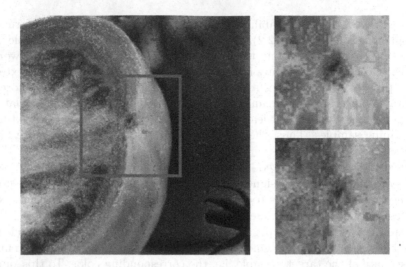

Fig. 3. Histogram normalization: Left: Ground truth image (a green tomato); Right: Colorization results. Without normalization (top) the tip of the tomato is falsely colored in green, while it is correctly colored brownish if all histograms are normalized according to the chrominance occurrence in the training data (bottom). (Image taken from our previous work [6].) (Color figure online)

value of the resulting histogram is assigned as chrominance estimate $\hat{a}^*\hat{b}^*$ to the corresponding pixel:

$$\hat{a}^*\hat{b}^* = \arg\max_{a,b} p(a,b|x) \tag{5}$$

$$p(a,b|x) = \frac{1}{N_T} \sum_{t=1}^{N_T} p_{n_t}(a,b|x) \tag{6}$$

The estimated $\hat{a}^*\hat{b}^*$-values together with the grayscale value of the query image provide the complete CIE L*a*b*-vector which is then converted to the RGB color space and saved at the corresponding image position.

3   Evaluation

3.1   Data

The proposed method assumes a small database of images similar to the query image (see Fig. 1). The difficulty of the colorization task depends on the content of the query images and how well their statistics match the statistics of the training data. These two factors are somewhat connected: If scenes have a limited color variation and a clear relationship between texture and color, it is more likely to sufficiently represent them with a few training images. If scene content is diverse and similar textures are colored differently, the training data might not suffice to extract all necessary information and even if, the estimated mapping will be ambiguous. In order to evaluate the performance without having a selection bias towards too easy (or too hard) image types, we collected data for seven different and diverse categories, namely Sanssouci, RedbrickHouse, GarbageCan, PolarLight, Airport, Train, Grapes (see for example Fig. 6). Those are used during the final evaluation (see Sect. 3.3), while parameter tuning was performed on the separate eight category Forest (see for example Fig. 8). These categories include man-made as well as natural objects, homogeneous as well as strongly textured regions, and cover a wide range of color distributions.

3.2 Random Forest Statistics

The colorization results depend solely on the performance of the applied RF since no other type of processing (e.g. label smoothing as post processing) is involved.

That is why this section briefly analyzes two example instances of a RF that were trained on images of the category Sanssouci and PolarLight, respectively, with image patches of variable size (see Sect. 2.2). It consists of 16 trees that have been grown until maximal height. A node needed to contain at least 10 samples to continue splitting. In this case, 300 possible split candidates are created randomly and evaluated based on the drop of impurity (see Eq. 3). If the drop of impurity of the best split was below 10^{-4} or other stopping criteria became valid, the recursive partitioning stopped. In this case, a leaf node is created containing a 2D histogram over possible a*b* values discretized into a 128×128 grid.

Figure 4(a) shows the number of leafs existing at a specific tree height within a tree of the forest. The longest path within the forest only reached a height of 34. Most paths end before height 20, which shows that the trees are fully grown. Increasing the maximal tree height will not change the tree topology unless they are induced with a larger set of samples during tree creation.

Instead of acting as a pure black-box system, RFs allow some insights into their decision making process. One example is the frequency how often certain node tests have been performed. Figure 4(b) shows the selection frequency of the implicitly calculated features (see Sect. 2.2). The luminance difference of pixels inside a patch (test type Ψ_2) has been used most often, followed by the luminance value itself (test type Ψ_1). While the latter distinguishes between dark and bright patches, the former analyses the local texture by approximating the luminance gradient. As spatial prior information the circular region prior (see Sect. 2.2) is preferred over the x-y-position.

Each internal node within a tree aims at dividing the data in a way such that the corresponding child nodes are as "pure" as possible, i.e. contain samples mostly having similar colors. One way to measure the "pureness" of a node in a regression tree is to compute the average distance of the samples to their mean value (see Eq. 4). The left side of Fig. 5(a) shows the number of leafs with different impurity levels of the proposed approach for an example image from the PolarLight category. Most of the leafs contain samples that concentrate within a

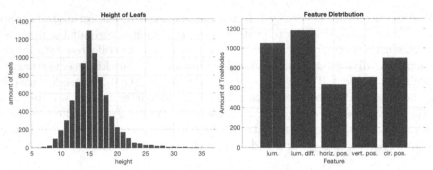

(a) Amount of leafs at different tree levels (b) Frequency how often a certain node test within a tree of the forest.   is performed within a tree of the RF.

Fig. 4. Forest statistics.

very small region around the mean value (e.g. less than 5), while only a few leafs contain a set of colors of mediocre diversity (e.g. average distance between 10 and 20). The right side of Fig. 5(a) shows the same information for our previous work [6] which treated the color regression task rather as a classification problem and used the Gini impurity for optimization. This measure minimizes only the amount of different hues, but does not take the distance between them into account, e.g. two different tones of red lead to the same level of impurity as one red and one blue tone. Consequently, the hues within the leaf histograms tend to span a much wider range in comparison with the newly proposed implementation that optimizes the sample standard deviation explicitly.

Figures 5(b)–(d) show estimated histograms of three different leaf examples with different impurities (see Eq. 4) ranging from a very pure leaf to a very impure leaf. As can be seen, even for leafs with high impurity the colors have been well clustered by the forest and stay within close proximity to each other.

Figure 5(e) shows the distribution of the colorization error within an example image and illustrates that only very few pixels deviate much from their true color, while most pixels have been assigned with a color close to the reference value.

3.3   Results

Image colorization is an ill-posed problem: The same texture might have very different colors. One example is the color of the hair of a person, which can - taken artificial hair colors into account - be practically anything despite having very similar textures. On the other hand, the goal of image colorization is often not to assign the "correct" color (i.e. the color the object had when the grayscale picture was taken), but to assign a realistic color (i.e. the color objects of this category usually have). Thus, achieving a visually pleasing result is often more important than a "correct" result or - in other words - a "wrong" result can still be acceptable for a human observer.

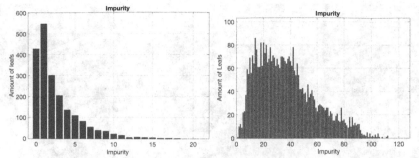

(a) Frequency of leafs with different levels of impurity measured as average sample distance to sample mean. Left: This work. Right: Previous work [6].

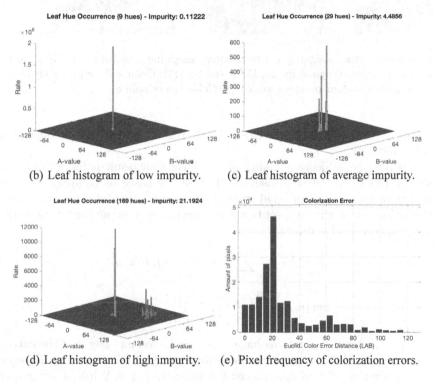

(b) Leaf histogram of low impurity.   (c) Leaf histogram of average impurity.

(d) Leaf histogram of high impurity.   (e) Pixel frequency of colorization errors.

Fig. 5. Leaf impurities and resulting colorization error for an image of category PolarLight. (Color figure online)

This is illustrated in Fig. 6, which shows the colorization result of the proposed method on the right and the result of the reference method [17] in the center. Both results are not correct in a numerical sense: The proposed method colors the blurry background in blueish colors giving it a flowerbed-like look, while it is supposed to be green. The reference method colors the grapes in a

Fig. 6. Rather than assigning a correct color, assigning a realistic color is important. From left to right: Original image; Colorized by [17]; Colorized by proposed method. (Image taken from our previous work [6]) (Color figure online)

greenish-brownish color. Nevertheless, both results look equally plausible and visually pleasing.

However, the subjective quality of a colorization result is hard to measure. Thus, we rely on objective measurements that are based on comparing the estimated color image to the ground truth. In particular, we state the error $Err(E)$ of the estimation E with respect to a reference image R as the Euclidean distance of the respective color values.

$$Err(E) = \sum_{(x,y) \in E} err(E(x,y), R(x,y)) \tag{7}$$

$$err(e,r) = \left\| \begin{pmatrix} e_{a*} - r_{a*} \\ e_{b*} - r_{b*} \end{pmatrix} \right\|_2 \tag{8}$$

All parameter optimizations have been conducted on images of the category Forest of which Fig. 7 shows example training images. These images have been used to train the RF that has colored the image in Fig. 8. While showing a very similar scene, the actual image content is general enough (given the category) to easily find colored examples.

Figure 8 shows the corresponding colorization result. The top row shows the original image on the left and the corresponding grayscale image on the right. The second row shows the colorization result obtained by the proposed method with the corresponding error map on the right where black means a correct colorization and white corresponds to the maximum Euclidean distance between estimated and reference chrominance. The third row shows the colorization result

Fig. 7. Training images for result in Fig. 8.

obtained by the reference method [17] together with the corresponding error map[1].

Figure 9(a) shows the influence of the number of trees on this error for images of the category Forest. As expected for RFs, there is a steady decrease of the error with increasing number of trees. However, the change saturates quickly for RFs with more than 20 trees. It should be noted that the various system

---

[1] The error maps are contrast enhanced for better visibility in print.

Fig. 8. Results of example image from the Forest category; The top row shows the original color image on the left as well as the grayscale version on the right. The second and third row show on the left the colorization results of the proposed and the reference method, respectively, as well as the corresponding error maps (See footnote 1) on the right.

parameters have been optimized for images of this category alone, but not on any of the categories of the final performance evaluation described next.

Even within a category, the image content can vary largely, e.g. day vs. night images of a building or summer vs. winter images of a landscape. That is why the training images within a category are divided into three groups: Similar to the query, dissimilar to the query, and mixed. A separate RF is trained on each of these three groups and evaluated on common query images.

(a) Dependency of the regression error on the number of trees within the forest (tested in images of the Forest category).

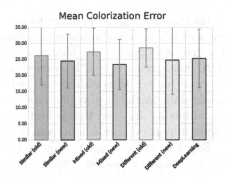

(b) Comparison of the previous approach in [6] with the proposed method for three different scenarios (i.e. similarity between training set and query image) as well as a reference method based on deep learning [17].

Fig. 9. Results of the proposed method, i.e. Euclidean error between estimated and reference color image.

The first six columns of Fig. 9(b) show the corresponding performance for all three scenarios using the approach in [6] (denoted by "old") and the newly proposed approach (denoted by "new"). The proposed method outperforms the previous approach in all three cases. Furthermore, while the previous method showed a clear decrease in performance if the diversity in the training set increases, the proposed approach shows rather robust results.

The last column shows the performance of the reference method proposed by [17]. It should be noted that this method is based on training a deep convolutional network on millions of images. This tremendous effort during training allows the network to colorize general images during prediction. Our method, on the other side, is trained on a rather small database of training images which have to be of the same category as the query image. The results of the deep network are slightly worse than the performance of the RF in all three considered training scenarios. The differences, however, are well within the standard deviation of the results of both methods and are thus not significant. Thus, the proposed framework presents a viable alternative to the deep network in the case where training on many images is either not possible or not desired.

4 Conclusions

Similar to our previous work in [6], we address the specific use case of having a small but specific training database available that comprises the texture-color statistics of the query images. This is in contrast to other related works that instead aim for colorization of arbitrary images and allows us to keep training time at a minimum and to lessen ambiguities.

Instead of using hand-crafted features we use a Random Forest variant that is able to learn meaningful features automatically by analysing the local structure of a grayscale patch. The hue information is saved within the terminal nodes as 2D histograms over a*b* values of the CIE L*a*b* color space. Applying a spatial prior that is also learnt from the data, relating the sampling rate of trainig data to the local region size based on a coarse segmentation, and using a local quality criterion that is better suited for regression further improved the results in particular in comparison to our previous work in [6].

Experiments over a different image categories including several man-made and natural scenes indicate that the proposed method is able to colorize grayscale images, if a suitable database of training images is available. The obtained colorization results are on par with a reference method which is based on a deep convolutional network trained on millions of images and used for general colorization tasks.

The proposed approach works particular well if the training images match the color statistics of the query image. This requirement will be addressed in future work by using more and more diverse images, which - in principle - allow the colorization of images from less specific topics or scenes. This not only requires the usage of more and deeper trees which leads to an increase in time and memory cost, but also to a more sophisticated pipeline that is able to distinguish between different topics in order to reduce ambiguities.

A second future research direction is how the estimated colors can be adjusted in a post-processing step. In particular global optimization schemes, such as conditional random fields, should allow to not only obtain local color consistency but also to achieve a colorization that is plausible on a global level.

References

1. Mulligan, T., Wooters, D.: Geschichte der Fotografie. Von 1839 bis heute. TASCHEN (2015)
2. Welsh, T., Ashikhmin, M., Mueller, K.: Transferring color to greyscale images. ACM Trans. Graph. **21**, 277–280 (2002)
3. Bugeau, A., Ta, V.T., Papadakis, N.: Variational exemplar-based image colorization. IEEE Trans. Image Process. **23**, 298–307 (2014)
4. Horiuchi, T.: Estimation of color for gray-level image by probabilistic relaxation. In: Object Recognition Supported by User Interaction for Service Robots, vol. 3, pp. 867–870 (2002)
5. de Queiroz, R.L., Braun, K.M.: Color to gray and back: color embedding into textured gray images. IEEE Trans. Image Process. **15**, 1464–1470 (2006)
6. Mohn, H., Gaebelein, M., Hänsch, R., Hellwich, O.: Towards image colorization with random forests. In: Proceedings of the 13th International Joint Conference on Computer Vision, Imaging and Computer Graphics Theory and Applications, vol. 4, pp. 270–278. VISAPP, INSTICC, SciTePress (2018)
7. Karthikeyani, V., Duraiswamy, D.K., Kamalakkannan, P.: Conversion of gray-scale image to color image with and without texture synthesis. Int. J. Comput. Sci. Netw. Secur. **7**, 11–16 (2007)

8. Irony, R., Cohen-Or, D., Lischinski, D.: Colorization by example. In: Proceedings of the Sixteenth Eurographics Conference on Rendering Techniques, EGSR 2005, pp. 201–210 (2005)
9. Levin, A., Lischinski, D., Y.W.: Colorization using optimization. ACM Trans. Graph. (TOG) (2004). Proceedings of ACM SIGGRAPH
10. Huang, Y.C., Tung, Y.S., Chen, J.C., Wang, S.W., Wu, J.L.: An adaptive edge detection based colorization algorithm and its applications. In: Proceedings of the 13th Annual ACM International Conference on Multimedia, MULTIMEDIA 2005, pp. 351–354 (2005)
11. Yatziv, L., Sapiro, G.: Fast image and video colorization using chrominance blending. IEEE Trans. Image Process. **15**, 1120–1129 (2006)
12. Hertzmann, A., Jacobs, C.E., Oliver, N., Curless, B., Salesin, D.H.: Image analogies. In: Proceedings of the 28th Annual Conference on Computer Graphics and Interactive Techniques, SIGGRAPH 2001, pp. 327–340 (2001)
13. Charpiat, G., Hofmann, M., Schölkopf, B.: Automatic image colorization via multimodal predictions. In: Forsyth, D., Torr, P., Zisserman, A. (eds.) ECCV 2008. LNCS, vol. 5304, pp. 126–139. Springer, Heidelberg (2008). https://doi.org/10.1007/978-3-540-88690-7_10
14. Liu, X., et al.: Intrinsic colorization. ACM Trans. Graph. **27** (2008)
15. Gupta, R.K., Chia, A.Y.S., Rajan, D., Ng, E.S., Zhiyong, H.: Image colorization using similar images. In: Proceedings of the 20th ACM International Conference on Multimedia, MM 2012, pp. 369–378 (2012)
16. Cheng, Z., Yang, Q., Sheng, B.: Deep colorization. In: Proceedings of the 2015 IEEE International Conference on Computer Vision (ICCV), ICCV 2015, pp. 415–423 (2015)
17. Zhang, R., Isola, P., Efros, A.A.: Colorful image colorization. In: Leibe, B., Matas, J., Sebe, N., Welling, M. (eds.) ECCV 2016. LNCS, vol. 9907, pp. 649–666. Springer, Cham (2016). https://doi.org/10.1007/978-3-319-46487-9_40
18. Cao, Y., Zhou, Z., Zhang, W., Yu, Y.: Unsupervised diverse colorization via generative adversarial networks. In: Ceci, M., Hollmén, J., Todorovski, L., Vens, C., Džeroski, S. (eds.) ECML PKDD 2017. LNCS (LNAI), vol. 10534, pp. 151–166. Springer, Cham (2017). https://doi.org/10.1007/978-3-319-71249-9_10
19. Breiman, L.: Random forests. Statistics Department University of California Berkeley, CA, 94720 (2001)
20. Lepetit, V., Fua, P.: Keypoint recognition using randomized trees. IEEE Trans. Pattern Anal. Mach. Intell. **28**, 1465–1479 (2006)

A Survey on Databases of Facial Macro-expression and Micro-expression

Raphaël Weber[1,2,3]($\boxtimes$), Jingting Li[1], Catherine Soladié[1], and Renaud Séguier[1]

[1] FAST Team, IETR Lab., CentraleSupelec, Avenue de la Boulaie,
35576 Cesson-Sévigné, France
{raphael.weber,jingting.li,catherine.soladie,
renaud.seguier}@centralesupelec.fr
[2] Univ. Rennes, LTSI - UMR_S 1099, 35000 Rennes, France
raphael.weber@univ-rennes1.fr
[3] INSERM, U1099, 35000 Rennes, France

Abstract. A crucial step for developing and testing a system of facial expression analysis is to choose the database which suits best the targeted context application. We propose in this paper a survey based on the review of 69 databases, taking into account both macro- and micro-expressions. To the best of our knowledge, there are no other surveys with so many databases. We review the existing facial expression databases according to 18 characteristics grouped in 6 categories (population, modalities, data acquisition hardware, experimental conditions, experimental protocol and annotations). These characteristics are meant to be helpful for researchers when they are choosing a database which suits their context application. We bring to light the trends between posed, spontaneous and in-the-wild databases, as well as micro-expression databases. We finish with future directions, including crowd sourcing and databases with groups of people.

Keywords: Facial expression · Micro-expression · Database · Multimodal · Survey

1 Introduction

Automatic facial expression analysis has attracted an increasing attention in the past decades. Such methods have been widely used in many domains, such as human-computer interaction or medical applications. That's why facial expression databases are fundamental especially for the performance evaluation of a facial expression analysis system.

In the late 1990s, the first public databases of facial macro-expressions [32,44, 45] were created when automatic facial expression analysis was taking off. The samples of these first databases are posed expressions which were acquired in the

Supported by China Scholarship Council and ANR French Reflet (AAP Generique 2017).

laboratory environment. Nowadays, some of these databases are still used for the comparison to other existing methods. Yet, most databases are now presenting spontaneous expressions. They are different from posed expressions, for they are expressions that a person naturally shows on the face in daily life [10,62,72]. The differences between posed and spontaneous expression can be distinguished both by the intensity and the dynamics of the expression. Testing on spontaneous expressions with a system trained on posed expressions, leads to bad performance. Thus, more and more spontaneous expressions databases began to appear in the 2000s [63,69]. Furthermore, new available spontaneous macro expression databases were built almost every year. Lately, to extend the applications in real life conditions, the communities has been tackling the one of the most challenging issues, which is automatic facial expression analysis in in-the-wild conditions [47]. Since the beginning of the 2010s, databases which gather samples from an unconstrained environment get a growing interest.

Unlike macro-expression, micro-expression is an involuntary local brief facial expression [22], particularly occurring in the case of high stress. Its involuntary nature helps to analyze the real emotions of a person [21]. On the one hand, research on automatic detection and recognition of micro-expression has emerged in the current decade [53]. On the other hand, there are still a limited number of available micro-expression databases. Indeed, to the best of our knowledge, only 10 databases with such data are published. Around 2010, four databases appeared: Canal9 [74], York-DDT [76], Polikvsky's database [56] and USF-HD [64]. However, these databases are not used nowadays because the first two are not created specifically for micro-expression research and the last two contain posed micro-expressions. In the following years, several spontaneous micro-expression databases were created, including: SMIC [40] and its extended version SMIC-E [39], CASME I [79], CASME II [78], SAMM [13]. Besides, in 2017, two databases are published: $CAS(ME)^2$ [57] which contains both macro-and micro-expression, and MEVIEW [31] which contains in-the-wild data.

A facial expression database can be defined by many characteristics going from the number of subjects to the annotations describing the data. They have a direct impact on the use of the database. For instance, if we would like to build a system aimed at analyzing in-the-wild expressions, a database of frontal posed expressions is not suitable neither for the training nor for the test. Hence, before creating or choosing a database, one must properly identify the targeted application context, so that the desired database characteristics can be defined. In this article, we propose to group the different characteristics of a database into 6 categories: population, modalities, data acquisition hardware, experimental conditions, experimental protocol and annotations.

To the best of our knowledge, the existing surveys on databases of facial expressions are not very comprehensive. For instance, there are only about 15 databases [6], 20 databases [12,26,37,57] or 30 databases [33]. In [77], 61 databases are reported but it focuses only on macro-expression databases. In this paper, we propose a survey based on the review of 69 databases of both macro-and micro-expression, considering unimodal databases (only facial expressions) as well as multimodal databases (facial expressions combined with other modalities). In Sect. 2, we review the databases according to their characteristics while indicating the different trends between posed, spontaneous and in-the-wild databases. In Sect. 3, we discuss the future directions. We conclude the paper in Sect. 4.

2 Survey According to the Characteristics

In this section, we review the existing databases according to their characteristics as listed in Table 1. Each subsection corresponds to one of the 6 categories. The characteristics are coded in order to refer to them easily in the following tables. When the databases of posed, spontaneous and in-the-wild expressions are compared under the same circumstance, the following formatting are utilized to distinguish them in tables: no particular formatting for posed databases, bold for spontaneous databases and italic for in-the-wild databases. To simplify the table of this section, the references of the databases are not reported. They can be found in the appendix.

Table 1. Characteristics of a database (taken from [77]). We propose a codification of these characteristics in order to refer to them easily in the following tables.

Category	Characteristic	Code
Population	# of subjects	P.1
	Women/Men %	P.2
	Age range	P.3
	Ethnic group(s)	P.4
Modalities	Available modalities	M.1
Data acquisition hardware	# of cameras	AE.1
	Resolution	AE.2
	FPS	AE.3
Experimental conditions	Background	EC.1
	Lightning	EC.2
	Occlusions	EC.3
	Head pose	EC.4
Experimental protocol	Method of acquisition	EP.1
	Available expressions	EP.2
Annotations	Facial features	A.1
	Action units (FACS)	A.2
	Emotional labels	A.3
	Emotional dimensions	A.4

2.1   Population

The characteristics of population consist of the number of subjects (P.1), the women/men distribution (P.2), the age range of the subjects (P.3) and the ethnic groups contained in the population (P.4). The choice of population is essential because of interpersonal variability: shape and texture of the face varies with identity, gender, age and ethnic group. In order to develop a method that is robust to interpersonal variability, the database should contain the widest range of ethnic groups and a balanced distribution of age and sex among the subjects, *i.e.* an interpersonal variability as great as possible.

Number of Subjects (P.1). Table 2 reports a classification of macro-expression databases according to the number of subjects (P.1). A majority of the databases of posed expressions have less than 50 subjects. Comparatively, databases with more than 90 subjects are mostly spontaneous and in-the-wild databases.

Table 2. Classification of macro-expression databases according to the characteristic P.1 (number of subjects). The following formatting distinguishes databases: no particular formatting for posed databases, bold for spontaneous databases and italic for in-the-wild databases.

P.1	Macro-expression databases
≤ 50	University of Maryland, JAFFE, PICS - Pain Expressions, MMI, GEMEP, FABO, D3DFACS, ICT-3DRFE, ADFES, MPI, B3D(AC)^2, DISFA+, **ENTERFACE, SAL, EmoTABOO, IEMOCAP, MMI+, MUG, SEMAINE, CAM3D, MAHNOB-HCI, DEAP, DISFA, RECOLA, CAS(ME)^2, BP4D-Spontaneous, BAUM-1**, *EmoTV*
$\in (50, 90)$	KDEF, OULU-CASIA, MUG, Radboud Faces, **BINED - Set 2 and 3**
$\in (90, 130)$	BU-3D FE, BU-4D FE, Bosphorus, **Smile Database, RU-FACS, BINED - Set 1, UNBS-McMaster Shoulder Pain Expression Archive, PICS - Stirling ESRC 3D Face DB, BioVid Emo, GFT**, *Belfast Naturalistic, VAM*
$\in (170, 250)$	CK, FACES, **CK+, NVIE**, *AM-FED, Vinereactor, CHEAVD*
≥ 280	Multi-PIE, **UT-Dallas, DynEmo, AVEC 2013 AViD-Corpus**, *AFEW, SFEW, HAPPEI, Aff-Wild, AFEW-VA, AffectNet, AM-FED+*

Table 3 reports a classification of micro-expression databases according to the number of subjects (P.1). Unlike the situation for macro-expression databases, most of micro-expression databases contain less than 50 subjects, whether they are posed or spontaneous. This is because the micro-expression sequences are more difficult to produce, which requires more strict recording environment and more professional eliciting methods.

Table 3. Classification of micro-expression databases according to the characteristic P.1 (number of subjects) (adapted from [77]). The following formatting distinguishes databases: no particular formatting for posed databases, bold for spontaneous databases and italic for in-the-wild databases.

P.1	Micro-expression databases
≤ 50	Polikovsky's Database, USF-HD, **SMIC, SMIC-E, CASME I, CASME II, SAMM, CAS(ME)^2,** *MEVIEW*
$\in (50, 90)$	**York-DDT**
$\in (180, 250)$	*Canal9*

Women/Men Percentage (P.2). For macro-expression database, the women/men percentage is most of the time between 40/60 and 60/40. However, there are exceptions such as JAFFE [45] only containing women. Databases with mostly women ($\geq 70\%$) are CK [32], Belfast Naturalistic [19] and UT-Dallas [69]. Databases with mostly men ($\geq 70\%$) are Multi-PIE [29], NVIE [75] and ICT-3DRFE [67].

However, the women/men percentage (P.2) for micro-expression databases is not quite balanced. Canal9 [74], CASME I [79] and SMIC [40] contain more male subjects than female subjects, while the number of female subjects in York-DDT [76] is almost twice the number of male subjects. Nevertheless, the women/men percentage is between 40/60 and 60/40 in the three most recent databases (CASME II [78], SAMM [13] and CAS(ME)^2 [57]).

Age Range (P.3). For macro-expression database, there are two main trends for age range: low (18–30 years old) and moderate (18–40 to 18–60 years old). Radboud Faces [38], AFEW [15] and AffectNet [54] are the exceptions since they also contain children. FACES [20] is also an interesting database in order to study facial expression across age since it has a well balanced population with an age range of 19–80 years old.

Meanwhile, the age range (P.3) for most micro-expression databases is quite low, since the recruited subjects are mainly undergraduate students. The average age is around 25 years old and the standard deviation is around 3. Even though, York-DDT [76] has a moderate age range (18–45), and the average age of SAMM [13] is 33.24 with a large standard deviation (11.32).

Ethnic Groups (P.4). Most of the macro-expression databases contain various ethnic groups such as Caucasian, African Subaharian or Asian. In this case, Caucasian group is the majority. However, there are some databases which contain only one or two specific ethnic groups as following: Caucasian and Asian (OULU-CASIA [2]), Caucasian and Mediterranean (Radboud Faces [38], ADFES [73]), Caucasian and South-American (BINED - Set 3 [65]), Caucasian only (GEMEP [7], FACES [20], D3DFACS [11], BINED - Set 1 and 2 [65],

DynEmo [68]), Asian only (JAFFE [45], NVIE [75], CAS(ME)^2 [57], CHEAVD [41] and Turkish only (BAUM-1 [86]).

Micro-expression databases do not have too many ethnic groups (P.4). In the three databases built by China Academy of Science (CAS) (CASME I [79], CASME II [78] and CAS(ME)^2 [57]), there is only one ethnic group: Asian. Meanwhile, there are 2 databases with 3 ethnic groups: Polikovsky's database [56] (Asian, Caucasian and Indian) and SMIC [40] (Asian, Caucasian and African). Furthermore, SAMM [13] contains 13 ethnic groups, which makes it the most varied micro-expression database in term of ethnic groups (P.4).

2.2 Modalities

Modalities represent the nature of the acquired signals. Databases can be distinguished according to the number of modalities: unimodal (only one modality) vs. multimodal (two or more modalities). The earliest published macro-expression databases are unimodal with 2D video (University of Maryland [8], CK [32]) or image (JAFFE [45], KDEF [44]) of the face. 2D video allows us to study the dynamics of facial expression. In the 2000s, bimodal databases began to be created for the audio-visual emotion analysis [85]. The first database combining facial expression and audio is Belfast Naturalistic [19]. Meanwhile, in order to analyze smile, Smile Database [63] is first published combining 2D video of face and physiological signals. Two new modalities are further investigated: body movement and 3D face model. FABO [30] and GEMEP [7] are the first published databases combining facial expression and body movement. GEMEP also added audio. BU-3D FE [82] is the first database which contains static 3D models of facial expression. Soon after, the same research team built BU-4D FE [81] with dynamic 3D model.

Depending on the above introduction, the available modalities for macro-expression databases are facial expression (2D or 3D), audio, body movement and physiological signals. NVIE [75] is an exception, which combines facial expression both in the visible and infrared domain. Table 4 shows a classification of macro-expression databases according to these modalities (M.1). It is worth noticing that spontaneous databases are often multimodal and cover every possible modality. MAHNOB-HCI [66] and RECOLA [58] attract lots of attention because they combine facial expressions, audio and physiological signals, which makes them ideal databases for multimodal emotion analysis. In the meantime, in-the-wild databases are either unimodal (facial expression) or audio-visual. Since body movement, 3D model and physiological signals require a heavy hardware setup, it is indeed a very huge challenge to obtain a high interpersonal variability with these modalities.

Table 5 reports a classification of micro-expression databases according to the modalities (M.1). Until now, micro-expression databases are unimodal with 2D video. SMIC [40] and SMIC-E [39] are the exception since they also contain infrared video. However, there are no audio, 3D model or body movements in these databases, as the eye blinks and subtle head movement have already been a great challenge for micro-expression detection and recognition.

Table 4. Classification of macro-expression databases according to the characteristic M.1 (modalities) (adapted from [77]). The following formatting distinguishes databases: no particular formatting for posed databases, bold for spontaneous databases and italic for in-the-wild databases. "Physio. sig." refers to physiological signals.

M.1	Macro-expression databases
2D image	JAFFE, KDEF, PICS - Pain Expressions, Multi-PIE, FACES, Radboud Faces, *SFEW*, *HAPPEI*, *AffectNet*
2D video	University of Maryland, CK, OULU-CASIA, DISFA+, **CK+**, **MUG**, **UNBC-McMaster Shoulder Pain Expression Archive**, **DISFA**, **CAS(ME)**^{2}, **GFT**, *AM-FED*, *Vinereactor*, *AFEW-VA*, *AM-FED+*
2D video + 2D image	MMI, ADFES, **UT-Dallas**, *Aff-Wild*
2D video + infrared video	**NVIE**
2D video + audio	**SAL**, **MMI+**, **SEMAINE**, **AVEC 2013 AViD-Corpus**, **BAUM-1**, *Belfast Naturalistic*, *EmoTV*, *AFEW*, *CHEAVD*
2D video + 2D image + audio	*VAM*
2D video + audio + 3D image	MPI
2D video + body movement	FABO, **RU-FACS**, **BINED**, **DynEmo**
2D video + body movement + audio	GEMEP, **EmoTABOO**
Motion capture + audio	**IEMOCAP**
2D video + physio. sig.	**Smile Database**, **ENTERFACE**, **DEAP**
2D video + audio + physio. sig.	**RECOLA**
2D video + body movement + physio. sig. + audio	**MAHNOB-HCI**
2D video + 3D video + physio. sig.	**BioVid Emo**
3D image	BU-3D FE, Bosphorus, ICT-3DRFE
2D video + 2D image + 3D image	**PICS - Stirling ESRC 3D Face Database**
3D video	BU-4D FE, D3DFACS, **BP4D-Spontaneous**
3D video + audio	B3D(AC)^2
2D video + 3D video + audio	**CAM3D**

The use of 2D video is explained by the fact that micro-expression is subtle on the face, so it is unlikely to be detected and recognized by a single image. The video modality is necessary for analyzing the dynamics of the facial motion. The duration of a micro-expression sequence is quite short: most videos last less than 10 s. For micro-expression recognition, most methods only use the frames between the onset and the offset. In order to develop a method for spotting micro-expression in long video sequences, SMIC-E [39] extended the duration of micro-expression samples compared to SMIC [40]. Similarly, SAMM [13] contains videos with long duration: the average duration is 35.3 s. Moreover, CAS(ME)^2 [57] provides video samples whose duration can reach to 148 s.

Table 5. Classification of micro-expression databases according to the characteristic M.1 (modalities). The following formatting distinguishes databases: no particular formatting for posed databases, bold for spontaneous databases and italic for in-the-wild databases.

M.1	Micro-expression databases
2D video	*Canal9*, **York-DDT**, Polikovsky's Database, USF-HD, **CASME I, CASME II, SAMM, CAS(ME)^2**, *MEVIEW*
2D video + infrared video	**SMIC, SMIC-E**

2.3 Data Acquisition Hardware

We focus here on the data acquisition hardware for image and video. We consider 3 characteristics: number of cameras (AE.1), camera resolution (AE.2) and frame per second (FPS, AE.3).

Number of Cameras (AE.1). Concerning the number of cameras, about half of the reviewed macro-expression databases use only 1 camera facing the subject. Yet, with regard to the 3D acquisition (multi-view acquisition and body movement acquisition), several cameras are used. For instance, 2 stereo cameras and 1 texture video camera are used in BU-4D FE [81] and BP4D-Spontaneous [88] for 3D acquisition. Multi-view acquisition means simultaneous image or video acquisition of the face from different views. The cameras are usually installed on different angles of profile view (angle of yaw). Multi-PIE [29] and Bosphorus [60] are two exceptions. In these two databases, additional cameras are mounted above the subjects, thus combining yaw and pitch angles. Body movement acquisition also needs several cameras. In most cases, facial expressions are recorded by 1 camera and body movements are acquired by 1 or more cameras. The following are the concerned databases (in brackets the number of cameras for body movement acquisition): FABO [30] (1), EmoTABOO [84] (1), GEMEP [7] (2) and RU-FACS [1] (3). In MAHNOB-HCI [66], 5 cameras are utilized for the multi-view acquisition and 1 camera for body movement acquisition. IEMOCAP [9] is a singular database, in which a motion capture system is used to capture facial expression and hand movements.

For micro-expression databases, there is only 1 camera facing the subject. The exception is SMIC [40] where 3 cameras are used: a high speed camera, a normal visual camera and a near-infrared camera. It is worth noting that the facial area in MEVIEW [31] varies because the camera is often zooming, as well as changing the angle and the scene.

Camera Resolution (AE.2) and FPS (AE.3). The camera resolution and the FPS are chosen by researchers depending on the application context or the topic of study. For example, concerning the samples which come from real-life condition, it is likely that the camera resolution and/or FPS are low (e.g. with low-cost webcam). On the other side, a high FPS can help to study facial expression dynamics. These two characteristics of the majority of macro-expression databases are related to the typical parameters of consumer cameras, i.e. images/videos with a resolution (AE.2) of approximately 720×576 pixels and videos with a FPS (AE.3) between 24 and 30.

Concerning camera resolution (AE.2), a few macro-expression databases are built with a low resolution of approximately 320×240 pixels: VAM [28], OULU-CASIA [2], AM-FED [51], Vinereactor [34], AffectNet [54] and AM-FED+ [50]. Except OULU-CASIA [2], these are in-the-wild databases, which indicates that the resolution is likely to be low in real-life conditions. Contrarily, for both posed and spontaneous macro-expression, there are much more databases with a high resolution of approximately 1024×768 or more: FABO [30], BU-3D FE [82], BU-4D FE [81], Bosphorus [60], FACES [20], Multi-PIE [29], D3DFACS [11], ICT-3DRFE [67], BINED - Set 3 [65], DISFA [49], PICS - Stirling ESRC 3D Face Database [3], DISFA+ [48], RECOLA, BP4D-Spontaneous, BioVid Emo.

Few macro-expression databases contain samples with a low or high FPS (AE.3). The following databases have a FPS smaller or equal to 20: AM-FED, AM-FED+, DISFA+, DISFA, FABO, MUG. The following databases have a FPS greater than 50: D3DFACS, IEMOCAP, MPI, MAHNOB-HCI. Until now, IEMOCAP has the greater available FPS (equals to 120), which makes it an valuable database to study the dynamics of spontaneous macro expressions.

As the higher resolution (AE.2) and FPS (AE.3) will help to capture more subtle facial movements, most micro-expression databases have at least a FPS equal to 60 with a camera resolution larger than 150×190. The FPS in Polikovsky's Database [56], CASME II [78] and SAMM [13] reach 200, while the camera resolution in SAMM [13] is 400×400. These micro-expression sequences were produced in a strictly controlled laboratory environment. Meanwhile, USF-HD [64], SMIC [40], MEVIEW [31] and CAS(ME)^2 [57] contain micro-expression clips with low FPS (lower or equal to 30).

2.4   Experimental Conditions

Experimental conditions consist of the background (EC.1), lightning condition (EC.2), head pose variation (EC.3) and occlusions (EC.4). Background and lightning conditions are related to environment variability, whereas head pose variation and occlusions concern intra-personal variability. These characteristics are important to be considered if one wants to test the robustness of an application in real life conditions.

Background (EC.1) and Lightning Condition (EC.2). Most macro- and micro-expression databases are acquired in the laboratory with a plain background and uniform or ambiant lightning. In this case, face detection and facial landmarks tracking are eased. The background may not be plain, then it remains the same. In-the-wild databases propose to tackle this problem since they consist in video or audio-visual corpus or crowd sourcing (see Subsect. 2.5), offering high variability in background and lightning condition.

Only a few databases of posed and spontaneous macro-expressions propose several lightning conditions (EC.2). Three lightning conditions are available in OULU-CASIA [2] (normal, weak and dark) and NVIE [75] (front, left and right), whereas Multi-PIE [29] proposes 19 lightning conditions. ICT-3DRFE [67] goes further with a static 3D model of the face that is relightable thanks to a light stage with 156 LEDs. In the case of micro-expression databases, CASME I [79] has two lightning conditions: natural lightning and uniform lightning with two LED lights.

Occlusions (EC.3). Five kinds of occlusions are considered: wearing glasses, hair on face, data acquisition hardware, hands in front of face and others. Occlusions caused by data acquisition hardware may affect databases which contain physiological signals (e.g. Smile Database [63] and ENTERFACE [61]) or audio (RECOLA [58]). Table 6 shows the classification of macro-expression databases according to occlusions (EC.3). As expected, there are very few posed databases that have occlusions, while in-the-wild databases contain a wide range of occlusions.

For micro-expression databases, the only existing occlusion so far is when the subject wears glasses. It is worth noting that this occlusion can be found in almost all the micro-expression databases.

Head Pose Variation (EC.4). Head pose variation is very rare in micro-expression databases, so only macro-expression databases are considered here. There are three ways to obtain head pose variation (EC.4). First, multi-view acquisition (see Subsect. 2.3) consists in acquiring the face simultaneously from several views. In the existing databases, we can find variation for the yaw angle, the pitch angle or the combination of yaw and pitch. Second, 3D databases allow to generate 2D face with any pose. Third, there are databases where the subject can freely move her head, hence a natural head pose variation.

Table 7 reports the classification of macro-expression databases according to head pose variation (EC.4). Multi-view acquisition is split in variation of yaw, pitch and combination of both. Most of the posed databases contain yaw variation or 3D model, whereas most of the spontaneous and in-the-wild databases contain natural variation. 3D databases are ideal to investigate facial expression analysis robust to head pose variation. Yaw variation is a good alternative and easier to set up. Multi-PIE [29] and Bosphorus [60] are the only database containing pitch variation combined with yaw variation.

Table 6. Classification of macro-expression databases according to the characteristic EC.3 (occlusions) (adapted from [77]). The following formatting distinguishes databases: no particular formatting for posed databases, bold for spontaneous databases and italic for in-the-wild databases. If the database contains several kinds of occlusions, it appears in each corresponding row.

EC.3	Macro-expression databases
Glasses	MMI, Multi-PIE, Bosphorus, DISFA+, **Smile Database, EmoTABOO, MMI+, MUG, NVIE, CAM3D, DEAP, PICS - Stirling ESRC 3D Face Database, DynEmo, RECOLA**, *EmoTV, AFEW, SFEW, AM-FED, Aff-Wild, Vinereactor, AFEW-VA, AffectNet, AM-FED+*
Hair on face	Bosphorus, **MUG, CAM3D, PICS - Stirling ESRC 3D Face Database, RECOLA**, *EmoTV, AFEW, SFEW, AM-FED, Aff-Wild, Vinereactor, AFEW-VA, AffectNet, AM-FED+*
Data acquisition hardware	**Smile Database, ENTERFACE, RECOLA**
Hands	Bosphorus, **CAM3D, RECOLA, GFT**, *Aff-Wild, AffectNet*
Others	*AFEW, SFEW, HAPPEI, Aff-Wild, AFEW-VA, AffectNet*

Table 7. Classification of macro-expression databases according to the characteristic EC.4 (head pose variation) (adapted from [77]). The following formatting distinguishes databases: no particular formatting for posed databases, bold for spontaneous databases and italic for in-the-wild databases. For yaw and pitch variations, the number of poses (including frontal) is in brackets.

EC.4	Macro-expression databases
Yaw	KDEF (5), PICS - Pain Expressions (3), MMI (2), Multi-PIE (13), Bosphorus (7), Radboud Faces (5), ADFES (2, continuous), MPI (3), **UT-Dallas (9), BioVid Emo (3), BAUM-1 (2)**
Pitch	Bosphorus (4)
Yaw + pitch	Multi-PIE (2), Bosphorus (2)
3D	BU-3D FE, BU-4D FE, D3DFACS, ICT-3DRFE, B(3D)AC2, **BP4D-Spontaneous**
Natural	University of Maryland, **Smile Database, RU-FACS, SAL, EmoTABOO, BINED, IEMOCAP, MMI+, SEMAINE, CAM3D, UNBC-McMaster Shoulder Pain Expression Archive, DISFA, PICS - Stirling ESRC 3D Face Database, DynEmo, RECOLA, GFT**, *Befast Naturalistic, EmoTV, VAM, AFEW, SFEW, AM-FED, HAPPEI, Aff-Wild, Vinereactor, CHEAVD, AFEW-VA, AffectNet, AM-FED+*

2.5   Experimental Protocol

Experimental protocol represents the expressive/emotional content of the database (available expressions, EP.2) and the way it is acquired from the subjects (method of acquisition, EP.1). As mentioned in the introduction, there are 3 kinds of databases: posed, spontaneous and in-the-wild. The experimental protocol differs from one to another, so that we introduce each kind of database in three separate subsections.

We have included some spontaneous macro-expression databases in this subsection because they also contain posed expressions (IEMOCAP [9], MUG [5], NVIE [75], PICS - Stirling ESRC 3D Face Database [3], BAUM-1 [86]).

Posed Expressions

Methods of Reproduction (EP.1). Posed expressions are displayed on purpose by the subject by reproducing specific facial movements. There are three reproduction methods: free reproduction, ordered reproduction and portrayal.

Concerning free reproduction, the subject is just informed about the emotion to reproduce and then they must do it in an expressive manner without any other instruction. The following macro-expression databases gathered samples by this method: University of Maryland [8], JAFFE [45], FABO [30], BU-3D FE [82], ICT-3DRFE [67].

Regarding ordered reproduction, the subject is guided compared to free reproduction. It could be possible that either the subject is trained in advance to reproduce the expressions, or during the acquisition, she is in the presence of an expert who gives her an order. The following databases use this method: KDEF [44], CK [32], MMI [55], BU-4D FE [81], Bosphorus [60], OULU-CASIA [2], Multi-PIE [29], MUG [5], NVIE [75], Radboud Faces [38]. The micro-expression databases USF-HD [64] and Polikovsky's Database [56] are also based on ordered reproduction.

With portrayal of the emotion, the subject is required to improvise on an emotionally rich scenario. This is an interesting option to obtain more realistic posed expressions. Besides these databases often include professional actors as subjects. The following databases are created by this method: GEMEP [7], IEMOCAP [9], MPI [33], B3D(AC)^2 [25], BAUM-1 [86]. FACES [20] uses both portrayal and ordered reproduction for the data acquisition. Then, the two most prototypical images for each subject and each expression are selected. Even though images are showed to the subject to induce an emotion during the first step of the acquisition, we still consider that this database contains posed expressions because the image selection focus on the two most prototypical images.

Available Expressions (EP.2). Regarding the available expressions, there are 6 prototypic expressions and possibly other expressions in posed databases. These prototypic expressions correspond to the 6 basic emotions [23] (i.e. anger, disgust, fear, joy, sadness, surprise). Meanwhile, secondary emotions may exist in databases. Secondary emotions, also known as mental states, correspond to non-basic emotions such as frustration, shame, anxiety. A few databases just include a subset of these 6 expressions along with secondary emotions or non-emotional expressions: IEMOCAP [9], B3D(AC)^2 [25], Multi-PIE [29] and BAUM-1 [86].

The classification of the posed databases based on the available expressions (EP.2) is shown in Table 8. We identify if the databases only contain the 6 basic emotions (if neutral is added, it gives 7 expressions), if they also include contempt, secondary emotions, pain expressions, combinations of action units (AUs) or non-emotional expressions. AUs describe the local activation of facial muscles that produce facial expressions and they are used in the FACS system [24].

Table 8. Classification of databases of posed expressions according to the characteristic EP.2 (available expressions) (adapted from [77]). Neutral face is included in the number of expressions. The following formatting distinguishes databases: no particular formatting for macro-expression databases and italic for micro-expression databases. NB: FACES [20] contains 5 basic emotions (surprise is excluded) and the neutral expression, USF-HD [64] contains 4 basic emotions (disgust and fear are excluded) and the neutral expression.

# of expressions	Only 6 basic emotions	Incl. contempt	Incl. AUs	Incl. secondary emotions	Incl. pain expres-sions	Incl. non emotional expressions
4	*USF-HD (+ neutral)*	-	-	-	-	-
5	FACES (+ neutral)	-	IEMOCAP	-	-	-
6	University of Maryland, BU-4D FE, OULU-CASIA, NVIE	-	-	-	-	Multi-PIE
7 (6 + neutral)	JAFFE, KDEF, BU-3D FE, MUG, PICS - Stirling ESRC 3D Face Database	-	-	-	-	-
∈ (8, 25)	-	Radboud Faces, ADFES	GEMEP, FABO, ADFES, *Polikovsky's Database*	PICS - Pain Expressions	CK	ICT-3DRFE
≥ 34	-	MPI	B3D(AC)^2, MPI, BAUM-1	-	MMI, Bospho-rus, D3DFACS, DISFA+	-

Spontaneous Expressions. Contrary to posed expressions, spontaneous expressions are not controlled by the subject and they occur naturally. Basically, there are two acquisition methods (EP.1) to obtain spontaneous expressions. The first one is emotion elicitation methods that are used to induce a specific emotional state. And the second one is the interaction between two (or more) protagonists in order to get emotionally rich content.

Acquisition Method (EP.1): Emotion Elicitation Methods. There are some difficulties for the setup of emotion elicitation methods [65]. It is impossible to identify objectively what emotion is felt by the subject, how it is perceived by a third party and how much the facial expression reflects it. The more spontaneous the expressions are, the less easy they can be captured, the less information is available about the emotional state and the less the experimental protocol is reproducible. In contrast, the reproducibility of the experimental protocol could be controlled perfectly based on the acquisition of posed expressions. Yet, the posed expressions are not able to deliver any information on the genuine emotional state. The emotion elicitation methods is proposed to find a compromise by controlling the experimental protocol, since the relatively standardized tasks could collect emotional state information while it also allows the subject to react naturally to the task [65]. There are 2 emotion elicitation methods: passive tasks and active tasks.

Passive tasks means watching videos or images that are intended to induce specific emotions. It is worth noting that in the case of DEAP [35], the subject watches musical clips that intend to span the 4 quadrants of the arousal/valence emotional space [59] instead of specific emotions.

All the spontaneous micro-expression databases use passive task as emotion elicitation method. The most common method is neutralization paradigm, i.e. asking participants to watch videos containing strong emotions and try to neutralize during the while time or try to suppress facial expressions when they realized there is one. Since the micro-expressions are too subtle, it is difficult to detect and recognize them by human eyes. Hence, in SMIC [40], SMIC-E [39] and SAMM [13], in order to label the micro-expression sequence, the subjects are required to fill a self-report about their emotions when watching the eliciting videos. In addition, the micro-expression sequences in CASME I [79], CASME II [78] and CAS(ME)^2 [57] are also evaluated by psychological researchers.

Active tasks were popularized by BINED [65]. By definition, during the active tasks, the subject is directly involved to induce specific emotions. For instance, to induce disgust emotion, the subject is asked to put his non-dominant hand in a box containing cold, cooked and cut spaghetti in sauce, while he cannot see what is inside [65]. In the case of AVEC 2013 AViD-Corpus [71], the active tasks are not used to induce specific emotions. Meanwhile, some databases combine active and passive tasks.

Acquisition Method (EP.1): Interaction. The methods of interaction include: human-human interaction and human-computer interaction.

Concerning human-human interaction, there are 2 situations. For the first one, one of the subject may be aware of the protocol and thus try to manage the interaction in order to make it emotionally rich (RU-FACS [1], EmoTA-BOO [84]). For the second one, both subjects need to interact naturally in a precise context (RECOLA [58]). GFT [27] database extends the latter case to 3 subjects interacting together.

In human-computer interaction, the subject interacts with a virtual agent. The agent is remotely monitored by the experimenter. This is the wizard-of-Oz setup. The experimenter can choose several characters for the virtual agent, and thus the emotional content of the interaction could be influenced.

Available Expressions (EP.2). Table 9 lists the classification of the spontaneous databases according to the acquisition method (EP.1) and the available expressions (EP.2). The available expressions (EP.2) are usually the same as with posed databases (basic and secondary emotions, see Table 8). As the passive task is the easiest protocol to set up, most of the spontaneous databases use it to obtain samples. It is also worth noting that all of the spontaneous micro-expression databases contain only basic emotions.

In-the-Wild Expressions. Like the situations that we can meet in real life, in-the-wild conditions refer to an unconstrained environment in terms of population (see Subsect. 2.1) and experimental conditions (see Subsect. 2.4). To obtain in-the-wild expressions, there are roughly 2 methods of acquisition (EP.1): corpus of videos/images (containing posed and/or spontaneous expressions) and crowd sourcing.

Corpus of Videos/Images. Since 2000s, several macro-expression databases begin to meet the criteria of in-the-wild: Belfast Naturalistic [19], EmoTV [4] and VAM [28]. The samples in these databases are a corpus of videos of spontaneous expressions which are extracted from television programs. Thus the spontaneous expressions result from human-human interaction. These databases are considered as in-the-wild databases since the emotional content is totally uncontrolled, as well as the experimental conditions. However, they lack of variability in population.

More recently, videos in Aff-Wild [83] are extracted from Youtube. The selected videos show the spontaneous expressions when the subject are watching a video, practicing an activity or reacting to a joke or surprise. This database also contains images from Google Image. This database helps to provide a wide variability in population (500+ for videos and 2000+ for images) and experimental conditions. Furthermore, AffectNet [54] is also created based on the same protocol. It consists of more than 1,000,000 images extracted with three search engines.

AFEW [15] contains corpus of videos or images of posed. Subtitles for deaf and hard of hearing contain information about emotional context of actors. By analyzing them, the selection of videos is processed automatically among 54

Table 9. Classification of databases of spontaneous expressions according to the characteristics EP.1 (acquisition method) and EP.2 (available expressions) (adapted from [77]). The row 'Various' (available expressions) refer to databases where the acquisition methods do not intend to induce specific emotions. "HHI" and "HCI" refer to human-human interaction and human-computer interaction respectively. The following formatting distinguishes databases: no particular formatting for macro-expression databases and italic for micro-expression databases.

EP.2	EP.1				
	Emotion elicitation methods			Interaction	
	Passive tasks	Active tasks	Passive + active tasks	HHI	HCI
Basic emotions	ENTERFACE, MMI+, MUG, NVIE, CAS(ME)^2, *York-DDT, SMIC, SMIC-E, CASME I, CASME II, CAS(ME)^2, SAMM*	-	-	-	-
Basic and secondary emotions	UT-Dallas, MAHNOB-HCI, BioVid Emo, BAUM-1	CAM3D	BINED, PICS - Stirling ESRC 3D Face Database, DynEmo, BP4D-Spontaneous	Emo-TABOO, IEMO-CAP, CAM3D	-
Various	DEAP	AVEC 2013 AViD-Corpus	-	RU-FACS, RECOLA, GFT	SAL, SEMAINE
Smile	Smile Database	-	-	CK+	-
AUs	DISFA	-	-	-	-
Pain expressions	-	UNBC-McMaster Shoulder Pain Expression Archive, BP4D-Spontaneous	-	-	-

movies. SFEW [17] is a static version of AFEW [15], and it contains images extracted from the latter. The advantage of these two databases is that they provide a high variability in population (330 subjects ranging from 1 to 70 years old) and experimental conditions. However, the available expressions are posed expressions which correspond to the 6 basic emotions. Lately, AFEW-VA [36] extends the corpus of AFEW [15]. Its particularity is providing continuous annotations of emotional dimensions arousal and valence.

There are also macro-expression databases which have the combination of a corpus of videos of posed expressions and spontaneous. In HAPPEI [16], the images are selected on Flickr and contain a group of people (2 or more subjects) showing different levels of happiness (from neutral to thrilled). This database is regarded as containing both posed and spontaneous expressions because it is likely that people may be posing on pictures taken in social events. In CHEAVD [41], the posed expressions are extracted from movies and television series. However, spontaneous expressions of this database are extracted from television programs.

So far, we reported only 2 in-the-wild micro-expression databases: Canal9 [74] and MEVIEW [31]. They both consist in a corpus of videos of spontaneous expressions. Canal9 [74] contains 70 political debates recorded by the Canal9 local station. This database provides the micro-expression when the politicians tried to hide their real emotion. MEVIEW [31] contains 31 video clips from poker games and TV interviews downloaded from the Internet. The poker game can help to trigger micro-expression thanks to the stress factor and the need to hide emotions. However, it is challenging to detect and recognize the micro-expression automatically since there are too many other irrelevant movements.

Crowd Sourcing. In order to get a high variability in population and experimental conditions for spontaneous expressions, crowd sourcing has been developed. The idea is to recruit subjects through the Internet for a study and then to film them directly at home via their webcam. The subject's reaction is recorded when she watches an inducing video.

To the best of our knowledge, there are only 3 macro-expression databases using this method: AM-FED [51], AM-FED+ [50] and Vinereactor [34]. In AM-FED [51], only the smile is induced. AM-FED+ [50] is an extended version of the latter with more recordings. Vinereactor [34] has the similar situation. Since the subjects are just required to note how much the induction video amused them, the induced emotions appear to be related only to amusement.

2.6   Annotations

The annotations are meta-data provided with the database, which could be low-level information (facial features A.1 or action units A.2) or high-level (emotional labels A.3 or emotional dimensions A.4). As the annotations will be regarded as ground-truth, they are chosen depending on the problem that the database is meant to tackle. Emotional labels are used for facial expression recognition, action units annotations are aimed at action units recognition and emotional dimensions are targeted for emotional dimension estimation (such as arousal or valence [59]). Facial features (e.g. facial landmarks, LBP, ...) could make a database interesting since they could be directly used to rapidly design a system (no need to compute). Table 10 lists the classification of macro-expression databases according to the annotations (A.1, A.2, A.3, A.4).

Table 10. Classification of macro-expression databases according to the annotation characteristics A.1 (facial features), A.2 (AUs), A.3 (emotional labels) and A.4 (emotional dimensions) (adapted from [77]). The following formatting distinguishes databases: no particular formatting for posed databases, bold for spontaneous databases and italic for in-the-wild databases.

Annotation	Macro-expression databases
A.1 (facial features)	BU-3D FE, BU-4D FE, Bosphorus, B3D(AC)^2, **Smile Database, IEMOCAP, CK+, MUG, NVIE, UNBC-McMaster Shoulder Pain Expression Archive, DISFA, AVEC 2013 AViD-Corpus, BP4D-Spontaneous, GFT**, *AFEW, SFEW, AM-FED, Vinereactor, AFEW-VA, AM-FED+*
A.2 (AUs)	CK, MMI, D3DFACS, ICT-3DRFE, DISFA+, **Smile Database, RU-FACS, CK+, MMI+, UNBC-McMaster Shoulder Pain Expression Archive, DISFA, CAS(ME)^2, BP4D-Spontaneous, GFT**, *AM-FED, Aff-Wild, Vinereactor, AM-FED+*
A.3 (Emotional labels)	JAFFE, CK, FABO, FACES, Radboud Faces, **UT-Dallas, EmoTABOO, BINED, IEMOCAP, CK+, SEMAINE, NVIE, CAM3D, DynEmo, CAS(ME)^2, BioVid Emo, BAUM-1**, *Belfast Naturalistic, EmoTV, VAM, AFEW, SFEW, AM-FED, HAPPEI, CHEAVD, AffectNet*
A.4 (Emotional dimensions)	GEMEP, Radboud Faces, **SAL, EmoTABOO, BINED, IEMOCAP, SEMAINE, NVIE, UNBC-McMaster Shoulder Pain Expression Archive, MAHNOB-HCI, DEAP, DynEmo, RECOLA, AVEC 2013 AViD-Corpus**, *Belfast Naturalistic, EmoTV, VAM, AM-FED, Aff-Wild, AFEW-VA, AffectNet*

Regarding micro-expression databases, action units (A.2) and emotional labels (A.3) are the only available annotations to the best of our knowledge. Table 11 reports the classification of micro-expression databases according to the annotations (A.2, A.3).

Table 11. Classification of micro-expression databases according to the annotation characteristics A.2 (AUs) and A.3 (emotional labels). The following formatting distinguishes databases: no particular formatting for posed databases, bold for spontaneous databases and italic for in-the-wild databases.

Annotation	Micro-expression databases
A.2 (AUs)	Polikovsky's Database,**CASME I, CASME II, SAMM, CAS(ME)^2**, *MEVIEW*
A.3 (Emotional labels)	USF-HD, **York-DDT**, SMIC, SMIC-E, **CASME I, CASME II, SAMM, CAS(ME)^2**, *MEVIEW*

Almost all the micro-expression databases provide emotional labels. However, there are two kinds of emotional labels, depending on the considered classification problem. On one hand, the emotional labels are the 6 basic emotions (York-DDT [76], CASME I [79], CASME II [78] and SAMM [13]). On the other hand, the emotion is divided into three or four classes (SMIC [40], SMIC-E [39] and CAS(ME)^2 [57]): positive, negative, surprise and others.

Meanwhile, there are less micro-expression databases annotated with AUs. But it tends now to be a very important annotation for micro-expression. Indeed, a method for an objective micro-expression classification using AUs has been proposed recently in [14], and in the Facial Micro-Expression Grand Challenge organized by 2018 FG [80], micro-expression must be classified according to AUs combinations.

3   Future Directions

3.1   Macro-expression Databases

In this sub-section, we present 3 future directions for macro-expression databases that have already been addressed by only very few databases.

In the past 5 years, it has been made clear that facial expression analysis in an unconstrained environment is one of the main challenging problems [47]. Hence, in-the-wild databases have drawn a growing interest. As introduced in the Subsect. 2.5, there are 2 methods of acquisition of in-the-wild expressions up to now: corpus of videos/images and crowd sourcing. Crowd sourcing appears to be a promising method to acquire realistic data because of its high variability in population and experimental conditions. To the best of our knowledge, thus far, only positive emotions have been gathered by this method in the databases AM-FED [51], AM-FED+ [50] and Vinereactor [34]. In order to extend the available in-the-wild expression data scale, enhancing crowd sourcing by acquiring not only positive but also negative emotions could be an interesting direction to explore. However, it would be a complex problem in the real-life due to ethical concerns.

Another direction that has been studied recently is building a database with groups of people. To the best of our knowledge, there are only two databases that propose such kind of data. In HAPPEI [16], the size of groups varies but the database only contains different levels of happiness expressions. This database is targeted to study the happiness intensity of the group. In GFT [27], 3 subjects interact naturally in the videos. The subjects stay facing each other, so the same video cannot have all 3 frontal face at the same time. This database aims at studying social interaction and the originality is to have 3 subjects rather than 2 as in RU-FACS [1] or RECOLA [58]. Thus, two directions within databases of groups of people could be considered: (1) images or videos with a group of people facing the camera for estimating the overall emotion of the group; (2) videos of a group interaction to study social interaction.

Regarding the third direction, we find that there are very few databases with time lapse between acquisitions for each subject. To the best of our knowledge, this exists only in 3 databases. The Smile Database [63] acquires only spontaneous smiles in two sessions which are recorded a year apart. In Multi-PIE [29], 4 acquisitions of 5 expressions were gathered over the course of 6 months. In AVEC 2013 AViD-Corpus [71], there are between 1 and 4 acquisitions for each subject recorded two weeks apart. It is worth exploring further in this direction in order to study the stability of facial expression reaction to a particular event or the variation of behavior over time. In addition, these situations could be meaningful for human-computer interaction or medical application such as monitoring an individual's emotional state.

3.2 Micro-expression Databases

Nowadays, research on micro-expression analysis focuses the experiments on spontaneous expressions. CASME II [78] and SMIC [40] are the two most commonly used databases thanks to their sufficient micro-expression samples.

In fact, each database has its own advantages. CASME I [79], CASME II [78] and SAMM [13] have both emotional labels and AU labels. SMIC [40] and SAMM [13] respond to the necessity of multi ethnic groups. In addition, CAS(ME)^2 [57] contains both macro and micro expressions, which can be used to enhance the ability of distinguishing micro-expression from other facial movements.

Nevertheless, there are still large amounts of works to do for micro-expression databases. First of all, there are too few subjects and most of them are undergraduate students. The age range need to be extended, for example the wrinkle on the face of an older person may influence the recognition results. Furthermore, the undergraduate students do not have much experience in hiding their emotions in high-stakes situations. In order to perform micro-expression analysis in real world conditions, e.g. national security or medical care, it is needed to recruit more subjects from civil society.

Secondly, almost all the micro-expression database were built in a strict controlled laboratory environment. So, a future direction could be to build in-the-wild micro-expression databases with more occlusions, such as pose variation, hair on face or lightning change.

4   Conclusions

In this paper, we presented a survey for both macro- and micro-expression databases based on 69 databases. We review the existing facial expression databases according to 18 characteristics grouped in 6 categories (population, modalities, data acquisition hardware, experimental conditions, experimental protocol and annotations). We proposed the future directions according to whether the databases are about macro- or micro-expressions. Regarding macro-expression database, this could include: enhancing crowd sourcing to build in-the-wild databases with a greater variety of expressions, building databases with groups of people and building databases with time lapse between acquisition for each subject. Regarding micro-expression databases, this could include: broadening the recruited subjects (so far most of them are undergraduate students) in order to extend the available age range and have subjects with more experience in hiding their emotions in high-stakes situations, and building in-the-wild databases with more occlusions.

Appendix

For a purpose of clarity, the references are not included in the tables of Sect. 2. We report here the corresponding references to all the databases we review (Tables 12 and 13).

Table 12. References of macro-expression databases.

Posed		Spontaneous		In-the-wild	
Database	Reference	Database	Reference	Database	Reference
ADFES (2011)	[73]	AVEC 2013 AViD-Corpus (2013)	[71]	AFEW (2012)	[15]
B3D(AC)^2 (2013)	[25]	BAUM-1 (2016)	[86]	AFEW-VA (2017)	[36]
BAUM-1 (2016)	[86]	BINED (2012)	[65]	Aff-Wild (2016)	[83]
Bosphorus (2008)	[60]	BioVid Emo (2016)	[87]	AffectNet (2017)	[54]
BU-3D FE (2006)	[82]	BP4D-Spontaneous (2014)	[88]	AM-FED (2013)	[51]
BU-4D FE (2008)	[81]	CAM3D (2013)	[46]	AM-FED+ (2018)	[50]
CK (2000)	[32]	CAS(ME)^2 (2017)	[57]	Belfast Naturalistic (2000)	[19]
D3DFACS (2011)	[11]	CK+ (2010)	[42]	CHEAVD (2016)	[41]
DISFA+ (2016)	[48]	DEAP (2012)	[35]	EmoTV (2005)	[4]
FABO (2006)	[30]	DISFA (2013)	[49]	HAPPEI (2015)	[16]
FACES (2010)	[20]	DynEmo (2013)	[68]	SFEW (2011)	[17]
GEMEP (2006)	[7]	EmoTABOO (2007)	[84]	VAM (2008)	[28]
ICT-3DRFE (2011)	[67]	ENTERFACE (2006)	[61]	Vinereactor (2016)	[34]
IEMOCAP (2008)	[9]	GFT (2017)	[27]		
JAFFE (1998)	[45]	IEMOCAP (2008)	[9]		
KDEF (1998)	[44]	MAHNOB-HCI (2012)	[66]		
MMI (2005)	[55]	MMI+ (2010)	[70]		
MPI (2012)	[33]	MUG (2010)	[5]		
MUG (2010)	[5]	NVIE (2010)	[75]		
Multi-PIE (2010)	[29]	PICS - Stirling ESRC 3D Face Database (2013)	[3]		
NVIE (2010)	[75]	RECOLA (2013)	[58]		
OULU-CASIA (2009)	[2]	RU-FACS (2006)	[1]		
PICS - Pain Expression (2013)	[3]	SAL (2008)	[18]		
PICS - Stirling ESRC 3D Face Database (2013)	[3]	SEMAINE (2010)	[52]		
Radboud Faces (2010)	[38]	Smile Database (2001)	[63]		
University of Maryland (1997)	[8]	UNBC-McMaster Shoulder Pain Expression Archive (2011)	[43]		
		UT-Dallas (2005)	[69]		

Table 13. References of micro-expression databases.

Posed		Spontaneous		In-the-wild	
Database	Reference	Database	Reference	Database	Reference
Polikovsky's Database (2009)	[56]	CASME I (2013)	[79]	Canal9 (2009)	[74]
USF-HD (2011)	[64]	CASME II (2014)	[78]	MEVIEW (2017)	[31]
		CAS(ME)^2 (2017)	[57]		
		SAMM (2018)	[13]		
		SMIC (2013)	[40]		
		SMIC-E (2015)	[39]		
		York-DDT (2009)	[76]		

References

1. http://mplab.ucsd.edu/grants/project1/research/rufacs1-dataset.html (2006)
2. http://www.cse.oulu.fi/CMV/Downloads/Oulu-CASIA (2009)
3. http://pics.stir.ac.uk (2013)
4. Abrilian, S., Devillers, L., Buisine, S., Martin, J.C.: EmoTV1: annotation of real-life emotions for the specification of multimodal affective interfaces. In: HCI International (2005)
5. Aifanti, N., Papachristou, C., Delopoulos, A.: The mug facial expression database. In: 2010 11th International Workshop on Image Analysis for Multimedia Interactive Services (WIAMIS), pp. 1–4. IEEE (2010)
6. Anitha, C., Venkatesha, M., Adiga, B.S.: A survey on facial expression databases. Int. J. Eng. Sci. Technol. **2**(10), 5158–5174 (2010)
7. Bänziger, T., Pirker, H., Scherer, K.: GEMEP-GEneva multimodal emotion portrayals: a corpus for the study of multimodal emotional expressions. In: Proceedings of LREC, vol. 6, pp. 15–019 (2006)
8. Black, M.J., Yacoob, Y.: Recognizing facial expressions in image sequences using local parameterized models of image motion. Int. J. Comput. Vision **25**(1), 23–48 (1997)
9. Busso, C., et al.: IEMOCAP: interactive emotional dyadic motion capture database. Lang. Resour. Eval. **42**(4), 335–359 (2008)
10. Cohn, J.F., Schmidt, K.L.: The timing of facial motion in posed and spontaneous smiles. Int. J. Wavelets Multiresolut. Inf. Process. **2**(02), 121–132 (2004)
11. Cosker, D., Krumhuber, E., Hilton, A.: A FACS valid 3D dynamic action unit database with applications to 3D dynamic Morphable facial modeling. In: 2011 IEEE International Conference on Computer Vision (ICCV), pp. 2296–2303. IEEE (2011)
12. Cowie, R., Douglas-Cowie, E., Cox, C.: Beyond emotion archetypes: databases for emotion modelling using neural networks. Neural Netw. **18**(4), 371–388 (2005)

13. Davison, A.K., Lansley, C., Costen, N., Tan, K., Yap, M.H.: SAMM: a spontaneous micro-facial movement dataset. IEEE Trans. Affect. Comput. **9**(1), 116–129 (2018)
14. Davison, A.K., Merghani, W., Yap, M.H.: Objective classes for micro-facial expression recognition. arXiv preprint arXiv:1708.07549 (2017)
15. Dhall, A., Goecke, R., Lucey, S., Gedeon, T.: Collecting large, richly annotated facial-expression databases from movies (2012)
16. Dhall, A., Goecke, R., Gedeon, T.: Automatic group happiness intensity analysis. IEEE Trans. Affect. Comput. **6**(1), 13–26 (2015)
17. Dhall, A., Goecke, R., Lucey, S., Gedeon, T.: Static facial expression analysis in tough conditions: data, evaluation protocol and benchmark. In: 2011 IEEE International Conference on Computer Vision Workshops (ICCV Workshops), pp. 2106–2112. IEEE (2011)
18. Douglas-Cowie, E., Cowie, R., Cox, C., Amier, N., Heylen, D.: The sensitive artificial listner: an induction technique for generating emotionally coloured conversation (2008)
19. Douglas-Cowie, E., Cowie, R., Schröder, M.: A new emotion database: considerations, sources and scope. In: ISCA Tutorial and Research Workshop (ITRW) on Speech and Emotion (2000)
20. Ebner, N.C., Riediger, M., Lindenberger, U.: FACES–a database of facial expressions in young, middle-aged, and older women and men: development and validation. Behav. Res. Methods **42**(1), 351–362 (2010)
21. Ekman, P.: Lie catching and microexpressions. In: The Philosophy of Deception, pp. 118–133 (2009)
22. Ekman, P., Friesen, W.V.: Nonverbal leakage and clues to deception. Psychiatry **32**(1), 88–106 (1969)
23. Ekman, P., Friesen, W.V.: Constants across cultures in the face and emotion. J. Pers. Soc. Psychol. **17**(2), 124 (1971)
24. Ekman, P., Friesen, W.V.: Facial action coding system (1977)
25. Fanelli, G., Gall, J., Romsdorfer, H., Weise, T., Van Gool, L.: A 3-D audio-visual corpus of affective communication. IEEE Trans. Multimedia **12**(6), 591–598 (2010)
26. Fu, S., Yang, G., Kuai, X., Zheng, R.: A parametric survey for facial expression database. In: Zhang, H., Hussain, A., Liu, D., Wang, Z. (eds.) BICS 2012. LNCS (LNAI), vol. 7366, pp. 373–381. Springer, Heidelberg (2012). https://doi.org/10.1007/978-3-642-31561-9_42
27. Girard, J.M., Chu, W.S., Jeni, L.A., Cohn, J.F., De la Torre, F.: Sayette group formation task (GFT) spontaneous facial expression database (2017)
28. Grimm, M., Kroschel, K., Narayanan, S.: The Vera am Mittag German audio-visual emotional speech database. In: 2008 IEEE International Conference on Multimedia and Expo, pp. 865–868. IEEE (2008)
29. Gross, R., Matthews, I., Cohn, J., Kanade, T., Baker, S.: Multi-pie. Image Vis. Comput. **28**(5), 807–813 (2010)
30. Gunes, H., Piccardi, M.: A bimodal face and body gesture database for automatic analysis of human nonverbal affective behavior. In: 18th International Conference on Pattern Recognition, ICPR 2006, vol. 1, pp. 1148–1153. IEEE (2006)
31. Husák, P., Čech, J., Matas, J.: Spotting facial micro-expressions "in the wild". In: Proceedings of the 22nd Computer Vision Winter Workshop, Pattern Recognition and Image Processing Group (PRIP) and PRIP Club (2017). http://cvww2017.prip.tuwien.ac.at/papers/CVWW2017_paper_17.pdf
32. Kanade, T., Cohn, J.F., Tian, Y.: Comprehensive database for facial expression analysis. In: Fourth IEEE International Conference on Automatic Face and Gesture Recognition, Proceedings, pp. 46–53. IEEE (2000)

33. Kaulard, K., Cunningham, D.W., Bülthoff, H.H., Wallraven, C.: The MPI facial expression database a validated database of emotional and conversational facial expressions. PLoS ONE **7**(3), e32321 (2012)
34. Kim, E., Vangala, S.: Vinereactor: crowdsourced spontaneous facial expression data. In: International Conference on Multimedia Retrieval (ICMR). IEEE (2016)
35. Koelstra, S., et al.: DEAP: a database for emotion analysis; using physiological signals. IEEE Trans. Affect. Comput. **3**(1), 18–31 (2012)
36. Kossaifi, J., Tzimiropoulos, G., Todorovic, S., Pantic, M.: AFEW-VA database for valence and arousal estimation in-the-wild. Image Vis. Comput. **65**, 23–36 (2017)
37. Krumhuber, E.G., Skora, L., Küster, D., Fou, L.: A review of dynamic datasets for facial expression research. Emot. Rev. **9**(3), 280–292 (2017)
38. Langner, O., Dotsch, R., Bijlstra, G., Wigboldus, D.H., Hawk, S.T., van Knippenberg, A.: Presentation and validation of the radboud faces database. Cogn. Emot. **24**(8), 1377–1388 (2010)
39. Li, X., et al.: Reading hidden emotions: spontaneous micro-expression spotting and recognition. arXiv preprint arXiv:1511.00423 (2015)
40. Li, X., Pfister, T., Huang, X., Zhao, G., Pietikäinen, M.: A spontaneous micro-expression database: inducement, collection and baseline. In: 2013 10th IEEE International Conference and Workshops on Automatic Face and Gesture Recognition (FG), pp. 1–6. IEEE (2013)
41. Li, Y., Tao, J., Chao, L., Bao, W., Liu, Y.: CHEAVD: a Chinese natural emotional audio-visual database. J. Ambient Intell. Humaniz. Comput. **8**, 1–12 (2016)
42. Lucey, P., Cohn, J.F., Kanade, T., Saragih, J., Ambadar, Z., Matthews, I.: The extended Cohn-Kanade dataset (CK+): a complete dataset for action unit and emotion-specified expression. In: 2010 IEEE Computer Society Conference on Computer Vision and Pattern Recognition Workshops (CVPRW), pp. 94–101. IEEE (2010)
43. Lucey, P., Cohn, J.F., Prkachin, K.M., Solomon, P.E., Matthews, I.: Painful data: the UNBC-McMaster shoulder pain expression archive database. In: 2011 IEEE International Conference on Automatic Face & Gesture Recognition and Workshops (FG 2011), pp. 57–64. IEEE (2011)
44. Lundqvist, D., Flykt, A., Öhman, A.: The Karolinska Directed Emotional Faces - KDEF, CD ROM from Department of Clinical Neuroscience, Psychology Section, Karolinska Institutet (1998)
45. Lyons, M., Akamatsu, S., Kamachi, M., Gyoba, J.: Coding facial expressions with Gabor wavelets. In: Third IEEE International Conference on Automatic Face and Gesture Recognition, Proceedings, pp. 200–205. IEEE (1998)
46. Mahmoud, M., Baltrušaitis, T., Robinson, P., Riek, L.D.: 3D corpus of spontaneous complex mental states. In: D'Mello, S., Graesser, A., Schuller, B., Martin, J.-C. (eds.) ACII 2011. LNCS, vol. 6974, pp. 205–214. Springer, Heidelberg (2011). https://doi.org/10.1007/978-3-642-24600-5_24
47. Martinez, B., Valstar, M.F.: Advances, challenges, and opportunities in automatic facial expression recognition. In: Kawulok, M., Celebi, M.E., Smolka, B. (eds.) Advances in Face Detection and Facial Image Analysis, pp. 63–100. Springer, Cham (2016). https://doi.org/10.1007/978-3-319-25958-1_4
48. Mavadati, M., Sanger, P., Mahoor, M.H.: Extended DISFA dataset: investigating posed and spontaneous facial expressions. In: Proceedings of the IEEE Conference on Computer Vision and Pattern Recognition Workshops, pp. 1–8 (2016)
49. Mavadati, S.M., Mahoor, M.H., Bartlett, K., Trinh, P., Cohn, J.F.: DISFA: a spontaneous facial action intensity database. IEEE Trans. Affect. Comput. **4**(2), 151–160 (2013)

50. McDuff, D., Amr, M., El Kaliouby, R.: AM-FED+: an extended dataset of naturalistic facial expressions collected in everyday settings. IEEE Trans. Affect. Comput. **10**, 7–17 (2018)
51. McDuff, D., El Kaliouby, R., Senechal, T., Amr, M., Cohn, J.F., Picard, R.: Affectiva-MIT facial expression dataset (AM-FED): naturalistic and spontaneous facial expressions collected "in-the-wild". In: 2013 IEEE Conference on Computer Vision and Pattern Recognition Workshops (CVPRW), pp. 881–888. IEEE (2013)
52. McKeown, G., Valstar, M.F., Cowie, R., Pantic, M.: The semaine corpus of emotionally coloured character interactions. In: 2010 IEEE International Conference on Multimedia and Expo (ICME), pp. 1079–1084. IEEE (2010)
53. Merghani, W., Davison, A.K., Yap, M.H.: A review on facial micro-expressions analysis: datasets, features and metrics. arXiv preprint arXiv:1805.02397 (2018)
54. Mollahosseini, A., Hasani, B., Mahoor, M.H.: AffectNet: a database for facial expression, valence, and arousal computing in the wild. arXiv preprint arXiv:1708.03985 (2017)
55. Pantic, M., Valstar, M., Rademaker, R., Maat, L.: Web-based database for facial expression analysis. In: IEEE International Conference on Multimedia and Expo, ICME 2005, p. 5. IEEE (2005)
56. Polikovsky, S., Kameda, Y., Ohta, Y.: Facial micro-expressions recognition using high speed camera and 3D-gradient descriptor (2009)
57. Qu, F., Wang, S.J., Yan, W.J., Li, H., Wu, S., Fu, X.: CAS(ME)2: a database for spontaneous macro-expression and micro-expression spotting and recognition. IEEE Trans. Affect. Comput. **9**, 424–436 (2017)
58. Ringeval, F., Sonderegger, A., Sauer, J., Lalanne, D.: Introducing the RECOLA multimodal corpus of remote collaborative and affective interactions. In: Proceedings of EmoSPACE 2013, Held in Conjunction with FG 2013. IEEE, Shanghai, April 2013
59. Russell, J.A., Pratt, G.: A description of the affective quality attributed to environments. J. Pers. Soc. Psychol. **38**(2), 311 (1980)
60. Savran, A., et al.: Bosphorus database for 3D face analysis. In: Schouten, B., Juul, N.C., Drygajlo, A., Tistarelli, M. (eds.) BioID 2008. LNCS, vol. 5372, pp. 47–56. Springer, Heidelberg (2008). https://doi.org/10.1007/978-3-540-89991-4_6
61. Savran, A., et al.: Emotion detection in the loop from brain signals and facial images (2006)
62. Schmidt, K.L., Ambadar, Z., Cohn, J.F., Reed, L.I.: Movement differences between deliberate and spontaneous facial expressions: Zygomaticus major action in smiling. J. Nonverbal Behav. **30**(1), 37–52 (2006)
63. Schmidt, K.L., Cohn, J.F.: Dynamics of facial expression: normative characteristics and individual differences. In: ICME. Citeseer (2001)
64. Shreve, M., Godavarthy, S., Goldgof, D., Sarkar, S.: Macro-and micro-expression spotting in long videos using spatio-temporal strain. In: 2011 IEEE International Conference on Automatic Face & Gesture Recognition and Workshops (FG 2011), pp. 51–56. IEEE (2011)
65. Sneddon, I., McRorie, M., McKeown, G., Hanratty, J.: The belfast induced natural emotion database. IEEE Trans. Affect. Comput. **3**(1), 32–41 (2012)
66. Soleymani, M., Lichtenauer, J., Pun, T., Pantic, M.: A multimodal database for affect recognition and implicit tagging. IEEE Trans. Affect. Comput. **3**(1), 42–55 (2012)

67. Stratou, G., Ghosh, A., Debevec, P., Morency, L.P.: Effect of illumination on automatic expression recognition: a novel 3D relightable facial database. In: 2011 IEEE International Conference on Automatic Face & Gesture Recognition and Workshops (FG 2011), pp. 611–618. IEEE (2011)
68. Tcherkassof, A., Dupré, D., Meillon, B., Mandran, N., Dubois, M., Adam, J.M.: DynEmo: a video database of natural facial expressions of emotions. Int. J. Multimedia Appl. 5(5), 61–80 (2013)
69. Toole, A.J., et al.: A video database of moving faces and people. IEEE Trans. Pattern Anal. Mach. Intell. 27(5), 812–816 (2005)
70. Valstar, M., Pantic, M.: Induced disgust, happiness and surprise: an addition to the MMI facial expression database. In: Proceedings 3rd International Workshop on EMOTION (satellite of LREC): Corpora for Research on Emotion and Affect, p. 65 (2010)
71. Valstar, M., et al.: AVEC 2013: the continuous audio/visual emotion and depression recognition challenge. In: Proceedings of the 3rd ACM International Workshop on Audio/Visual Emotion Challenge, pp. 3–10. ACM (2013)
72. Valstar, M.F., Gunes, H., Pantic, M.: How to distinguish posed from spontaneous smiles using geometric features. In: Proceedings of the 9th International Conference on Multimodal Interfaces, pp. 38–45. ACM (2007)
73. Van Der Schalk, J., Hawk, S.T., Fischer, A.H., Doosje, B.: Moving faces, looking places: validation of the amsterdam dynamic facial expression set (ADFES). Emotion 11(4), 907 (2011)
74. Vinciarelli, A., Dielmann, A., Favre, S., Salamin, H.: Canal9: a database of political debates for analysis of social interactions. In: 3rd International Conference on Affective Computing and Intelligent Interaction and Workshops, ACII 2009, pp. 1–4. IEEE (2009)
75. Wang, S., et al.: A natural visible and infrared facial expression database for expression recognition and emotion inference. IEEE Trans. Multimedia 12(7), 682–691 (2010)
76. Warren, G., Schertler, E., Bull, P.: Detecting deception from emotional and unemotional cues. J. Nonverbal Behav. 33(1), 59–69 (2009)
77. Weber, R., Soladié, C., Séguier, R.: A survey on databases for facial expression analysis. In: Proceedings of the 13th International Joint Conference on Computer Vision, Imaging and Computer Graphics Theory and Applications (VISIGRAPP 2018), Volume 5, VISAPP, Funchal, Madeira, Portugal, 27–29 January 2018, pp. 73–84 (2018). https://doi.org/10.5220/0006553900730084
78. Yan, W.J., et al.: CASME II: an improved spontaneous micro-expression database and the baseline evaluation. PLoS ONE 9(1), e86041 (2014)
79. Yan, W.J., Wu, Q., Liu, Y.J., Wang, S.J., Fu, X.: CASME database: a dataset of spontaneous micro-expressions collected from neutralized faces. In: 2013 10th IEEE International Conference and Workshops on Automatic Face and Gesture Recognition (FG), pp. 1–7. IEEE (2013)
80. Yap, M.H., See, J., Hong, X., Wang, S.J.: Facial micro-expressions grand challenge 2018 summary. In: 2018 13th IEEE International Conference on Automatic Face and Gesture Recognition (FG), pp. 675–678. IEEE (2018)
81. Yin, L., Chen, X., Sun, Y., Worm, T., Reale, M.: A high-resolution 3D dynamic facial expression database. In: 8th IEEE International Conference on Automatic Face & Gesture Recognition, FG 2008, pp. 1–6. IEEE (2008)
82. Yin, L., Wei, X., Sun, Y., Wang, J., Rosato, M.J.: A 3D facial expression database for facial behavior research. In: 7th International Conference on Automatic Face and Gesture Recognition, FGR 2006, pp. 211–216. IEEE (2006)

83. Zafeiriou, S., et al.: Facial affect "in-the-wild": a survey and a new database. In: International Conference on Computer Vision (2016)
84. Zara, A., Maffiolo, V., Martin, J.C., Devillers, L.: Collection and annotation of a corpus of human-human multimodal interactions: emotion and others anthropomorphic characteristics. In: Paiva, A.C.R., Prada, R., Picard, R.W. (eds.) ACII 2007. LNCS, vol. 4738, pp. 464–475. Springer, Heidelberg (2007). https://doi.org/10.1007/978-3-540-74889-2_41
85. Zeng, Z., Pantic, M., Roisman, G., Huang, T.S., et al.: A survey of affect recognition methods: Audio, visual, and spontaneous expressions. IEEE Trans. Pattern Anal. Mach. Intell. **31**(1), 39–58 (2009)
86. Zhalehpour, S., Onder, O., Akhtar, Z., Erdem, C.E.: BAUM-1: a spontaneous audio-visual face database of affective and mental states. IEEE Trans. Affect. Comput. **8**, 300–313 (2016)
87. Zhang, L., et al.: "BioVid Emo DB": a multimodal database for emotion analyses validated by subjective ratings. In: 2016 IEEE Symposium Series on Computational Intelligence (SSCI), pp. 1–6. IEEE (2016)
88. Zhang, X., et al.: BP4D-spontaneous: a high-resolution spontaneous 3D dynamic facial expression database. Image Vis. Comput. **32**(10), 692–706 (2014)

Real-Time Head Pose Estimation by Tracking and Detection of Keypoints and Facial Landmarks

Jilliam M. Díaz Barros[1,2]($\boxtimes$), Bruno Mirbach[3]($\boxtimes$), Frederic Garcia[3]($\boxtimes$),
Kiran Varanasi[1]($\boxtimes$), and Didier Stricker[1,2]($\boxtimes$)

[1] Augmented Vision Department, German Research Center for Artificial Intelligence
(DFKI), 67663 Kaiserslautern, Germany
{Jilliam_Maria.Diaz_Barros,kiran.varanasi,Didier.Stricker}@dfki.de
[2] Computer Science Department, Technische Universität Kaiserslautern,
67663 Kaiserslautern, Germany
[3] IEE S.A., 5326 Contern, Luxembourg
{Bruno.Mirbach,Frederic.Garcia}@iee.lu
http://av.dfki.de/members/barros/

Abstract. We introduce a novel fusion framework for real-time head pose estimation using a tailored Kalman Filter. This approach estimates the pose from intensity images in monocular video data. The method is robust to extreme head rotations and varying illumination, with real-time capability. Our framework incorporates the head pose computed from a keypoint-based tracking scheme into the prediction step of the Kalman Filter and the head pose computed from a facial-landmark-based detection scheme into the correction step. The head pose from the tracking scheme is estimated from 2D keypoints tracked in two consecutive frames in the region of the head and their 3D projection on a simple geometric model. In contrast, the head pose from the detection scheme is estimated from 2D facial landmarks detected in each frame and their 3D correspondences retrieved through triangulation. In each scheme, the head pose results from the minimization of the reprojection error from the 3D-2D correspondences. In each iteration, we update the state transition matrix of the filter and subsequently the estimated covariance. We evaluated our approach on a publicly available dataset and compared with related methods of the state of the art. Our approach could achieve similar performance in terms of mean average error, while operating in real time. Furthermore, we tested our method on our own dataset, to evaluate its performance in the presence of large head rotations. We show good results even in cases where facial landmarks are partially occluded.

Keywords: Head pose estimation · Kalman Filter · Keypoints ·
Facial landmarks · Tracking · Detection · Real time

© Springer Nature Switzerland AG 2019
D. Bechmann et al. (Eds.): VISIGRAPP 2018, CCIS 997, pp. 326–349, 2019.
https://doi.org/10.1007/978-3-030-26756-8_16

1   Introduction

Head pose estimation (HPE) denotes the task of calculating the orientation and location of a person's head, *i.e.*, its pose, with respect to a given coordinate system. The estimation is generally performed for 6 degrees of freedom (*D.o.F.*), 3 rotation angles and 3 translation parameters. It is used for different purposes, either to increase the robustness of other computer vision tasks, such as face alignment [1], face recognition [2], facial expression recognition [3] or gaze estimation [4,5], or in a wide variety of applications, including human-computer interaction, driver monitoring [6,7] and augmented reality [8].

Our goal is to provide a head pose estimation method that can operate under realistic scenarios, given a set of restrictions: the method should be able to recover the pose for different users, regardless of age, gender or ethnicity, with no need of any additional calibration step; it should estimate the pose even for cases with large head rotations, where part of the face is occluded; the initialization should be performed as soon as the face is detected, without requiring the user to be in a specific initial pose, *i.e.*, facing the camera; and it should be able to estimate the pose in real time, with no power demanding devices like graphic hardwares.

For this task, the input data can be 2D images, such as intensity images, RGB or infrared (IR) data, depth images or a combination of both. Recently, more consumer RGB-D cameras have become available to the general public, causing an increase in the number of HPE methods using them [7,9,10]. We have opted to use intensity images, where the gaze could be extracted in a follow-up project. The advantage of not using additional sensors or depth images is that our method is suitable for applications where only 2D images are available.

We present a HPE approach that integrates two different pipelines operating in parallel: a keypoint-based HPE method, where the pose is computed from 2D tracked keypoints and using a simple geometric model, and a facial-landmark-based HPE method, where the pose is estimated from detected 2D facial landmarks and 3D facial landmarks refined through triangulation. Both pipelines are fused using a tailored Kalman Filter, which combines the strengths of both schemes: the robustness to handle large head pose variations of HPE from keypoints tracking and the precision and ability to recover from the facial-landmark based method. We show that our approach can perform in real time and is able to estimate the pose also for extreme head rotations.

Extending our previous works [11,12], the major contributions in this paper are:

- An updated facial-landmark-based head pose estimation technique, where the 3D facial landmarks are refined over time. The refinement is performed by triangulating 2D facial landmarks extracted from different frames. The 3D points obtained from triangulation are recursively added to a Kalman Filter, where for every new measurement, the observation noise covariance is updated with the covariance matrix computed during the triangulation.

- A re-evaluation of the head pose estimation approach with the updated 3D facial landmarks. We evaluated not only the fusion approach, but also the facial-landmark-based scheme individually. As before, we used the Boston University dataset for uniform illumination and compared to our previous results.
- A verification of the robustness of our approach under varying illumination. To do so, we evaluated our method on the Boston University video sequences under varying illumination and compared to other methods in the state of the art.
- A new dataset for head pose estimation under extreme head rotations, that we will be shared publicly. We included highly accurate groundtruth acquired with an optical tracking system.

2 Related Work

Following the classification proposed in [7,12], HPE methods can be classified in three main categories: model-based, appearance-based and 3D head model registration approaches. It should be noted that some methods might fall in more than one category.

Model-Based Approaches. These approaches are characterized for using rigid or non-rigid face models, facial landmark detection and/or any other prior information regarding the geometry of the head. La Cascia *et al.* in [13] proposed a HPE method based on registration of texture map images with a cylindrical head model. Choi and Kim [14] used templates for HPE, combining a particle filter with an ellipsoidal head model (EHM). Sung *et al.* [15] combined active appearance model (AAM) with a CHM. An and Chung [2] used an EHM to formulate the HPE as a linear system, assuming a rigid body motion under perspective projection. Kumano *et al.* [3] used a face model given by a variable-intensity template with a particle filter, for simultaneous HPE and facial expression recognition. Jang and Kanade [16,17] designed a user-specific CHM-based framework, by combining into a Kalman Filter the estimated motion and a pose retrieved from a dataset of SIFT feature points. In [4,5], Valenti *et al.* used a CHM for simultaneous HPE and eye tracking, based upon a crossed feedback mechanism, which compensated the estimated values and allowed to re-initialize the head pose tracker. Asteriadis *et al.* [18] used a facial-feature tracker with Distance Vector Fields (DVFs) for HPE. In [19], Prasad and Aravind computed the pose using POSIT from the 3D-2D correspondences from a parametrized 3D face mask and SIFT feature points. Diaz *et al.* [20], used random feature points and a CHM to estimate the pose by minimizing the reprojection error of the 3D features and the 2D correspondences. On the other hand, Vicente *et al.* [6] used facial landmarks and a deformable head model, namely parameterized appearance models, to minimize the reprojection error for HPE. Yin and Yang [21] used a pixel intensity binary test for face detection, with pose regression along with local binary feature for face alignment. From a rigid head model, the pose was retrieved by solving the 2D-3D correspondences. Wu *et al.* in [22] presented a pipeline for simultaneous facial landmark detection, HPE and deformation estimation using a cascade iterative procedure augmented with model-based HPE. Similarly, Gou et al. [23] proposed a Coupled Cascade Regression (CCR) framework for simultaneous facial landmark detection and HPE. In [11], we presented a first approach to combine the head pose estimated from facial landmarks with the head pose estimated from salient features. 3D points for both type of features were recovered from the intersection on a simple geometric head model. The estimated poses were integrated into a linear Kalman Filter as new measurements in the correction stage. In [12], we introduced a second approach to fuse both estimated poses. In this case, 3D facial landmarks were extracted from a reference head mesh and used through the entire video sequence. Similarly to this work, head pose estimated from keypoints was used to update the state transition matrix at the prediction stage, while the pose computed from facial landmarks was used as a new measurement at the correction stage.

Appearance-Based Approaches. These HPE methods are based on machine learning, using visual features of the face appearance. Even though they are robust to extreme head poses, usually the output corresponds to discrete head poses, thus assigning the pose to specific ranges instead of continuous estimation. These approaches usually have a higher performance for low-resolution face images [24,25]. In [26], Fanelli et al. used random regression forests for HPE and facial feature detection, from depth data. Patches from different parts of the face were used to recover the pose through a voting scheme. For the training, it was necessary a large dataset with annotated data. Wang et al. presented in [27] a head tracking approach from invariant keypoints. Simulation techniques and normalization were combined to create a learning scheme. Ahn et al. [24] introduced a deep-learning-based approach for RGB images, with a particle filter to refine and increase the stability of the estimated pose. In [28], Liu et al. used convolutional neural networks, where HPE was formulated as a regression problem. The network was trained using a large synthetic dataset obtained from rendered 3D head models. [24,28] used a GPU to reach real-time capabilities. Tulyakov et al. introduced in [29] a person-specific template scheme using a depth camera, which combined template-matching-based tracking with a frame-by-frame decision-tree-based estimator. Borghi et al. [7] presented a real time deep-learning-based approach for HPE from depth images, using a regression neural network, POSEidon, which integrated depth with motion features and appearance. In [30], Schwarz presented a deep learning method for HPE which fused IR and depth data with cross-stitch units. Derkach et al. [31] proposed a system intended for depth input data, which integrated three different approaches for HPE, two based on landmark detection and one on a dictionary-based method for extreme head poses.

3D Head Model Registration Approaches. These methods register the measured data to reference 3D head models. Meyer et al. [32] combined particle swarm optimization and the iterative closest point (ICP) algorithm to register a 3D morphable model (3DMM) to a measured depth face. Yu et al. [33] extended this with an online 3D reconstruction of the full head, to handle extreme head rotations. Ghiass *et al.* [34] estimated the pose through a fitting process with a 3D morphable model and RGB-D data. Papazov *et al.* [35] introduced triangular surface patch descriptors for HPE from depth data. The pose was computed from a voting scheme resulting from matching the descriptors to patches from synthetic head models. Jeni *et al.* [36] presented an approach for 3D registration of a dense face mesh from 2D images, through a cascade regression framework trained using a large database of high-resolution 3D face scans. Tan *et al.* [10] used RGB-D data to regress the 3D head pose using random forest in a temporal tracking scheme.

Other methods define HPE as an optimization problem. That is the case of [37], where Morency *et al.* presented a probabilistic scheme, namely Generalized Adaptive View-based Appearance Model (GAVAM), using an EHM. The pose was estimated by solving a linear system with normal flow constraint (NFC). Baltrusaitis *et al.* presented in [38] an extension, which combined head pose tracking with a 3D constrained local model, using both depth data and intensity information. Saragih *et al.* introduced in [39] a HPE approach which fits a deformable model using an optimization strategy through a non-parametric representation of the likelihood maps of landmarks locations. Drouard *et al.* [25] used a Gaussian mixture of locally-linear mapping model to map HOG features extracted on a face region to 3D head poses.

One of the issues of most tracking-based methods is that their robustness to initial HPE when the head is not frontal is not clear [31]. For facial-landmarks-based HPE methods, the accuracy of the head pose relies on the precision of the estimated facial landmarks. Since they strongly depend on the detection of facial landmarks, the misalignment of the landmarks in a frame might lead to erroneous estimations. Hence, these methods might be sensitive to extreme head poses, partial occlusions, facial expressions and low resolution images.

In this work, we introduce a model-based HPE approach based on intensity images. Two independent pipelines are fused on a Kalman Filter for pose estimation, extending the working range to large head rotations. The proposed method does not have any constraint for initialization, as facing the camera for the first frame, and is suitable for real time applications, making it useful for HPE in realistic scenarios.

3   Proposed HPE Pipeline

Several methods of the state of the art rely on facial landmarks for HPE. Even though they might be a reliable source for HPE for frontal and near-frontal faces, facial landmarks are sensitive to extreme head rotations and (self-) occlusions, where important reference regions of the face such as the eyes or nose are partially or totally occluded. In order to tackle this problem, we propose to integrate the head pose computed from a set of keypoints that can be tracked continuously, even when the facial landmarks are not visible. Although a keypoint-based HPE approach could be used alone, it might suffer from drifting in long sequences [16, 17,20]. Accordingly, a mechanism to reinforce and correct the head pose from keypoint tracking, using the facial-landmark HPE scheme must be included.

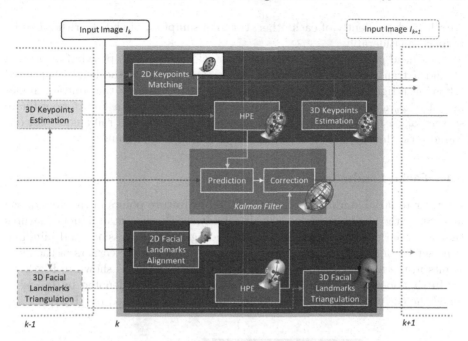

Fig. 1. Proposed HPE pipeline, from Keypoints (blue) and Facial Landmarks (red). (Color figure online)

A diagram of the proposed approach is presented in Fig. 1. On top, inside the blue rectangle, the HPE scheme from keypoints is depicted. At the bottom, inside the red rectangle, is the facial-landmark-based HPE method. The Kalman filter used to fuse both schemes is depicted in the center, inside the green rectangle.

For an input image at time k, I_k, we compute separately the head pose using keypoints and the head pose using facial landmarks. For the keypoint based method (see Fig. 1), we use a temporal tracking scheme, where the correspondences of 2D keypoints are estimated pairwise using optical flow. Then, these 2D keypoints are projected on a simple geometrical head model, to recover 3D keypoints. From the 2D keypoints at the current input image at time k and the 3D keypoints from the previous frame, $k - 1$, we obtain an estimation of the head pose.

For the facial-landmark-based HPE scheme, we align 2D facial landmarks in every input image, independently of the previously alignments (see Fig. 1). 3D facial landmarks are refined by triangulating 2D facial landmarks detected over time. Afterwards, we compute the head pose from the 2D facial landmarks at the current frame and the refined 3D facial landmarks at a fixed pose.

The head poses from both independent frameworks are later integrated into a Kalman filter as follows: HPE from keypoints is included at the prediction stage, while HPE from facial landmarks is used as a new measurement at the correction stage of the filter. As the two different strategies for HPE run in parallel independently of each other, time consumption of the algorithm can be reduced considerably.

The head pose is represented with a transformation, composed of a rotation $\mathbf{R}$ and a translation $\mathbf{t}$. The pose of every 3D point $\mathbf{P}$ in the head is updated following a rigid transformation. $\mathbf{R}$ can also be denoted by the rotation angles $\boldsymbol{\omega} = [\omega_x, \omega_y, \omega_z]$ with respect to the X, Y and Z axes of a known coordinate system. ω_x, ω_y, and ω_z are usually termed as pitch, yaw and roll angles. For our framework, the calibration of the camera is required in advance.

3.1   Facial Landmarks

We refer to facial landmarks as a specific set of feature points in the area of the face. Since the head is modeled as a rigid body, we chose a set of fiducial features that are robust to non-rigid motions, including facial expressions and blinking. This set is composed of 13 features, which encompasses the corners of the eyes, points in the nasal bridge and points around the nostrils, as shown in Fig. 2.

In this document, the set of n 2D facial landmarks is denoted by $\{\mathbf{p}_F\}_{i=1}^n$, while the corresponding set of n 3D facial features is denoted by $\{\mathbf{P}_F\}_{i=1}^n$.

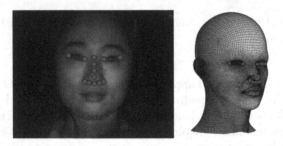

Fig. 2. Facial Landmarks in 2D (left) and 3D (right).

2D Facial Landmarks Detection. For every input image, the set of 2D facial landmarks is detected using the method proposed by Kazemi and Sullivan [40]. This method aligns the facial landmarks by using an ensemble of regression trees, from a sparse subset of intensity values indexed to an initial estimate of the shape. The resulting facial landmarks are depicted in Fig. 2 (left).

It should be noted that the face is not always detected in every frame, thus the facial landmarks cannot be properly aligned to the input image. In those cases, the head pose is only estimated from the keypoints, as detailed in Sect. 3.4.

3D Facial Landmarks Triangulation. Given the set of robust 2D facial landmarks described before, the corresponding 3D facial landmarks are extracted and refined progressively. For the initial frame, we use 3D points that were retrieved offline on a reference head mesh, as shown in Fig. 2 (right). These pre-defined 3D features were manually annotated from an open-source 3D face model [41].

Afterwards, as new 2D facial landmarks are detected along the video sequence, 3D facial landmarks are refined using triangulation. This is possible as the extrinsic camera parameters, *i.e.* the camera pose, is known. Following the linear triangulation method described in [42], from two camera poses $\mathbf{C}$ and $\mathbf{C}'$ and the corresponding sets of 2D facial landmarks, $\{\mathbf{p}_F\}_{i=1}^n$ and $\{\mathbf{p}'_F\}_{i=1}^n$, the relation of each 2D point x and its corresponding 3D point X is defined by $x \propto \mathcal{P}X$, where $\mathcal{P}$ is the 3×4 camera projection matrix. Given two views, we can re-write for each point an equation in the form $AX = 0$, as detailed in [42]. This equation is then solved using the Jacobi's method for finding eigenvalues of symmetric matrices [43,44].

By using the Jacobi's method, we apply singular value decomposition on matrix A, as follows:

$$A = U\Sigma V^T, \tag{1}$$

where U is an orthogonal matrix, Σ is a diagonal positive definite matrix and V is an orthogonal matrix. From this decomposition, we can compute the covariance matrix of A, given by:

$$\mathbf{cov} = V\Sigma^2 V^T. \tag{2}$$

To incorporate new camera poses, and thus refine the 3D facial landmarks, we include a linear Kalman filter where the 3D points are corrected when a new measurement is obtained. This measurement corresponds to the output of the triangulation method from two camera views described before. In each iteration, we use the covariance computed in Eq. (2), as the observation noise covariance of the Kalman filter.

With the previous procedure, we avoid the time-consuming process of manual [36] or semi-automatic facial landmarks annotation [38] on large datasets of 3D face scans, yet providing a robust estimated head pose as long as the facial features are visible in the image.

3.2 Keypoints

We denote the set of 2D keypoints by $\{\mathbf{p}_K\}_{i=1}^m$ and the set of 3D keypoints by $\{\mathbf{P}_K\}_{i=1}^m$. The number of keypoints per frame, m, is not fixed as in the facial landmarks, since it depends on the number of feature points tracked between two frames.

2D Keypoints Extraction. In every frame, we extract 2D keypoints in the area of the head and find their correspondences from the previous frame. These keypoints can be located in the area of the face, but also on the back side or top of the head, for large head rotations.

2D keypoints are detected using the Features from Accelerated Segment Test algorithm [45], also known as FAST. With this method, we are able to detect robust 2D features with low computation time.

Given the set of keypoints extracted from the previous frame, we find the 2D correspondences at the new input image using optical flow. To that end, we use the pyramidal Lucas-Kanade feature tracker detailed in [46].

3D Keypoints Computation. In contrast to 3D facial landmarks estimation, where points are first extracted offline on a 3D head mesh and later refined using triangulation, 3D keypoints are recovered by using a simple geometric model. Similarly to our previous works [11,12], this model corresponds to an ellipsoid as it resembles the shape of the head. Other methods of the state of the art use 3D morphable models for HPE [32,33,38]. These complex head models can be computationally expensive, requiring the use of graphics hardware. We demonstrate in Sect. 4 that the ellipsoid yields good results for the tracking task.

As depicted in Fig. 3, each 3D keypoint $\mathbf{P}_K$ results from the intersection of the projection line l on the ellipsoidal head model (EHM). This line passes through the optical center of the camera $\mathbf{C}$ and the corresponding 2D keypoint $\mathbf{p}_K$ in the image plane $\mathbf{I_0}$, The orientation, position and dimension of the ellipsoid on the 3D space are known in advance, as explained in Sect. 3.3.

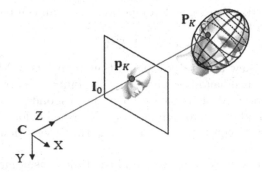

Fig. 3. Computation of 3D keypoints. Source: [12].

The equation of the projection line is given by $\mathbf{l} = \mathbf{C} + \lambda \mathbf{d}$, where $\mathbf{d}$ represents a line parallel to l and λ is a scalar retrieved from the quadratic equation of the ellipsoid [11,12] as follows:

$$|\mathbf{a}|^2 \lambda^2 + 2(\mathbf{a} \cdot \mathbf{b}) \lambda + |\mathbf{b}|^2 - 1 = 0 \tag{3}$$

Given an ellipsoid with radii $\{\frac{1}{r_x}, \frac{1}{r_y}, \frac{1}{r_z}\}$, rotation matrix $\mathbf{R}$ and having its center at $\mathbf{E_0}$, $\mathbf{a}$ and $\mathbf{b}$ are defined as $\mathbf{a} = \mathbf{GR}^T \mathbf{d}$ and $\mathbf{b} = \mathbf{GR}^T(\mathbf{C} - \mathbf{E_0})$, with $\mathbf{G}$ being a 3×3 diagonal matrix of the inverses of the ellipsoid radii.

Area for 2D Keypoint Detection. For every new input image, 2D keypoints are extracted exclusively from a defined area of the head. As mentioned earlier, this area might not only be on the face, but also on top or on the back side of the head. Some methods propose to extract salient features from the area given by a face detection algorithm [47]. Besides being time consuming, this approach would fail when the face is not detected, *i.e.*, for large head rotations.

We propose to continuously update the area for feature detection, by projecting the 3D ellipsoidal head model on the image plane in every frame, as shown in

Fig. 4. To that end, we first estimate the plane π parallel to the horizontal axis of the image plane and to the vertical axis of the ellipsoid, and which divides it in two parts. We then find the elliptical surface that results from the intersection of π and the ellipsoid. Finally, this surface is projected in the image, assuming a perspective camera model.

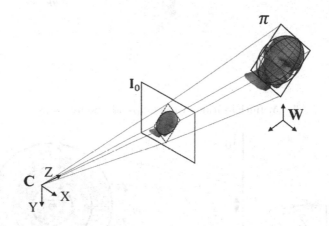

Fig. 4. Update area for keypoint detection. Source: [11].

3.3 Initialization

Similarly to [12], we adjust the dimension of the ellipsoid according to the size of the user's head. The 2D facial landmarks detected in the first frame are used for this step. Since the calibration of the camera is known, we can use the relation between the interpupillary distance of the eyes in pixels, δ_{px}, extracted from the input image and an approximate distance between a person's eyes in cm, δ_{cm} for the initialization. Measurements reported in [48,49] found that the averaged interpupillary distance for men is around 6.47 cm, while for women is 6.23 cm. We assumed this distance to be of 6 cm in our experiments.

As shown in Fig. 5, we define the 2D bounding box of the detected head by points $\{\mathbf{p}_{TL}, \mathbf{p}_{TR}, \mathbf{p}_{BL}, \mathbf{p}_{BR}\}$. Additionally, the corresponding 3D bounding box is defined by points $\{\mathbf{P}_{TL}, \mathbf{P}_{TR}, \mathbf{P}_{BL}, \mathbf{P}_{BR}\}$. The radii of the ellipsoid on the X and Z axes, r_x and r_z, are set equal to half of the width of the 3D bounding box, i.e., $\frac{1}{2}|\mathbf{P}_{TL} - \mathbf{P}_{TR}|$ and are computed directly from Eq. (4) [12]. On the other hand, the radius r_y of the ellipsoid is given by half of the height of the 3D bounding box, i.e., $\frac{1}{2}|\mathbf{P}_{TL} - \mathbf{P}_{BL}|$ and is calculated from Eq. (5) [12].

$$r_x = r_z = \frac{1}{2}|\mathbf{P}_{TR} - \mathbf{P}_{TL}| \cdot \frac{\delta_{cm}}{\delta_{px}} \tag{4}$$

$$r_y = \frac{1}{2}|\mathbf{P}_{TL} - \mathbf{P}_{BL}| \cdot \frac{\delta_{cm}}{\delta_{px}} \tag{5}$$

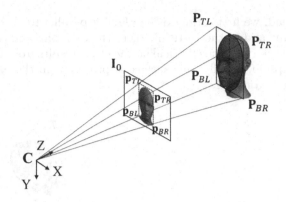

Fig. 5. Initialization of the ellipsoid. Source: [11].

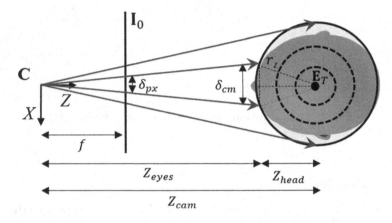

Fig. 6. Estimation of the ellipsoid's depth. Source: [12].

The estimation of the initial depth of the ellipsoid with respect to the camera's optical center $\mathbf{C}$ is depicted in Fig. 6. Z_{cam}, the distance between $\mathbf{C}$ and $\mathbf{E}_T$, the center of the ellipsoid, is given by $Z_{cam} = Z_{eyes} + Z_{head}$. Z_{eyes} is the distance from $\mathbf{C}$ to the eyes' baseline and is computed from Eq. (6) [11,12], where f is the focal length of the camera. Z_{head} corresponds to the distance from the eyes' baseline to $\mathbf{E}_T$ and is given by Eq. (7) [11,12].

$$Z_{eyes} = f \cdot \frac{\delta_{cm}}{\delta_{px}} \tag{6}$$

$$Z_{head} = \sqrt{r_z{}^2 - (\delta_{cm}/2)^2} \tag{7}$$

3.4   Head Pose Estimation

The head pose estimated from each independent pipeline is computed by minimizing the reprojection error between the 3D features points $\{\mathbf{P}\}_{i=1}^{\eta}$ on the image plane and the 2D correspondences on the image $\{\mathbf{p}\}_{i=1}^{\eta}$ at time k. For the keypoint-based scheme, the 3D and 2D features correspond to $\{\mathbf{P}_K, \mathbf{p}_K\}$ respectively, $\eta = m$ and $\{\mathbf{P}_K\}_{i=1}^{m}$ is given at time $k-1$. For the facial-landmark-based scheme, the 3D and 2D features correspond to $\{\mathbf{P}_F, \mathbf{p}_F\}$ respectively, $\eta = n$ and $\{\mathbf{P}_F\}_{i=1}^{n}$ is given at the initial frame. The minimization is expressed by Eq. (8) [12], where $\pi(\mathbf{P}) : \mathbb{R}^3 \mapsto \mathbb{R}^2$ denotes the perspective projection operator and i the index of the i-th feature point. Equation (8) [12] is minimized in the least squared sense with respect to the rotation $\mathbf{R}$ and translation $\mathbf{t}$, using Levenberg-Marquardt iteration.

$$\arg\min \sum_{i=1}^{\eta} \|\pi(\mathbf{R}\mathbf{P}_i + \mathbf{t}) - \mathbf{p}_i\|_2^2 \tag{8}$$

Before introducing the fusion scheme to combine both estimated head, it is important to understand the difference between both estimates.

For the keypoint-based scheme (Sect. 3.2), we calculate the head pose resulting from tracking keypoints in two consecutive frames. This implies that we compute a transformation from the frame at time $k-1$ to the frame at time k. This frame-to-frame transformation is referred to as a local transformation and is denoted by $\mathbf{R}_{k-1}^{k}$ and $\mathbf{t}_{k-1}^{k}$.

Head pose estimated from the facial-landmark-based scheme (Sect. 3.1) is computed with respect to 3D facial landmarks fixed to an initial head pose, $\mathbf{R}_0$ and $\mathbf{t}_0$. Although the 3D facial landmarks are refined over time, the pose is not updated. Therefore, the pose retrieved from this scheme maps the head pose from the first given frame at time k_0, to a pose at time k. This transformation is referred to a global transformation and is denoted by $\mathbf{R}_0^{k}$ and $\mathbf{t}_0^{k}$.

Given a local and a global transformation, we need to formulate our Kalman Filter in a way that we can integrate both head poses. We define the state vector $\mathbf{x}$ of the filter to be composed of the rotation and translation from the first given frame, i.e., the global head pose. The head rotation is represented using a quaternion $\mathbf{q} = [q_x, q_y, q_z, q_w]^T$, where q_w is the scalar part and $\{q_x, q_y, q_z\}$ the vector part. The translation is denoted in homogeneous coordinates as $\tilde{\mathbf{t}} = [t_x, t_y, t_z, 1]^T$. Consequently, the state vector is given by $\mathbf{x} = [\mathbf{q}^T, \tilde{\mathbf{t}}^T]^T$, with a dimension of 8×1.

Initial HPE. For the first given frame, the head pose $\mathbf{R}_0$ and $\mathbf{t}_0$ is computed from facial landmarks only, as 3D keypoints are not available. The pose is recovered by minimizing Eq. (8) with the 3D facial landmarks $\{\mathbf{P}_F\}_{i=1}^{n}$ extracted offline from the reference head model and the 2D facial landmarks $\{\mathbf{p}_F\}_{i=1}^{n}$ aligned at the first frame. We initialize the Kalman Filter using the computed head pose.

HPE for the Other Frames. We define a linear Kalman Filter to fuse the pose estimated from keypoints and the pose estimated from facial landmarks. This is possible, as a linear process model can be built by representing the rotation with quaternions and the translation with homogeneous coordinates. The predicted or *a priori* state estimate of the filter $\hat{\mathbf{x}}_k^{-}$ at time k is calculated using Eq. (9), where $\mathbf{A}$ represents the state transition matrix of the process model, with a normal distributed process noise with covariance $\mathbf{Q}$.

$$\hat{\mathbf{x}}_k^- = \mathbf{A}_k \hat{\mathbf{x}}_{k-1} \qquad (9)$$

In order to integrate the keypoint-based HPE into the prediction step of the filter, we update $\mathbf{A}$ in every iteration with the pose estimated at the tracking scheme, as shown in Eq. (10) [12]. The resulting $\mathbf{A}$ is a matrix of size 8×8.

$$\mathbf{A} = \begin{bmatrix} \mathbf{A}_\rho & 0 \\ 0 & \mathbf{A_t} \end{bmatrix} \qquad (10)$$

$\mathbf{A}_\rho$ corresponds to the state transition sub-matrix to project the rotation ahead and is computed from the local rotation $\mathbf{R}_{k-1}^k$. We convert this rotation matrix to a quaternion $\boldsymbol{\rho} = [\rho_x, \rho_y, \rho_z, \rho_w]^T$, and calculate $\mathbf{A}_\rho$ as follows [12]:

$$\mathbf{A}_\rho = \begin{bmatrix} \rho_w & -\rho_z & \rho_y & \rho_x \\ \rho_z & \rho_w & -\rho_x & \rho_y \\ -\rho_y & \rho_x & \rho_w & \rho_z \\ -\rho_x & -\rho_y & -\rho_z & \rho_w \end{bmatrix} \qquad (11)$$

$\mathbf{A_t}$ represents the state transition sub-matrix to update the translation, and is defined by (12) [12]. The new translation estimate t_0^{k-} is given by (13) [12].

$$\mathbf{A_t} = \begin{bmatrix} \mathbf{R}_{k-1}^k & t_{k-1}^k \\ 0 & 1 \end{bmatrix}, \qquad (12)$$

$$t_0^{k-} = \mathbf{R}_{k-1}^k t_0^k + t_{k-1}^k. \qquad (13)$$

The covariance $\mathbf{P}^-$ at the prediction step is computed from Eq. (14).

$$\mathbf{P}_k^- = \mathbf{A}_k \mathbf{P}_{k-1} \mathbf{A}_k^T + \mathbf{Q} \qquad (14)$$

The measurement model of the Kalman Filter is given by Eq. (15). The new measurement $\mathbf{z}_k$ at time k corresponds to the head pose retrieved from the facial-landmark-based scheme, $i.e.$, the global head pose. $\mathbf{H}$ is a 7×8 matrix that relates the current state $\mathbf{x}_k$ to the measurement and is given by $\mathbf{H} = [\mathbf{I}_7 \ 0]$, where $\mathbf{I}_7$ is a 7×7 identity matrix. $\mathbf{v}_k$ denotes the measurement noise in the observation with covariance $\mathbf{R}$.

$$\mathbf{z}_k = \mathbf{H}\mathbf{x}_k + \mathbf{v}_k \qquad (15)$$

The updated or a $posteriori$ state estimate $\hat{\mathbf{x}}_k$ is calculated from Eq. (16), where $\mathbf{K}_k$ represents the Kalman gain.

$$\hat{\mathbf{x}}_k = \hat{\mathbf{x}}_k^- + \mathbf{K}_k(\mathbf{z}_k - \mathbf{H}\hat{\mathbf{x}}_k^-) \qquad (16)$$

The covariance is updated at the correction step using Eq. (17).

$$\mathbf{P}_k = (\mathbf{I} - \mathbf{K}_k\mathbf{H})\mathbf{P}_k^- \tag{17}$$

Occlusion Handling and Pose Recovery. One challenge in HPE is to compute the head pose when the face is occluded due to large head rotations or when it is not detected at all. The facial-landmark-based scheme fails to provide an estimation in these cases, so our fusion approach uses only the head pose computed from the keypoint-based scheme. This implies that the head pose calculated at the Kalman Filter is given only from the prediction step, as no new measurement is available. Thereby, our approach is able to provide an estimated pose even when the face has not been detected.

When the face is detected again, the output of the facial-landmark-based scheme is integrated again at the Kalman Filter to correct the estimated pose. This step is fundamental in our approach, especially if the face has not been detected for several consecutive frames. If the pose has been computed only from keypoints for a long sequence, the estimation might suffer from drifting, while increasing the state covariance (uncertainty) of the filter (from Eq. (14)) over time. When a new measurement is available, the recovery takes place rapidly, since the weight of the predicted state covariance is relatively small.

In contrast to our previous method presented in [12], we do not update in each iteration the covariance of the process noise and measurement noise, but set it fixed for all the sequences.

4 Experiments and Results

We have evaluated the proposed approach using a publicly available database for HPE and compared to other methods of the state of the art. Additionally, we have evaluated the performance of our approach under extreme head poses using our own dataset. We have also analyzed the contribution of each HPE scheme in our approach, by assessing them individually. We implemented both pipelines in C++ and tested the algorithms in an Intel® Xeon(R) W3520 processor with 8 Gb of RAM.

4.1 Comparison with Other HPE Methods

We evaluated our method using the Boston University (BU) head tracking database presented in [13]. This database is composed of short video sequences with subjects performing several head movements inside an office. The database is divided in two sets of videos, one recorded under uniform illumination and the other under varying illumination. The first set contains 45 video sequences from 5 different subjects, while the second set has 27 video sequences from 3 subjects. Ground truth was acquired using the Flock of Birds magnetic tracker attached to the head, reporting nominal accuracies of 0.5° in rotation and 1.8 mm in translation.

We used three metrics for comparison with other relevant HPE methods of the state of the art: root mean square error (RMSE), mean absolute error (MAE) and standard deviation (STD). These three estimation errors were computed from Eqs. (18), (19) and (20) respectively, where n represents the number of frames, s_i the ground truth $\mathbf{s}$ at time i and $\hat{s}_i$ the estimate of the position or angle $\hat{\mathbf{s}}$, at time i.

$$RMSE = \sqrt{\frac{1}{n}\sum_{i=1}^{n}(s_i - \hat{s}_i)^2} \tag{18}$$

$$MAE = \frac{1}{n}\sum_{i=1}^{n}|s_i - \hat{s}_i| \tag{19}$$

$$STD = \sqrt{\frac{1}{n-1}\sum_{i=1}^{n}|(s_i - \hat{s}_i) - \mu|^2} \tag{20}$$

μ corresponds to the mean of $(\mathbf{s} - \hat{\mathbf{s}})$ and is given by, (21).

$$\mu = \frac{1}{n}\sum_{i=1}^{n}(s_i - \hat{s}_i) \tag{21}$$

Tables 1 and 2 present the results of our approach and related works on the BU database, with uniform and varying illumination, respectively. We have also included the average of the rotation MAE for each method.

The last three rows of each table present the angular accuracies from the individual HPE approaches, using only keypoints (K.P.) or facial landmarks (F.L.) and HPE from fusion. It should be noted that the latter performs better for every angle estimation, yaw, pitch and roll, than each individual method. Only for the varying illumination set, Table 2, the performance of the facial-landmark-based method is comparable to the fusion approach.

Regarding other methods of the state of the art, we can observe that the proposed approach has an outstanding performance. For the uniform illumination set, Table 1, only [36] presents a similar average error with a higher estimation rate. Other methods as [27,38] present lower MAE, but with much lower estimation rate. On the other hand, on the varying illumination set, Table 2, our fusion approach presents the best performance, with the lowest average of the MAE and real-time capability.

For the BU database, no calibration data is provided. For that reason, most of related work do not report their translation estimation errors. We have included our results in Tables 3 and 4, for the uniform and varying illumination sets, respectively. It can be noted that in average, the fusion scheme presents the lowest errors for both sets, with a similar performance of the keypoint-based HPE scheme. This can be explained as this pipeline uses frame-by-frame tracking, so the 2D estimation of the features is robust. In contrast, in the facial-landmark-based scheme the feature detection is not always precise and there are small displacements in the alignments between frames even when the person is not moving.

Table 1. Comparison with other methods of the state of the art on BU dataset with uniform illumination set.

Method	Year	RMSE ± STD			MAE				Time (FPS)
		Roll	Pitch	Yaw	Roll	Pitch	Yaw	Average	
La Cascia et al. [13]	2000	-	-	-	9.8	6.1	**3.3**	6.4	-
Sung et al. [15]	2008	-	-	-	3.1	5.6	5.4	4.7	-
Morency et al. [37]	2008	-	-	-	2.91	3.67	4.97	3.85	6
Jang and Kanade [16]	2008	-	-	-	2.1	3.7	4.6	3.46	-
An and Chung [2]	2008	-	-	-	2.83	3.95	3.94	3.57	-
Choi and Kim [14]	2008	-	-	-	2.82	3.92	4.04	3.59	14
Kumano et al. [3]	2009	-	-	-	2.9	4.2	7.1	4.73	-
Lefevre and Odobez [50]	2009	-	-	-	2.0	3.3	4.4	3.23	3
Asteriadis et al. [18]	2010	3.56	4.89	5.72	-	-	-	-	-
Prasad and Aravind [19]	2010	-	-	-	3.6	**2.5**	3.8	3.3	-
Jang and Kanade [17]	2010	-	-	-	2.07	3.44	4.22	3.24	-
Saragih et al. [39]	2011	-	-	-	2.55	4.46	5.23	4.08	8
Valenti et al. [4]	2012	3.00 ± 2.82	5.26 ± 4.67	6.10 ± 5.79	-	-	-	-	-
Wang et al. [27]	2012	-	-	-	**1.86**	2.69	3.75	2.76	15
Baltrusaitis et al. [38]	2012	-	-	-	2.08	3.81	**3.00**	2.96	-
Tran et al. [51]	2013	-	-	-	2.4	3.9	5.4	3.90	5
Vicente et al. [6]	2015	-	-	-	3.2	6.2	4.3	4.56	25
Jeni et al. [36]	2017	-	-	-	2.41	**2.66**	3.93	**3.0**	**50**
Wu et al. [22]	2017	-	-	-	3.1	5.3	4.9	4.43	-
Diaz Barros et al. [20]	2017	3.36 ± 2.98	4.46 ± 3.84	5.09 ± 4.56	2.56	3.39	3.99	3.31	56
Gou et al. [23]	2017	-	-	-	3.3	4.8	5.1	4.4	-
Diaz Barros et al. [11]	2018	3.36 ± 2.99	4.32 ± 3.62	5.25 ± 4.70	2.54	3.27	4.07	3.29	23
Diaz Barros et al. [12]	2018	3.06 ± 2.78	4.38 ± 3.76	4.93 ± 4.56	2.32	3.41	3.90	3.21	40
HPE from K.P.	2018	3.42 ± 3.05	4.53 ± 3.78	5.46 ± 4.81	2.61	3.45	4.27	3.44	-
HPE from F.L.	2018	2.46 ± 2.31	4.43 ± 3.61	5.23 ± 4.85	**1.92**	3.49	4.17	3.19	-
HPE from fusion	2018	**2.41 ± 2.20**	**4.11 ± 3.26**	**4.92 ± 4.40**	1.91	3.26	3.92	**3.03**	40

Table 2. Comparison with other methods of the state of the art on BU dataset with uniform illumination set.

Method	Year	RMSE ± STD			MAE				Time (FPS)
		Roll	Pitch	Yaw	Roll	Pitch	Yaw	Average	
Lefevre and Odobez [50]	2009	-	-	-	2.3	3.5	**4.1**	3.3	3
Jang and Kanade [17]	2010	-	-	-	2.8	4.25	5.92	4.32	-
Jeni et al. [36]	2017	-	-	-	2.24	**2.72**	4.87	3.27	50
HPE from K.P.	2018	3.44 ± 2.77	5.31 ± 4.38	6.67 ± 5.56	2.73	4.20	5.21	4.04	-
HPE from F.L.	2018	2.70 ± 2.17	4.14 ± 3.59	5.21 ± 4.51	**2.18**	3.22	**4.12**	3.17	-
HPE from fusion	2018	**2.66 ± 2.08**	**4.11 ± 3.42**	**5.15 ± 4.05**	2.16	3.23	**4.12**	**3.17**	40

Time Consumption Analysis. To estimate the time consumption of our approach, we have evaluated the runtime for each step on the BU dataset (see Table 5). A comparison with other methods of the state of the art is presented in the last column of Tables 1 and 2.

Table 3. Errors on the translation estimation on BU dataset with uniform illumination set.

Method	RMSE ± STD			MAE			
	Trans. X	Trans. Y	Trans. Z	Trans. X	Trans. Y	Trans. Z	Average
HPE from K.P.	4.09 ± 3.76	**2.10 ± 1.68**	1.58 ± 1.23	3.27	**1.64**	1.22	2.04
HPE from F.L.	4.30 ± 4.07	2.49 ± 2.05	1.45 ± 1.19	3.48	1.99	1.13	2.2
HPE from fusion	**3.89 ± 3.65**	2.31 ± 1.91	**1.40 ± 1.07**	**3.15**	1.86	**1.13**	2.04

Table 4. Errors on the translation estimation on BU dataset with varying illumination set.

Method	RMSE ± STD			MAE			
	Trans. X	Trans. Y	Trans. Z	Trans. X	Trans. Y	Trans. Z	Average
HPE from K.P.	3.17 ± **2.63**	**2.41 ± 1.82**	1.53 ± 1.09	2.58	**1.94**	1.24	1.92
HPE from F.L.	3.69 ± 3.26	2.66 ± 2.12	1.11 ± 0.89	3.00	2.18	0.91	2.03
HPE from fusion	**3.10 ± 2.85**	2.76 ± 2.16	**0.96 ± 0.75**	**2.54**	2.29	**0.77**	1.87

Table 5. Errors on the translation estimation on BU dataset with uniform illumination set.

Process	Time (ms)
Initial face detection	22.34
Initial head pose estimation	2.01
Total	24.35
2D feature detection and matching	21.27
Estimation of 3D keypoints	0.3
HPE and refinement of 3D facial landmarks	3.12
Total	24.68

As can be noted in Table 5, the HPE in our method for both the initialization step and the other frames took around 40 FPS. If we compare to previous works, only [36] and our previous approaches [12,20] could reach >40FPS, with estimation errors similar to the proposed approach. In contrast to [36], we did not need manual annotation on a large dataset of high-resolution 3D face scans.

4.2   Experiments with Our Own Dataset

We have also evaluated the HPE fusion approach and both independent schemes on our own video sequence. We made this video publicly available for research purposes at [52], and included groundtruth with the respective calibration file. The video contains 1263 images of a person sitting, while moving her head with large rotations. In some frames, the head is partially self-occluded, due to rotations larger that $45°$ in the X or Y axes (pitch and yaw). The most challenging estimations are the yaw and pitch rotation, where facial landmark detectors usually present higher error.

(a) Frame 9   (b) Frame 132   (c) Frame 199   (d) Frame 318

(e) Frame 417   (f) Frame 500   (g) Frame 581   (h) Frame 609

(i) Frame 749   (j) Frame 886   (k) Frame 1005   (l) Frame 1209

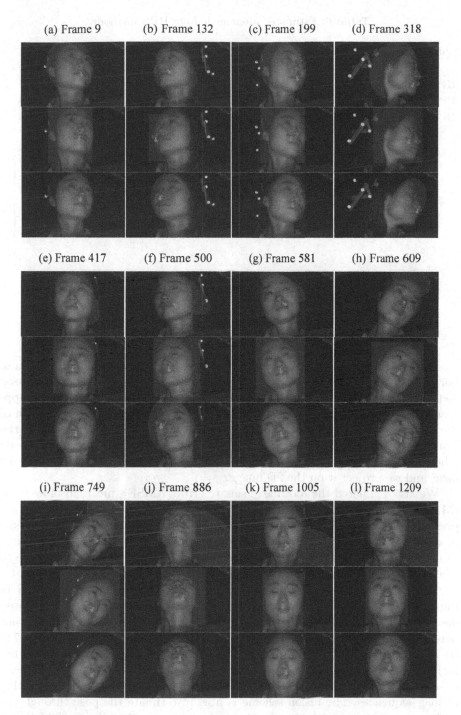

Fig. 7. HPE from the provided sequences with keypoints (top), facial landmarks (center) and the fusion scheme (bottom) for each frame.

Table 6. Estimated pitch angle from HPE methods.

Method	RMSE ± STD			MAE			
	Roll	Pitch	Yaw	Roll	Pitch	Yaw	Average
HPE from K.P.	57.63 ± 30.20	55.04 ± 54.02	32.78 ± 25.15	52.94	46.02	25.70	41.55
HPE from F.L.	16.34 ± 16.16	16.66 ± 16.61	9.82 ± 9.73	9.72	12.61	5.66	9.33
HPE from fusion	14.87 ± 14.69	16.85 ± 16.81	9.69 ± 9.42	8.24	12.09	5.65	8.66

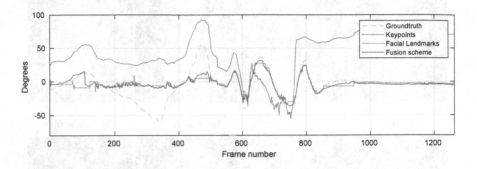

Fig. 8. Estimated roll angle from the three HPE methods.

Figure 7 presents the results for different frames from the three HPE schemes. For each frame, the results are shown as follows: on top is the keypoint-based method; the facial-landmark-based scheme is on the middle; and the fusion approach is at the bottom. The blue area around the face depicts the projection of the ellipsoid onto the 2D image, while the coordinate system representing the estimated pose is displayed with the RGB arrows. For the facial-landmark-based scheme, we define a plane parallel to the image plane with the dimensions of the head and we project it on the 2D image.

We also estimated the root mean square error (RMSE), mean absolute error (MAE) and standard deviation (STD) for the three rotation angles. Results are presented in Table 6. Similar to the Boston University dataset, the fusion scheme presents the lowest errors. The high errors in the keypoint-based scheme is due to the fact that the estimated head pose started drifting and it was not able to recover (see Fig. 7 from frame 417 (e) onwards).

The estimated angles in degrees for the three schemes are presented in Figs. 8, 9 and 10. For some frames, the pose from the facial-landmark-based method could not be updated from the last estimate, since the face was not detect. This can also be noted in Fig. 7 in frames 9 (a), 132 (b), 318 (d), 749 (i) and 886 (j). However, as soon as the face is correctly detected again, the facial-landmark-based approach is able to recover. On the other hand, the head pose from the keypoint-based method is continuous, but suffers from drifting in long sequences. The fusion scheme is able to estimate the pose through the entire sequence, even with large head rotations (frames 318 (d) and 886 (j)) and recover in case it starts drifting, exploiting the advantages from both pipelines.

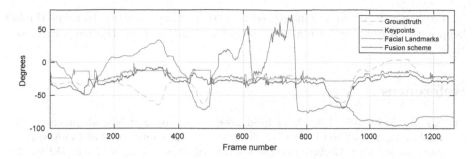

Fig. 9. Estimated pitch angle from the three HPE methods.

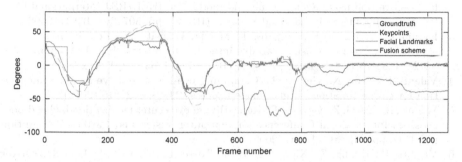

Fig. 10. Estimated yaw angle from the three HPE methods.

5 Conclusions

We have presented a method for head pose estimation in real time from monocular video data. The proposed approach integrates into a tailored Kalman Filter the head poses estimated from two different pipelines, one based on tracked keypoints and the other based on detected facial landmarks. Its particular strength is that it combines the advantages of both HPE methods. On the one hand, it benefits from the robustness of detecting keypoints, which is nearly always possible, regardless of the head pose and (limited) occlusions. On the other hand, it benefits from the absolute (i.e. not relative to a previous head pose) determination of the head pose based on facial landmarks, which is unaffected by drift or similar effects. Another great advantage is that the head pose from keypoints and the head pose from facial landmarks can be determined independently of each other, *i.e.*, the corresponding calculations can be performed in an arbitrary sequence, *e.g.* in parallel. These greatly help to provide a real-time head pose estimation, which is robust to large head rotations.

We have evaluated and compared our approach to other methods of the state of the art obtaining similar results, with an average runtime of 40FPS. We also demonstrated that our approach provides a reliable estimation even for extreme head poses and under varying light conditions.

For future work, we are interested in investigating a method to refine the 3D keypoints, in order to have a more robust estimation from the keypoint-based HPE scheme.

References

1. Xu, X., Kakadiaris, I.A.: Joint head pose estimation and face alignment framework using global and local CNN features. In: 12th International Conference on Automatic Face & Gesture Recognition (FG 2017), vol. 2, pp. 642–649. IEEE, May 2017
2. An, K.H., Chung, M.J.: 3D head tracking and pose-robust 2D texture map-based face recognition using a simple ellipsoid model. In: IEEE/RSJ International Conference on Intelligent Robots and Systems (IROS), pp. 307–312. IEEE (2008)
3. Kumano, S., Otsuka, K., Yamato, J., Maeda, E., Sato, Y.: Pose-invariant facial expression recognition using variable-intensity templates. Int. J. Comput. Vis. **83**(2), 178–194 (2009). https://doi.org/10.1007/s11263-008-0185-x
4. Valenti, R., Sebe, N., Gevers, T.: Combining head pose and eye location information for gaze estimation. Trans. Image Process. **21**(2), 802–815 (2012)
5. Valenti, R., Yucel, Z., Gevers, T.: Robustifying eye center localization by head pose cues. In: International Conference on Computer Vision and Pattern Recognition (CVPR), pp. 612–618. IEEE (2009)
6. Vicente, F., Huang, Z., Xiong, X., De la Torre, F., Zhang, W., Levi, D.: Driver gaze tracking and eyes off the road detection system. Trans. Intell. Transp. Syst. **16**(4), 2014–2027 (2015)
7. Borghi, G., Venturelli, M., Vezzani, R., Cucchiara, R.: Poseidon: face-from-depth for driver pose estimation. In: International Conference on Computer Vision and Pattern Recognition (CVPR). IEEE (2017)
8. Mohr, P., Tatzgern, M., Grubert, J., Schmalstieg, D., Kalkofen, D.: Adaptive user perspective rendering for handheld augmented reality. In: Symposium on 3D User Interfaces (3DUI), pp. 176–181. IEEE (2017)
9. Fanelli, G., Dantone, M., Gall, J., Fossati, A., Van Gool, L.: Random forests for real time 3D face analysis. Int. J. Comput. Vis. **101**(3), 437–458 (2013)
10. Tan, D.J., Tombari, F., Navab, N.: Real-time accurate 3D head tracking and pose estimation with consumer RGB-D cameras. Int. J. Comput. Vis. **126**, 1–26 (2017)
11. Diaz Barros, J.M., Garcia, F., Mirbach, B., Varanasi, K., Stricker, D.: Combined framework for real-time head pose estimation using facial landmark detection and salient feature tracking. In: Proceedings of the 13th International Joint Conference on Computer Vision, Imaging and Computer Graphics Theory and Applications (VISAPP), vol. 5, pp. 123–133. INSTICC, SciTePress (2018)
12. Diaz Barros, J.M., Mirbach, B., Garcia, F., Varanasi, K., Stricker, D.: Fusion of keypoint tracking and facial landmark detection for real-time head pose estimation. In: IEEE Winter Conference on Applications of Computer Vision (WACV), pp. 2028–2037. IEEE, March 2018
13. La Cascia, M., Sclaroff, S., Athitsos, V.: Fast, reliable head tracking under varying illumination: an approach based on registration of texture-mapped 3D models. Trans. Pattern Anal. Mach. Intell. **22**(4), 322–336 (2000)
14. Choi, S., Kim, D.: Robust head tracking using 3D ellipsoidal head model in particle filter. Pattern Recogn. **41**(9), 2901–2915 (2008)

15. Sung, J., Kanade, T., Kim, D.: Pose robust face tracking by combining active appearance models and cylinder head models. Int. J. Comput. Vision **80**(2), 260–274 (2008)
16. Jang, J.S., Kanade, T.: Robust 3D head tracking by online feature registration. In: 8th International Conference on Automatic Face & Gesture Recognition (FG 2008). IEEE (2008)
17. Jang, J.S., Kanade, T.: Robust 3D head tracking by view-based feature point registration. People Image Analysis (PIA) Consortium, Carnegie Mellon University, Technical report (2010)
18. Asteriadis, S., Karpouzis, K., Kollias, S.: Head pose estimation with one camera, in uncalibrated environments. In: Workshop on Eye Gaze in Intelligent Human Machine Interaction, pp. 55–62. ACM (2010)
19. Prasad, B.H., Aravind, R.: A robust head pose estimation system for uncalibrated monocular videos. In: 7th Indian Conference on Computer Vision, Graphics and Image Processing, pp. 162–169. ACM (2010)
20. Diaz Barros, J.M., Garcia, F., Mirbach, B., Stricker, D.: Real-time monocular 6-DoF head pose estimation from salient 2D points. In: International Conference on Image Processing (ICIP), pp. 121–125. IEEE, September 2017
21. Yin, C., Yang, X.: Real-time head pose estimation for driver assistance system using low-cost on-board computer. In: 15th ACM SIGGRAPH Conference on Virtual-Reality Continuum and Its Applications in Industry, vol. 1, pp. 43–46. ACM (2016)
22. Wu, Y., Gou, C., Ji, Q.: Simultaneous facial landmark detection, pose and deformation estimation under facial occlusion (2017)
23. Gou, C., Wu, Y., Wang, F.Y., Ji, Q.: Coupled cascade regression for simultaneous facial landmark detection and head pose estimation. In: International Conference on Image Processing (ICIP). IEEE (2017)
24. Ahn, B., Park, J., Kweon, I.S.: Real-time head orientation from a monocular camera using deep neural network. In: Cremers, D., Reid, I., Saito, H., Yang, M.-H. (eds.) ACCV 2014. LNCS, vol. 9005, pp. 82–96. Springer, Cham (2015). https://doi.org/10.1007/978-3-319-16811-1_6
25. Drouard, V., Ba, S., Evangelidis, G., Deleforge, A., Horaud, R.: Head pose estimation via probabilistic high-dimensional regression. In: International Conference on Image Processing (ICIP), pp. 4624–4628. IEEE (2015)
26. Fanelli, G., Gall, J., Van Gool, L.: Real time head pose estimation with random regression forests. In: International Conference on Computer Vision and Pattern Recognition (CVPR), pp. 617–624. IEEE (2011)
27. Wang, H., Davoine, F., Lepetit, V., Chaillou, C., Pan, C.: 3D head tracking via invariant keypoint learning. Trans. Circuits Syst. Video Technol. **22**(8), 1113–1126 (2012)
28. Liu, X., Liang, W., Wang, Y., Li, S., Pei, M.: 3D head pose estimation with convolutional neural network trained on synthetic images. In: International Conference on Image Processing (ICIP), pp. 1289–1293. IEEE (2016)
29. Tulyakov, S., Vieriu, R.L., Semeniuta, S., Sebe, N.: Robust real-time extreme head pose estimation. In: 22nd International Conference on Pattern Recognition (ICPR), pp. 2263–2268. IEEE (2014)
30. Schwarz, A., Haurilet, M., Martinez, M., Stiefelhagen, R.: Driveahead - a large-scale driver head pose dataset. In: International Conference on Computer Vision and Pattern Recognition Workshops (CVPRW). IEEE (2017)
31. Derkach, D., Ruiz, A., Sukno, F.M.: Head pose estimation based on 3-D facial landmarks localization and regression. In: 12th International Conference on Automatic Face & Gesture Recognition (FG 2017), pp. 820–827. IEEE, May 2017

32. Meyer, G.P., Gupta, S., Frosio, I., Reddy, D., Kautz, J.: Robust model-based 3D head pose estimation. In: International Conference on Computer Vision (ICCV), pp. 3649–3657. IEEE (2015)

33. Yu, Y., Funes Mora, K.A., Odobez, J.M.: Robust and accurate 3D head pose estimation through 3DMM and online head model reconstruction. In: 12th International Conference on Automatic Face & Gesture Recognition (FG 2017), pp. 711–718. IEEE, May 2017

34. Ghiass, R.S., Arandjelović, O., Laurendeau, D.: Highly accurate and fully automatic head pose estimation from a low quality consumer-level RGB-D sensor. In: 2nd Workshop on Computational Models of Social Interactions: Human-Computer-Media Communication, pp. 25–34. ACM (2015)

35. Papazov, C., Marks, T.K., Jones, M.: Real-time 3D head pose and facial landmark estimation from depth images using triangular surface patch features. In: International Conference on Computer Vision and Pattern Recognition (CVPR). IEEE (2015)

36. Jeni, L.A., Cohn, J.F., Kanade, T.: Dense 3D face alignment from 2D video for real-time use. Image Vis. Comput. 58, 13–24 (2017)

37. Morency, L., Whitehill, J., Movellan, J.: Generalized adaptive view-based appearance model: integrated framework for monocular head pose estimation. In: 8th International Conference on Automatic Face & Gesture Recognition (FG 2008), pp. 1–8. IEEE (2008)

38. Baltrušaitis, T., Robinson, P., Morency, L.P.: 3D constrained local model for rigid and non-rigid facial tracking. In: International Conference on Computer Vision and Pattern Recognition (CVPR). IEEE (2012)

39. Saragih, J.M., Lucey, S., Cohn, J.F.: Deformable model fitting by regularized landmark mean-shift. Int. J. Comput. Vision 91(2), 200–215 (2011)

40. Kazemi, V., Sullivan, J.: One millisecond face alignment with an ensemble of regression trees. In: International Conference on Computer Vision and Pattern Recognition (CVPR), pp. 1867–1874. IEEE (2014)

41. Makehuman: Open source tool for making 3D characters (2017). http://www.makehumancommunity.org/. Accessed 31 May 2018

42. Hartley, R.I., Sturm, P.: Triangulation. Comput. Vis. Image Underst. 68(2), 146–157 (1997)

43. Atkinson, K.E.: An introduction to numerical analysis. Wiley, New York (2008)

44. Press, W.H., Teukolsky, S.A., Vetterling, W.T., Flannery, B.P.: Numerical Recipes in C: The Art of Scientific Computing, Cambridge (1992)

45. Rosten, E., Porter, R., Drummond, T.: FASTER and better: a machine learning approach to corner detection. Trans. Pattern Anal. Mach. Intell. 32, 105–119 (2010)

46. Bouguet, J.Y.: Pyramidal implementation of the affine Lucas-Kanade feature tracker description of the algorithm. Intel Corporation 5, 1–10 (2001)

47. Kun, J., Bok-Suk, S., Reinhard, K.: Novel backprojection method for monocular head pose estimation. Int. J. Fuzzy Logic Intell. Syst. 13(1), 50–58 (2013)

48. Dodgson, N.A.: Variation and extrema of human interpupillary distance. In: Stereoscopic Displays and Virtual Reality Systems XI, vol. 5291, pp. 36–46. SPIE (2004)

49. Gordon, C.C., et al.: Anthropometric survey of U.S. army personnel: methods and summary statistics. In: Technical report 89–044, U.S. Army Natick Research, Development and Engineering Center, Natick, MA (1989)

50. Lefevre, S., Odobez, J.M.: Structure and appearance features for robust 3D facial actions tracking. In: International Conference on Multimedia and Expo, pp. 298–301. IEEE, June 2009

51. Tran, N.-T., Ababsa, F.-E., Charbit, M., Feldmar, J., Petrovska-Delacrétaz, D., Chollet, G.: 3D face pose and animation tracking via eigen-decomposition based bayesian approach. In: Bebis, G., et al. (eds.) ISVC 2013. LNCS, vol. 8033, pp. 562–571. Springer, Heidelberg (2013). https://doi.org/10.1007/978-3-642-41914-0_55
52. German Research Center for Artificial Intelligence (DFKI): Head pose estimation dataset (2018). http://av.dfki.de/publications/real-time-head-pose-estimation-by-tracking-and-detection-of-keypoints-and-facial-landmarks/

Contact-Less, Optical Heart Rate Determination in the Field Ambient Assisted Living

Christian Wiede[(✉)], Julia Richter, and Gangolf Hirtz

Chemnitz University of Technology, Reichenhainer Str. 70, 09126 Chemnitz, Germany
{christian.wiede,julia.richter,g.hirtz}@etit.tu-chemnitz.de

Abstract. A continuous monitoring of vital parameters, such as the heart rate, can be beneficial in order to quantify a person's health status. Especially in the field ambient assisted living (AAL) such of information can support elderly persons with their self-determined living. In this study, we propose a new contact-less, optical method to determine the heart rate. This approach is based on an individual, situation dependent skin colour model, an advanced tracking, an independent component analysis (ICA) and an adaptive filtering. Moreover, this method was evaluated in a general setting with twelve different scenarios and three AAL specific scenarios. Overall, the findings indicate that this approach can be used in the field AAL.

Keywords: AAL · rPPG · KLT · Skin colour model · Vital parameters

1 Introduction

Due to the demographic change in developed countries, the number of elderly people is continuously rising. Unfortunately, the number of medical and nursing personnel is not increasing to the same extent, which leads to a shortage of care giving. In the research field AAL this problem is addressed. AAL supports elderly people with their daily activities by providing technical assistant systems. Current systems are able to detect persons falling [1] or to analyse their behaviour based on their daily activities [2,3].

Heretofore, these technical assistance systems cannot monitor a person's current health status in terms of vital parameters. This, however, is one essential requirement for living longer in a self-determined way in the own flat. By continuously determining vital parameters such as the heart rate, the respiration rate or the blood pressure this gap could be closed. In this work, we focus on the remote determination of the heart rate. One possibility to realise that is by using RGB-cameras.

The benefit of this contact-less working principle is that patients do not have to wear additional devices, which are inconvenient in long-term use. Additionally,

© Springer Nature Switzerland AG 2019
D. Bechmann et al. (Eds.): VISIGRAPP 2018, CCIS 997, pp. 350–368, 2019.
https://doi.org/10.1007/978-3-030-26756-8_17

heart rate monitoring in the own flat allows to immediately inform an emergency doctor in case of sudden health issues such as heart attacks. Furthermore, the remote heart rate determination can be beneficial in other applications as well. Such applications are the monitoring of training in rehabilitation centres, the prevention of sudden infant death syndrome, sleep monitoring and the monitoring of a driver's well being.

In the field of remote heart rate determination there exist two principle methods. The first method is based on intensity, such as suggested by Poh et al. [4]. The second method relies on motion changes in the image, such as proposed by Balakrishnan [5]. However, both methods are facing problems of motion and intensity artefacts in the setting of AAL: When a person moves in its flat, the determined heart rate will be less accurate due to motion artefacts. Equally, intensity artefacts, such as reflections and shadows, reduce the accuracy of the heart rate determination as well. We propose a new robust method to determine a person's heart rate to overcome these issues. This method is based on a person dependent skin colour model, an advanced Kanade-Lucas-Thomasi (KLT) tracking, an ICA and an adaptive filtering.

This paper is organised as follows: In Sect. 2, a survey about the existing literature in the field of remote heart rate determination is conducted and the research gap is highlighted. This is followed by Sect. 3, where the proposed method, which overcomes intensity and motion artefacts, is presented. Based on this, two experimental studies for multiple scenarios are introduced in Sect. 4. This includes a general evaluation and an evaluation in the field of AAL. Finally, the findings are summarised and future work is outlined in Sect. 5.

2 Related Work

The determination of vital parameters is a relevant field in medicine to monitor a person's current health status. The heart rate, respiration rate, oxygen saturation and blood pressure are considered as the four main vital parameters. In this work, we focus on remote heart rate determination by means of optical sensors using principles of photoplethysmography (PPG). In contrast to that, the heart rate is normally obtained in clinical environments by electrocardiography (ECG) or by using pulse oximeters.

In 1937, Hertzman and Spealman [6] described the basics of PPG for the first time. PPG measures the volumetric changes of the blood flow by means of optical sensors. The transmissive PPG measures the transmitting light, which is not absorbed in thin body parts such as fingers or earlobes [7]. In contrast to that, the reflective PPG measure the light that is reflected from a tissue. The signal-to-noise-ratio (SNR) for this reflective PPG is by a ten-fold than for the transmissive PPG. Both methods share the problem that decives have to be attached to the body. Humphreys et al. were the first to develop a concept to overcome this issue and named the new method remote photoplethysmography (rPPG) [8]. That concept was verified in experiments in the visible light spectrum [9] and the infra-red spectrum [10].

Verkruysse et al. were able to determine the heart rate in colour image sequences by manually defining a region of interest (ROI) within a face, by performing a spatial averaging on each colour channel and by extracting the frequency with a Fast Fourier Transform (FFT) [9]. This approach was extended by Poh et al. [4,11], which automatised the ROI selection and introduced an ICA. Lewandoska et al. [12] suggested to use a principal component analysis (PCA) instead of an ICA to improve the computational speed. Further extensions exist in the use of temporal filters [13], autoregressive models [14] or adaptive filtering [15]. All these methods are considered as intensity-based methods.

A different category are the so-called motion-based methods, which were first introduced by Balakrishnan et al. [5]. Due to the 3rd Newtonian law, the blood flow caused by the heart bump induces a counter movement of the head. This small motion of the head can be tracked by means of an optical flow. The further processing includes a PCA of the trajectory points and a peak detection of the principal components.

Both, intensity- and motion-based methods have different advantages and disadvantages. Intensity-based approaches are less sensitive to motion artefacts, whereas motion-based methods suffer from arbitrary motions [16]. The reason for that is that motion artefacts and the motion signal induced by the heart bump share the same frequency bands. But, motion-based methods are less susceptible to illumination artefacts, such as shadows and reflections. These facts are the fundamentals for the ratio-based method [16], which switches between the intensity-based and motion-based approach in dependency of occurring artefacts.

Nevertheless, this method only quantifies and weights the artefacts instead of eliminating them. If the present artefacts could be eliminated or at least be reduced, an increased accuracy will be the consequence. For that aim, we propose a method based on a person dependent skin colour model, an advanced KLT tracking, an ICA and an adaptive filtering.

Moreover, to date there is no study that evaluates a patient's heart rate remotely in the field of AAL. Determining the accuracy of the estimated heart rate in AAL is a further aim of that study.

3   Methods

3.1   Overview

In Fig. 1, the principal steps for our robust remote heart rate determination method are shown. An individual, scene dependent skin colour is determined by performing an automatic white balancing, a face detection, an ROI selection and a skin colour estimation on the first frame of the sequence. After having acquired the skin colour model, an automatic white balancing, an advanced KLT face tracking, a skin pixel selection and a signal extraction are carried out in every image of the sequence. The resulting three colour channels are normalised and bandpass filtered. An ICA determines the three independent components and a channel selection selects the best channel for the subsequent frequency analysis. In order to obtain achieve a robust heart rate measurement, an adaptive filtering is applied.

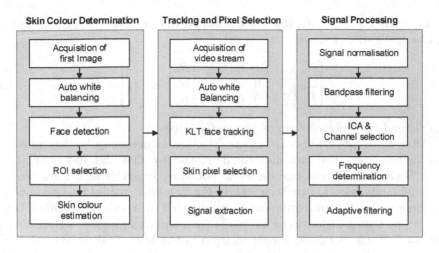

Fig. 1. Overview of the steps to remotely determine the heart rate.

3.2 Skin Colour Determination

An individual skin colour model is necessary to make the algorithm invariant to the person's individual skin colour. Furthermore, location, day time, weather and external illumination affects the perceived person's skin colour as well.

In order to determine the skin colour in an accurate fashion, a white balancing is needed. A white balancing adjusts the colours of an image by scaling and shifting the intensities in such a way that real white surfaces are finally represented by equally distributed RGB values. This means that former bluish or yellowish white representations can be corrected. For our implementation, the fast auto white balancing algorithm proposed by Garud et al. [17] was adjusted. This algorithm is based on the source illuminant values $[\iota_r, \iota_g, \iota_b]$. The correlated colour temperature (CCT) is given and the gain factors κ and the offset values τ can be determined. The gain factors are defined in the following way:

$$\kappa_r = \frac{\iota_g}{\iota_r}, \tag{1a}$$

$$\kappa_g = 1, \tag{1b}$$

$$\kappa_b = \frac{\iota_g}{\iota_b}. \tag{1c}$$

Hereby κ_r, κ_g and κ_b denote for the gain factors in the red, the green and the blue colour channel respectively.

The corresponding offset values are computed as:

$$\tau_r = max(1, \frac{\text{CCT} - \text{CCT}_{ref}}{100}) \cdot (\kappa_r - 1), \tag{2a}$$

$$\tau_g = 0, \tag{2b}$$

$$\tau_b = max(1, \frac{\text{CCT}_{ref} - \text{CCT}}{100}) \cdot (\kappa_b - 1), \tag{2c}$$

where CCT_{ref} indicates the CCT of the canonical illuminant.

By using these factors, the white balanced colour channels R_w, G_w and B_w can be specified as follows:

$$\begin{bmatrix} R_\mathrm{w} \\ G_\mathrm{w} \\ B_\mathrm{w} \end{bmatrix} = \begin{bmatrix} \kappa_\mathrm{r} & 0 & 0 \\ 0 & \kappa_\mathrm{g} & 0 \\ 0 & 0 & \kappa_\mathrm{b} \end{bmatrix} \cdot \begin{bmatrix} R_o \\ G_o \\ B_o \end{bmatrix} + \begin{bmatrix} \tau_\mathrm{r} \\ \tau_\mathrm{g} \\ \tau_\mathrm{b} \end{bmatrix}. \tag{3}$$

R_o, G_o and B_o denote for original intensity values.

After the white balancing, a face detection is necessary to determine the skin colour later. The face detector developed by Zhu and Ramanan [18] is used. Besides the actual face detection bounding box, this algorithm provides 68 facial landmarks, as can been seen in Fig. 2, which enables to determine the face orientation. For our requirements, we changed the resulting bounding box in such a way that it includes the forehead region and excludes the neck region. To achieve that, the bounding box is enlarged in the horizontal direction by 20%, at the upper boundary by 30% and narrowed at the lower boundary by 10%. The results of that operation are shown in Fig. 2.

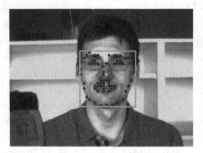

Fig. 2. Left: Original bounding box and facial landmarks. Right: Original bounding box (green) and adjusted bounding box (yellow). (Color figure online)

In order to obtain an accurate skin colour model, only those regions in the image are selected, which represent skin. Regions that contain hair, eyebrows, eyes, lips or glasses are rejected. Under that condition, the regions of the forehead, the nose and the two cheeks are selected for the skin colour estimation.

Next to that, the RGB colour space is not suitable for creating a skin colour model, because the distribution of the skin pixels does not follow any linear or concentrated coherency. Therefore, a conversion to another colour space that separates luminance and chrominance is necessary. One colour space which fulfils this requirement, is the HSV colour space. It consists of the three colour channels hue H, saturation S and value V. For the conversion the rules of Smith [19] are applied. The brightness value V can be determined as follows:

$$V = \max(R_w, G_w, B_w). \tag{4}$$

By introducing the auxiliary variable C, a chrominance value can be obtained:

$$C = V - \min(R_w, G_w, B_w). \tag{5}$$

S can be calculated by using V and C:

$$S = \begin{cases} 0, & \text{if } V = 0, \\ \frac{C}{V}, & \text{otherwise.} \end{cases} \tag{6}$$

Finally, the hue H is determined as follows:

$$H = \begin{cases} \text{undefined}, & \text{if } C = 0, \\ 60° \cdot (\frac{G_w - B_w}{C}), & \text{if } V = R_w, \\ 60° \cdot (\frac{B_w - R_w}{C} + 2), & \text{if } V = G_w, \\ 60° \cdot (\frac{R_w - G_w}{C} + 4), & \text{if } V = B_w. \end{cases} \tag{7}$$

Thereby, the HSV colour space is based on a cylindrical coordinate system. Due to the fact that only the chrominance of the skin pixels is relevant, the value V can be omitted and only the hue-saturation-plane is considered. In the next step, the thresholds H_{low} and H_{high} for the hue as well as the thresholds S_{low} and S_{high} for the saturation of the skin have to be determined. However, it has to be taken into consideration that shadows and reflections can occur, e. g. shadows can appear around the nose or reflections occur on the forehead. In order to avoid the inclusion of these artefacts on the skin colour model, a two-dimensional Gaussian distribution is used to model the distribution of the ROIs. In consequence, only 90% of the distribution is used to exclude outliers. Therefore, the final thresholds are denoted as $H_{\text{low},90}$ and $H_{\text{high},90}$ for the hue, and $S_{\text{low},90}$ and $S_{\text{high},90}$ for the saturation. After applying these rules to the distribution for one exemplary proband shown in Fig. 3, the following thresholds are the results:

$$H_{\text{low},90} = 12° \tag{8a}$$
$$H_{\text{high},90} = 19° \tag{8b}$$
$$S_{\text{low},90} = 45\% \tag{8c}$$
$$S_{\text{high},90} = 56\% \tag{8d}$$

The application of these thresholds to the original image results in the rejection of a certain amount of pixels as shown in Fig. 4. It can be observed that the regions of the eyes, hairs, lips, nostrils, shadows and reflections do not influence the skin colour model.

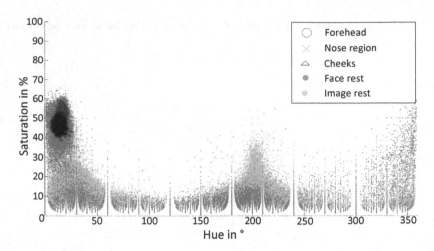

Fig. 3. Exemplary illustration of the pixel distributions in the hue-saturation-plane with respect to different regions: The blue circles represent the pixels of the forehead region, the magenta crosses the nose region, the black triangles the cheek region, the green points the rest of the face and the yellow points the rest of the image [20]. (Color figure online)

Fig. 4. Selected skin pixels after applying the thresholds $H_{\text{low},90}$, $H_{\text{high},90}$, $S_{\text{low},90}$ and $S_{\text{high},90}$. Unselected pixels are shown in black colour.

3.3   Tracking and Skin Pixel Selection

In order to apply the skin colour model not only for the first image but for the whole frame sequence a continuous tracking is needed to assure an invariance against motion artefacts. A possibility for tracking consist in the optical flow method. This method estimates the motion between two subsequent frames at a certain time t and $t + \Delta t$. That fact can be described with the general optical flow equation:

$$I_x V_x + I_y V_y = -I_t, \tag{9}$$

where I_x, I_y and I_t denote the partial derivatives of the image at the position (x, y) at a time t. V_x, V_y represent the x and y components of the velocity or the optical flow of $I(x, y, t)$. Because of two unknown variables, this equation cannot be solved directly. To resolve that issue, it can be assumed that the motion is constant in a small local neighbourhood of an image. As a consequence, n equations denoting n different patches in the image:

$$
\begin{aligned}
I_x(p_1)V_x + I_y(p_1)V_y &= -I_t(p_1), \\
I_x(p_2)V_x + I_y(p_2)V_y &= -I_t(p_2), \\
&\vdots \\
I_x(p_n)V_x + I_y(p_n)V_y &= -I_t(p_n),
\end{aligned}
\tag{10}
$$

where $p_1, p_2, \ldots, p_n$ stand for the pixels inside the image patch. This solution is known as KLT tracking [21]. The former single equations can be written as well in matrix form $Av = b$:

$$
A = \begin{bmatrix} I_x(p_1) & I_y(p_1) \\ I_x(p_2) & I_y(p_2) \\ \vdots & \vdots \\ I_x(p_n) & I_y(p_n) \end{bmatrix},
\tag{11a}
$$

$$
v = \begin{bmatrix} V_x \\ V_y \end{bmatrix},
\tag{11b}
$$

$$
b = \begin{bmatrix} -I_t(p_1) \\ -I_t(p_2) \\ \vdots \\ -I_t(p_n) \end{bmatrix}.
\tag{11c}
$$

By applying the least squares principle this equation system can be solved:

$$
A^T A v = A^T b.
\tag{12}
$$

Tracking all image pixels is a time challenging task. To avoid that, only certain striking image regions, so-called features, are selected. In this work, the minimum Eigenvalue features proposed by Shi and Tomasi [22] are selected. They are designed especially for the tracking and show a high robustness.

Still, these feature points can vanish over time due to perspective distortions in the person's face. By re-detecting the person's face in every image, that problem can be solved. For that aim, we use the online face detector of Liao et al. [23], which is based on the normalised pixel difference (NPD). The NPD features are the input for a classifier of a quadratic tree structure. In case the NPD detector is not able to detect a subject's face, there is still the KLT tracker to track the minimum Eigenvalue features. The result of the tracking is a 2-D geometric transform from one frame to the next frame. This 2-D geometric transform can be applied on the face bounding box as well.

By fusing the NPD face detector and the 2-D geometric transform estimation of the feature tracking, a person's face region can be accurately followed even in cases of complex head motions.

Under the assumption that the lighting conditions do not drastically change from the first frame on, the previous determined skin colour model can be applied for the total frame sequence. All pixel $\mathbf{P}_j$ matching the four thresholds of the skin colour model are defined as follows:

$$\mathbf{P}_j \in \{\mathbf{p} \in \mathbf{P}; H_{\text{low},90} < H(\mathbf{p}) < H_{\text{high},90}; S_{\text{low},90} < S(\mathbf{p}) < S_{\text{high},90}\}. \quad (13)$$

In order to improve the reliability of the skin pixel selection, a distance threshold D is defined. For every skin pixel $\mathbf{P}_j$, the distance to the closest non-skin pixel $\mathbf{P}_g$ is calculated. If this distance becomes smaller than D, this skin pixel is rejected. This procedure is equivalent to an erosion and applies for all finally selected skin pixels $\mathbf{P}_l$:

$$\mathbf{P}_l \in \{\|(\mathbf{P}_j, \mathbf{P}_g)\| > D\}. \quad (14)$$

To extract a time signal from the remaining pixels, these pixels $\mathbf{P}_l$ are averaged in the RGB domain. Due to the fact that we operate in the discrete domain, n is used as time variable.

$$\bar{R}(n) = \frac{1}{L} \sum_{l=1}^{L} R_l(n) \quad (15a)$$

$$\bar{G}(n) = \frac{1}{L} \sum_{l=1}^{L} G_l(n) \quad (15b)$$

$$\bar{B}(n) = \frac{1}{L} \sum_{l=1}^{L} B_l(n) \quad (15c)$$

In these equations, R_l, G_l and B_l belong to the lth selected skin pixel in the frame n. L denotes the number of all selected skin pixels in this frame. $\bar{R}(n)$, $\bar{G}(n)$ and $\bar{B}(n)$ represent the mean values of the facial skin colour for a certain frame n. The result are three time varying signals for the skin colour as shown in Fig. 5.

3.4   Signal Processing

To remove remaining noise sources, a further signal processing of the three extracted colour channels is necessary.

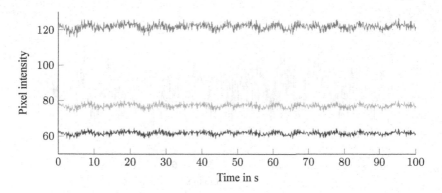

Fig. 5. Accumulated pixel intensities $\bar{R}$, $\bar{G}$ and $\bar{B}$ over the time.

In a first step, the signal is normalised to attain a zero mean and a standard deviation of one:

$$\hat{R}(n) = \frac{1}{\sigma_R}(\bar{R}(n) - \mu_R), \tag{16a}$$

$$\hat{G}(n) = \frac{1}{\sigma_G}(\bar{G}(n) - \mu_G), \tag{16b}$$

$$\hat{B}(n) = \frac{1}{\sigma_R}(\bar{B}(n) - \mu_B), \tag{16c}$$

whereby $\hat{R}$, $\hat{G}$ and $\hat{B}$ denote as the normalised colour channels. μ_C is the mean value and σ_C is the standard deviation of the corresponding colour channel $C \in \{R, G, B\}$, which can be calculated as follows:

$$\mu_C = \frac{1}{N} \sum_{n=1}^{N} \bar{C}(n), \tag{17}$$

$$\sigma_C = \sqrt{\frac{1}{N} \sum_{n=1}^{N} (\bar{C}(n) - \mu_C)^2}, \tag{18}$$

where $\bar{C}(n)$ refers to the original colour channels $\bar{R}(n)$, $\bar{G}(n)$ as well as $\bar{B}(n)$. N denotes the number of samples for a single channel. The result of the normalisation is shown in Fig. 6.

The second step consists of a bandpass filter BP, which excludes implausible frequencies in the normalised colour channels.

$$R_{\mathrm{BP}}(n) = \mathrm{BP}(n) * \hat{R}(n) \tag{19a}$$

$$G_{\mathrm{BP}}(n) = \mathrm{BP}(n) * \hat{G}(n) \tag{19b}$$

$$B_{\mathrm{BP}}(n) = \mathrm{BP}(n) * \hat{B}(n) \tag{19c}$$

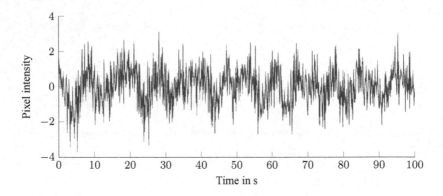

Fig. 6. Normalised pixel intensities $\hat{R}$, $\hat{G}$ and $\hat{B}$ over the time

Hereby, R_{BP}, G_{BP} and B_{BP} denote the filtered colour channels. All frequencies lower than 0.7 Hz and higher than 4 Hz are cut off. In order to ensure a constant group delay, 128 symmetric filter coefficients are chosen. The three filtered colour channels are shown in Fig. 7.

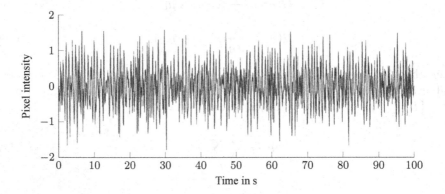

Fig. 7. Filtered colour channels R_{BP}, G_{BP} and B_{BP} over the time.

However, these three filtered colour channels can still be affected by noise sources. In order to separate the wanted pulse signal from noise parts, a decomposition of the colour channels is needed. By applying an ICA, three new independent components IC_1, IC_2 and IC_3 are determined:

$$\begin{bmatrix} IC_1(n) \\ IC_2(n) \\ IC_3(n) \end{bmatrix} = \begin{bmatrix} a_{11} & a_{12} & a_{13} \\ a_{21} & a_{22} & a_{23} \\ a_{31} & a_{32} & a_{33} \end{bmatrix}^{-1} \cdot \begin{bmatrix} R_{BP}(n) \\ G_{BP}(n) \\ B_{BP}(n) \end{bmatrix}. \tag{20}$$

Hereby, a_{xx} refers to one element of the mixing matrix A. For this implementation, the FastICA approach of Hyvärinen [24] is utilised.

At this point, the question arises which of the independent components contains our target pulse signal. It can be assumed that the independent component with the highest periodicity p represents the pulse signal. For that case, the periodicity p of an independent component is calculated as the ratio between the accumulated coefficients in a range of 0.05 Hz around the dominant frequency f_d and the accumulated coefficients of the total power spectrum, see Eq. 21.

$$p = \frac{\sum_{f_d-0.025}^{f_d+0.025} \hat{S}_{xx}^{av}(k)}{\sum_0^{f_s} \hat{S}_{xx}^{av}(k)} \tag{21}$$

In this equation, f_s denotes the sampling frequency. A precondition to calculate p is to determine the spectrum of each independent component. This can be solved by using the Welch's estimate of the power spectrum density (PSD) $\hat{S}_{xx}^{av}(k)$:

$$\hat{S}_{xx}^{av}(k) = \frac{1}{N} \sum_{n=1}^{N} \hat{P}_n(k). \tag{22}$$

Hereby, $\hat{P}_n(k)$ is the periodogram and k refers to the discrete iterator in the frequency domain. A hamming window is applied to each segment in order to determine the periodogram.

The best independent component IC_i is split into segments of 10 s with an overlap of 90% between the segments. Selecting this small segmented size guarantees to recognise natural changes of the heart rate. Subsequently, the dominant frequency f_{FFT} for each segment ϕ is determined by calculating the FFT in this segment and by obtaining the maximum in the spectrum:

$$f_{\text{FFT}}(\phi) = \max_n \left(|\text{FFT}(IC_i(n))| \right). \tag{23}$$

However, in presence of large motions, the spectrum shows multiple high peaks, which leads to misinterpretations of the real heart rate. Under the assumption that the heart rate does not change by more than 15 beats per minute (BPM) between two subsequent frames, which corresponds to 0.25 Hz, an adaptive filtering is introduced. This alteration is equivalent to a change of the heart rate by 150 BPM within a second in case of a recording rate of 10 frames per second. Therefore, a guide frequency f_{gui} is defined as the mean value of the two previous segments.

$$f_{\text{gui}}(\phi) = \frac{f_{\text{FFT}}(\phi-1) + f_{\text{FFT}}(\phi-2)}{2} \tag{24}$$

For the current frequency $f_{\text{FFT}}(\phi)$, only frequency peaks within the range of $f_{\text{gui}} \pm 0,25$ Hz are considered. This is visualised in Fig. 8. Hence, the calculation of $f_{\text{FFT}}(\phi)$ changes to:

$$f_{\text{FFT}}(\phi) = \max_n \left(|\text{FFT}(IC_i(n))| \right) \in (f_{\text{gui}}(\phi) \pm 0,25 \text{ Hz}) \tag{25}$$

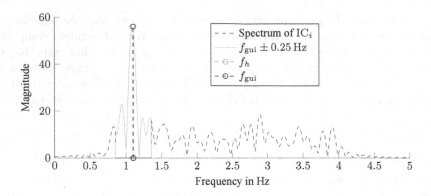

Fig. 8. Working principle of the adaptive filtering: Only frequency peaks in the range of $f_{\text{gui}} \pm 0.25\,\text{Hz}$ are considered. f_{gui} represents the guide frequency and f_h the final heart rate [20].

In order to obtain the final heart rate f_h in BPM, the frequency f_{FFT} is multiplied by the factor of 60:

$$f_h(\phi) = f_{\text{FFT}}(\phi) \cdot 60 \ [\text{BPM}]. \tag{26}$$

4   Results and Discussion

This evaluation section is split into two parts: The first part assesses the general parameters of the proposed algorithm, whereas the second part investigates the accuracy in an AAL scenario.

4.1   General Accuracy Evaluation

For all recordings, an industrial camera, i. e. an Allied Manta G201c, was chosen. The automatic exposure time control and the automatic white balancing were disabled in order not to influence the measurements. The video sequences have a length of 1,000 frames and were recorded with a fixed frame rate of 10 FPS.

For the general evaluation, we created a database with 117 videos in total. Eleven probands of different age, gender and skin colour guarantee a high variability in the data set. Overall, twelve different scenarios are chosen for the evaluation, which are listed in Table 1: The control scenario indicates the optimal case, where no additional noise sources are present. Subsequently, we recorded scenarios with illumination artefacts caused by a lighting source placed above the face or placed at one side of the face, which results in different kinds of shadows and reflections. Furthermore, the probands performed different movements to evaluate the influence of motion artefacts such as translation, rotation of the head (pitch, yaw and roll), scaling and non-rigid movements. Moreover, a combination of motion artefacts and intensity artefacts was considered in one scenario. Also, videos directly after sport and during cycling were recorded to investigate scenarios where a person has a more varying heart rate.

As reference system a Polar FT1 heart rate monitor is chosen. The reference heart rate is determined by means of a chest strap and shown on a display that was recorded by the camera. With this procedure, the reference heat rate and the estimated heart rate can be obtained simultaneously.

In order to determine differences between the estimated heart rate f_h and the reference heart rate f_{ref}, both values are plotted in the same graph, as shown in Fig. 9. It can be seen that the estimated heart rate is very close to the reference heart rate.

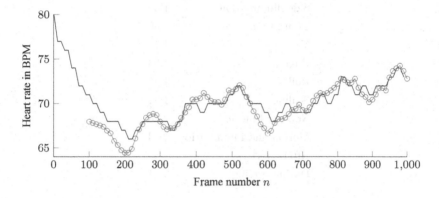

Fig. 9. Comparison of the computed heart rate (blue dots) and the reference heart rate (black curve) for a control sequence. (Color figure online)

A more significant evaluation criterion for the accuracy analysis is the root-mean-square error (RMSE). The definition of the RMSE for a sequence m is as follows:

$$\text{RMSE}_m = \sqrt{\frac{1}{\Phi} \sum_{\phi=1}^{\Phi} |f_h(\phi) - f_{ref}(\phi)|^2}. \tag{27}$$

Hereby, f_h denotes the estimated heart rate and f_{ref} the reference heart rate. Φ is the absolute number of segments within one video. The RMSE of all videos of one scenario can be averaged as $\overline{\text{RMSE}}$:

$$\overline{\text{RMSE}} = \frac{1}{M} \sum_{m=1}^{M} \text{RMSE}_m \tag{28}$$

Thereby, M is the total number of videos for a single scenario. All videos consist of 91 segments ϕ, which results in 10,647 evaluated segments in 117 videos. This consolidates the statistical relevance of the database.

The results for the single scenarios are shown in Table 1. As expected, the control scenario without external artefacts shows the best $\overline{\text{RMSE}}$ with 1.19 BPM. Since the error of the reference system can be quantified with ±1 BPM, this result proves to be of high quality.

Table 1. $\overline{\text{RMSE}}$ for all scenarios in BPM [20].

Evaluated scenario	RMSE
Control	1.19
Upper illumination	1.49
Side illumination	1.38
Translation	1.36
Yaw	1.70
Pitch	1.93
Roll	1.86
Scaling	1.81
Non-rigid motion	2.46
Motion and illumination	2.93
After sport	1.53
During cycling	2.11

The $\overline{\text{RMSE}}$ for external illumination rises up to 1.38 BPM for the side illumination and 1.48 BPM for the upper illumination, which is due to the influence of shadows and reflections.

When translational movement occurs only isolated, the $\overline{\text{RMSE}}$ is quite accurate with 1.36 BPM. The $\overline{\text{RMSE}}$ is increasing for the scenarios of scaling and rotation up to 1.81 BPM and 1.93 BPM respectively. This grow can be explained by the perspective view point change and in consequence with the different projection of the face to the image sensor. This affects the size of the bounding box and the following tracking process. The largest $\overline{\text{RMSE}}$ with 2.46 BPM exists for the scenario of non-rigid movement. This can be explained by a change of the shape of the face due to speaking and facial expressions. Consequently, the size and the location of the bounding box are strongly influenced by that.

The $\overline{\text{RMSE}}$ increases significantly up to 2.92 BPM when motion and intensity artefacts are combined in one scenario. In the scenarios after the sport and during the cycling an $\overline{\text{RMSE}}$ of 1.53 BPM and 2.11 BPM can be observed respectively. It can be stated that especially the scenario with the cycling is challenging due to its periodically motions, especially if the motion frequency is similar to the heart rate.

Overall, the scenarios showed an $\overline{\text{RMSE}}$ below 3 BPM, which seems to be accurate and robust for the use case AAL. The performance for AAL scenarios has to be verified within the next section.

4.2   Accuracy Evaluation in AAL Scenarios

In order to evaluate the proposed heart rate determination method in the field of AAL, further measurements were carried out. The AAL test flat of Chemnitz University of Technology was used as the test location to place the measurements in a realistic home environment. The used RGB camera, i. e. an Allied Manta G201c, was mounted on the ceiling to avoid occlusions by other objects in the image. Due to the perspective viewpoint change, this setting is quite challenging. The frame rate was fixed to 10 FPS.

For the evaluation, six probands were recruited in three different scenarios as shown in Fig. 10. In order to reduce the effect of motion artefacts, which has proven to be a large noise source in the previous section, only scenarios were chose, where the person does not move extremely. Therefore, the scenarios comprise sitting on a chair, sitting on an armchair and lying in a bed.

Fig. 10. Scenarios to determine the heart rate in AAL from left to right: Proband sits on a chair, proband sits on an armchair, proband lies in a bed.

As a reference system a Polar FT1 heart rate monitor was used as well for this evaluation. A time curve of the estimated heart rate and the reference heart is shown in Fig. 11. It can be seen that the estimated heart rate from the proposed method is very close to the reference heart rate. This demonstrates the high accuracy of the proposed method.

For a quantitative assessment, the error measures RMSE and $\overline{\mathrm{RMSE}}$ are chosen. The overview of the results is shown in Table 2. It can been seen that the results show an accurate and robust determination of the heart rate. The $\overline{\mathrm{RMSE}}$ is always below 3 BPM. But it can be recognised that the error varies between the different probands. Proband 2 has higher RMSEs than proband 1. The lowest $\overline{\mathrm{RMSE}}$ with 1.56 BPM is present in the scenario of sitting on a chair. That value increases for the scenario sitting on the armchair up to 2.16 BPM. Essentially, this value is influenced by proband 4, who turns his head very fast and abruptly during the complete video. In that case, motion artefacts influence the determination of the correct peak in spectrum. Even though the distance to the camera is the highest for that scenario, the scenario lying in a bed shows an $\overline{\mathrm{RMSE}}$ of 1.94 BPM, although. At the same time, less motion artefacts appear in that scenario because the head lies still on a pillow and has less degrees of freedom compared to the other scenarios.

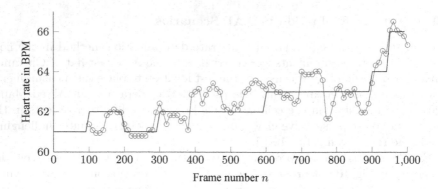

Fig. 11. Comparison of the computed heart rate (blue dots) and the reference heart rate (black curve) in the scenario of lying in a bed. (Color figure online)

Table 2. RMSE and $\overline{\text{RMSE}}$ in BPM for different scenarios and probands in the application field AAL.

Scenario/Proband	1	2	3	4	5	6	$\overline{\text{RMSE}}$
Sitting on a chair	2.8	0.68	1.43	1.48	1.17	1.79	1.56
Sitting on an armchair	2.39	0.75	1.8	4.22	1.32	2.46	2.16
Lying in a bed	3.6	1.05	1.5	1.6	1.63	2.28	1.94

The results clearly indicate that the proposed optical heart rate determination method is suitable for the field AAL.

5   Conclusions

In this work, a new method to determine the heart rate in a contact-less and optical way is presented. The aim is to eliminate intensity and motion artefacts from the signal. This is realised by an accurate tracking, an individual, situation depending skin colour determination, an ICA and an adaptive filtering.

In order to evaluate the accuracy of the proposed method, a general evaluation and a specific evaluation in the field of AAL is carried out. In the general setting, all values for the $\overline{\text{RMSE}}$ are below 3 BPM. Even in scenarios with a high occurrence of intensity and motion artefacts this method proved to be robust. The tested AAL scenarios show that the heart rate can be reliably determined. Therefore, the remote determination of the heart rate as a vital parameter in the field of AAL is now possible.

In further work, we plan to make this method even more robust against motion artefacts, which showed to have the largest impact on the measurements. Moreover, it is intended to evaluate this method in other applications fields, such as automotive and e-rehabilitation.

Acknowledgements. This project is supported by the European Social Fund (ESF). We express our thanks to all volunteers who took part in the recordings.

References

1. Wohlrab, D., et al.: Hom-e-call - an enhanced fall detection system based on accelerometer and optical sensors applicable in domestic environment. In: Jaffray, D.A. (ed.) World Congress on Medical Physics and Biomedical Engineering, June 7-12, 2015, Toronto, Canada. IP, vol. 51, pp. 1461–1464. Springer, Cham (2015). https://doi.org/10.1007/978-3-319-19387-8_356
2. Meinel, L., Richter, J., Schmidt, R., Findeisen, M., Hirtz, G.: OPDEMIVA: An integrated assistance and information system for elderly with dementia. In: 2015 IEEE International Conference on Consumer Electronics (ICCE), pp. 76–77 (2015)
3. Meinel, L., et al.: OPDEMIVA: Optimierung der pflege demenzkranker menschen durch intelligente verhaltensanalyse. In: AAL-Kongress 2015 (AAL 2015), vol. 8, pp. 496–503, 29–30 April 2015
4. Poh, M.Z., McDuff, D., Picard, R.: Non-contact, automated cardiac pulse measurements using video imaging and blind source separation. Opt. Express **18**, 10762–10774 (2010)
5. Balakrishnan, G., Durand, F., Guttag, J.: Detecting pulse from head motions in video. In: 2013 IEEE Conference on Computer Vision and Pattern Recognition (CVPR), pp. 3430–3437 (2013)
6. Hertzman, A.B., Spealman, C.R.: Observations on the finger volume pulse recorded photoelectrically. Am. J. Physiol. **119**, 334–335 (1937)
7. Allen, J.: Photoplethysmography and its application in clinical physiological measurement. Physiol. Meas. **28**, R1–R39 (2007)
8. Humphreys, K., Markham, C., Ward, T.: A CMOS camera-based system for clinical photoplethysmographic applications. Proc. SPIE **5823**, 88–95 (2005)
9. Verkruysse, W., Svaasand, L.O., Nelson, J.S.: Remote plethysmographic imaging using ambient light. Opt. Express **16**, 21434–21445 (2008)
10. Garbey, M., Sun, N., Merla, A., Pavlidis, I.: Contact-free measurement of cardiac pulse based on the analysis of thermal imagery. IEEE Trans. Biomed. Eng. **54**, 1418–1426 (2007)
11. Poh, M.Z., McDuff, D., Picard, R.: Advancements in noncontact, multiparameter physiological measurements using a webcam. IEEE Trans. Biomed. Eng. **58**, 7–11 (2011)
12. Lewandowska, M., Ruminski, J., Kocejko, T., Nowak, J.: Measuring pulse rate with a webcam - a non-contact method for evaluating cardiac activity. In: 2011 Federated Conference on Computer Science and Information Systems (FedCSIS), pp. 405–410 (2011)
13. van Gastel, M., Zinger, S., Kemps, H., de With, P.: e-health video system for performance analysis in heart revalidation cycling. In: Consumer Electronics Berlin (ICCE-Berlin), pp. 31–35 (2014)
14. Tarassenko, L., Villarroel, M., Guazzi, A., Jorge, J., Clifton, D.A., Pugh, C.: Non-contact video-based vital sign monitoring using ambient light and auto-regressive models. Physiol. Meas. **35**, 807–831 (2014)
15. Wiede, C., Richter, J., Apitzsch, A., KhairAldin, F., Hirtz, G.: Remote heart rate determination in RGB Data. In: Proceedings of the 5th International Conference on Pattern Recognition Applications and Methods, Rome, pp. 240–246 (2016)

16. Wiede, C., Richter, J., Hirtz, G.: Signal fusion based on intensity and motion variations for remote heart rate determination. In: 2016 IEEE International Conference on Imaging Systems and Techniques (IST), pp. 526–531 (2016)
17. Garud, H., Ray, A.K., Mahadevappa, M., Chatterjee, J., Mandal, S.: A fast auto white balance scheme for digital pathology. In: 2014 IEEE-EMBS International Conference on Biomedical and Health Informatics, BHI 2014, pp. 153–156 (2014)
18. Zhu, X., Ramanan, D.: Face detection, pose estimation, and landmark localization in the wild. In: Proceedings of the IEEE Computer Society Conference on Computer Vision and Pattern Recognition, pp. 2879–2886 (2012)
19. Smith, A.R.: Color gamut transform pairs. In: ACM SIGGRAPH Computer Graphics **12**, pp. 12–19 (1978)
20. Wiede, C., Sun, J., Richter, J., Hirtz, G.: Robust remote heart rate determination for e-rehabilitation - a method that overcomes motion and intensity artefacts. In: Proceedings of the 13th International Joint Conference on Computer Vision, Imaging and Computer Graphics Theory and Applications - Volume 4: VISAPP, INSTICC, SciTePress, pp. 491–500 (2018)
21. Tomasi, C., Kanade, T.: Detection and Tracking of Point Features. Technical report, Carnegie Mellon University (1991)
22. Shi, J., Tomasi, C.: Good features to track. Technical report, Cornell University, Ithaca, NY, USA (1993)
23. Liao, S., Jain, A.K., Li, S.Z.: A fast and accurate unconstrained face detector. IEEE Trans. Pattern Anal. Mach. Intell. **38**, 211–223 (2016)
24. Hyvärinen, A.: Fast and robust fixed-point algorithms for independent component analysis. IEEE Trans. Neural Networks **10**, 626–634 (1999)

Effective Facial Expression Recognition Through Multimodal Imaging for Traumatic Brain Injured Patient's Rehabilitation

Chaudhary Muhammad Aqdus Ilyas[1]($\boxtimes$), Mohammad A. Haque[1]($\boxtimes$), Matthias Rehm[2]($\boxtimes$), Kamal Nasrollahi[1]($\boxtimes$), and Thomas B. Moeslund[1]($\boxtimes$)

[1] Visual Analysis of People Laboratory and Interaction laboratory Aalborg University (AAU), Aalborg, Denmark
{cmai,mah,kn,tbm}@create.aau.dk
[2] Robotics Aalborg U, Aalborg University, Aalborg, Denmark
matthias@create.aau.dk

Abstract. This article presents the issues related to applying computer vision techniques to identify facial expressions and recognize the mood of Traumatic Brain Injured (TBI) patients in real life scenarios. Many TBI patients face serious problems in communication and activities of daily living. These are due to restricted movement of muscles or paralysis with lesser facial expression along with non-cooperative behaviour, and inappropriate reasoning and reactions. All these aforementioned attributes contribute towards the complexity of the system for the automatic understanding of their emotional expressions. Existing systems for facial expression recognition are highly accurate when tested on healthy people in controlled conditions. However, their performance is not yet verified on the TBI patients in the real environment. In order to test this, we devised a special arrangement to collect data from these patients. Unlike the controlled environment, it was very challenging because these patients have large pose variations, poor attention and concentration with impulsive behaviours. In order to acquire high-quality facial images from videos for facial expression analysis, effective techniques of data preprocessing are applied. The extracted images are then fed to a deep learning architecture based on Convolution Neural Network (CNN) and Long Short-Term Memory (LSTM) network to exploit the spatiotemporal information with 3D face frontalization. RGB and thermal imaging modalities are used and the experimental results show that better quality of facial images and larger database enhance the system performance in facial expressions and mood recognition of TBI patients under natural challenging conditions. The proposed approach hopefully facilitates the physiotherapists, trainers and caregivers to deploy fast rehabilitation activities by knowing the positive mood of the patients.

© Springer Nature Switzerland AG 2019
D. Bechmann et al. (Eds.): VISIGRAPP 2018, CCIS 997, pp. 369–389, 2019.
https://doi.org/10.1007/978-3-030-26756-8_18

Keywords: Computer vision ·
Multi-visual (RGB, thermal) modalities · Face detection ·
Facial landmarks · Facial Expressions Recognition ·
Convolution Neural Networks · Long-Short Term Memory ·
Traumatic Brain Injured Patients

1   Introduction

Traumatic Brain Injury (TBI) lead to life-long harm to physical, cognitive, emotional and behavioral abilities depending upon the area of the brain damage. For example if frontal lobe is damaged, person lacks skills of planning, organizing, emotional and behavioral control, aggression, problem solving, attention, social skills, flexible thinking, consciousness and hand-eye coordination [1]. Similarly if temporal lobe is impaired, it can lead to complications in memory, recognition of faces, emotions elicitation, sequencing and speaking abilities. Moreover, occipital lobe is controlling the visual functions and parietal lobe is responsible for perception, spatial consciousness, objects manipulations and spelling [2]. Rehabilitation after brain injury is complex, long and expensive process, that can vary greatly depending upon the intensity of the injury and some times can result in permanent disabilities [3]. In America almost one million people suffer from brain injury and almost same number of people suffer in Europe each year, with approximately 4 million people are living globally having long-term disability after TBI [4,5].

Researchers are putting high emphasis on fast and efficient rehabilitation to lessen the suffering and low quality life of TBI patients. Physiotherapists, trainers and caregiver face severe complications in performing rehabilitation tasks as these patients have limited ability to perceive social signals associated with sudden changes in behavior including aggression, negative emotions, reduced motor and reasoning skills [6–8]. Experts, psychologists, trainers and researchers strongly believe that rehabilitation process can be made fast by accurately assessing the emotions of these patients [7,9]. Researchers are enforcing computer vision (CV) techniques for automatic assessment of mental states [10,11], monitoring elderly people [12] and measuring various physiological parameters like heartbeat rate, fatigue, blood pressure and respiratory rate [13], in a contactless manner by analyzing facial features [6,14]. Therefore, researchers are focusing with greater intensity in the development of accurate, reliable and robust facial expression recognition (FER) system. Automatic detection and identification of facial features by utilizing CV techniques are cost and time effective with 24/7 monitoring facility and lesser human assessment errors. Due to this, it has wide range of applications in various fields like monitoring, medical examination, forensics, biometric, defense and surveillance [6].

Most of the current computer vision techniques for Facial Expression Recognition (FER) are working effectively and robustly only on the healthy people in controlled environment. But when these systems are applied on TBI patients in real environment, we have to face unique challenges incurred from data collection, pre- and post-processing, expression recognition and environmental conditions. However, to the best of our knowledge there is neither research on data collection techniques from TBI patients nor public database from real patients for facial expression analysis. Thus, we created a database of TBI patients as in [6] and identified that emotional states of TBI patients are quite different from the healthy people with large imbalance of six common expressions along with higher negative emotional states.

The methods proposed by [15] and [16] perform exceptionally well for FER, and its modeling and structuring as social signals for healthy people in controlled environment. However, these systems demonstrated challenges and complications when applied in real environment on real Traumatic Brain Injured (TBI) patients residing at specialized centers like neuro-centers or care-homes [6]. These challenges are associated with non-cooperative and non-compliance patient's behavior, along with varied level of aggression both verbal and physical, agitation, anxiety, disorientation, dis-inhibition, improper reasoning, lack of concentration, judgment and mental inflexibility [17]. In addition to that, brain injured patients also suffer with limited facial expressions such as smile, laugh, cry, anger or sadness or they may exhibit disproportionate responses. On the other hand, some TBI patients also displays intense responses like abrupt tears, laughter or anger outbursts. This is due to inability to control emotions due to injury. We tested state of the art FER systems, like [15] and [16], on real data of TBI patients in challenging scenarios with variable environmental conditions and figured out there is need of reliable system for FER with high quality facial images that are collected when patients are well-posed towards the camera [6]. Nevertheless, due to the above mentioned reasons, TBI patients do not pose toward camera thus illustrating very large pose variation with poor quality of facial frames. In [6], we employed Face Quality Assessment (FQA) method prior to deep architecture, to remove low quality and unwanted facial images. We also performed 3D face frontalization to acquire more frontal faces. We also developed unique data collection techniques in uniform scenarios to get reliable data from TBI patients in Neuro-centers. Exploiting facial expressions from TBI patients using computer vision techniques is not much explored field, with no database of these patients. To the best of our knowledge, we are the pioneer in developing database of these patients to understand their facial expressions and analyzing mood for rehabilitation purposes.

This article aims to provide the solution for TBI individuals by developing new tool and extended database for determining and monitoring facial expressions. It also presents unique experience in enhancing communication with patients and care givers, as well as extraction of physiological and psychological signals and interpreting them as social signals. In this article, we compare the results for six expressions as well as classify the facial characteristics into positive and negative states [14]. Experts and psychologists have annotated our collected data and featured negative expressions as fear, disgust, anger, sad, stress and fatigue. Some patients exhibits unique expressions like lip trembling, teeth grinding and frequent eye blinking, which have also characterized as negative expression by the experts [18]. On the contrary, positive expressions have featured as laugh, smile, surprise and few other unique neutral expressions. It is seen that in case of TBI patients, negative expressions are much more abundant then positive expressions during the data collection sessions. With the help of experts, trainers, physiologists, psychologists and caregivers, we determined three uniform scenarios for reliable data collection of TBI patients. Details are explained in Sect. 3.1. We have employed a linear cascading of a Convolutional Neural Network (CNN) and a Long Short Term Memory (LSTM) network [16], with Face Quality Assessment (FQA) and 3D face frontalization on the facial images obtained through RGB and thermal sensors with early and feature level late fusion techniques. Unlike [15, 16], Our approach addressed additional challenges of non-frontal faces, less cooperative and aggressive subjects, high occlusion, low quality of images that required a lot of preprocessing before feeding into system and varied expressions from normal/healthy people. We have also extended the database with more subjects and more effective pre-processing techniques like faster facial landmark detector with D-LIB and 3D-face frontalization than our previous methods in [6, 14]. Experimental results acquired by utilizing deep learning architecture, demonstrated that RGB and thermal modalities in different fusion states assist each other on classifying patients mental states accurately.

The rest of the paper is organized as follows. Next section will describe the related work on FER systems. Section 3.1 describes the creation of the new extended database including camera specifications, data collection arrangements and pre-processing techniques. Section 3 provides the methodology proposed for facial feature extraction and expression recognition. Section 4 demonstrates the results achieved from experimentation. Finally, Sect. 5 concludes the paper.

2 Related Work

Prevailing FER systems can be distinguished generally on the basis of the techniques used for facial features extraction and classification methods [19]. Facial feature extraction methods can be based on: geometric features, appearance based methods and hybrid ones [20, 21].

- Geometric feature extraction methods make use of geometric shape and position of facial components like nose, cheeks, eyebrows, lips, mouth, chin, related to time sequenced information of movement of these salient features. Facial characters movement is analyzed from the previous frame to the current frame [22, 23]. Geometric features are immune to lightning condition fluctuation, that gives flexibility to deal with non-frontal head positions by altering the figure to frontal head pose to extract the features by measuring distance of fixed reference points [24, 25]. Researchers applied effective shape models by using 58 facial landmarks like Pantic et al. [20].
- Facial feature extraction methods based on appearance utilize the characteristics of a surface of face like skin texture, wrinkles, bulges and furrows. It is not resistant to illumination variation [26, 27].
- Facial feature extraction methods that make use of both geometric features as well as characteristics of surfaces fall in the category of hybrid methods

[24]. Hybrid techniques have produced the best results in the development of automatic FER systems.

We can further distinguish the facial expression recognition (FER) systems on the basis of the classification approaches. Since last decade more and more efforts are converged towards deep learning approaches due to fast computational powers and state of art performances. As mentioned in [14] deep learning architecture involving Convolutional Neural Networks (CNN) outperformed traditional methods and provided state of art results for face recognition [28–30], facial expressions recognition [15,16,31–37] and emotional states identification [38–41]. These newer approaches like CNN learn the features from the image data for aforementioned computer vision problems, unlike traditional machine learning approaches those use handcrafted features. Handcrafted features such as Local Binary Pattern (LBP), Support vectors, SIFT, Histogram of Oriented Gradient (HoG), Linear Discriminant Analysis (LDA), Non-Negative Matrix Factorization (NMF) and Discriminant NMF and Local Quantized Pattern (LPQ) applied in [42–49]. Although their computational costs are low, CNN-based deep neural networks surpassed them in accuracy. This is because handcrafted features are accompanied with unintended features that have no or less impact on classification. Similarly as these features made by human experts, so not all possible cases are included for features classification. Due to modern advancement in computation devices and invention of many-core GPUs, more and more research is focused around CNNs that has illustrated remarkable success for classification challenges [16,50–53]. The major advantage of deep learning methods over common machine learning models is the simultaneous performance of feature extraction and classification. Moreover, deep learning methods apply iterative approach for feature extraction and optimize error by back propagation, thus resulting in those important features that human experts can miss while handcrafting features. CNNs are very good at feature learning through training datasets.

Authors in [31], applied deep CNN with Support Vector Machines (SVM) and won first prize in 2013-FER competition. Liu [33] accomplished three tasks-feature learning, feature selection and classification in a consolidated manner and outperformed other methods in extracting extremely complex features from facial images through Boosted Deep Belief Networks (BDBN). The problem of linear feature selections in previous method is addressed by [36] through DBN models. In 2015, Yu and Zang [34] demonstrated their work for Emotion recognition in Wild challenge for FER based on static images. They have employed multiple deep CNN where each network is randomly initialized thus reduced likelihood and hinge loss, resulting in significantly exceeding the challenge standard criteria. In year 2016, Yoshihara et al. proposed a feature point detection method for qualitative analysis of facial paralysis using DCNN [52]. For initial feature point detection, Active Appearance Model (AAM) is used as an input to DCNN for fine tuning. Kharghanian et al. [53] used DBN for pain assessment from facial expressions, where features were extracted with the help of Convolution Deep Belief Networks (CDBN) to identify the pain. They have further explored Deep

Belief Network (DBN) for robust FER. Rodriguez et al. [15], in 2017 exploited the temporal information by linking Long Short Term Memory (LSTM) with CNN fine tuned with features from VGG-Faces. Their method was boosted by [16] through involvement of deep CNN for fast features extraction and categorization into facial appearances and reinforcing the CNN+LSTM system with super-resolved facial images.

3   The Proposed Method

This section describes the main steps of the proposed methods for FER analysis of TBI patients in real challenging scenarios. The block diagram of the proposed method is illustrated in Fig. 1. First step is face detection from input video streams like [15], followed by face alignment by landmark identification to reduce erroneous face detection. These detected landmarks are tracked and then faces are cropped according to the landmark positions. In the next step face quality is assessed by following [54] and only good quality faces are stored in face log. Faces are then fed to a CNN. This network was pre-trained with VGG-16 faces as used by [16] and [15]. These steps of the system are further explained in the following subsections.

Fig. 1. Deep learning architecture based upon CNN+LSTM with pre-processing algorithm for Facial Expression Recognition (FER).

3.1   Creating TBI Patient Database

TBI patients have mild to severe injury, accompanied with paralysis, coordination and speech inhibition, and higher level of emotional instability. For facial expression analysis, data is collected from patients who lived in neuro-center for at least 10 weeks prior to commence the data collection so that trainers or care givers can understand their different mental states. This helped in accurate annotation of the data. Physiotherapist, trainers and caregivers devised the rehabilitation strategies by accessing their health indicators, and neuro-psychological and cognitive test results [55]. Data is collected from 9 TBI patients in three predefined rehabilitation scenarios in two imaging modalities: RGB and Thermal. These special scenarios are selected with the help of experts, trainers, physiotherapist and care givers by considering the reliability of data as well as disability of patients due nature of injury as described in Table 1. These scenarios are: (1) Cognitive Rehabilitation, (2) Physical Rehabilitation, and (3) Social Rehabilitation. These are described below.

Cognitive Rehabilitation Scenario. In this scenario, data is collected while patient is performing activities to train the patient's ability to understand particular information and perform function accordingly. Experts perform set of repetitive activities with gradual increase in complexity to asses the memory, attention, visual perception, communication, problem solving and learning skills [56,57]. In neuro centers, aforementioned task is accomplished by use of calenders, memory devices, drawing clocks, playing quizzes and games, reading or listening books or music, watching movies or other visual aids. Subjects are also given specific tasks like placing room keys at fixed places, telling their daily routine and activities, setting deadlines or time slots for their favourite tasks. These activities are tailored to patients requirements as it is observed while performing aforementioned tasks patients have large pose variations, attention inhibition, less frontal facial pose, emotional instability and aggravated aggression. Different strategies are adopted to enrich the attention and memory of the patient, particularly it is make sure when any subject tells his story or daily routine his or her face must face the camera by placing a mirror just behind the camera and asked them to visualize themselves. Moreover quiz questions, time clocks, calenders, movies and etc. are displayed over tablet placed next to camera, ensuring more frontal images.

Physical Rehabilitation Scenario. In this mode of data collection, patients are performing activities of physical rehabilitation to assess the functionality of sensory motor neurons. Depending upon the nature of the stroke, muscle movements are reduced or ceased. Physiotherapists conducts cardiovascular, skeletal-muscular and vestigial activities to assess the activity tolerance, muscle-action coordination and postural control. These activities are performed through mild walk or running, cycling, push-ups, arms raise, hands or neck moves and other similar activities depending upon a particular subject disability. These physical exercises are modified to have better and reliable facial and upper body data. It is observed that when subjects walk, cycle, or perform similar physical activity, pose varied largely resulting in very less usable data. To avoid such problems, patients are asked to cycle over stationary bike while keeping their upper body still as much as possible and visualize themselves in specific camera-mirror arrangement as described in previous rehabilitation scenario. Similarly hand pressers, leg raises, walking and other tasks are performed.

Social Rehabilitation Scenario. TBI individuals face severe complexity in social integration due to behavioral and cognitive malfunctions. In this scenario, data is collected while TBI patients are either eating, playing music or discussing or sharing stories, and playing cards or console games in a group of at least 4 or more people. Social communication and integration strategies are also modified according to need of the patients and to have good quality of data. Best results were obtained, when subjects were playing games with the help of consoles and cameras are adjusted next to monitor or screens. It is observed that clear variations in expressions are recorded with changes in the game situations such as happy faces are captured when subjects were winning, sad expression while losing, tense look in difficult situation, even angry looks were observed when cheats are applied in the game.

Table 1. Database of TBI patients with activity participation.

Subjects	Number of sessions	Activities participated		
		Cognitive	Social comm	Physiotherapy
Subject A	7	Y	Y	Y
Subject B	5	Y	Y	Y
Subject C	5	Y	Y	Y
Subject D	7	Y	X	Y
Subject E	3	Y	X	X
Subject F	4	Y	Y	Y
Subject G	3	X	Y	Y
Subject H	6	Y	Y	Y
Subject H	5	Y	X	Y

3.2   Data Acquisition and Preprocessing

Ilyas et al. [6] established the TBI database with only RGB images where TBI subjects are filmed by Axis RGB-Q16 camera with the resolution of 1280×960 to 160×90 pixels at 30 fps (frames per second) in aforementioned specialized scenarios with tailored techniques. Along with RGB, in this work we have obtained the thermal images with Axis Thermal-Q1922 camera having 10 mm of focal length. After collecting the raw data from both modalities, time synchronization is achieved by the time stamps in the RGB frames captured with variable frame rate. Furthermore, 8-point homography estimation is employed for approximate image registration by determining homography matrices from RGB to thermal by [58]. These collected images are passed to facial image acquisition system with the following steps.

Face Detection and Tracking. In [6], face detection is performed by Viola Jones (VJ) algorithm. VJ uses Haar like features and employs a classifier based on AdaBoost algorithm to detect the face and discard background. However, due to large pose variation and non cooperative behaviour of TBI patients, VJ detector misses many faces in the video frames when subject has even small non-frontal pose. To address this issue, we have employed deep face detection [50] that gives the more flexibility to detect face even with large pose variation. Deep face detector able to detect face with minimum confidence of 74.24% even when subject has more than 90° of non frontal pose and challenging illumination conditions. After deep-face detection we employed facial landmarks identification and tracking. We have also employed a face alignment method called Supervised Decent Method (SDM) [59] that tracks the facial landmarks in subsequent frames to capture maximum facial images. SDM helped in better enrolment of the face and fast extraction of geometric structures. This also reduces the miss-detection. In SDM, 49 facial landmarks at the apex of nose, curve of eyes, eye borrows, lips and corner of the face are applied. SDM utilizes the optical flow vectors and pixel by pixel neighbourhood measurement which are resulting in high computational efficiency and precise tracking for longer time by avoiding window based point tracing [54]. After aligning the face, the face boundary is determined by landmarks, followed by face cropping. Another advantage of facial landmarks tracking is the reduction of possible erroneous detection by avoiding face detection in each of the video frames.

Face Quality Assessment and Face Logging. Face quality assessment is performed before lodging the facial frames into face log system as it is seen that even capturing the facial images followed by face tracking, there is still presence of unwanted features in the cropped facial images such as hands or hairs over the face or downward faces. As the performance of the system is greatly dependant upon the quality of facial data so these unwanted and erroneous images must be removed. In our case, data is collected from TBI patients who have non cooperative behaviour with continuous head or face movement, and most of the time these movements are combined with hand motion in front of face or camera. Figure 2 is demonstrating such cases of occluded faces resulting low quality of cropped facial image. In order to avoid such complications, we have devised a filter that discard the faces of low quality on the basis of pixel intensities, image resolution, sharpness and face rotation as shown in [6]. Low quality facial frames are identified by setting first frame as a standard reference frame and discarding rest of the frames who are not 80% or more similar with the first frame in a particular event of video [60]. Similarity of frames is calculated by the following equation:

$$S_{RBG} = \frac{\sum_{m=1}^{M} \sum_{n=1}^{N} (\mathbf{A}_{mn} - \overline{A})(\mathbf{B}_{mn} - \overline{B})}{\sqrt{\sum_{m=1}^{M} \sum_{n=1}^{N} (\mathbf{A}_{mn} - \overline{A})^2 \sum_{m}^{M} \sum_{n}^{N} (\mathbf{B}_{mn} - \overline{B})^2}} \times 100\% \qquad (1)$$

In the above equation A and B are the reference faces whereas $\overline{A}$ and $\overline{B}$ are average pixels levels of the current frame. M and N are number of rows and columns in an image matrix. The degree of dissimilarity calculated from the above equation forms the basis for face quality score. The more the dissimilarity the more the possibility of a low quality face. During face logging, when the low quality facial frame in RGB is discarded based on the filter, it's corresponding thermal image is also removed to maintain the synchronization in both modalities. Images are cropped to specific neutral network input size (224×224 pixels in our experiment) after ensuring the best quality of faces.

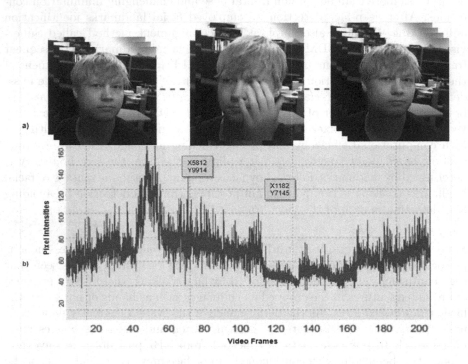

Fig. 2. Face Quality Assessment overview: (a) Input image with and without occlusion (b) Varying image pixel intensities due to presence and absence of obstruction in front of the facial image thus aiding in identifying low quality of images to be discarded [6].

Face Frontalization. FER is dependant upon the pose of the subject and frontalization can boost the performance of the system many folds. Frontalization is the process of manufacturing frontal facing visual frames showing up in single unconstrained photos [61]. In case of TBI patients with continues and large pose variation, this method has increased the FER accuracy to considerable extent. We have employed the simpler approach of using single, unmodified 3D face, termed as reference face for all the images under observation to produce frontalized sights like [61]. This resulted in better image alignment providing accurate comparison of local facial features of different facial images. Facial features are detected by SDM [59], where pose is estimated by specifying a reference projection matrix C_M consist of intrinsic A_M and extrinsic $[R_M \quad t_M]$ matrices.

$$C_M = A_M * [R_M \quad t_M] \tag{2}$$

The extrinsic matrix comprises of rotational matrix R_M and translation vector t_M. Frontal pose is synthesized by taking the transpose of feature points in query image and projecting it on the reference image using geometry of 3D model as seen in Fig. 3. As out of plane head rotation leads to less visibility of facial features, this results in occlusion. This is reduced by employing soft symmetry by taking approximation of 3D reference image and single view query image to estimate the visibility in second image. This may result in replication of occlusion as appearances from one side are transferred to another side of the face. In order to avoid this we take the advantage of facial features of aligned images that appear at the same face image locations regardless of the actual shape of the query image.

Fig. 3. Face frontalization process: (a) Query image, (b) Facial features detection by SDM, (c) Reference face image, (d) Soft symmetry and facial appearance estimation by corresponding symmetric image locations to have frontalized image.

3.3 Linear Cascading of CNN and LSTM as Deep Learning Architecture for FER

The frontalized facial images obtained by face logging are fed into deep learning architecture composed of CNN and LSTM. CNNs are specialized set of artificial neuron networks with learnable weights and biases. These have multiple input and output layers to analyze the visual information by creating features maps of the image. A schematic diagram demonstrating vital steps in convolutional neural network is represented in the Fig. 4. A typical 2-Dimensional (2D) CNN takes 2D images as input and considers each image as a $n \times n$ matrix. Generally, parameters of the CNN are randomly initialized and learned by performing gradient descend using a back propagation algorithm. It uses a convolution operator in order to implement a filter vector. The output of the first convolution will be a new image, which will be passed through another convolution by a new filter. This procedure will continue until the most suitable feature vector elements $\{V_1, V_2, ..., V_n\}$ are found. Convolutional layers are normally alternated with another type of layer, called Pooling layer, which function is to reduce the size of the input in order to reduce the spatial dimensions and gaining computational performances and translation invariant [41]. CNN performed remarkably well in facial recognition [62] as well as automatic facial detection [50]. In order to take advantage of its good results for FER we have applied this method on TBI patients data to extract facial features relevant to FER.

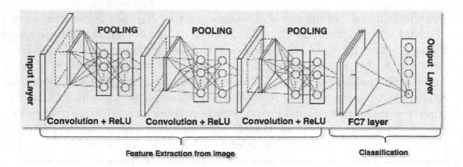

Fig. 4. Convolution Neural Network (CNN) working paradigm with input, convolution, pooling layers and feature vectors.

In general, like any other neural network, CNN deals with images that are isolated. However, in our case we are dealing with the events in a video that happened in time sequential approach so providing the notion of using temporal information. In order to utilize the temporal information associated with facial expression in video, we have used a special kind of Recurrent Neural Network (RNN) that is capable of absorbing the sequential information as well as learning long-term dependencies, called LSTM model from [15]. The LSTM states are controlled by three gates associated with forget (f), input (i), and output (o) states. These gates control the flow of information through the model by using point-wise multiplications and sigmoid functions σ, which bound the information flow between zero and one by the following steps.

In the first step, the forget (f) gate controls the information that is passed through the LSTM cell. It perceive information at $h(t-1)$ and $x(t)$ and produce output numbers between 0 and 1, zero to forget and 1 to keep the information in the cell state $C(t-1)$ as seen in Fig. 5a.

$$f(t) = \sigma(W_{(x \to f)}x(t) + W(h \to f)h(t-1) + b_{(1 \to f)}) \tag{3}$$

In the next step, input gate i with sigmoid σ layer identifies which values will be updated and with *tanh* layers creates the vector to update the state from C(t−1) to C(t).

$$i(t) = \sigma(W_{(x \to i)}x(t) + W_{(h \to i)}h(t-1) + b_{(1 \to i)}) \tag{4}$$

$$\widetilde{C}(t) = tanh(W_{(x \to c)}x(t)) + W_{(h \to c)}h(t-1) + b_{(1 \to c)}) \tag{5}$$

$$C(t) = f(t) * C(t-1) + i(t)\widetilde{C}(t), \tag{6}$$

In the last step, output is decided on the basis of the state of the cell but with filtered version. It is done by first running sigmoid σ layer that decides which information of the cell will go to the output then *tanh* evaluates the values between (-1 and 1) and multiply it with output of the input *i*gate as demonstrated in the Fig. 5d.

$$o(t) = \sigma(W_{(x \to o)}x(t) + W_{(h \to o)}h(t-1) + b_{(1 \to o)}) \tag{7}$$

$$h(t) = o(t)tanh(C(t)), \tag{8}$$

where $C(t)$ is the input to the cell at time t, C is the cell, and h is the output. $W_{(x \to y)}$ are the weights from x to y.

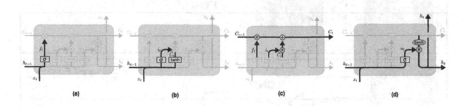

(a)   (b)   (c)   (d)

Fig. 5. Depiction of steps LSTM system with forget, input and output states.

In this paper, linear architecture of CNN and LSTM have been employed, to extract the facial features with the help of CNN from the input faces of TBI patients and then feed to LSTM to exploit the temporal relation on the basis of extracted features in timely manner. For feature extraction we have fine tuned the CNN with off the shelf pre-trained VGG-16CNN model [63]. Features are obtained as fc7 layer of CNN with VGG-16 model that is feed into LSTM model to analyze the performance of combined CNN + LSTM deep neural architecture. Figure 1 is exhibiting the main steps of this neural network along with pre-processing techniques.

3.4 Fusion of RGB and Thermal Modalities

We have employed two fusion approaches in order to analyze the performance of both RGB and thermal modalities for FER as we did it in [14]. These techniques are: (a) Early fusion approach and (b) Feature level late fusion approach. In the early fusion, both RGB and thermal modalities are combined into single array for feature extraction through CNN. In the feature level fusion technique, feature vectors obtained separately from RGB and thermal data with the help of CNN and then combined as a single input to LSTM model for classification. Block diagrams of both of the fusion approaches are demonstrated in Fig. 6.

4 Experimental Results

In this section, we will discuss the database structure and its utilization in our experiments. We then demonstrate the performance of the proposed system.

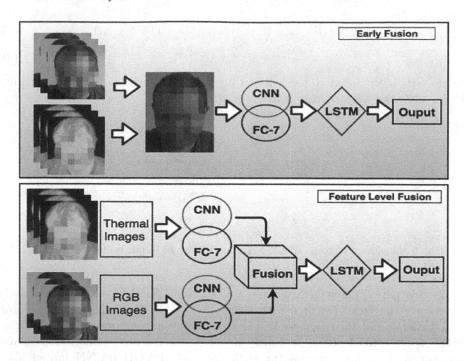

Fig. 6. Early and feature level fusion schemes for RGB and thermal modalities [14].

4.1   The Database Structure

TBI patients database is established for FER as described in Sect. 3.1. We have collected data from 9 TBI patients in multiple phases in 45 sessions with the help of experts, trainers and physiotherapists in specialized scenarios. We collected the data from OSterskoven Neurocenter Hobro and SCN Frederikshavn, Denmark. It is noteworthy that all the patients did not participate in all the activities due to nature of disability. We analyzed 6 basic emotional expression of the participated TBI patients, which are happy, sad, anger, fatigue, surprise and neutral. Data collection scenario are adjusted to get more frontal images with clearer expressions. A tablet displaying emotional scenes is placed just parallel to camera while recording their facial expressions. One interesting observation is that all the TBI patients have taken deep interest in mind game, and movie or picture illustration regardless of their disability nature. This allows us to collect more neutral, happy and angry expressions. However, we could not collect much expressions of sadness, surprised and fatigue due to non-cooperation, traumatic disabilities and other social and technical issues. Another complication is associated with large pose variation due extensive head motions of few TBI patients. We got 935 video events, each of maximum 5 s of duration comprising almost 140,000 frames. However, as data were highly imbalance with most of the events are captured with neutral expressions so we have applied data augmentation techniques to avoid over fitting.

4.2 Performance Evaluation

Table 2 demonstrates the performance comparison of VJ face detector vs deep face detector. From the results it is clearly evident that deep face detector [50] is much better than VJ. This is because VJ is unable to detect faces when there is large pose variations, whereas deep face detector [50] has successfully identified the face that is 90 out of plane with 74.24% confidence. Also, VJ produce false detection of facial images due to change in illumination condition. On the other deep face detector out performed the VJ in challenging conditions with accuracy and speed. Last but not least, when face quality assessment is applied on database of VJ it produced 14,875 false frames detection that account error percentage of 12.56%. On the contrary when FQA is applied over deep face detector database, it detected 4,169 erroneous frames. That accumulates only 2.97% false frames as seen in Table 2. These erroneous frames in both cases are either due to false detection or obstruction in front of the face resulting in lower quality of the facial images.

Table 2. The performance comparison of Viola Jones face detector vs deep face detector.

	Viola Jones	Deep face
Total no. of frames	118502	140250
Training frames	94800	112200
Testing frames	23700	28005
Miss-detection	14875	4169
Miss detection percentage	12.56%	2.97%
Frames missed	21748	0

We have employed a number of techniques to evaluate the performance of the system, such as by illustrating FER accuracy by Area Under Curve (AUC) and by displaying confusion matrix for both early and feature level fusion. Table 3 depicts the FER accuracy by measuring AUC. In this scenario number of epochs of CNN-LSTM system is gradually increased by the steps of 5, from 5 to 50 keeping other parameters such as RHO, recurrent depth, and drop-out probability constant. From the results we observe that the accuracies of RGB database are increased with gradual increase in epochs up to 25 epochs. It reached up to level of 83.25% at the 25th epoch. On the other hand, with fusion of RGB and thermal at early stage, AUC is gradually increased to 83.54% untill 25th epochs and then decreased with further increase in epochs to 50th level. It is also observed that with thermal data only, FER accuracy is also gradually increased from 68.951 to maximum value of 73.04% at the 25th epoch. It is also noted that all the databases such RGB with non-frontalization, frontalization, thermal and fused datasets exhibited optimal performance at the 25–30 epochs.

Table 3. AUC results for FER of TBI patients data with gradual increase in epochs.

Epochs	AUC			
	RGB non-frontalized	RGB frontalized	Thermal	Early fusion RGB+T
10	74.91	75.55	68.95	75.01
15	75.40	78.87	69.51	78.42
20	78.01	80.25	71.68	79.85
25	79.36	83.26	73.04	83.54
30	77.85	82.97	72.16	82.45
35	76.29	80.56	70.21	81.03
40	75.06	78.17	68.55	79.49
45	72.63	76.81	67.86	78.03
50	72.31	74.86	67.52	76.46

In contrast to Table 3, we have gradually changed the RHO values, while keeping the other parameters such as epochs, recurrent depth and drop-out probability constant as seen in Table 4. It is observed that the RGB non- frontalized dataset reached maximum the accuracy of 79.04% when RHO value is 7. RHO value is gradually changed at steps of 2, from 1 to 13, means giving more temporal information for FER. AUC values showed the RGB frontalized dataset exhibited slightly higher accuracy of 83.75% at the same 7th RHO. In contrast, thermal data got the accuracy above 70% in all steps with maximum value of 75.02% at 5th RHO and minimum value of 71.19%. Maximum AUC is observed with RGB+T early fusion data base with maximum value of 80.44% when RHO value is increased to 7. It is clearly evident from the experiment results for TBI patients data, despite of the challenging data set accuracy of system is increased to certain extent as compared to [6].

Tables 5 and 6 illustrated the confusion matrix obtained by the early feature level fusion of the RGB and Thermal modalities respectively. Early fusion of

Table 4. AUC results for FER of TBI patients data with gradual increase in RHO.

RHO	AUC			
	RGB non-frontalized	RGB frontalized	Thermal	Early fusion RGB+T
1	75.46	77.59	73.55	72.42
3	76.51	79.08	73.83	75.73
5	78.49	83.75	75.02	78.67
7	79.04	83.41	74.89	80.45
9	78.42	81.46	74.16	79.03
11	77.11	79.27	73.68	78.33
13	74.22	78.07	72.10	76.70

both modalities has demonstrated the maximum accuracy of 88% for neutral expressions, along with 85% for angry, 82% for happy and 78% for sad emotions. However, 67% accuracy is for fatigue feelings due to the less training data for this expressions. Feature level fusion showed better results for neutral 89%, happy 85% and for fatigue 71% accuracy in Table 6 as compared to early fusion. Both early and feature level fusion exhibited accuracy 71% for surprised feelings.

Table 5. FER confusion matrix for early fusion of RGB and thermal modalities.

	Neutral	Happy	Angry	Sad	Fatigued	Surprised
Neutral	0.88	0.03	0.02	0.04	0.02	0.01
Happy	0.04	0.82	0.02	0.03	0.02	0.07
Angry	0.02	0.02	0.85	0.05	0.06	0.02
Sad	0.06	0.01	0.04	0.78	0.11	0.01
Fatigued	0.07	0.01	0.05	0.2	0.67	0.09
Surprised	0.02	0.08	0.1	0.02	0.06	0.71

Table 6. FER confusion matrix for feature level fusion of RGB and thermal modalities.

	Neutral	Happy	Angry	Sad	Fatigued	Surprised
Neutral	0.89	0.02	0.03	0.05	0.01	0.01
Happy	0.03	0.85	0.02	0.03	0.02	0.04
Angry	0.02	0.02	0.82	0.05	0.06	0.02
Sad	0.05	0.01	0.04	0.81	0.11	0.01
Fatigued	0.06	0.01	0.05	0.3	0.71	0.02
Surprised	0.05	0.04	0.1	0.02	0.06	0.71

5 Conclusions

In this paper, we investigated the performance of FER for real TBI patients in uncontrolled natural challenging conditions. The study depicts the complexities that are associated with TBI patient data collection for database establishment due to varying illumination and changing pose conditions. Data is captured from TBI patients residing in neurocenters in real scenarios to have reliable data. We proposed an effective approach for FER for these subjects. Facial images are extracted from the video frames by employing different methods followed by various pre-processing techniques ensuring high quality of images that are fed into a CNN+LSTM based deep learning architecture to exploit both spatio-temporal information to detect the patients mental status in terms of facial expressions. The results are demonstrated for 6 basic facial expressions classification by using multimodal data in both early and feature level fusion. The results showed clear improvement over our previous approach in [14]. We observed that deep face detector has enhanced the detection rate of facial images even in poor lightening and extensive non-frontal images. However, for future work, TBI patients upper body movements, larger dataset for training and subject specific knowledge base incorporation can be explored for mood and emotion recognition to better facilitate rehabilitation procedure.

References

1. Stuss, D.T., Levine, B.: Adult clinical neuropsychology: lessons from studies of the frontal lobes. Annu. Rev. Psychol. **53**, 401–433 (2002). PMID: 11752491
2. Levin, H.S., et al.: Relationship of depth of brain lesions to consciousness and outcome after closed head injury. J. Neurosurg. **69**, 861–866 (1988)
3. Khan, F., Baguley, I.J., Cameron, I.D.: 4: Rehabilitation after traumatic brain injury. Med. J. Aust. **178**(6), 290–295 (2003). Wiley Online Library
4. Koskinen, S., Hokkinen, E.M., Sarajuuri, J., Alaranta, H.: Applicability of the ICF checklist to traumatically brain-injured patients in post-acute rehabilitation settings. J. Rehabil. Med. **39**(6), 467–472 (2007). Medical Journals Limited
5. Taylor, C.A., Bell, J.M., Breiding, M.J., Xu, L.: Traumatic brain injury–related emergency department visits, hospitalizations, and deaths–United States, 2007 and 2013. MMWR Surveill. Summ. **66**(9), 1 (2017). Centers for Disease Control and Prevention
6. Ilyas, C.M.A., Haque, M.A., Rehm, M., Nasrollahi, K., Moeslund, T.B.: Facial expression recognition for traumatic brain injured patients. In: Proceedings of the 13th International Joint Conference on Computer Vision, Imaging and Computer Graphics Theory and Applications - Volume 4: VISAPP, INSTICC, SciTePress, pp. 522–530 (2018)
7. Dang, B., Chen, W., He, W., Chen, G.: Rehabilitation treatment and progress of traumatic brain injury dysfunction. Neural Plast. **2017**, 6 (2017)
8. Bird, J., Parente, R.: Recognition of nonverbal communication of emotion after traumatic brain injury. NeuroRehabilitation **34**, 39–43 (2014)
9. Bender, A., et al.: Longterm-rehabilitation in patients with acquired brain injury. Dtsch. Ärztebl. Int. **113**, 634–641 (2016)
10. Hyett, M.P., Parker, G.B., Dhall, A.: The utility of facial analysis algorithms in detecting Melancholia. In: Kawulok, M., Celebi, M.E., Smolka, B. (eds.) Advances in Face Detection and Facial Image Analysis, pp. 359–375. Springer, Cham (2016). https://doi.org/10.1007/978-3-319-25958-1_13
11. Chen, Y.: Face perception in schizophrenia spectrum disorders: interface between cognitive and social cognitive functioning. In: Ritsner, M. (ed.) Handbook of Schizophrenia Spectrum Disorders, vol. II, pp. 111–120. Springer, Dordrecht (2011). https://doi.org/10.1007/978-94-007-0831-0_5
12. Klonovs, J., et al.: Monitoring technology. Distributed Computing and Monitoring Technologies for Older Patients. SCS, pp. 49–84. Springer, Cham (2016). https://doi.org/10.1007/978-3-319-27024-1_4

13. Haque, M.A., Irani, R., Nasrollahi, K., Moeslund, T.B.: Facial video-based detection of physical fatigue for maximal muscle activity. IET Comput. Vision **10**, 323–329 (2016)
14. Ilyas, C.M.A., Rehm, M., Nasrollahi, K., Moeslund, T.B.: Rehabilitation of traumatic brain injured patients: patient mood analysis from multimodal video. In: IEEE Signal Processing Society. IEEE Xplore (2018)
15. Rodriguez, P., et al.: Deep pain: exploiting long short-term memory networks for facial expression classification. IEEE Trans. Cybern. **99**, 1–11 (2017)
16. Bellantonio, M., et al.: Spatio-temporal pain recognition in CNN-based super-resolved facial images. In: Nasrollahi, K., et al. (eds.) FFER/VAAM -2016. LNCS, vol. 10165, pp. 151–162. Springer, Cham (2017). https://doi.org/10.1007/978-3-319-56687-0_13
17. Lauterbach, M.D., Notarangelo, P.L., Nichols, S.J., Lane, K.S., Koliatsos, V.E.: Diagnostic and treatment challenges in traumatic brain injury patients with severe neuropsychiatric symptoms: insights into psychiatric practice. Neuropsychiatr. Dis. Treat. **11**, 1601–1607 (2015)
18. Lander, K., Metcalfe, S.: The influence of positive and negative facial expressions on face familiarity. Memory **15**, 63–69 (2007). PMID: 17479925
19. Tian, Y.I., Kanade, T., Cohn, J.F.: Recognizing action units for facial expression analysis. IEEE Trans. Pattern Anal. Mach. Intell. **23**, 97–115 (2001)
20. Pantic, M., Patras, I.: Dynamics of facial expression: recognition of facial actions and their temporal segments from face profile image sequences. IEEE Trans. Syst. Man Cybern. Part B (Cybern.) **36**, 433–449 (2006)
21. Jiang, B., Valstar, M., Martinez, B., Pantic, M.: A dynamic appearance descriptor approach to facial actions temporal modeling. IEEE Trans. Cybern. **44**, 161–174 (2014)
22. Ghimire, D., Lee, J.: Geometric feature-based facial expression recognition in image sequences using multi-class adaboost and support vector machines. Sensors **13**, 7714–7734 (2013)
23. Haque, M.A., Nasrollahi, K., Moeslund, T.B.: Constructing facial expression log from video sequences using face quality assessment. In: 2014 International Conference on Computer Vision Theory and Applications (VISAPP), vol. 2, pp. 517–525 (2014)
24. Poursaberi, A., Noubari, H.A., Gavrilova, M., Yanushkevich, S.N.: Gauss-laguerre wavelet textural feature fusion with geometrical information for facial expression identification. EURASIP J. Image Video Process. **2012**, 17 (2012)
25. Saeed, A., Al-Hamadi, A., Niese, R., Elzobi, M.: Frame-based facial expression recognition using geometrical features. Adv. Hum.-Comput. Interact. **2014**, 1–13 (2014)
26. Lyons, M.J., Budynek, J., Akamatsu, S.: Automatic classification of single facial images. IEEE Trans. Pattern Anal. Mach. Intell. **21**, 1357–1362 (1999)
27. li Tian, Y.: Evaluation of face resolution for expression analysis. In: 2004 Conference on Computer Vision and Pattern Recognition Workshop, pp. 82–82 (2004)
28. Li, H., Hua, G.: Hierarchical-pep model for real-world face recognition. In: 2015 IEEE Conference on Computer Vision and Pattern Recognition (CVPR), pp. 4055–4064 (2015)
29. Huang, Z., Wang, R., Shan, S., Chen, X.: Face recognition on large-scale video in the wild with hybrid euclidean-and-riemannian metric learning. Pattern Recogn. **48**, 3113–3124 (2015). Discriminative Feature Learning from Big Data for Visual Recognition

30. Yang, J., Ren, P., Chen, D., Wen, F., Li, H., Hua, G.: Neural aggregation network for video face recognition. CoRR abs/1603.05474 (2016)
31. Tang, Y.: Deep learning using support vector machines. CoRR abs/1306.0239 (2013)
32. Kahou, S.E., et al.: Combining modality specific deep neural networks for emotion recognition in video. In: Proceedings of the 15th ACM on International Conference on Multimodal Interaction, ICMI 2013, pp. 543–550. ACM, New York, NY, USA (2013)
33. Liu, P., Han, S., Meng, Z., Tong, Y.: Facial expression recognition via a boosted deep belief network. In: 2014 IEEE Conference on Computer Vision and Pattern Recognition, pp. 1805–1812 (2014)
34. Yu, Z., Zhang, C.: Image based static facial expression recognition with multiple deep network learning. In: Proceedings of the 2015 ACM on International Conference on Multimodal Interaction, ICMI 2015, pp. 435–442. ACM, New York, NY, USA (2015)
35. Liu, M., Li, S., Shan, S., Wang, R., Chen, X.: Deeply learning deformable facial action parts model for dynamic expression analysis. In: Cremers, D., Reid, I., Saito, H., Yang, M.-H. (eds.) ACCV 2014. LNCS, vol. 9006, pp. 143–157. Springer, Cham (2015). https://doi.org/10.1007/978-3-319-16817-3_10
36. Kim, B.K., Roh, J., Dong, S.Y., Lee, S.Y.: Hierarchical committee of deep convolutional neural networks for robust facial expression recognition. J. Multimodal User Interfaces 10, 173–189 (2016)
37. Ofodile, I., et al.: Automatic recognition of deceptive facial expressions of emotion. CoRR abs/1707.04061 (2017)
38. Liu, M., Wang, R., Li, S., Shan, S., Huang, Z., Chen, X.: Combining multiple kernel methods on riemannian manifold for emotion recognition in the wild. In: Proceedings of the 16th International Conference on Multimodal Interaction, ICMI 2014, pp. 494–501. ACM, New York, NY, USA (2014)
39. Fan, Y., Lu, X., Li, D., Liu, Y.: Video-based emotion recognition using CNN-RNN and C3D hybrid networks. In: Proceedings of the 18th ACM International Conference on Multimodal Interaction, ICMI 2016, pp. 445–450. ACM, New York, NY, USA (2016)
40. Ranganathan, H., Chakraborty, S., Panchanathan, S.: Multimodal emotion recognition using deep learning architectures. In: 2016 IEEE Winter Conference on Applications of Computer Vision (WACV), pp. 1–9 (2016)
41. Noroozi, F., Marjanovic, M., Njegus, A., Escalera, S., Anbarjafari, G.: Audio-visual emotion recognition in video clips. IEEE Trans. Affect. Comput. 10, 1–1 (2017)
42. Uddin, M.Z., Hassan, M.M., Almogren, A., Alamri, A., Alrubaian, M., Fortino, G.: Facial expression recognition utilizing local direction-based robust features and deep belief network. IEEE Access 5, 4525–4536 (2017)
43. Zhao, X., Zhang, S.: Facial expression recognition based on local binary patterns and kernel discriminant isomap. Sensors 11, 9573–9588 (2011)
44. Albiol, A., Monzo, D., Martin, A., Sastre, J., Albiol, A.: Face recognition using HOG-EBGM. Pattern Recogn. Lett. 29, 1537–1543 (2008)
45. Berretti, S., Ben Amor, B., Daoudi, M., del Bimbo, A.: 3D facial expression recognition using sift descriptors of automatically detected keypoints. Vis. Comput. 27, 1021 (2011)
46. Shan, C., Gong, S., McOwan, P.W.: Facial expression recognition based on local binary patterns: a comprehensive study. Image Vis. Comput. 27, 803–816 (2009)
47. Uddin, M.Z., Hassan, M.M.: A depth video-based facial expression recognition system using radon transform, generalized discriminant analysis, and hidden markov model. Multimed. Tools Appl. 74, 3675–3690 (2015)

48. de Vries, G.-J., Pauws, S., Biehl, M.: Facial expression recognition using learning vector quantization. In: Azzopardi, G., Petkov, N. (eds.) CAIP 2015. LNCS, vol. 9257, pp. 760–771. Springer, Cham (2015). https://doi.org/10.1007/978-3-319-23117-4_65

49. Ravichander, A., Vijay, S., Ramaseshan, V., Natarajan, S.: Automated human facial expression recognition using extreme learning machines. In: Cao, J., Mao, K., Wu, J., Lendasse, A. (eds.) Proceedings of ELM-2015 Volume 2. PALO, vol. 7, pp. 209–222. Springer, Cham (2016). https://doi.org/10.1007/978-3-319-28373-9_18

50. Farfade, S.S., Saberian, M.J., Li, L.J.: Multi-view face detection using deep convolutional neural networks. In: Proceedings of the 5th ACM on International Conference on Multimedia Retrieval, ICMR 2015, pp. 643–650. ACM (2015)

51. Triantafyllidou, D., Tefas, A.: Face detection based on deep convolutional neural networks exploiting incremental facial part learning. In: 2016 23rd International Conference on Pattern Recognition (ICPR), pp. 3560–3565 (2016)

52. Yoshihara, H., Seo, M., Ngo, T.H., Matsushiro, N., Chen, Y.W.: Automatic feature point detection using deep convolutional networks for quantitative evaluation of facial paralysis. In: 2016 9th International Congress on Image and Signal Processing, BioMedical Engineering and Informatics (CISP-BMEI), pp. 811–814 (2016)

53. Kharghanian, R., Peiravi, A., Moradi, F.: Pain detection from facial images using unsupervised feature learning approach. In: 2016 38th Annual International Conference of the IEEE Engineering in Medicine and Biology Society (EMBC), pp. 419–422 (2016)

54. Haque, M.A., Nasrollahi, K., Moeslund, T.B.: Quality-aware estimation of facial landmarks in video sequences. In: 2015 IEEE Winter Conference on Applications of Computer Vision, pp. 678–685 (2015)

55. Barman, A., Chatterjee, A., Bhide, R.: Cognitive impairment and rehabilitation strategies after traumatic brain injury. Indian J. Psychol. Med. **38**, 172–181 (2016)

56. McKenna, K., Cooke, D.M., Fleming, J., Jefferson, A., Ogden, S.: The incidence of visual perceptual impairment in patients with severe traumatic brain injury. Brain Inj. **20**, 507–518 (2006)

57. Tsaousides, T., Gordon, W.A.: Cognitive rehabilitation following traumatic brain injury: assessment to treatment. Mt. Sinai J. Med. J. Transl. Personalized Med. **76**, 173–181 (2009)

58. Hartley, R., Zisserman, A.: Multiple View Geometry in Computer Vision, 2nd edn. Cambridge University Press, New York (2003)

59. Xiong, X., la Torre, F.D.: Supervised descent method and its applications to face alignment. In: 2013 IEEE Conference on Computer Vision and Pattern Recognition, pp. 532–539 (2013)

60. Irani, R., Nasrollahi, K., Dhall, A., Moeslund, T.B., Gedeon, T.: Thermal superpixels for bimodal stress recognition. In: 2016 Sixth International Conference on Image Processing Theory, Tools and Applications (IPTA), pp. 1–6 (2016)

61. Hassner, T., Harel, S., Paz, E., Enbar, R.: Effective face frontalization in unconstrained images. In: 2015 IEEE Conference on Computer Vision and Pattern Recognition (CVPR), pp. 4295–4304 (2015)

62. Ji, S., Xu, W., Yang, M., Yu, K.: 3D convolutional neural networks for human action recognition. IEEE Trans. Pattern Anal. Mach. Intell. **35**, 221–231 (2013)

63. Parkhi, O.M., Vedaldi, A., Zisserman, A.: Deep face recognition. In: British Machine Vision Conference (2015)

Author Index